FATHER PAUL

AND

CHRISTIAN UNITY

Dec 8, 1963

In Jesus and Mary —

f. Titus S.A.

FATHER PAUL

AND

CHRISTIAN UNITY

An Anthology on Christian Reunion
prepared from the
Writings, Sermons and Addresses
of Father Paul James Francis, S.A.
(1863-1940)

Compiled and Edited by
TITUS CRANNY, S.A., M.A., S.T.D.

Foreword by
GREGORY PETER CARDINAL AGAGIANIAN

CHAIR OF UNITY APOSTOLATE
Graymoor, Garrison, New York

Library of Congress
Catalog Card No. 63-21981

270.8
CRt

Printed and bound in the United States of America
at Graymoor Press, Peekskill, N. Y.

TO MARY:

Mother of God and

Mother of all men,

Humble Instrument of the Incarnate Word,

Inseparable Associate of the Atoning King,

Mother, Queen, and Patroness of Unity,

OUR LADY OF THE ATONEMENT

Table of Contents

IV. Our Separated Brethren • 133

V. OUR LADY AND UNITY • 199

General Introduction

THE THOUGHTS and ideas of a great man are his legacy to posterity. In the work of Christian Unity the words of Fr. Paul James Francis, S.A. have a special message for all concerned with this vital apostolate. He was an apostle of Unity in our own century, perhaps ahead of his time, intensely interested in the reunion of Christendom and the extension of the Catholic Church throughout the world.

His long and dedicated life give testimony to the ardor and range of his apostleship. He was born in the middle of the Civil War in 1863; he died in 1940, about a year and half before the United States entered World War II. He spent forty-six years as a devout member of the Episcopalian communion; he lived the other thirty-one years as a prominent priest of the Catholic Church.

Fr. Paul was somewhat like Cardinal Newman in this respect—half of his life he was Protestant and half of his life he was Catholic. He was not as great as the English prelate in his thinking or in his leadership as an intellectual; but perhaps, in another sense, he was even greater. For he established a religious family of which he was the father and guide, to whom he committed the message and the mission of Christian Unity which has become so much a part of contemporary religious life.

Our present work is a collection or compilation of the more important statements and ideas of Fr. Paul on Christian Unity. They have a special meaning today when the whole religious world is interested in Christian Unity; they have an application for Catholics especially, since Fr. Paul was such a capable and persevering leader in his devotedness to the Church and in his abiding interest to those outside the One Fold of the Good Shepherd. The finest praise surely, for this noble man, came from the pen of Pope John XXIII, who in a letter to the Father General of the Society of the Atonement wrote: "Prayer, in fact, is the first and principal means to be used to bring about this yearned-for unity, as your beloved founder, Father Paul Wattson so clearly saw; and he therefore promoted the Chair of Unity Octave. . . ."

It is fitting to publish a work about Fr. Paul and Christian Unity during this grace-laden age of the Second Vatican Council. Pope John himself was the providential leader in this holy enterprise and were the Graymoor founder living today he would be enthusiastic and warm in his praise and admiration of the holy Pope, who stood before the world as the living expression of the voice and example of the Good Shepherd in longing to fulfill the prophetic vision of leading the "other sheep" to the life-giving pastures of the One Fold.

Pope Paul VI sets the tone and gives the direction in efforts for Christian Unity. He will implement the noble work of Pope John, deepen and develop it as he promised in his first address after his election to the papacy. All mankind may take inspiration and courage from his words: "The common aspiration to re-integrate the Unity sorrowfully broken in the past will find us an echo of fervent will and moving prayer, in awareness of the office bestowed on us by Jesus. . . . We open our arms to all those who glory in the name of Christ. We call them by the sweet name of brothers, and let them know they will find in us constant comprehension and benevolence, that they will find in Rome the paternal house that underlies with new splendor the treasuries of their history, of their cultural patrimony, and of their spiritual heritage" (June 21, 1963.)

In tribute to Pope John he promised to pursue "the great work launched with so much hope and with bright expectancy . . . the achievement of *that all may be one* so awaited by all and for which Pope John gave his life."

There is another reason for wishing to publish this compilation at this time. 1963 marks the centenary of the birth of Father Paul who came into this world on January 16, 1863 in Millington, Md. The volume may serve as a tribute to his labors and his leadership. It is a presentation of his ideas and ideals in that Unity to which he gave his life and dedicated all the energies of his mind and heart. May this volume serve to make him better known in the field of Ecumenism and reveal the character and magnitude of his apostolic zeal.

This collection does not represent all that Fr. Paul wrote and said on Unity for there would be much more material if we were to present everything. But it does represent his more important statements on the matter and provides an adequate sampling of what he taught and believed. We have made some slight changes, such as in punctuation or in a thread of thought that seems obscure, for such would be of little service to him or to us. Some statements, made forty or fifty years ago, are remarkable, almost prophetic, and seem just as useful today as then. But that is the characteristic of a herald and an apostle: to be ahead of his times and to lead the way for others.

This anthology is rather uneven in form; that is, some selections are formal writings, or radio talks, or articles from publications, while other statements are remarks at meditation, sermons recorded by a faithful secretary, or letters written for some members of the community. Though the form is varied, the content is not. It is a constant, recurring theme: unity with God, unity with each other, unity through Our Lady and the need of unity for all who are separated from Christ and the Vicar of His love, the Holy Father. Unity was indeed the compelling passion of Fr. Paul's life.

To His Eminence, Cardinal Agagianian I am indebted for writing the expressive foreword. To our Father General, Very Rev. Bonaventure Koelzer, S.A. I am grateful for his permission to collate and publish this volume.

This collection of the words of Father Paul on Christian Reunion is divided into six parts: on Christian Unity; on the Papacy; on our Separated Brethren; on the Chair of Unity Octave; on Our Lady of the Atonement; and on Fr. Paul himself. They cover a period of about forty years, from 1897, shortly before his coming to Graymoor, until his death in 1940. I have given the original reference and where this was impossible I have stated it so. A complete analysis and synthesis of the value of Father Paul's greatness in the field of Christian Unity is the task of another time. This collation shows simply that he was an effective pioneer and apostle of Christian Unity, and that his ideas and efforts have meaning and importance for the world today. His enthusiasm and selfless courage merit our deepest praise and sincerest imitation.

Feast of the Lady of the Atonement

July 9, 1963

Foreword

One of the essential notes or marks by which the Church reveals herself as the true "spouse of Christ" is her oneness or unity. While the unity willed by Christ for His Church, which consists in the unified and immutable character of its teachings, its Sacraments and its authority, has always been present, the same cannot be said for that visible union of all its members, made such by Baptism, with the Apostolic See, which is necessary for the accomplishment of its divinely-bestowed sanctifying mission to all men.

Past history and present-day happenings provide us with many examples of the Church's ardent and loving interest in her separated children and of the efforts which have been made and are being made today to enable them to share fully in the spiritual rights and privileges reserved for them. These efforts, of course, serve only as a preparation for the action of the Holy Spirit, Who alone can give our separated brothers the light and strength needed to overcome their many difficulties.

It is all too evident that Christian reunion will not be achieved overnight, but that it will come about as the result of a long and patient preparation. Those who undertake this preparatory work must be men of deep faith, great clarity of thought, profound religious learning and, above all, holy men. Such a man, I believe, was Father Paul James Francis, the founder of the Society of the Atonement and one of the outstanding apostles of Christian unity of our day.

It is my fervent hope and prayer that this present collection of Father Paul's writings, addresses and sermons on the subject of Christian reunion, so competently prepared by Father Titus Cranny, will receive the wide circulation which it merits and be a source of inspiration and encouragement to work and pray that "all may be one."

GREGORY PETER CARDINAL AGAGIANIAN
Prefect of Sacred Congregation for the Propagation of the Faith
Cardinal Protector of the Friars and Sisters of the Atonement.

I

Features of Christian Unity

IN THE HEART *of Fr. Paul, love of Christ and devotion to the Church were identical. With St. Joan of Arc he would have said: "Jesus and the Church are one." To both the Word Incarnate and to its extension, the Mystical Body, the Graymoor founder consecrated all the energies of his mind and heart. He gave unstinted service to both Our Lord and the Church and sought to lead souls outside the One Fold to that imperishable unity which the Church possesses by virtue of her Unity with the Divine Redeemer.*

In the soul of Fr. Paul there was no rancor or bitterness; there was no spirit of competition in his allegiance to the Church. He was forthright in his attitude and single-minded in his approach. No one could ever mistake his position. But the same love that held him to Christ and drew him to the Church was poured out upon the souls of men, that they might attain religious unity in the Fold of Peter. In the spirit of the Good Shepherd he sought to work for the "other sheep" that they might enter the One Fold.

The selections chosen here reflect various aspects of Christian Unity—St. Francis and Unity, the Precious Blood and Unity, the Sacred Heart and Unity, and the Church as the Ark of Salvation. For Fr. Paul, everything was in some way related to Unity: the soul is made for God and for union with Him; sin is a breach of that love. The Eucharist is the Sacrament of Unity, Holy Mass is the Sacrifice of Unity, Our Lady is the principal aide in heaven to achieve Unity. Our Lord founded but one Church upon Peter (the Rock) and on his successors in the Chair of Unity in Rome.

Fr. Paul realized that reunion would not be attained quickly. He knew the difficulties and the dangers, but he was supremely confident that Unity would be realized through God's divine

1

power and love, and with the intercession of the Mother of God, whom he joyfully honored as Our Lady of the Atonement.

The religious climate in which we live today is charged with a desire and longing for unity. The future is bright with hope—and never before has the desire for unity been so universal and so compelling. May the inspiration and example of Fr. Paul prove an effective factor in helping to achieve Christian Unity—for those who are apostles of this noble work and for those who seek for this blessing that God desires to give all mankind.

1. Can We Know the Doctrine?

The Lamp, August, 1910

Weary of four hundred years of strife among themselves, sect against sect, the divided forces of Protestantism have made a truce with each other, agreeing to ignore their doctrinal differences and the "World's Missionary Conference" was organized and carried on through on that principle.

We are heartily glad to see a spirit of love and fellowship taking the place of hatred and sectarian rivalry among our Christian brethren outside the Catholic Church, but that does not close our eyes to the glaring fallacy in Mr. Roosevelt's scriptural argument in support of the Protestant makeshift for real and vital Christian Unity.

The Protestant assumption, which Mr. Roosevelt voices, is that doctrinal differences among Christians, even of a fundamental nature, are inevitable and unavoidable, and being taken entirely for granted, they are to be overlooked or treated as of small importance. For instance, the Baptists do not baptize infants and confine the baptism of adults to the one form of immersion; the Lutherans, on the other hand, baptize infants and practice aspersion. Yet, for the sake of intercommunion, this doctrinal difference is to be ignored with the logical result that Protestants for the most part now teach that baptism is not a saving ordinance and its administration under any form or at any age is immaterial, but what then becomes of the doctrine of Christ. "He that believeth, and is baptized shall be saved; he that believeth not shall be condemned?" When in fact every saving doctrine of Christ is denied by some sect or deviation of His followers and all positive affirmations of other Christian bodies must be tacitly ignored or sacrificed as the price of universal fellowship and intercommunion, what becomes of Christ's description of Himself: "I am the Truth"?

2. Reconciliation: The Word of the New Century

The Talisman of Unity

The Lamp, September, 1910

Reconciliation is the Christian Talisman of the Twentieth Century. And surely none should be more alive to this than we Catholics.

Amid the decay of religious thought, we cannot but note the compelling power of one generally felt force, the Church Unity idea, an idea or ideal which appears to have taken fast grip upon the minds and hearts of so many within the non-Catholic bodies.

If the phenomenon can be explained by the hypothesis that it is the work of the Holy Spirit, and if we accept such an explanation for the sake of a working principle, then as Catholics we may very readily believe that the end of such a movement is, in the mind of God, the reconciliation of all sincere Christians with the divine Center of Unity, the Rock of Peter. Suppose we bear this possible hypothesis in mind and allow it to be a guiding principle in the attitude we assume toward our separated brethren, who are working and praying for Unity, however much they may still be in the dark as to the destined end of their efforts. And lest we be misunderstood, let us add, that this attitude on our part as Catholics, by no means stultifies the work of individual conversions; on the contrary, we know by experience that it is the best way of facilitating them.

Here in America, as well as in England, there is no body of Christians, who approach so nearly the borderland of reconciliation with the Vicar of Christ as the so-called "Advanced" or "Catholic" Wing of the Anglican Church. It must have been these whom Dr. Barry had in mind, when he said, "From Melrose to Oxford, from Oxford to the whole Anglican Communion, that spirit has penetrated into a thousand homes where no voice of ours had been heard. Not Protestant, but Catholic is the watchword."

For Catholic-minded Anglicans above all others among our separated brethren, *The Lamp* be-speaks and pleads, the spirit of brotherliness, of intelligent comprehension, of cordial sympathy.

The serious and self-sacrificing labors of the Tractarian

leaders and their successors to purge out the leaven of Protestantism from the English mind and to rebuild the fabric which the Tudor Trio so ruthlessly tore down represent a worthy ambition surely, whatever *sine-qua-non* the Anglican builders still lack for the successful completion of their labors.

If Dr. Barry's interpretation of what Anglicans themselves call the "Catholic Revival" in the Anglican Church is the correct one; if as he says, it has been "Providence, meanwhile, (who) was acting by secret ways to bring again the Old Church, cleansed and renewed, in due course to be enlarged by English people, whose genius for reconciliation (has shown itself) in laws, government, politics, language, (and) empire," ought there to be any difference of opinion among Catholics as to whether this Romeward tendency among Anglicans is to be fusilladed with the stones of controversy and pelted with the stinging thorns of sarcasm and contempt, or whether in the spirit of loving reconciliation, it is to be met as the Prodigal Son was met, when once his face was homeward turned? Can anyone doubt the answer that would be given in reply were the question put to our Holy Father, Pope Pius X?

In marked contrast to this utter confusion of doctrinal belief among Protestants stands the unity of doctrine and oneness in faith of the Roman Catholic Church. Surely among the Church's children, we find the verification of Our Lord's saying: "If any man will do the will of God he will know the doctrine." From the least unto the greatest in the Catholic Church all know but one doctrine of Christ and the reason is that all revere and obey the voice of the Church as the mouthpiece of the Holy Spirit.

The voice of God speaking from Heaven to Peter, James and John on Mount Thabor and to John the Baptist at the river Jordan said of Christ: "This is My beloved Son, hear ye Him."

To His Apostles Christ in turn said: "All power is given to Me in heaven and on earth. Go ye therefore, teach ye all things whatsoever I have commanded you" (St. Matt. 28: 18-20) and again He promised to send them the Holy Ghost, saying: "When He, the Spirit of truth, is come, He will teach you all truth" (St. John 16:13). But that they might always bear the yoke of obedience and do the will of the Father, He chose one of their number as His special Vicar, saying to St. Peter: "Feed my lambs; feed my sheep" (St. John 21:17,18).

5

Thus to a Catholic is very plain that one cannot do the will of God who does not obey Jesus Christ, and one cannot obey Jesus Christ who does not obey His Church, and one cannot obey the Church without obeying the successors of the Apostles and their Christ-appointed Head, the successor of St. Peter.

3. The Sacred Heart and Church Unity

The Lamp, June, 1913

June is the month of the Sacred Heart and devotion to the Sacred Heart implies devotion to the interests and desires of the Sacred Heart. To love what He loves and to desire what He desires should constitute the ruling passion of every Catholic soul that is devoted to the most Sacred Heart of Jesus Christ.

There is a two-fold desire of the Sacred Heart, which has persevered through the centuries ever since that awful night of His betrayal, in which Our Lord prayed that His disciples might be one, to the end that the world might believe that the Father had sent Him to be its Redeemer and Savior.

Not only has this two-fold desire of Our Lord for the Unity of the faithful and the conversion of the world continued like the current of a deep and mighty river down the course of the ages, but, if that were possible, we believe it to be more intense now than ever before.

Because Our Lord foresaw the necessity of Unity among His disciples as a means to the world's conversion, we cannot conceive of any failure on His part to make provision for the continuance and perpetuation of such unity; and in some form and to some degree Church unity must have manifested itself in every successive period of ecclesiastical history. Indeed, we know that organic unity is one of the four infallible marks of the Church founded by Jesus Christ and so it must be in some degree always in evidence in every generation, even as holiness and catholicity and apostolicity must always exist to some appreciable degree in the Church and persevere from the day of Pentecost to the second coming of Christ, otherwise the confession of our faith is untrue, "I believe in One, Holy Catholic and Apostolic Church."

Now as a matter of historic fact the only unity among Christians that has persevered for 1900 years and consequently the only unity that can continue to persevere in unbroken continuity from the first Whitsunday, until the end of the world is that which now and ever has been in the Catholic Church, as she herself defines the limitations and the extent of that unity.

We know that many millions of our fellow Christians outside the visible unity of the Catholic Church claim to be either the whole Catholic Church, as do the schismatic Orientals, or to be a *branch*, at least, of the Catholic Church, as do the Anglicans. But the only Body of Christians now extant which has preserved its unity unbroken from the days of the blessed Apostles until now is that Church which has ever been in visible communion with the Apostolic See of Rome. And it is this Church which takes in her hand the Holy Gospels and out of them expounds to her children the *fiat* of Jesus Christ concerning the unalterable constitution of His Church and the provisions for unity that He himself has made. She begins with the words of Christ to Simon the Son of John, *"And I say to thee: that thou art Peter; and upon this rock I will build My Church, and the gates of hell shall not prevail against it. And I will give to thee the keys of the kingdom of heaven. And whatsoever thou shalt bind upon earth, it shall be bound also in heaven; and whatsoever thou shalt loose upon earth, it shall be loosed in heaven"* (St. Matt. 16:18,19); she recounts how after the institution of the Blessed Sacrament Jesus again addressing His Vicar, says: *". . . Simon, Simon, behold Satan hath desired to have you"* (that is, the whole body of the Apostles—for the *"you"* is plural) *"that he may sift you as wheat; but I have prayed for thee, that thy faith fail not; and thou, being once converted, confirm thy brethren."* (St. Luke 22:31-32) And she ends the long array of Petrine texts from the Holy Gospels with Christ's commission to Peter: *"Feed my lambs; feed my sheep"* (St. John 21:16-17).

Thus to every Catholic it is as clear as the sunlight that, in the person of St. Peter and his successors, Christ has provided for His Church an unalterable and indestructible Center of Unity; and that whenever the prayer of Our Lord that His disciples "that all be one" (St. John 17:21), shall be finally and fully realized, the center of that unity will be nowhere else than where He originally placed it, viz., in the Chair of St. Peter, His Vicar.

Nevertheless, it is incumbent upon the three hundred millions of Christ's disciples, now in visible communion with the

7

Apostolic See, to recognize that something more than authority is needed to bring the two hundred million "other sheep" of Christ into One Fold under the One Shepherd.

It was not enough for Jehovah to write His commandments upon two tablets of stone and to send Moses the Lawgiver with them in his hands back to the Congregation of Israel. In spite of the Tablets of the Decalogue, the Israelites continued to be a rebellious people; in vain was prophet after prophet sent to expound the word of God unto them. Something more than law and more than the knowledge of the will of God was required to save the human race. The love of God for sinners had to be manifested in the Person of His Son; and when Divine Love was incarnate among men, He said, "*And I, if I be lifted up from the earth, will draw all things unto Myself*" (St. John 12:32).

It is then, the attractive power of Christ crucified and the magnetism of the Sacred Heart which is to compel the multitude of believers to submit themselves to the sweet yoke of Christ, as divinely revealed in the rule of His Chief Steward, the Supreme Pontiff and Holy Father of Christendom.

When we turn back to the origin of the cleavage between the East and West, about a thousand years ago, we find the root causes to have been political jealousy and racial hatred; and that which stands today as a wall of division between the Latin and the Greek much more than the *filioque* of any dogmatic disagreements in this same deepseated jealousy and hatred, which a thousand years have intensified rather than lessened. So much is this the case, that since the triumph of the Balkan allies over the Turks, some conversant with conditions in the Orient go as far as to express the opinion that the Catholics in that portion of the world are likely to fare worse at the hands of the Christian Greeks than they did under Mohammedan rule.

Here also in the West the problem of Church Unity imposes upon Catholics something more than the work of proving by Holy Scripture, history and logic to our non-Catholic brethren that papal authority is *de jure divino;* most of all, ours is the superhuman task of overcoming anti-Catholic prejudice and even hatred, by the invincible power of Divine Love.

One of the most hopeful signs of reunion in the West is that the old-time bitterness of Protestants against Catholics has in large measure subsided. In spite of Socialistic agitators, it is a fact that our non-Catholic fellow Christians around us are much more charitably disposed towards Catholics now than was the case a generation or two ago, and it behooves us in union with the Sacred Heart to increase this good will and better feeling more and more in love toward our separated brethren.

The Lamp especially pleads with its readers to display the charity of the Sacred Heart towards our Anglican neighbors, particularly, towards those who approach the nearest to us in Catholic faith and practice. There is going on in the Anglican Body a constant approximation towards Rome, the Center of Catholic Unity, and the pains and struggles of the so-called "Catholic Party" in the Anglican Church should command our profoundest sympathy. Our Lord said we were to judge a tree by its fruits and already the tree of High Church Anglicanism has dropped into the lap of our Mother, the Catholic church, some of the choicest fruits it has been hers to enjoy during the last seventy years; so much so, that we have cause to wish long life to this tree and good luck in the Name of the Lord. It seems to us, that those Episcopalians in America are to be applauded who detest the name Protestant Episcopal and who wish to get rid of it; for is it not a praiseworthy ambition? As for ourselves, we are delighted at every victory which the more Catholic-minded Anglicans win over their low and broad Church associates, because we do not doubt, that the more they strive to be Catholic, the more will God open their eyes to see how impossible it is to be truly Catholic and yet ignore the Petrine foundation on which the Church is built. Because we believe that the secret power which is attracting Anglicans in a homeward direction emanates from the Sacred Heart, we hail every step that Anglicans take away from the far country of Protestantism, and back to their Father's House.

There is an old tradition concerning the founding of Rome that Romulus chose the Palatine Hill as the official site of the City and established about it a pomerium, or ceremonial line. Outside the fold, marked by this circular line, he established on the Capitoline Hill, an asylum for all friendly comers, who wished the Romans well and while basking in their friendship were ready in stress of attack from any common foe to bear arms in the City's defense. The subsequent history of Rome proved the wisdom of Romulus' policy. It is our humble conviction that the Roman party in the Anglican Church ought to be regarded as Romulus regarded his friends who lodged on the Capitoline Hill.

9

4. The Precious Blood and Church Unity

The Lamp, July, 1913

We headed our June editorial, "The Sacred Heart and Church Unity." We are now passing through the month of the Most Precious Blood and It too speaks eloquently of Church Unity. We recall to mind St. Paul's sermon on Mar's Hill, where speaking of God "Who made the world and all the things there," he says, "It is He who giveth to all life and health and all things and made both of one (blood) all mankind to dwell upon the whole face of the earth."

Perhaps never since the confounding of tongues of Babel, and the consequent scatterings of the human family over the face of the earth, has the civilized portion of mankind risen to a higher conception of universal brotherhood existing between the various peoples and races all over the globe, than is the case today when the Gospel of civil peace is preached from the courthouse steps as well as from the church pulpits and in the halls of parliament, as well as from the altars of great cathedrals.

But Christianity teaches of a yet more intimate brotherhood —of a brotherhood within a brotherhood—where the ties of kinship are far more closely drawn than those which bind together Jew and Gentile, Greek and Barbarian, American, European, African, Asiatic and Australian, namely, that the Children of the New Adam who have received the New Birth of Water and the Spirit and in whose veins flows the Royal Blood of the Redeemer of mankind.

Much as the Christian desires to "live peacefully with all men," and to love every man as his brother, he cannot ignore the existence of certain divisions and hostilities between the seed of God and the seed of the devil, which are as age-long as the human family itself. God proclaimed this unbridgeable gulf when He said: "I will put enmities between thee and the woman, and thy seed and her seed; she shall crush thy head and thou shalt lie in wait for her heel." (Gen. 3:15)

As the descendants of Ismael have made war from time immemorial on the seed of Isaac and as Esau has persecuted Jacob, so we find in the twentieth century, the seed of Satan persecuting as of old, the Children of Mary. Nor have we reason to expect that these enmities will be eliminated as the world grows older. Quite the contrary—for we read in the Apocalypse: "Woe to the earth, and to the sea, because the devil is come down unto you, having great wrath, knowing that he hath but a short time. And when the dragon saw that he was cast unto the earth, he persecuted the woman who brought forth the man child ... And the dragon was angry against the woman: and went to make war with the rest of her seed, who keep the commandments of God, and have the testimony of Jesus Christ" (Apoc. 12:12; 13:17).

As Satan's time grows shorter, both reason and prophecy lead us to anticipate that his wrath against the holy seed of the elect will increase and not diminish and that the persecutions that have reddened with the Royal Blood of Jesus Christ, the pathway of human history will grow yet more bloody as the end of the world draws near.

It has ever been the duty of Christians to love all men, and the Sister of Charity who ministers alike to Christian and Jew, to pagan and Mohammedan, to white man and Negro, is truly the personification of the Church's loving attitude towards all the children of Adam. But this does not destroy the divinely established fact that there is a more intimate fellowship between the elect of God and the oneness of Blood, which through Adam, makes the whole human race akin. "Let us work good to all men," exhorts the Apostle, "but especially to those who are of the household of the faith" (Gal. 6:10).

That which sometimes is called the Eleventh Commandment, was imparted by Jesus Christ to His disciples, on the night of His betrayal; and it was a commandment to love—not their enemies, for already He had taught them in the Sermon on the Mount to do that—but in that solemn hour He said: "A new commandment I give unto you: that you love one another." (Jn. 13:34)

In the thirteenth chapter of St. John's Gospel we read: "Jesus knowing that his hour was come, that He should pass out of this world to the Father, having loved His own who were in the world, He loved them unto the end."

That Our Lord entertained a very different affection towards His elect than He did towards mankind at large, is evident in the prayer which he addressed to the Father after He had instituted the Sacrament of His love and which is manifested in the seventeenth chapter of the same Gospel: "I have

11

manifested Thy name to those whom Thou hast given Me out of the world: I pray for them. I pray not for the world, but for those whom Thou hast given Me; for they are Thine."

And that He desired that the brotherhood between Christians should be far more intimate and close than what is commonly called the "universal brotherhood of man" is again plainly indicated in the prayer, for He continues: "Holy Father keep them in Thy name whom Thou hast given Me; that they may be one as We also are ... And not for them only do I pray; but for them also who through their word shall believe in Me; that they all may be one as Thou Father in Me and I in Thee, that they also may be one in Us."

Alas, that through the malice of the devil and man's own fallen nature divisions, separations, estrangements, misunderstandings, and even age-long hatred should find their existence among Christians! The shame and grief that the holy seed of God, surrounded by their enemies should be at strife among themselves! The Holy Spirit is arousing the consciences of the whole Christian family to realize the sadness and pity of all and the paramount duty of every Child of God in the twentieth century, is to emphasize both in thought and deed, our kinship in Christ Jesus, whether Catholic or Protestant, Roman, Greek or Anglican.

Who knows—it may be the sword of persecution and the fierce onslaught of the seed of the serpent, which in the end, will drive the children of Mary together and compel us in self-defense to make an end of disunity and to fight shoulder to shoulder under one Commander-in-Chief, against the serried-hosts of darkness and the powers of hell.

There is an old saying, "Blood will tell" and this we believe to be preeminently true of the Most Precious Blood, shed for the unity of God's elect on Mount Calvary.

5. Essentials of Unity

Antidote, February, 1922

On Sunday morning, January the 22nd, as the clocks of Rome struck the hour of six the soul of Pope Benedict the Fifteenth passed from the Sovereign Pontiff's body. Giacomo Della

Chiesa was the two hundred and sixtieth to ascend the Chair of Peter at Rome from which to rule the One, Holy, Roman and Catholic Church throughout the world. He was a little man like Saul of Tarsus in person, but a giant in spiritual accomplishment. Coming to the Throne of the Fisherman at one of the most critical times in the entire history of the world, he guided the Ship of Christ through the rocks, and shoals, and storms of the most tempestuous era in the history of the world. If there is one thing more than another which the short Pontificate of Pope Benedict XV should impress upon the mind of the world it is the solidarity and the indestructible unity of the Catholic Church.

While the social and political worlds are struggling with the problem of reconstruction, the prophets of non-Catholic Christianity are lamenting the almost endless divisions of Christendom and the problem of Church Unity is everywhere to the front. Yet all confess that, until now, the remedies humanly devised fall short of what is so urgently required, whether it be Protestant Federation, the Anglican Quadrilateral, or the Greco-Russian test of orthodoxy, viz., the first seven Ecumenical Councils. It is manifestly hopeless that the entire Christian world will ever get together under any of these three programs, nor under any other of man's own devising, no matter how clever or ingenious.

The Antidote believes it will immensely help to prepare the way for a real Reunion of Christendom, if all the "other sheep" of Christ "not of this Fold," i.e., not in communion with Peter and his unfailing successors, will come to recognize that Unity or Oneness is as much an unfailing and indestructible mark of the Church of Jesus Christ, as is her Apostolicity, Catholicity and Holiness.

At the General Council of Nicea, A.D. 325, the Catholic Church declared that besides her Catholicity, Apostolicity and Holiness, the Church of Jesus Christ is essentially *One*—one, not for the first century only, nor up to the time of the Greek Schism, nor up to the Reformation period with the innumerable Christian sects of the present day, or that Protestant principle of private judgment which gave them being, began; but one in that organic oneness and visible unity which is one of the fundamental and abiding marks of the Church.

When St. Peter came to Rome he established there the

Chair of Unity, and all who have succeeded him in that Chair until now have steadfastly borne witness to its being the will of Jesus Christ, the Church's Divine Head, that communion with that Chair should be the real test of Catholic Unity.

The extraordinary phenomenon which the Catholic Church presented during the late World War ought to impress itself upon the minds of men as an extraordinary evidence of the indestructible unity of that original Church which Christ built upon the Rock of Peter. In spite of the fact that Catholics belonging to the central powers were in deadly conflict with those of the entente, yet from the Vatican Pope Benedict XV with marvelous and supernatural tact, good judgment, and patience, that refused to waver in face of claims of his neutral policy—sometimes by the central powers, sometimes by England, or America, or France, or Italy—kept in touch with all the faithful through the world; never for a single instant was any Cardinal, Archbishop, Bishop, Priest or Layman, in all this immense network of conflicting interests out of communion with the head of the Catholic Church.

Christian Unity in the only proper sense of that term necessitates above all unity of faith, for there is "one Lord, one Faith and one Baptism." This unity of faith is found only in the Catholic Church. Among Protestants there is the widest possible divergence, ranging all the way from Unitarian denial of the divinity of Christ to High Church Episcopalian admission of the primacy of St. Peter and his successors, the Popes. This point does not have to be stressed. We address both the intellects and hearts of learned and devout Protestants themselves, who do not need to be shown that there is nothing in Protestantism approaching unity of faith.

Christian Unity necessitates unity of hope, in its essential features, at least. And Christian hope is linked up with a right faith, which alone enables us with united voice to give to every man that asketh us, a reason of the hope that is in us.

Christian Unity also requires charity. This is the greatest of the three only when it is the fruit of the other two; for how can the highest charity exist apart from a right faith and a certain hope? You may give a man a glass of cold water and earn a reward in heaven's eyes thereby; but suppose you tell him God did not make the heavens and the earth, or that Christ is not God, or that His Church is the sum of every conceivable

14

shade of error—what then? There must be a true charity as well as a right faith and a certain hope. True charity is found in the Catholic Church. The average Protestant does not realize how much this charity is taxed and expended on account of vicious attacks founded on groundless lies idly retailed; in charity the Catholic Church turns the other cheek like her Lord and prays for her enemies; for she knows that many who do these things really mean to serve God, and that like Saul of Tarsus, when the scales fall from their eyes, they may come to serve God, as only they can do perfectly, in His Church which before they persecuted.

That Church is *One*. Unity is essential to her very Being. By that Unity she has been identified in every Christian age and nation. This Unity cannot be broken. It is today a fact and reality and it has been in every age, whether in the Middle Ages, in the days of St. Augustine in the fifth century, at the time of St. Irenaeus in the second century, in the days of St. Clement of Rome or in the days of the Apostles when Our Lord associated with Himself, Peter, whose faith, ardently and positively expressed, had not been revealed by flesh and blood but by the Father in Heaven. That faith could only be preserved where there was Unity, and because His Church must have a visible head, like His Church of the old dispensation, whose Law and prophets He came to fulfill, He said to Peter in the midst of the other Apostles, "Thou art Peter and upon this Rock I will build My Church." Peter's name in Chaldaic—the language which our Blessed Lord spoke—was Cephas—meaning rock, and Peter's faith was also founded upon a rock. A rock does not shift. It is stable and the faith, to be stable, must hold its moorings and be voiced by authority—"Whatsoever thou shalt bind on earth, shall be bound in Heaven"—"I give unto thee the keys of the kingdom of heaven."

Christ is the Way, the Truth and the Life—He is also the Door, and to Peter and his successors He gave the keys. Hence the Church is the pillar and ground of the truth, and Unity of faith proceeds from Christ and is preserved through His Vicar on earth. The Chair of Peter is the visible center of Unity. It is the only Unity which the Catholic Church has ever known. It is the only Unity against which the gates of hell cannot prevail. It cannot be broken. Schism does not break this Unity; it simply

15

breaks away from it. If it could be broken, it would no longer be Unity.

There was no communion during the War between Protestants in Germany and Protestants in England, but through the center of the Catholic Church's life and the heart of her administration in the Vatican, and in the person of the occupant of the Vatican, the life-blood of the whole Catholic Church throughout the world circulated without let or hindrance. Why in view of all this do people continue to attribute it all to the political ambition of crafty ecclesiastics, and not recognize in it all the fulfillment of the promise of Christ to St. Peter and his successors and those associated with the Apostolic See from the days of the Apostles to the present time—"Lo! I am with you always, even unto the end of the world."

Instead of continuing to prophesy that the papacy has arrived at the end of its rope, and that soon we shall see the downfall of the last surviving autocracy of the world, it would be better for those who profess to believe in Christ to recognize such men as Leo XIII, Pius X, and Benedict XV, as true successors of the Apostle Peter, in whom dwelt the same Holy Spirit; who were protected from error in faith by the same divine guidance as those in the past; and to realize that as with them, so it will be with those that succeed them on the throne of the Fishermen until Christ Himself comes to judge the living and the dead, and to establish His Kingdom in righteousness for ever and ever.

6. The Unity of the Church

Sermon, July 5, 1925

St. John's Church, Graymoor

Now, at this time, instead of dealing with the standpoint of the individual and exhorting you as individuals to exercise yourselves in the spirit of the divine love, we will, rather, speak from the collective standpoint. Of course, we realize that a *collection,* whether of the nation, or of the Church, is made of individuals. The quality and nature of the Church is governed by the individual, and so indirectly, what we have to say applies to you, yet it is from the standpoint of the comprehensive, rather than the individual aspect.

The purpose of Our Lord in coming into this world was to establish the kingdom of heaven in the midst of this world. The human family by the seduction of our first parents and the malice of the devil had come under the sway of a ursurper. Our Lord speaks of him in the gospel as "the prince of this world" and St. Paul says: "We wrestle not with flesh and blood but with principalities and the powers of darkness."

The world from the fall of Adam until now, in spite of the Christian elements that have been thrown into it, has been a world of anxiety, hatred, greed, lust and passion, culminating in the outbreak of innumerable wars. Men have cultivated the cults of what they call "the enemy" and have stirred themselves up to glorify enmity and to think hatred the virtue of patriotism. You find this exemplified in the savages of the primeval forests of America. Their idea of friendship was limited to a narrow tribe and all that did not belong to their tribe were their enemies; thus the one pursuit of their lives was to hunt their enemies. Their great occupation was to decorate themselves with warpaint and regard it as the greatest virtue to run down these enemies and hang their scalps at their belts. Although nations have formed men into larger groups, we have seen in our day that these groups can out-Indian the Indian in the wholesale destructiveness of hate, when those aggregations of nations combine to immerse themselves in the struggle of a world war.

Now all this hatred, whether it be between the individual, the members of a family, fratricidal strife within the larger group of the nation, or of one nation warring against another, all this, I say, is against the teaching of Our Lord Jesus Christ and the peace of that Kingdom which He came to establish in the world. A kingdom which is not of this world, but which is to be transferred from the sphere of this world into those new heavens and new earth, which God said He would erect in that great realm of God, ruled over by justice and charity, a realm where there will be perfect harmony, perfect peace and perfect love, and where "God shall wipe away all tears from all eyes" in the final triumph of the Cross and the love of God.

Now, as we have just said, Our Lord came to establish this kingdom in the world and it was His will that it should be ever-extending, so that at last the prince of this world, the usurper, should be put down from his throne, and He, the rightful heir of the throne, reign from pole to pole and from sea to sea. And so in the Apocalypse, we have an angel proclaiming that the kingdom of this world shall become the Kingdom of Christ and of His anointed, and we must look forward to the day when Christ shall triumph over all the world, and all peoples shall bow down and recognize their Lord and their King, not only in the letter, but in the spirit.

It is also clearly stated that there shall be a great millenium, a reign of peace, before the end of the world, and as Christians and Catholics we should be recognizing this purpose of God and we should contribute our share towards the final evolution—if you want so to call it—from the present sad condition of human society. From this standpoint of the future, we may look forward with some degree of encouragement. The great war that has passed has not brought "safety to democracy" and we are disappointed in many of the immediate after-effects, but it was satisfactorily conducted as far as the American people were concerned and dominated by an altruistic motive. We sincerely thought that democracy in our land was in peril from the *German Kultur*, and we wanted to make the world "safe for democracy," so we threw ourselves into the conflict and poured out the blood of our youth and the treasure of our land without stint. Now we must not forget these ideals, or think that they were altogether wasted and ineffective. In spite of the outrageous Contract of Versailles, made by politicians who were influenced by sordid motives and by the hatred which rankled in their breast against their neighbor, there is still the hope for better things.

Yes, there is one hope, but one hope only, for a world-wide Christian democracy, and one possibility that our great nation shall go on developing along Christian lines, and that hope is the triumph of Catholicity in this country. Now in order that there may be this triumph, there must be the unity of those who believe in Christ, and not only unity but charity, the putting on of the divine love which burns in the heart of God, into the heart of man; this alone throws out the acidity and malice of lust, generated by the prince of this world, who is the author of hatred and who will ultimately generate a kingdom of unspeakable darkness where all warmth of love will be extracted and where undying death shall consume.

This is the situation. How can we overcome it? We will not

overcome it by opposing hatred to it, because that would contradict the teaching of Our Lord. St. Paul says we are to overcome evil with good, and hatred with love. Not to labor the point any more, we have before us the task as Catholics of working in a true patriotic spirit, for the evolution of everything that is good and beautiful and praiseworthy in our people, in other words, laboring to establish the peace of Christ. This can only mean the triumph of the principles of love, good fellowship, and charity. We shall oppose, therefore, the spirit of carnage with the spirit of charity. The way to triumph is not to show ourselves more hateful than our opponents, opposing weapon against weapon. Let them alone, because there is something in the mind of the American people that protests against bigotry, and if our people find Catholics full of a forgiving spirit, not giving back abuse, but rather turning away anger by a soft answer and not displaying otherwise than the charity of Christ, all this will have its infallible effect. Even so did the first martyrs triumph over the blood-thirsty Romans; they subjected themselves meekly to persecution and died in the arena, and from their holocaust was raised in Rome, the most Christian city in the world, its Christian capitol.

This is the spirit of St. Francis, the spirit of reconciliation, the spirit that overcomes evil with good. In my sermon this morning, I spoke of an incident in the life of St. Francis, how in the mountain country of Assisi there were depredations made by desperate bandits, who waylaid the people and lived on spoils. On one occasion St. Francis, knowing that these desperate men had been for some time unsuccessful in their raids and that they were hungry, sent some good bread to them by his brethren. Now these robbers were so impressed by this charity that the bandit band was actually broken up, and some of them went so far as to put on the brown habit and become Friars.

7. Saint Francis — The Apostle of Unity

The Lamp 1926
February, 56-7, March, 65-7

The present year of grace is signalized by being the seventh centenary of the passing of St. Francis of Assisi, from his earthly career, to the realm of heavenly glory. Undoubtedly the commemoration of the seven hundredth anniversary of the death of the Seraphic Patriarch will be one of the outstanding ecclesiastical events of 1926, for this great servant of God, "being dead yet speaketh" and the son of Peter Bernadone, the merchant Prince of Assisi, has left an indelible impression not only upon the age in which he lived but upon all succeeding ages, so that in all Christendom it would be difficult to find a spot that is not enriched because the Saint of Umbria determined to follow the gospel of Jesus Christ literally and because in so doing, under the inspiration of the Holy Ghost, he gave to the world an interpretation of the spirit and life of Jesus Christ of Nazareth, that came upon the nations almost as a new revelation of the Son of God from heaven.

Do we realize the full significance of the fact so often commented upon that there is no post-apostolic saint raised to the altars of the Church who wields such influence among Christians of every name as St. Francis? He is admired, talked of, and read about, and his example is held up as worthy of imitation by every denomination of Christians, even among the least orthodox. His name is one to conjure with. His record in the past and his increasing popularity constitutes him pre-eminently as the Saint of Church Unity. May we not hope, looking with discernment upon the signs of the times, that it is the purpose of God after the lapse of seven centuries to accomplish a reincarnation of the spirit of the Seraphic Patriarch among men and to call forth from the ranks of his disciples and spiritual children those who shall meet the peculiar needs of this generation, rekindling the fire of divine love on earth and recalling men once more to a realizing sense that "the Kingdom of God is not meat and drink, but righteousness, joy and peace in the Holy Ghost;" teaching them also that the prayer of Our Lord "Ut omnes unum sint" lays upon all Christians a grave responsibility and a sublime obligation?

The salutation with which Francis commanded his friars to address all whom they should meet, "the Lord give thee peace," and it is interesting to note that the international committee formed to celebrate the centenary above referred to, in addressing themselves to the lovers of St. Francis in every nation fittingly call him "the Lover and Apostle of Peace." It is this message which we desire to emphasize, for if there is one thing more than another which the Holy Spirit is pressing home to the hearts and minds of all Christians today, it is the necessity of peace among the hitherto warring factions of Christ's followers, that by once more returning to unity they may wage successful warfare against the Prince of Darkness and hasten the day when the "Kingdom of this world shall become the Kingdom of Christ."

It is a Franciscan tradition that the Poverello had his precursor in the streets of Assisi and that this herald of his advent uttered the two words "Peace and Good." The first triumph scored by St. Francis as a preacher of good will and peace was the political and social reformation of his own beloved Assisi. The cathedral could not hold the multitudes that sought to hear him. His fellow citizens not only listened, they acted, and the fruit of his preaching was the character of the commune drafted, signed and sealed in the year 1210. This remarkable document begins "In the Name of God, Amen" and decrees that henceforth there shall be peace and not strife between the *majors* and *minors* of Assisi. Then follows the enfranchisement of those who aforetime had been serfs.

This was the first link in the chain of mediaeval feudalism which Francis broke, but it was by no means the last. By a master stroke of inspiration, he later on founded the Third Order, the Brothers of Penance, and these, conjointly with the Friars Minor, became the "Militia of Jesus Christ" under his generalship to disperse the armies of the feudal princes and take from them the armor wherein they trusted. True to his gospel of peace, St. Francis decreed that all who joined his Third Order might take no oath of homage to any lord, save the Vicar of Christ, neither should they bear arms. The multitudes of the people weary with internecine war and bloodshed, wherein they fought each other to gratify the hatred and ambitions of the nobility, took refuge throughout Europe under the peace banner of the Prince of Assisi. In vain the feudal lords raged and protested. The Holy See threw over the Franciscan Tertiaries the aegis of its mighty protection, feudalism fell back defeated; the work of the Umbrian Emancipator stood like Gibraltar. *Christian Democracy was born.* It yet remains for his biographers to trace through the succeeding centuries of Old and New World History, the influence of Francis upon the social and political reforms, which have eventuated in the great popular governments of the day.

As an American citizen, I venture to say that the discovery of the western hemisphere and its present status as a land to which the oppressed and poor of Europe flocked at the rate of a million a year prior to the World War, is a consequence of the ministry and life of St. Francis, in much the same way that the possession of the Promised Land by the Israelites hundreds of years after his death, was a consequence of the faith and obedience of Abraham. The stamp of redestination was as much upon Christopher Columbus as it was upon Joshua. The name given him at baptism foretold his mission, he was the son of St. Francis, a member of the Third Order. After years of baffled hope, when ridicule and rejection had given birth to despair, another Franciscan Tertiary, the Spanish Queen, supplied the purchase money for the ships and so saved the cause. And the inspiration of Isabella was her confessor, another Franciscan, John Perez, guardian of the Friars Minor of La Rabida. Yes, and the very sailors that manned two ships were Tertiaries of St. Francis. They alone had faith enough to venture their lives on what the world thought a madman's enterprise. Again we are to remember that the first Christian evangelists of the new world were Franciscan missionaries. Lastly, it was the democratic principles preached five hundred years before, by St. Francis of Assisi, and afterwards, disseminated everywhere by his disciples, which found their national expression in the Declaration of American Independence.

And it is here that the political reformers of this generation need to learn an all-important lesson from the Great Reformer of seven hundred years ago. He did not make the mistake, which so many secularists are making, antagonizing two things which God wills to work in concert and concord, the Church of Jesus Christ and the Christian State. Francis was a Christian and a Catholic, from the core of his heart to the tip of his fingers. And he was a social reformer, not *in spite* of his being a Catholic and a cleric, but *because* he was first, the follower of the Divine Master and a loyal obedient son of that Church which the Lord founded on the Rock of Peter. And moreover, it was the Church, in the person of the Vicar of Christ, that stood behind the social reforms of Francis and shielded his Third Order from the opposition of the barons, who would certainly have crushed the militia of the Poverello had they not been so upheld.

But, however splendid the social reforms inaugurated by

St. Francis, they were a secondary consequence and not of the prime essence of his mission. Religion was everything with the Saint of Assisi and had he not inaugurated a religious reform, his social reformation would never have been. When, therefore, we entitle him the Apostle of Unity, we are thinking of him more as a peace-maker in the Kingdom of God, than as a citizen of Italy, or of the world.

Catholic biographers are quite as emphatic as M. Sabatier, in describing the perilous state of the Church, at the beginning of the thirteenth century and the prevalence everywhere among the masses of the seeds of revolt against her authority. The worldliness of the secular clergy, the decadence of missionary zeal, even among the regulars, had alienated the hearts of the people from their Catholic pastors and made them ready to follow the lead of heretical teachers, who abounded on all sides. A reformation was needed badly and had it not taken place at that time within the Church, the upheaval of the sixteenth century, with its wide sweeping revolt from the rule of the Catholic hierarchy, might have come then instead of three centuries later. St. Francis certainly fulfilled the vision of Innocent III, when, as it said, he beheld in his sleep the Church of St. John Lateran falling and a mendicant staying it up on his shoulders.

It is no exaggeration to say, that to St. Francis, as the Apostle of Church Unity, belongs pre-eminently, the credit of postponing the breakup of Western Christianity of three hundred years. And it is also to be noted, that on the soil which the feet of the Umbrian Saint trod in his apostolic journeys, Protestantism has never taken root and the unity of the Church has experienced no serious breach. Yet the same soil was the hotbead of heresy and schism at the time when kneeling before the crucifiz in St. Damian's, he received the command, *"Francis, go and rebuild My Church."*

As all the world knows, the methods employed by the chivalrous Knight of Lady Poverty, to recall the people to obedience to their Christ-appointed pastors, were never the repressive measure of the inquisition nor the unsheathing of the material sword. His remedy for all the ills of his own and subsequent ages was the return of the Church to simplicity, the piety, the faith and the love of Apostolic days, and he was leader enough to marshal an army to follow him, while he gained for his holy crusade the sanction of the Holy See. When the multitude of the people found that the gospel was preached to them by Catholics, whose saintliness, poverty and zeal rivaled that of the blessed Apostles themselves, they had no more use for heretics and love for the Holy Roman Church was marvelously increased among rich and poor alike.

(March)

It is to be noted that the new feast instituted by the Holy Father to celebrate the Kingship of Christ, as Sovereign Lord and Master of the World, will not only be celebrated by the Church at large in the same year in which Christendom celebrates the seventh centenary of the passing from earth to heaven of St. Francis of Assisi, but to make the coincidence more intimate, the feast of Our Lord as King will be kept on the last Sunday of October, whereas the celebration of the Seven Hundredth Anniversary of St. Francis' Death, will begin on the first Sunday of October.

When we regard St. Francis as the Apostle of Catholic Unity, the sequence of the two celebrations is all the more significant. Our Blessed Lord prayed Himself to the Father, that His disciples might all be one, in order that the world might believe in His Messiaship. Thus we learn from the very lips of Christ that His followers must first be one otherwise His reign as King among men will not be realized.

What is needed now is a double portion of Francis, the Seraphic Saint of Love, to descend upon his children in particular and all Christians at large, as the mantle of Elias fell upon Eliseus, in order that by united prayer and brotherly conferences and cooperation, the schisms and heresies of the past thousand years may be swept into oblivion and the Unity of the Holy Spirit reign among those who confess Jesus Christ to be their King, as on the day of Pentecost when, "the multitude of believers had but one heart and one soul." (Acts 4:32)

But to resume the narration of how St. Francis and his sons carried on their Apostolate of Unity.

The influence of the Seraphic Peacemaker was not to be confined to Western Christendom, he was also destined to stamp the impression of his apostleship upon the East. His famous expedition to the Sultan of Egypt and his incorporation in the Rule of the Friars Minor of the chapter on: "Those who go

24

among the Saracens and other infidels," has had more effect in rescuing the Holy Places of Palestine, from the desecration of the Turk, than the rivers of blood shed during the Crusades. The Latin Kingdom of Jerusalem fell centuries ago and perished with the sword that had established it, but ever since the knightly sons of Francis invaded the Holy Land, they have held their ground and, today, as they have been for ages, they are the guardians of the sacred places at Bethlehem, Nazareth and Mount Calvary. It is they who watch over the gnarled olive trees of Gethsemane and keep the flowers blooming where, in His agony, Jesus stained the earth with His blood.

Nor will our sketch of Francis, as the Apostle of Unity, be complete, without some mention of the part he and his disciples played in the all-but-successful efforts, which were made in the thirteenth, fourteenth and fifteenth centuries, to heal the breach between the East and West.

That the healing of the Greek Schism was in the heart of St. Francis there can be no doubt and soon after his death, it became one of the foremost objects which his sons in religion tried to accomplish.

As early as 1233 we find Brother Haymo of the English Province, and afterwards Minister General, deputed by Gregory IX, who had been the friend of Francis, to negotiate with the Patriarch of Constantinople terms of reunion. He and his fellow legates were cordially received by the Emperor and the Patriarch. By the latter they were invited to attend a synod, in which they argued before the Eastern prelates on the procession of the Holy Ghost, and that, so successfully, they returned to Rome bringing with them an orthodox profession of faith signed by the Easterns at the synod. About the year 1250 Blessed John of Parma, the eighth in succession from St. Francis, as Minister General, asked leave of Innocent IV to undertake a like mission to the Greeks and calling him "an angel of peace" the Pope gave him leave. The humble Franciscan in his poor coarse habit captivated the Greeks from the Emperor, John Vitalian, down to the lowest of the people. Anne MacDonell says, in *The Sons of St. Francis*: "All eyes were turned for the moment toward Rome and the Church that had bred this holy man. The mission seemed accomplished. The Emperor sent messages to Innocent to say that he favored the project and was willing to continue negotiations. But then the Emperor died. Shortly after, Innocent

25

died too. The matter was shelved for the time." John of Parma, however, had sowed the good seed. A score of years later the harvest was reached at the Council of Lyons (1274). Here the Greeks were present and the very life and inspiration of the Council was another famous Franciscan, St. Bonaventure, the successor of John of Parma, in the office of Minister General. At the opening of the synod, he sat at the Pope's right hand and was the first to address the assembly. The Eastern representatives, won by the sweetness and convinced by the logic of Bonaventure, agreed to all that was proposed by the Holy See. On the feast of Saints Peter and Paul, a grand Mass of thanksgiving was celebrated by the Pope. The great Franciscan preached the sermon on the Unity of the Church. Overwhelmed by the anxieties and the labors of the gigantic task laid upon him and consumed with zeal for the unity and peace of the household of faith, St. Bonaventure died after the fourth session of the Council, and the East and the West were of one heart and soul in paying the last tribute of honor to the illustrious saint. Time and space forbids more mention of how Brother Jerome of Ascoli, afterwards Pope Nicholas IV, went as Papal Nuncio to Greece in 1272 and how in 1289, at the extreme age of eighty, John of Parma again set out for the East, his journey ending not in Constantinople, the seat of earthly pride and strife, but in the City of celestial peace, the new Jerusalem.

At the Council of Florence, when again the schism between East and West was temporarily healed, once more we find the sons of Francis the leading spirits for unity. Towering over all his contemporaries was John of Capistran, one of the most sublime missionary spirits in the whole range of Church history. He it was, who had induced the Patriarchs of Jerusalem, Alexandria and Antioch to send delegates to the Council and brought with himself to Florence, ambassadors from the Armenians, who were eager to unite with Rome. Other Franciscans, who took part in the Council, were Brothers Bartholomew of Tano and Albert of Sarziano, both men of great learning and masters of the Greek language, who returned from Constantinople bringing with them the Patriarch Joseph, the Emperor Paleologus and a great number of Eastern prelates besides. Still other shining lights of the Council were Francis and Louis of Bologna, James of Trimadizzi, and last, but not least, St. Bernardino of Siena.

We especially look to St. Francis, to exert his apostleship

26

of Unity to restore the Ecclesia Anglicana to her ancient position of obedience and submission to the Holy See. Certainly the Franciscan traditions in England have always been those of unflinching loyalty to the Successor of St. Peter. They had been favorites of Henry VIII prior to his entanglement with Anne Boleyn, but when it became a question of their choice between the royal favor and fidelity to the Vicar of Christ, the Franciscans did not waver. Catherine, Henry's true wife, was herself a Franciscan Tertiary and wore the habit of the Third Order under her queenly attire. Henry attended Mass in the Franciscan Church at Greenwich on Easter Day, 1532. Father Peto, provincial of the Gray Friars (years after made a Cardinal and at the time, confessor to Princess Mary) preached the sermon. With dauntless courage he rebuked the King and prophesied that, "As dogs licked the blood of Ahab, so would a similar judgment be meted out to him by God." A prophecy, which it is said, was literally fulfilled, when the corpse of Henry was being conveyed to Windsor for interment. Friar Peto, for his boldness, was imprisoned and later banished from the realm. All the Friars suffered, more or less, and some were permitted to win the crown of martyrdom, along with the Carthusians and many others, who resisted unto blood, striving against the King's supremacy.

A name which Anglo-Catholics hold especially dear, is that of the eminent Franciscan, Santa Clara, a contemporary of Archbishop Laud, who wrote a treatise on the XXXIX articles of religion and dedicated the same to King Charles I, his design being to reconcile the official teaching of the Church of England with that of the Council of Trent and thus to pave the way for reunion with Rome. It was this treatise which inspired Newman's famous Tract XC. And this brings us to Oxford, where the great Catholic Revival in the Anglican Church had its rise seventy-five years ago. Referring to the Oxford Movement, Lord Halifax, addressing the English Church Union in 1904 said: "We are resolved that work begun by God's mercy amongst us shall, God helping us, be carried to its predestined end, which, whether in union with the State or not, shall be nothing less than the spread and maintenance of the Catholic Faith ... and the eventual reunion of all those who love Our Lord, Jesus Christ, in sincerity and truth, in one visible Fold, under One Shepherd." The scholarly Benedictine, Dom John

Chapman, in a recent book (*Bishop Gore on Catholic Claims*, p.19) says, "I think, then, that the Church of England, as a whole, (apart from the Broad Party) is moving steadily and corporately Romewards."

If, as Anglicans themselves are coming more and more to recognize, the *terminus ad quem*, of the Oxford Movement, is reunion with the Apostolic See, then the question easily suggests itself: How much of this is to be traced to the Franciscan tradition of the Oxford University? Mr. Gladstone (*Romanos Lectures*, 1892) said: "The greatest names belonging to Oxford in the thirteenth and fourteenth centuries are . . . in the ranks of the Seraphic Francis . . . The Franciscan Order gave to Oxford the larger number of those remarkable and even epoch-making men who secured, for this University, such a career of glory even in Mediaeval times." And Anthony Wood declares that by reason of Alexander Hales, Roger Bacon, Duns Scotus, and the other mendicants Oxford was deservedly styled at this time *Emporium optimarum disciplinarum* (The Tablet). The Return of the Franciscans to Oxford last April on St. Anselm's Day is as the shooting up of a vine killed by the frosts of a long winter and the earnest start of a new summer for the sons of St. Francis at the ancient University.

The Book of Malachi, the last of the Old Testament prophecies, ends thusly: "Behold, I will send you Elijah the prophet before the coming of the great and dreadful day of the Lord: And he shall turn the hearts of the children to their fathers, lest I come and smite the earth with a curse" (Mal. 4:5-6). This is precisely the crying need of Christendom today. It is the heart of the fathers that need to be turned to their children as the heart of Francis burned with love and sympathy for the people, and especially the poor and oppressed and it is the alienated millions, who confess the name of Christ, but who are separatists from the Church's visible unity, that need be turned once more in love to the Fathers, the bishops and priests of the Catholic Church. Will it not be that the spirit of Francis living and moving and having its being among men that will fulfill this prophecy as far as it is to be realized by the world in the twentieth century? Surely it is the faith and love of St. Francis that needs to be revived among us, if the schisms in the mystical body of Christ are to be healed and the vast company of baptized

Christians be made to dwell together as brethren who are at unity.

To the Fathers, St. Francis' message in the twentieth century is what it was in the thirteenth: "Feed not yourselves, feed the sheep. Lead them, mingle with them, go out before them, lay down your life for them. Be as the Good Shepherd."

To the children, St. Francis' message is the message of the faith once for all delivered to the saints and loving submission to the guardian of that faith to whom Our Lord said: "I have prayed for thee that thy faith fail not."

8. The Ark of Salvation

Radio Address, October 22, 1935

"And the Lord added unto the Church daily,
such as should be saved."   ACTS, 2:47

At the conclusion of my discourse last Tuesday on the "Valley of Destruction," I invited any among my listeners who felt themselves tangled up in the thickets and briars of that valley, and were finding difficulty in making their escape, to write me, promising to render them any assistance in my power. Correspondence so far resulting from that invitation reveals a confusion of mind upon the part of some, as to just how to deliver their souls from perdition and to win for themselves a place among the blessed ones, who will reign with Christ the King in heavenly glory forever.

We don't have to be learned theologians to save our souls and the mere searching of the scriptures, the studying of our Bibles, is no guarantee of our getting to heaven. The way of salvation has not changed since the time of the Apostles. As it was on the day of Pentecost, so it is in the 20th Century of the Christian era. As the Lord added to the Church daily such as should be saved when St. Peter preached in Jerusalem, John in Ephesus, Paul and Barnabas in Antioch, so the Lord adds daily to the membership of His Church such as shall be saved in this year of grace, 1935. Those whose names are written in the Lamb's Book of Life are they who, like the first Christians, "continue steadfastly in the doctrine and fellowship of the apostles, in the breaking of the bread and in prayer."

After the eternal Son of God assumed our flesh and at such tremendous cost to Himself, purchased the salvation of man, even by the shedding of His blood unto death, He did not abandon man to his own devices in so important a matter as the salvation of his soul, but as He commanded Noah to build an ark, through the instrumentality of which he and his family were to be saved from the deluge, so Christ created the Church as the ark of safety to carry His elect over the tempestuous sea of the present life and to bring them safely to the shores of eternity.

The process of salvation is in itself a simple one. Our Lord said to Nicodemus, "Except a man be born again of the Spirit and of water he cannot enter into the Kingdom of God." The Kingdom of God is the Church, which Christ Himself established, the congregation of those who have been incorporated into the Mystical Body of Christ. Just as God instituted circumcision when He made His covenant with Abraham, Isaac and Jacob, as the *sine qua non* to every male child born among the Israelites of admission to that covenant fellowship, so in the New Covenant, God instituted baptism as the door of entrance into the Church, which is the company of the redeemed. St. Peter says all those who have been baptized have become "partakers of the divine Nature;" they are the children of God the Father, members of Christ, and inheritors of the Kingdom of Heaven. Where the Church has been long established in a Christian land, adult baptism is confined almost exclusively to those who have experienced conversion to the faith late in life. As soon as a child is born to Christian parents, themselves members all their life long of Christ's true Church, the little one is hurried to the baptismal font, to be incorporated into the family of the redeemed. The children of the Old Covenant were circumcised on the eighth day, and became just as much members of the Jewish Church thereby, as though they had been circumcised after they had attained the full stature of manhood. So the Holy Ghost operates just as readily, if not more so, in accomplishing the new birth into the Kingdom of God, through the water of regeneration, when the subject is an infant of a few days only, as when the catechumen is as old as was Constantine, the first Christian Emperor of Rome when he received Baptism. Confirmation, under the Jewish covenant, took place and still takes place, when the child has arrived at years of discretion, so also is it in the Church of Christ, by the laying on of the hands of the bishop, seven-fold gifts of the Holy Ghost are conferred to strengthen and confirm the children of the Church in a way of sanctification. But most important of all, the boys and girls are brought early to the altar rail to the reception of the Most Blessed Sarcament of the Body and Blood of Christ, because thereby Christ more fully dwells in them and they dwell in Christ and they are nourished and strengthened on the journey that leads across the "Valley of the Shadow of Death" into the promised land, flowing with milk and honey, into the paradise of God.

To make their calling and election sure, it is only necessary for the faithful, supported by divine grace received through the sacraments of the Church, to obey the commandments of God, to keep themselves unspotted from the world and to prepare the wedding garment which is the justice of saints, then when they come into the heavenly Jerusalem to appear among the company of the redeemed they shall be clothed in white garments and carry in their hands the palm branch of victory, having triumphed in the battle of life over the temptations of the world, the flesh and the devil and at the end of their earthly pilgrimage they may be able to say with St. Paul: "I have fought a good fight, I have kept the faith, henceforth there is laid up for me a crown of justice which Christ, the righteous judge, shall give me at that day."

To those of our listeners who are outside the New Covenant which Christ as the Divine Savior, established in the shedding of His own blood for the redemption of mankind, my message today is: Try no longer to work out your salvation by your own efforts, as an independent "no church Member" but seek without delay admission to the Church which Christ established, as the Ark of Salvation of immortal souls.

Next Sunday many millions of Christians throughout the world will be celebrating the Feast of Christ the King. When Christ was arraigned before the judgment seat of Pilate, the Roman Governor, the latter addressed to Him the question: "Art thou a King then?" His answer was: "Thou sayest that I am a King." A moment before, Jesus said to Pilate: "My Kingdom is not of this world; if my Kingdom were of this world, My servants would certainly strive that I should not be delivered unto you, but now My Kingdom is not from hence." It is to be

31

borne in mind that Christ is the only begotten Son of God, the express image of His glory, to whom the Father hath given all jurisdiction and dominion and power in Heaven and on earth. St. John, speaking of Him, said, "In the beginning was the Word (the Logos) and the Word was with God, and the Word was God; all things were made by Him and without Him was made nothing that was made, and the Word was made Flesh and dwelt among us (and we saw His glory, the glory, as it were, of the only begotten Son of the Father) full of grace and truth."

Whereas the Kingdom of God is not of this world, the citizens of that Kingdom are drafted every day from among the sons of men dwelling upon the earth. They are the elect of God, the baptized children of God the Father, and the members of Christ, the only begotten Son of the Father, and they are indwelt by the Holy Ghost. Their numbers are destined to go on increasing until they outnumber all the rest of the citizens of the world who remain outside of Christ. We read in the Book of the Apocalypse, "And the seventh angel sounded the trumpet; and there were great voices in heaven saying: The kingdom of this world is become our Lord's and His Christ's, and he shall reign for ever and ever. Amen."

The Kingdom of heavenly glory, where Christ shall reign with His elect in radiant bliss, through all the ages of eternity, is reserved for those whose names are written in the Lamb's Book of Life, even for those who hail Jesus Christ, as King here on earth and they will be saved, those who through baptism become members of the Church and are added to her ranks from day to day, but those who refuse to have Christ reign over them as King and Lord and Master now, need not expect a place in His Kingdom hereafter.

9. The Good Shepherd

St. Anthony Hour, April 11, 1937

Who are these "other sheep" that the Good Shepherd said He must bring and that they would hear His voice, obey His call, and there would be "One Fold" and "One Shepherd"? Does that "One Fold" and "One Shepherd" exist in the world today?

32

If so, *where* is it? *Where* can it be found? Is it identical with the Catholic Church? That is what we Catholics believe. In the Catechism which every child in the Catholic Church is taught, we find this question: "What is the Church?" and the answer is: "The Church is the congregation of all those who profess the Faith of Christ, partake of the same Sacraments and are governed by their lawful pastors under one visible head." *Pastor,* as you know, is the Latin word for shepherd. The Good Shepherd, before He went up to Heaven, commissioned the lawful shepherds to watch over His sheep and to take His place and to act in His name.

Last Sunday we read in the Gospel how He appeared on Easter Sunday night in the midst of the Apostles in the upper room at Jerusalem and said unto them: "Peace be to you. As the Father hath sent Me, I also send you." And when He had said this, He breathed on them and said to them: "Receive ye the Holy Ghost. Whose sins you shall forgive, they are forgiven, and whose sins you shall retain, they are retained." The Father had sent Him to be the Good Shepherd and now the Good Shepherd, before He returned to the Father, sent His Apostles and their successors, the bishops and priests of His Church, to be shepherds. He gave them power to wash the sheep and the lambs of the flock in the Precious Blood of the Atonement, that they might be white and clean and He gave them power also to feed the sheep in that same upper room before His death, when He instituted the Blessed Sacrament, and said to them: "Do this in remembrance of Me." As He fed them upon His own precious Body and Blood, so were they to feed the sheep of the flock, by consecrating bread and wine in the Holy Eucharist at the altar, changing them into the Body and Blood of the Good Shepherd Himself, and then, as true pastors, to feed the sheep and the lambs upon that bread that "cometh down from heaven," so that, "he that eateth thereof shall live forever."

Now in order that there might be One Flock and one supreme shepherd over the flock of which all the other pastors are under-shepherds, Christ made St. Peter the Bishop of Rome, His Vicar *par excellence,* and the Supreme Shepherd. He did this some time after His resurrection from the dead, when the apostolic shepherds were gathered together, and in their presence He said to Peter three times: "Simon, son of John, lovest thou Me more than these?" Each time when Peter answered "Yes" Christ said to him: "Feed my lambs, feed my sheep, feed my sheep." Thus, they all understood that He, Jesus, made him the supreme shepherd, the one shepherd over all, the one shepherd over His own flock, that is to say, His Catholic Church, the Church which is described in the Creed as "One, Holy, Catholic, and Apostolic." So we Catholics understand the "One Fold" to be the Catholic Church and the "One Shepherd" to be the Vicar of Christ, the Successor of St. Peter, to whom Our Lord gave universal jurisdiction over all His sheep, saying: "Feed my lambs, feed my sheep, feed my sheep."

Now we have reason to think that there are many non-Catholics listening in to this broadcast every Sunday. I judge so from the letters I am constantly receiving where they say: "I am a non-Catholic but I believe in prayer and I want you to pray for me in the novena to St. Anthony." If you, therefore, as a non-Catholic, recognize yourself as one of the "other sheep" and the Catholic Church as the "One Fold" under the "One Shepherd", then do you not see how Our Lord wants you to come into the One Fold under the One Shepherd and to be subject to the One Supreme Shepherd who gave His life for His sheep? Did not the Good Shepherd say: "Other sheep I have that are not of this fold. Them also I must bring and they will hear my voice and there shall be one fold and one shepherd."

II

The Papacy

OF ST. JOHN BOSCO *it has been said: "After the Eucharist and Our Lady, the Pope was the object of his fervent and filial love." The same judgment might be made of Father Paul of Graymoor, who loved the Holy Father, the Vicar of Christ, in a very special way, and even for a long time before he became a Catholic.*

Father Paul was born on the eastern shore of Maryland while Pope Pius IX was reigning. He lived through the pontificate of Pope Leo XIII, for whom he had great admiration and whom he defended while still an Anglican clergyman. He loved St. Pius X and sent small annual offerings to him, but he loved him most of all because he allowed the Society of the Atonement to enter the Fold of Peter as a religious community in 1909 and to continue its work of Unity. The Graymoor founder was immensely grateful to Pope Benedict XV for granting papal approval and indulgences to the Chair of Unity Octave in 1916. He praised the leadership and integrity of Pope Pius XI and experienced the consolation of three audiences with him. He rejoiced in the election of Pope Pius XII and predicted great success for this enlightened Pontiff.

Were Father Paul living today, he would surely have rejoiced in the pontificate of Pope John XXIII, who did so much in a short time to promote the possibilities and interest of Christian Unity. He would glory in the reign of Pope Paul VI who has made Unity the goal and purpose of his pontificate. Father Paul loved the papacy with an intensity born of deep faith and of complete dedication to Our Lord and the Church.

With St. Ambrose of Milan, Father Paul would call the Holy Father "the Vicar of Christ's Love." For he considered the office of ruling in the name of the Savior as a work of love. The Papacy was created by the love of Jesus so that He might guide, rule and teach His sheep, through His Vicar on earth, in every century of human existence. Like St. Francis of Assisi, Father Paul loved the Pope with all his heart. Such love was simply the logical extension of loyalty to the Good Shepherd and in the expression of this love, he was eminently conspicuous.

1. In Defense of the Holy Father

Rose Leaves, November, 1902

My Dear Father:

You told me in your letter if I did not understand *Rose Leaves* I should tell you . . . You say we must look up to the Pope as our truest Father. Why, Father, the Old Man in Rome disowns us. To believe the Pope infallible, and our true Father, seems to me like a traitor to my Church. Please, Father, send me your answer soon.

Your child in the Atonement

The Answer

Society of the Atonement: Think what Atonement means. It means At-one-(ment), does it not? Our Society exists today not only to help make Catholic Christians *at one* with God, but at one with each other. Its mission is to help bring about the happy fulfillment of our Savior's Prayer, that His Church might be one.

The devil got up a great big quarrel in the Catholic family some four hundred years ago and ever since England and Rome have been at enmity. Before this quarrel started, the Pope had few, if any, more loyal and loving children in Christendom than his English children. But as a result of the sixteenth century rupture between the Church of England and the Holy See, Anglicans turned against their Father, the Pope, and began to call him all the abominable and outragous names they could lay their tongues to; and our Roman brethren, in their return, called us every bad name they could think of.

Anglicans said the Pope instead of being the Vicar of Christ, was anti-Christ; he was not the successor of St. Peter at all; that he had no more jurisdiction over the English Church than the Bishop of the Hindus; that the Catholic Church had no visible head anyway, and Our Lord did not mean St. Peter at all, when He said, "Thou art Peter, and on this Rock I will build My Church." Then the Church of Rome retaliated by asserting that the Church of England was no part of the Catholic Church, that it was a protestant sect founded by Henry VIII, that her priests were not priests, her Bishops mere creatures of the State, and her Sacraments worthless imitations and shameful shams.

Don't you think it is time something was being done to bring this breach between ourselves and the Holy Roman Church to an end? Should we not do our utmost to live in love and peace with all our Catholic brethren and stop fighting? I am sure Our Lord and His Blessed Mother think so, and that is the reason God has called the Society of the Atonement into existence.

It is our rule of life to feel and act towards all our Catholic brothers and sisters throughout the world, as far as possible, as though the schisms made by our forefathers no longer existed and we were in reality One Fold, under One Shepherd.

Then there will be the grandest love feast Christendom has ever seen, and the miserable breach between England and Rome will be at an end forever. "Blessed are the peacemakers, for they shall be called the children of God." When you think how glorious and truly divine its mission is, are you not proud and, oh, so glad, to belong to the Society of the Atonement and to be a Child of the Atonement! Only do be more reverent and never again speak of His Holiness, Leo XIII, as "the old man in Rome."

2. Ad Graecos

The Lamp, April, 1908

During the present month, we shall be directing our thoughts to those holy places in and about Jerusalem that are forever associated with the Passion, Death and Resurrection of our Divine Redeemer and not least among those hallowed memories to claim our thought will be the prayer, *Ut omnes unum sint,* uttered by the great High Priest at the institution of the Holy Eucharist, and the seven words of Christ from Calvary.

Surely it is not wandering far afield to associate with the prayer for Unity first pleaded at Mass on Maundy Thursday, that wonderful function at St. Peter's, Rome, mentioned in our last issue and more fully described in this, where on the occasion of the fifteenth centenary of St. John Chrysostom, the Greek, in a Latin chapel and the supreme Pontiff participated in both, something which has never happened before in the history of the Catholic Church (Pope Pius X).

On the day following, the members of the Committee for the Centenary, among whom were the Greek Melchite Patriarch of Antioch and other Eastern prelates, were presented to the Pope in the Consistorial Hall of the Vatican, and what the Holy Father said to them will harmonize much more effectively with the message of Our Lord, from Mount Calvary, than anything which we ourselves could write, and in offering the Pope's address to the Orientals in lieu of the customary editorial, we trust, our readers will find the same facility in applying to ourselves the Holy Father's fervent appeal to the Easterns to return to Catholic Unity as though his words had been addressed to the Occident instead of to the Orient.

3. "Love the Pope"

The Lamp, February, 1913

These words should have a new sacredness for every loyal Catholic in the whole world, since our Holy Father Himself has spoken them and mingled their utterance with his tears. As Our Lord wept over Jerusalem, it is reported that Pope Pius in the audience which he gave to the priests of the *L'Union Apostolique*, mentioned in our editorial last month, wept with emotion when he said: *"Truly enough have you said that it is the characteristic of the Union Apostolique that your emblem should be and is love for the Pope, inasmuch as that is another means of sanctifying ourselves, and to love him, it is enough to reflect— who is the Pope?"*

"It seems incredible, and it is indeed deplorable, that there should be priests to whom this recommendation need be made; but we are truly in these days under the hard, sad necessity of saying to some priests: Love the Pope."

The Lamp owes everything to the Pope. To bear witness to him as the Rock on which in union with Himself, Christ built His Church, and therefore, to point to Him as the divinely constituted Center of a reunited Christendom, for this *The Lamp* was lighted. The Pope is the very *raison d'etre* of its existence. In our Anglican days, for the love of the Pope, because he was the Vicar of Jesus Christ, the universal Shepherd and the Father of the faithful, we suffered poverty, ostracism and reproach. Now, as children in Peter's House, our hearts burn with zeal for His Holiness and especially for the fulfillment of that glorious promise of our Divine Redeemer: "Other sheep I have, that are not of this Fold, them also I must bring, and they shall hear My Voice, and there shall be one Fold and one Shepherd" (St. John 10:16).

4. The Death of Pius X

The Lamp, September, 1914

In the passing of His Holiness, Pope Pius X, from the Papal Chair in Rome to the companionship of St. Peter and his successors in the great assembly of the Church Triumphant, the Catholic Church on earth mourns the death of a saint.

Perhaps we have not appreciated the fact sufficiently, but it should be a reflection to fill the heart of every earnest Catholic with thanksgiving to Almighty God, that after the lapse of nineteen hoary centuries, the Catholic Church should have been ruled over by one whose faith in the verities and power of the Catholic religion seemed not one whit less virile and vivid than that of St. Peter himself. Though the miracles performed by Pope Pius X were not as numerous as those of the Church's first Vicar, concerning whom we read in the Acts of the Apostles that "the people brought forth the sick into the streets and laid them on beds and couches that the shadow of Peter passing by might deliver them from their infirmities," (Acts 5:15) yet the miracles of healing performed by Pius X, while occupying Peter's Chair are sufficiently numerous to demonstrate that the hand of the Lord was not shortened to work through Pius as He had worked through Peter.

One of the most striking of these miracles was recorded in *The Lamp* for January, 1913. At that time a former Church of England clergyman, well known to the Editor, was a student at Beda College, Rome, and in a letter to us said:

The Bishop of Salford (Dr. Casartolli), who is staying here, was up on the common room for recreation last night.

He told us he had been conversing with a Greek Bishop now living in Rome. The Bishop was a Greek schismatic and made his submission to the Holy See. He is a very old man —92 years of age. He was blind in both eyes and paralyzed in one arm and side. When he went to see the Pope, he asked him to breathe upon his eyes and lay his hand upon his arm. The Holy Father did so, and the aged Bishop came away healed. This happened a year ago; he told Bishop Casartolli about it himself. The Bishop heard the old Greek say Mass—he resided at the Convent of the Coenaculum.

The whole Church owes a debt to the late Sovereign Pontiff which is incalculable, and he will rank among the greatest of the Successors of St. Peter by reason of the reforms he has wrought in the Curia; the revision he inaugurated of the vulgate and of the breviary; the codifying of the Canon Law, a gigantic labor; the death blow he dealt to Modernism, the most subtle and dangerous of modern heresies; the defense of the Church in France against the destructive plots of her civil enemies; but more than any of these things, because he has brought the Church of the twentieth century nearer to the ideals of the first, in the re-establishment among the faithful, of the practice of daily communion and the bringing of little children to Our Lord in the Blessed Sacrament at the earliest age of spiritual perception. The noblest title with which the name of Pope Pius X will be handed down to posterity is that of the Pope of the Blessed Sacrament.

Whereas the Society of the Atonement shares with all the rest of the Church in the benefits which have flowed to the Church Universal through these far-reaching reforms, Graymoor owes a debt of far greater gratitude to the late Sovereign Pontiff, for he it was who opened the door of Peter's Fold and bade us welcome to its sacred inclosure when we knocked for entrance. He might have refused our petition to receive us in a corporate body and to preserve our Name and Institute. There was but a handful of us, and he might have rejected our extraordinary request and bade us make our individual submission and be content with that.

The Society of the Atonement, therefore, owes its very life as an Institute to him, whom we must ever call in a unique and special sense, *Our* Holy Father. Our Lord said of Mary Magdalene: "She hath loved much because she hath been forgiven much," and we know not among the children of Pius X any who have greater cause to love him, out of sheer gratitude, than the Children of the Atonement. It has already become our prayer that God will hasten the day of his canonization, and we hope ere long to see Joseph Sarto as Pius X elevated to the altars of the Church.

5. The Passing of Benedict XV

The Lamp, February, 1922

For the third time in its history, *The Lamp* records the death of a Pope. Leo XIII laid down the scepter of the Fisherman, which he had wielded so ably for nearly the years of Peter, shortly after *The Lamp* was lighted on the Mount of the Atonement. Then, in 1914, that "Pastor Bonus" and saint of God, Pius X, lay his snow-white head upon the pillow whence his gentle, holy spirit went to God, and now Giacomo (James) Della Chiesa, who bore the title, as Sovereign Pontiff, of Benedict XV, has once again left the Chair of Peter to his successor.

Every Catholic should be proud to have lived under the pontificate of three such illustrious and Christ-like successors of Simon, son of Jonas, whom Christ originally called from his fisher boat, on the lake of Galilee, to be first pilot of that ship of the Lord, the Catholic Church, which is to ride the storms of the centuries to the end of the world.

The Prophet Isaiah, describing the deathless life of the spirit, says that they that "wait upon the Lord, renew their strength, they shall mount up with wings as eagles, they shall run and not grow weary, they shall walk and not faint." How wonderfully have these words been fulfilled in that long succession of Sovereign Pontiffs who, as the Vicars of Christ, have ruled the Church of God and piloted Christ's Church through the storms and tempests that are forever lashing the sea of human passion into fury and constant unrest. The papacy is hoary with age but ever young. Nineteen hundred years have gone by since Christ sent the Holy Ghost upon the Prince of Apostles and his companions in the upper room of Jerusalem, and yet the Successors of St. Peter have in no wise spent their force nor grown old and decrepit with the lapse of time. From age to age the Popes of Rome "run and grow not weary, they mount up with wings as eagles," they are old, yet their strength is every day renewed.

Saint Peter, in his old age, was no more active and full of vigor in administering the affairs of the Church under the tyrant Nero than was the aged and venerable Leo XIII, who, at 93, by his intellectual alertness and spiritual power, was the most notable personality in the whole world of his day. Peter, in the streets of Jerusalem, worked miracles, yet his faith in the verities of the freshly heralded Gospel of Jesus Christ was not one whit stronger or more vivid than was that of Pius X, and the miracles which the latter wrought at the Vatican, though by no means so numerous and striking as were those wrought at the hand of Peter, yet in superhuman power, were essentially the same.

One who entered the Catholic Church from Anglicanism on the Mount of the Atonement and afterwards studied for the priesthood in Rome, in a certain letter to the Editor of *The Lamp*, once stated that the writer that morning had served Mass for a Greek Bishop over ninety years of age, who had become blind and paralyzed, until kneeling at the feet of Pius X he asked him to lay his hands upon him that he might once more celebrate Mass, and sight was restored by the Holy Father's prayer and touch at once and motion was given to his paralyzed arm.

Who could have lived a life more simple and Christ-like than that of Benedict XV? His family wealth he renounced as soon as he was elected Pope, that he might say with Saint Peter: "Silver and gold have I none." His breakfast, we are told, consisted of a cup of milk and a raw egg, his dinner was of the simplest kind, and supper more milk and eggs. Those seven years of his Pontificate were given to toil and prayer and sacrifice. He spared not himself, and we could hardly conceive even one of the original Apostles of Our Blessed Lord as imitating his Divine Master more perfectly than this latest occupant of Peter's Chair.

A man, in stature small and unassuming as Saul of Tarsus, he was truly a giant of divine energy and ubiquitous influence, ruling with firmness, yet charily, the world-wide flock of Christ, knowing and communing with every Bishop of the Catholic Church and yet, having time besides to reach out a helping hand to the starving, fever-stricken, war-ridden and afflicted ones of all lands, even though strangers and aliens from the Catholic Church. His last act being to drain the coffers of the Vatican to give relief to the famished, plague-smitten millions of unhappy Russia.

Assuredly, in these three illustrious Pontiffs we have a striking fulfillment of Christ's original promise to the Apostles when He breathed on them and said: "Receive ye the Holy Ghost" and "Lo, I am with you always even unto the end of the world."

There was a saying among the early Fathers, "Where Peter is, there is the Church" and truly in that Great Shepherd of Rome, Christ has ever illustrated His own words to Simon, Bar Jona, "Thou art Peter and upon this rock I will build My Church and the gates of hell shall never prevail against it."

6. Feast of St. Peter's Chains

Sermon, August 1, 1926
St. John's Church, Graymoor

"Peter therefore was kept in chains. . . ."

The thought of the Universal Church throughout the world by the call of the Sovereign Pontiff is centered today in Mexico. Picture to yourself by way of imagination, electric wires stretching from all over the world up to the center, to the great central office in heaven, Almighty God listening in, and then those wires, passing on to Mexico; and this will be a help to you perhaps to think of the tremendous bombardment of the great center of the universe by the prayers of all the faithful throughout the world, pleading with Almighty God to aid the afflicted Church in Mexico. The Holy Father, as the Vicar of Christ, is waiting in the Vatican to pronounce, if necessary, if things come to the worst, an interdict, which is one of the spiritual weapons that has been exercised in previous centuries against recalcitrant princes to bring them to a sense of their opposition to the Vicar of Chirst. It is an extreme measure and inflicts upon the people themselves great suffering. It is somewhat on the same principle as the strikes which are held from time to time by labor organizations to obtain the purpose for which they are contending. These strikes bring distress upon a whole nation oftentimes, but the workers argue that it is the only means of redress and, therefore, they use it. For instance, last winter everybody in the nation suffered because the miners were striking for higher wages in the anthracite fields of Pennsylvania, and finally through the agitation the miners gained certain of their points.

So it is that in the contest between the powers of darkness and the Kingdom of God on earth those extreme measures are sometimes judged by the Apostolic See to be necessary. They have in the past ages humbled some very proud princes in the world, as for example, when Henry II got into the battle against Thomas of Canterbury, he expelled him from the country, and the Archbishop went into exile. The Holy Father took the matter in hand and excommunicated the king. For a long time Henry held out, but the pressure was too great for him ultimately and he recalled the Archbishop. It was only afterwards in a violent fit of temper that he cried out against the same Archbishop: "Is there nobody that will rid me of this man?" Taking the hint, certain of his officials went and put the Archbishop to death in the very cathedral; and then there arose such terrific protest that the king himself cast himself upon his knees before the representative of the Vicar of Christ and declared that he was innocent of any intention of murdering the Archbishop and was willing to do any penance whatsoever; and he went through a very severe penance, with a bare back passing through a line of ecclesiastics, who gave him a whack on the back. But more than that, he gave up the contest that he had made, wherein he claimed jurisdiction over those who are the special spiritual subjects of the bishop; so after the long contest, the Church was victorious, although it took a long period of many years for the final triumph of the Church.

Now our Holy Father does not want to pronounce that interdict, but the pressure has been brought to bear by councillors, seeing that the Mexican Government has gone to such an extreme that the dominant thought of an interdict is the only remedy that will bring them to their senses. The Holy Father hesitates because he knows it is going to bring terrible suffering. Calles, the president, has threatened, that if the Bishops and priests break, if they refuse to administer the Sacraments,

45

the churches will be taken over for public libraries, and the faithful will be deprived of their places of worship; that is one of the threats made. The Holy Father is relying upon our prayers to save the situation, to storm heaven that God will intervene in some way to bring Calles to repentance, so that matters may be adjusted.

So we are to pray. God is the same yesterday, today and forever, and we see things repeated in the history of the Church, so this particular feast of St. Peter in Chains has been chosen by the Holy Father as the time for this united prayer.

Let us look at the situation as it was in Jerusalem. Herod the King had begun to put forth his hand against the little band of the faithful in Jerusalem to please the Jews. He had put James, one of the Apostles, to death, one of the three whom Our Lord had brought up with Him to the Mount of the Transfiguration, Peter, James and John. James had been put to death and because Herod saw it pleased the Jews, he proceeded next to take Peter, the very head and Prince of the Apostles. He arrested him; he put a guard of soldiers before the door of the prison; and after Easter, the feast of the Pasch, he was going to bring him and deliver him to death, to please the Jews. But what did the Church do? They knew that their head was in danger; so they stormed heaven, all the faithful prayed, prayed earnestly, prayed night and day, prayed to save the Prince of the Apostles, the Vicar of Christ, the Chief Shepherd of the little flock of the faithful. They were apparently weak, they were only a handful in comparison with the great multitude of the Jews and Herod's representatives, the power of the great mistress of the world, the Roman Empire, and yet their prayers prevailed. God sent an angel into the prison while they slept, struck the chains that bound Peter to the bodies of the guards and woke him up, beckoning him to follow quietly; so he stepped out of prison. When they came to the door of the prison, an invisible hand opened it, and they passed out into the street; and the Vicar of Christ was free.

Now this principle, my dear brethren, is precisely the same today. It is not the Vicar of Christ himself who is in danger, but one of the members of the Mystical Body, one of the portions of the great flock over which he has been constituted the Universal Shepherd and, therefore, his father-heart has gone out; he has taken counsel with God what he is to do; and God has inspired him through our bishops to ask the faithful everywhere throughout the Church today to assemble in their various places of worship, to expose before them the Blessed Sacrament. And as Christ the King is enthroned there, to invoke the Divine Majesty to come to the assistance of our afflicted brethren, where a brutal, savage government, filled with anti-Christian sentiments, is boasting that they will by brute force eliminate the priesthood and the episcopate of Mexico, that they will compel the people to do what they wish, contrary to their consciences or else suffer the consequences.

Now let us respond to this call, let us respond with the faith of Catholics. Let us realize that these who are with us are more than those who are with Calles, even though he may muster two million working men whom he claims to have, backing him and supporting him. I hardly imagine there are that many; but we know that the labor unions of Mexico are being dominated by and infused with Bolshevist principles; and yet they are with us, those behind the Vicar of Christ are more than those who are with Calles.

Long ago there lived in Israel a prophet by the name of Eliseus; these were times of trouble for Israel, Syria had gone up against Samaria, the capital of Israel at that time; and one morning the little town where Eliseus lived was surrounded by the Syrian hosts and his servant rushed in in terror and said: "Master, Master, we are lost; the Syrians have surrounded the town." Eliseus just simply said, "Giezi, they who are with us are more than they who be against us," and he prayed that God might open the eyes of his servant Giezi. When the eyes of Giezi were opened, behold all around the children of Israel were chariots of fire, and rank upon rank of angel hosts had been sent down to minister to the people of God. And again Eliseus shut his eyes and prayed: "Lord, smite them with blindness," and these invisible hosts smote the Syrians with blindness. They knew not where they were and Eliseus, the prophet, went out and led them as a blind man is led sometimes by a string to his little dog; and he led them on to Samaria through the gates. And inside the gates he prayed again and God opened their eyes; and lo and behold, they were taken captive by their enemies, the king and the people of Israel. After that great manifestation of power through the prayers of Eliseus, there was peace and Israel triumphed. It is a very easy thing if God wishes it, to

47

smite Calles with blindness, or to open his eyes as the eyes of Giezi were opened, or as the eyes of Elezeno, the great tyrant of Italy, were opened in the days of St. Anthony.

When Elezeno was about to capture their beloved city of Padua, the citizens of Padua came in distress to St. Anthony to help them. Then St. Anthony prayed to God and said: "Take me into the presence of Elezeno," and he went into the presence of the tyrant, and to the astonishment of his soldiers, Elezeno's face blanched with terror. He fell on his knees and cried for mercy, promising to withdraw his armies and leave Padua free. Who had done it? The same power that had operated through Eliseus in the Old Testament, had operated through St. Anthony of Padua in the New Covenant. God had opened the eyes of this man to see the terrors of the Lord and for the time being he was brought to his knees. It may be that in answer to all our prayers God will show Calles a thing or two that will cause him to tremble within his soul with terror and he will no longer lift himself up against the Lord, lest a dreadful retribution come upon him.

Let us, therefore, pray with faith, with the realization of this tremendous power that is behind the prayer of faith, that which, humanly speaking, seems quite incredible, will come to pass; and our Holy Father's earnest petition, supported by your prayers and my prayers, will be realized, and the extreme measure of an interdict, which has not been imposed upon a nation for three centuries, may be withheld from unhappy Mexico.

Now to be practical, pray during the Mass, enter into the spirit of the litany which will be sung before the exposed Blessed Sacrament at the end of the Mass. And then come this afternoon, at some sacrifice to yourselves and assemble yourselves again before the Blessed Sacrament in this church and pray. Unite your prayer to the prayers of the Vicar of Christ, that those who oppose themselves against the Church south of the Rio Grande may be paralyzed with fear, or may be dealt with in some way by God that will make them realize their disdain, and make them docile to concede to whatever the Holy Father may ask of them in the interest of the Church in Mexico.

7. The Holy Father, Pope Pius XI

Sermon, February 12, 1929
St. John's Church, Graymoor

Sapientiam ipsorum narrent populi, et laudem eorum nuntiet Ecclesia. Let the people show forth their wisdom and the Church declare their praise.

The purpose of this solemn Mass today is to commemorate the seventh anniversary of the coronation of our Sovereign Pontiff, Pope Pius XI, successor to St. Peter on the Throne of the Fisherman in the Eternal City. Our Lord caused the scribes and high priests to cry out and rend their garments because He pronounced Himself the Son of God, and this to them seemed to be rank blasphemy. Among those sayings of Our Lord, which illustrate more and more as time goes on, His own proclamation that He was the Truth and all things have been committed unto Him, was the saying with which He ratified the proclamation of Simon Peter, the son of Jona, whom being asked along with the other disciples whom they thought Christ was, Simon Peter replied, "Thou art the son of the living God." And Our Lord replied, "Blessed art thou, Son of Jona, for flesh and blood hath not revealed it unto thee, but My Father in Heaven; and I say unto thee that thou art Peter and on this rock I will build My Church, and the gates of hell shall not prevail against it." I say that those words, spoken by Christ to Simon Peter, and their validity, as the centuries go by, set forth and illustrate and proclaim with loud voice the Divinity of Christ, the Founder of the Catholic Church. In our own day and generation there have sat upon the Throne of Peter in the City of Rome, the imperial mistress of the world, very wonderful successors of the Fisherman.

Although the Church is in the twentieth century of her existence, she has not grown old and decrepit with time as the kingdoms of this world do, decaying by age and falling to pieces. She is possessed by an eternal youth, and this has been illustrated in the visible head of the Church, the successor of St. Peter, in the City of Rome. As I said a moment ago, wonderful have been the Popes who have reigned over the Church in this day and generation. I remember as a boy of thirteen years of age, visiting during the Centennial celebration in Philadelphia,

49

and although I was outside the Fold of Peter at that time, among the multitudes of things that I remember having made an impression upon me at the time and which has continued since, was a bust of Pope Pius IX, who was then reigning over the Church, the one who is illustrious for having presided over the General Council and also for having made the proclamation concerning the Immaculate Conception of the Blessed Virgin. Yesterday we celebrated the anniversary of the Apparition of the Blessed Virgin to a child of poor parents, in a mountain town of France called Lourdes, in which she proclaimed to this child: "I am the Immaculate Conception." That occurred just four years after Pope Pius IX set up as a dogma in the Catholic Church, by his sovereign authority, the Immaculate Conception of the Blessed Virgin, and it seems fitting that yesterday on the anniversary of that proclamation the treaty between Italy and the Vatican should have been signed by the representatives of the Holy Father and Victor Emmanuel and Mussolini.

That brings to an end a contest of nearly sixty years that has raged between the Kingdom of Italy and the Vatican. Victor Emmanuel by his representatives, and the Pope by his representatives, have now signed a treaty which is, as far as we are able to understand the text of the treaty, full recognition of the sovereignty of the Holy Father, and sets aside a bit of territory over which the Pope himself will reign as sovereign lord, and at the same time the Kingdom of Italy recognizes the Pope as the Vicar of Christ in her official documents. The *L'Osservatore Romano* yesterday, in proclaiming this treaty being signed and this happy settling of the vexed Roman question, declared that Italy's recognition of the sovereignty of the Pope gave him a jurisdiction and nominal strength which would far exceed a material kingdom of the greatest magnitude, and so indeed it does. Thus we score and celebrate in connection with the Holy Father's seventh Coronation Day, one of the most signal triumphs of the Holy See recorded in the long history of its contests with the powers of the world, for we know that the prince of this world, as Our Lord designated Satan, the usurper, has lifted up the gates of his power repeatedly against the Throne of Christ's Vicar, and again and again the world seems to have prevailed, but again and again the words of Christ have been confirmed, the world has not prevailed and God's Church has triumphed.

50

Some of us are old enough to remember the great glee of some Protestant nations when Garibaldi broke into the city of Rome and stormed *Castel Sant Angelo* and took possession of the city over which the Pope had exercised a temporal jurisdiction for a considerable time. Then prophecies were freely passed around from pulpits in non-Catholic churches, declaring that this was the end at last of the papacy, that it was now a fallen power, and the days of its burial were soon to be celebrated. That prophecy has reacted on itself, so that today the papacy is stronger in its moral power, its judicial power, and in excellence of its government over the three hundred million subjects of the Pope than in any previous period of its history; and we trust that, like its Master, will continue to go on conquering and to conquer.

We must pay a tribute today to that glorious Pontiff who, in the good providence of God, now rules over us. As we said a little while ago, we have had wonderful popes during our own generation. Pope Pius IX was a very holy pope, and then came his successor, the tremendous Leo XIII, so brilliant, so wonderful in his encyclicals, demanding the admiration of the world. And before his death, all the nations of the world and all the great ones of the world paid tribute to him in the press, and the world proclaimed him emphatically one of the greatest men of its day independent of his great office. Then came that saintly pope, Pius X, who is treasured more particularly and gratefully in our memory at Graymoor because we owe to him our corporate reception into the Fold of Peter, and all that that means to our Holy Society, the Pope of the Holy Eucharist, the pope who was pre-eminently the pastor of souls and who led the people to practice daily Communion, thus increasing grace in the Church and the reception of the Heart of Jesus, Whose delight is to dwell in the hearts of men.

Then came the war. God spared that gentle priest the sufferings of that agony, and so he fell asleep and Benedict XV took his place, a man who had been trained in the diplomatic service of the Church in the courts of Europe, and who was gifted with those peculiar qualities, held the balance of power and preserved the neutrality of the Church where Catholics faced each other in the battle trenches so that their loyalty to their various nations was not put to a strain under which it might have snapped, and at the same time, their fidelity to the

Vicar of Chirst and to the Church of their Divine Master. And after that came the present Pope. What a wonderful selection the Holy Spirit made of the mountain-climber, the one who had been a student, who loved his books and acquired a mastery of a number of languages. He was called to succeed Benedict XV, and he has proven himself a great master of men. When he took hold of the administration of the Church, he was not content to let the affairs of the Church be managed by heads of congregations, but he himself took a personal interest in those matters and assumed their direction and administration, making the heads of the congregations simply the ministers to carry out his orders and directions. The signing of the treaty with Italy no doubt will go down to posterity as one of the signal glories of his reign.

It was a Pius who was taken captive by Napoleon and carried away into France and made a prisoner that he might be forced to do the will of the emperor, in which matter, however, even Napoleon found out that the Rock of Peter could not be intimidated; and when he came up against that rock, he found he was up against Gibraltar, even though he were a prisoner. Then there was Pius IX, another Pope by that name, who was taken away from his temporal jurisdiction, had it stripped away from him, and said, "Very well, I will be the prisoner of the Vatican." A certain sum of money was offered by the Italian Government to the Pope for his maintenance, and he would not accept it under these conditions.

And now another Pius comes to the Throne, and once more the pendulum swings, this time to triumph, not for the prince of this world, but for the Vicar of Chirst; and by the negotiations we understand a certain part of this money was set aside by the Italian Government under the condition that the Pope would not accept it as an indemnity for the wrongs that were done the Church when she was robbed of her patrimony. And so we rejoice that these times have come to pass with a Pius on the Throne, and a very pious Pius, indeed. What a wonderful inspiration—to think of that aged Pontiff, who is this year celebrating his Golden Jubilee, fifty years a priest, over seventy years of age and yet bearing upon his shoulders the tremendous weight of the administration of the greatest empire on earth, for, indeed, it is the only world-wide empire. Rome in her glory with the extension of her domain, did not reach the extent of that

kingdom over which the successor of the Fisherman rules, because the subjects of Peter are found in every land and under
every sun and upon every continent and upon every considerable island in the sea, whether it be the Pacific Ocean or the
Atlantic Ocean, or the Indian Ocean, or whatever part of the
world one might chance to visit. And there this Sovereign
Pontiff over seventy years of age, takes the burden of this great
world-wide kingdom in his representatives over the various sections of kingdom, in the bishops with their dioceses with special
jurisdiction. There is not one of those bishops who can be
assigned to his see except by the voice of the Sovereign Pontiff;
and he has to keep in touch, therefore, with them as his representatives, and they travel once in five years to the threshold of
St. Peter's that they may make their report to the Holy Father
and tell him about their special jurisdiction. When you think that
there are over a thousand bishops scattered over the world, just
think of the burden of this man over seventy years old, and all
the other people he has to see. Wonderful, wonderful, how he is
sustained under the fever heat of the Roman summer; while
others take flight into the mountains, he, until now, the prisoner
of the Vatican, has labored on and stood his ground and kept
up his life of the utmost regularity, rising early in the morning,
taking care of the recitation of the Divine Office, which he
does not shirk, nor the saying of his Mass, and then going to his
various duties, having a certain time of the day set aside for each
one. Then he receives all kinds of delegates and all kinds of
petitions, and administers the affairs of the Church with vigor,
and in nothing is this vigor more illustrated than in the position
he has taken in this Roman question just settled.

In the papers it said that it was fortunate that over the
government of the nation should have ruled at this time a man
of great strength (referring to Mussolini) and that over the
Church was a man of great strength and personal will, because
if the Pope had listened to all the voices that would have given
him counsel in regard to this matter, it would have all come to
naught. He listened, he watched, he directed the negotiations
with a hundred meetings that have taken place in the last two
years. And he has quietly gone on with the administration of the
Church, and even in opposition, and contrary to the advice of
some very prominent ecclesiastics, he has held steadfastly to his

purpose and now he pronounces what seems to be the will of God.

How could such a man at such an age, carry the administration of so vast an empire on his shoulders were he not supernaturally sustained and had not Our Lord promised that He would be with him, not only as with the other Apostles, but preeminently with St. Peter. In the midst of the Apostles He said: "Satan hath desired to sift you as wheat," twist you around his finger, then He turned to Peter and said: "I prayed for thee that thy faith fail not and when thou art converted, strengthen thy brethren." Here again we have an illustration of the divinity of Christ in the fulfillment of that promise that He has guided the successors of St. Peter down through the ages to stand like the rock of Gibraltar in the defense and confession of the Catholic faith, not allowing themselves to be swayed to the right hand or the left by the influence of others, and the same time leading the people with wisdom, and that wisdom is Divine and the power that is sustained and quickened and emphasized, not only in Leo XIII, over ninety years of age, although he had been an invalid all his days, but in this glorious Pontiff more than seventy years of age and yet with such vigor, such intellectual clearness and such supernatural wisdom and strength. We may well glorify God today in the fulfillment of Christ's promise to His Church and unite our praises with the praises of all the faithful everywhere for the wisdom and the courage and the strength and the holiness of Pope Pius XI, and praise him with the Church as God has set him up and glorified him among the strongest and noblest and most illustrious among the successors of St. Peter.

8. The Holy Father, Pius XI

Radio Address, February 15, 1939

Our Radio Broadcast this afternoon assumes, as is fitting, the character of a memorial of Pope Pius XI, who, on Friday last, was summoned by the Great High Priest of our Profession, Jesus Christ, to join the company on high of the Chief Shepherd, who, in succession to St. Peter, have ruled the flock of Christ since the day of Pentecost until now, two hundred and sixty-one of them all told, including St. Peter, himself.

54

Let me bring before your imagination three scenes depicted in the Holy Gospels, the first one at Caesarea-Phillippi when Jesus, surrounded by His Apostles, put to them the question: "Whom do men say that the Son of Man is? But they said: Some, John the Baptist, the other some Elias, and others Jeremias or one of the prophets. Jesus saith to them: "But whom do you say that I am?" Simon Peter answered and said: "Thou are Christ, the Son of the living God." and Jesus answering, said to him: "Blessed art thou, Simon Bar-Jona; because flesh and blood hath not revealed it to thee, but My Father who is in heaven. And I say to thee: That thou art Peter, and upon this rock I will build My Church. And the gates of hell shall not prevail against it. And I will give to thee the keys of the kingdom of heaven. And whatsoever thou shalt bind upon earth, it shall be bound also in heaven; and whatsoever thou shalt loose upon earth, it shall be loosed also in heaven."

The second scene was at the Last Supper in the upper room of Jerusalem on the night of His betrayal. He had instituted the Blessed Sacrament of His Body and Blood. Judas Iscariot, having received a morsel of bread dipped in the dish, had gone out from their midst, and, turning to St. Peter, Jesus says: "Simon, Simon, behold Satan hath desired to have you that he may sift you as wheat, but I have prayed for you, that thy faith fail not and when thou art converted, strengthen thy brethren."

The third scene is on the Sea of Tiberias, after Christ's Resurrection from the dead. Seven Apostles, altogether were in the group, Simon Peter, James, Thomas, Nathaniel and two other of Christ's disciples. They had breakfasted together; and then, turning to Simon Peter, Jesus said three times: "Simon, son of John, lovest thou Me more than these?" And when Peter answered in the affirmative, Jesus said unto him: "Feed My lambs, feed My lambs, feed My sheep."

My purpose in bringing these three scenes before you is that you may reflect upon the wonderful way Jesus has fulfilled the words that He spoke unto Peter. First He gave unto him the commission. Then He explained to Simon, son of John, why He had named him "Peter", the Rock; for he was to be the Rock upon which the Rock of Ages was to erect and build His Church. He said He would give unto him the keys of the Kingdom of Heaven, which is another word for His Church. Simon Peter went and established the Chair of his supreme authority at Rome. And not only did Our Lord thus fulfill His promise to give unto him the keys of jurisdiction and government; but His Church was to live on through the ages, and Jesus Christ must provide vicars for He had gone into Heaven. Consequently, we have a chain of Pontiffs, unbroken through a period of nineteen hundred years. The kingdoms of this world have failed. Governments of all kinds have succeeded to governments of greater or less duration. We see in our own day upstarts over the people, the son of a blacksmith and a paper hanger, ruling as masters over two great nations at the present time; but they will have gone the way of all dictators a few years hence. Yet that endless chain of the successors of St. Peter has continued without a broken link through the line of Pontiffs until now.

And while the ceremonies of the burial of Pope Pius XI are still going on, a new Pope will be elected to take his place within the next fortnight; and, in the meantime, the words of Christ will be fulfilled; "And the gates of hell shall not prevail against My Church." For the first three hundred years of the Church's history, scarcely a pope died in his bed. As Peter was crucified in the likeness of his master, only with his head downward, pope after pope was put out of the way at the same instigation which nailed the Son of God to the Cross and put Jesus, the Saviour, to death.

In the last century when Garibaldi took Rome, men were prophesying that at last the papacy was done for, and the Roman Catholic Church would soon cease to exist. And yet Pope Pius XI, during his reign of 17 years, ruled over more spiritual subjects than any of his predecessors. Catholics of the world today are estimated at 350,000,000. It was not long ago her membership was spoken of as 300,000,000, minus the fifty million added in recent years. The original commission given to St. Peter, "Feed My Lambs; feed My sheep," has been exercised by Pope Pius XI over a vaster flock than all his predecessors, shepherded in the name of Christ. Then, too, how remarkably have been fulfilled the words of Christ to St. Peter, "I have prayed for thee, that thy faith fail not, and when thou art converted, strengthen thy brethren."

The world is full of heresies and false doctrines and denial of the Christian faith, fuller today than ever before. The enemies of Christ have grown so bold that they now have formed one of the mightiest kingdoms on earth on a political platform of atheism, something unheard of in the history of the world before. But the faith of Peter has never failed, and I am frank to express the opinion that the faith of Pius XI in Jesus Christ, as the Son of God and the Divine Redeemer of mankind, was every whit as strong as the faith of St. Peter, himself; and as for that vast multitude of bishops and priests associated with him, as well as layfolk throughout the world, the Pope has confirmed and strengthened them in their faith; and the Catholics of today are just as strong and united in faith as in the days of the Apostles themselves. And as for character, St. Paul said: "It is no longer I that live, but Christ that liveth in me." St. Peter, I think, said the same, and Pope Pius XI could say it with equal truth. As the Vicar of Christ he displayed the love for the sheep that the Good Shepherd did, who said: "The good shepherd layeth down his life for the sheep."

It was on the Feast of St. Michael, only September 29th of last year, when the Pope sent out his message of peace, when we were on the verge of what seemed inevitable, a war which might have taken upon itself the dimensions of the war of 1914; and he said, that for the sake of peace, he had offered his life to God—and God took it. So, in reality, Pope Pius XI, like his Master and like St. Peter, laid down his life for his sheep. The love that burned in the heart of the Holy Father for all his children scattered throughout the world, vaster in its extent than the British Empire, upon which the sun is never to set. The love that burned in that heart was the love of the Sacred Heart united to the heart of His servant. For Jesus said: "Whosoever eateth My Flesh and drinketh My Blood abideth in Me and I in him." It was the indwelling Heart of Christ united to His vicar that filled the heart of the Holy Father to the point of breaking with an indescribable love for the sheep that Christ, the Good Shepherd, had committed unto him.

In the world a man is retired on a pension when he arrives at the age of sixty. Rarely do they elect a Pope who is not over sixty years of age. Pope Pius was sixty-five when he began to reign. And, oh, how he labored! How he toiled! He worked up to the very last day of his life, and though his body was wracked with pain, he struggled and battled on. This aged Pontiff gave himself without stint to all the duties of his office, neglecting nothing, and all this, mark you, because of the grace of God that operated within his soul. Jesus Christ possessed him for Himself, and it was through him that He ruled His flock, through his voice, loving through his heart and energy by the power of the Holy Ghost, and in his hands to discharge so faithfully the manifold duties imposed upon him as the Lord of the vastest kingdom on the face of the earth today, the Kingdom of Christ the King, the Catholic Church of the ages.

9. Pope Pius the Great

February, 1939

Nineteen hundred years ago the Eternal Son of God, having dwelt upon the earth as man for thirty-three years, returned through the door of suffering and death to His Father in Heaven. Being true God as well as true Man, our Divine Savior, while not continuing to walk the earth as the Man of Sorrows, yet has the power of perpetuating His presence in the world He loves so much, and which He came to save. This He has done in a twofold manner. First, on the night before He sacrificed His life in atonement for our sins, He left for our spiritual nourishment His Body and Blood, establishing the sacrament of the Blessed Eucharist. We know that the presence of our Divine Lord in the Eucharist is a true, real, substantial presence. Secondly, as the Ruler of a Kingdom, as the King of Kings, He appointed a ruler to legislate and judge and govern His dominion, the Kingdom of God on earth. He transmitted to St. Peter, and following him in an unbroken succession for nineteen centuries, to each occupant of Saint Peter's Chair, the power of binding and loosing upon earth, a power that is ratified in Heaven. How these two phases of our Lord's presence on earth harmonize with, and are related to one another, was most aptly and beautifully described by the man whose memory we are now venerating, before he himself became clothed with supreme authority. He said, "The Vicar of Jesus Christ is the complement of the Eucharist. In the Eucharist you have Jesus Christ whole and entire without His visible presence. In His Vicar, He is visibly present. Jesus Christ the Divine Pilot of the Church, the 'veritable bishop of our souls' as Holy Scripture says, is present in His Vicar, with His authority and His government, by which He directs the mystical ship."

Unless one understands that the Pope is another Christ, possessing, as His Vicar, supreme power in a real kingdom; unless one grasps the nature of that kingdom and the actual presence of God in it, he cannot comprehend either the dignity or the sublimity of the office which Pius XI held. Christ's kingdom is a real substantial kingdom. It is a universal kingdom. It embraces all peoples, extends to all places, and when time has folded its wings and ceased its flight, the kingdom of Chirst will endure for all eternity. Christianity takes to its breast the infant newly born, and supports with a firm hand the feeble, worn with the weight of many years. It refreshes and sustains the toiler, but no less does it moderate the decrees of kings and governors. Seamen and soldiers, doctors and lawyers, farmers and fishermen, find satisfaction in its counsels; scientists and educators are enraptured by the height of its wisdom. Christianity is solace for the poor and the needy, and a director to the rich in the proper use of their wealth, and in the preservation of that more precious gift, everlasting life. Inhabitants of the tropics as well as those dwelling in domiciles of snow are grateful in being admitted to its membership. Primitive peoples speaking a gutteral language understand its teachings, the same teachings which answer the demands of those expressing their thoughts in the elegant French of a Parisian drawing room. Men holding various political beliefs, monarchists, democrats, laborites, all find the fulfillment of the desires of their souls in the doctrines of the Kingdom of God on earth.

The manifold differences of the members of Christ's Church establish beyond any question the universality of that Church. That any organization should be composed of members so diverse, even for a brief period of time in the world's history, is a remarkable phenomenon. But that such a universal membership should become a permanent characteristic of a living body, yet in no way diminishing its vigor, but rather augmenting it, century after century, is miraculous. Nevertheless, while members of Christ's spiritual kingdom agree in matters of faith and morals, their differences in culture and tradition, in race and nationality, in physcal environment, political atmosphere, and in their material welfare, are real, actual human differences. They are differences, entering into every phase of man's life, influencing

59

their philosophy, governing their actions, both as individuals and as communities, of which they are a part, often being the causes of inflaming men's passions with wrong desires, and at times of leading them into war.

To govern, to judge, to legislate and to be a high priest for this world-wide assembly of humanity, to rule them in peace and harmony, is the duty of the Vicar of Christ. It is an office calling for pre-eminence not only in executive ability and statesmanship, but excellence as well in all the virtues, united to, and fortified by, a stainless reputation and an unusual degree of love and zeal for the welfare of mankind. The office of Pope is an office exalted above all other positions on earth; for a Pope must not only be a leader, a man amongst men, he must be a shepherd, leading souls to God; and this he can do only by being himself a living saint. Unless he be the temple of the Holy Ghost, unless he be guided and directed in all his actions by the Spirit of the Father and the Son, he cannot worthily fulfill his sacred obligations.

To measure up to the requirements of the papacy, then, even under the most favorable circumstances, a man must indeed be a person of outstanding character. At the time Pius XI assumed his solemn obligations, external conditions were anything but favorable, and during his term of stewardship, they became aggravated. Moral degeneracy, political unrest, and economic ruin on a world-wide scale furnished the background for his scene of action. Enemies of the Church, as cruel and relentless as the early Roman persecutors at their worst, constantly harassed his efforts and caused him great pain. Worldliness and indifference on the part of many who should be zealous for truth and righteousness grieved him too. The work of Pius XI was carried on in a turbulent, hostile and constantly changing world. When we realize this, and when we realize that throughout his entire career he never deviated from his principles; when we realize that he carried on an aggressive fight against the forces of immorality by constantly and boldly proclaiming the unchangeable moral law; when we realize that in spite of all the adverse circumstances he nevertheless fulfilled the exacting requirements of the most critical; and when retrogression to many seemed imminent, raised the papacy to new heights of glory; when we realize that he did this in a manner so exemplary as to command the attention and respect of opponents, then we begin to understand that a really great man has passed in review, that we have seen a figure who will go down in history as a great leader of our modern period.

Merely to enumerate the accomplishments of this great man would require more time than is at our disposal. He has been described as the busiest man in the world. We shall, therefore, point out only his more important achievements, and having done this, we shall show why he became great.

The most outstanding event in the reign of Pius XI, the effects of which are impossible to measure, was the canonization of St. Therese of the Child Jesus, popularly known as the Little Flower. The disciplinary law of the Church, requiring a lapse of fifty years from the time of death had been dispensed, and this servant of God was accorded a unique privilege in modern history, having been born, having died, and having been given the highest honors in the Church within the lifetime of many of her contemporaries. Her canonization is a triumph of humility. From infancy she was conscious of God and of her absolute dependence upon Him, and she tried at every moment of her life to do what would please Him most, even relinquishing her own will and enduring extreme sufferings. Her doctrine was directly opposed to the spirit of the world. Worldly comfort, pride, and success meant nothing to her, except things to be despised. Her sole desire was "to love God as He never yet had been loved," and to be herself completely forgotten. She wanted ever to be a mere child, basing her desire upon the words of her Lord, "Unless you become as little children, you shall not enter the Kingdom of Heaven."

The fact that Pius XI, one of the most highly educated men in the world of our day, a man prominent in world affairs for half a century, has endorsed her doctrine of cheerfully accepting lowliness and suffering for the love of God, is in itself a proof of his humility, and hence a proof of his own greatness. "We desire," said the Holy Father on the occasion of her canonization, "above all that the faithful should study her in order to imitate her, by becoming children themselves, since otherwise, according to the words of the Master, they cannot enter the Kingdom of Heaven."

"If this way of spiritual childhood became general," he continued, "who is there who does not see how easily that reformation of human society, which we set ourselves to accomplish at

61

the beginning of our Pontificate, would be realized? We therefore make our own, the prayer of the new saint, Therese, with which she ends her precious autobiography: 'O Jesus, we beseech Thee to cast Thy glance upon a vast multitude of little souls, and choose out of this world a legion of little victims worthy of Thy Love. Amen.'"

The second important work of Pius XI was his program for spreading the light of Christianity in missionary countries. He became known as the Pope of the Missions, and there is not a single country in the world that has not felt the beneficial influence of his zeal. He centered the missionary organizations in Rome, transferring the Society for the Propagation of the Faith headquarters there, and creating the new *Fides Agency* for collecting and distributing news of the missions. He encouraged the development of a native ministry, and in one country alone, China, consecrated six native bishops. As a result of his appeal, religious vocations increased in Asia and Africa; while in China and Japan, the contemplative life was introduced and is now rapidly spreading. A missionary exhibition given in the Vatican Gardens, during the jubilee year, was so successful that it was afterwards given a permanent home in the Lateran Palace. He made it possible for hundreds of students for the priesthood from missionary lands to be educated at Rome, and finally he appointed as Protectress and Patroness of the Missions, St. Therese, the Carmelite Virgin of Lisieux, whom he had canonized, who offered up innumerable prayers and acts of self-denial for missionary work.

Thus far we have been considering Pius XI from a spiritual point of view. But from a purely secular light he also made much important history. For one great accomplishment alone he will be long remembered; namely, the Vatican Treaty. In 1870 all diplomatic relations between the Holy See and Italy were severed; and for more than half a century because of the delicate complications and sensitive feelings, no reconciliation was brought about. In 1926 representatives of both powers got together and a series of meetings followed. Cardinal Pacelli, now Secretary of State for the Vatican, represented the Holy Father in this matter. It is recorded that he held one hundred and ten meetings with Professor Baronne, the spokesman for Italy, but with the Holy Father himself he held one hundred and twenty-nine meetings, some of them extending to three and four hours duration. The Pope said afterwards; "There is not a line, not even an expression, in these agreements which has not been the subject of our personal study, meditation, and above all, of prayer." Previous to the negotiations, the people of Italy had voted 8,000,000 to 135,000 in favor of a reconciliation. How successful the Treaty and Concordat were framed may be judged by the vote of acceptance in the two Houses of Parliament. The House of Deputies showed 357 for and only 2 against; while in the Senate, there were 316 votes for and only 6 against.

These three events stand out, but had they not taken place, the reign of Pius XI would still be extraordinary. His great encyclical letters, numbering more than a score and dealing with as many different subjects, are of the highest caliber and will serve as guides in the solution of moral and social problems for generations to come. In his letter on the Reconstruction of the Social Order, he restored the world's interest to a consideration of Pope Leo XIII's great magna charta, to the laboring classes of the world. In his encyclical on the Sacred Heart, he pointed out the way in which souls might offer themselves to God in atonement for the evils of modern times. Not content with consecrating the world to the Sacred Heart of Jesus, he later introduced the Feast of Christ the King, describing that kingdom beautifully, and making clear the kind of allegiance we owe to our Supreme Ruler. In his letter on the priesthood, he presented the ideals for which the clergy must strive if they are to follow the Master. His disciplinary encyclicals were emphatic and fearless. In France arose the organization known as *Action Francaise* which he felt obliged in conscience to condemn outright, and he did so regardless of what the consequences might be. In Mexico, refusing to surrender to the tyrannical Communist regime, he issued a letter on "The Church and Mexico", and followed it up a few years later with another letter to the Hierarchy of Mexico. Finding the Church persecuted in Germany, he surprised the world, by boldly sending an encyclical letter to all the bishops of that nation. From the beginning of his pontificate till the very end, Pius XI was vigorous in the defense and promotion of the faith. Because of the unusual influence manifested by the Little Flower, her canonization has received first mention. This should in no way detract from the glory acquired by more than thirty other saints, and over three hundred beatified, whom Pius XI caused to be raised to the honors of the altar. Four of these, Albert the Great, John of the Cross, Peter Canisius, and Robert Bellarmine, were enrolled by him among the Doctors of the Church.

During his term as Pontiff, thousands of problems of one kind and another presented themselves to him for solution; problems of state rights and Church rights, problems of education, problems of domestic relations, problems in missionary lands. In addition the government of the Church as a working organization had to be looked after, the various congregations supervised, bishops to be consecrated, prelates to be appointed, priests to be ordained, seminarians to be educated, Brothers and Sisters to be trained. The needs of dioceses throughout the world had to be answered; the work of the religious orders, of which there are over four hundred, had to be regulated. It would hardly seem possible for any individual to be able to supervise so complex a society and yet find time for interviews with visitors and pilgrims to the Holy City of Rome. Yet we know that the Pope received callers and gave personal audiences to thousands of persons every year.

Pius XI was gifted with a vigorous constitution, a brilliant mind, and a good heart; and he developed these gifts to the honor and glory of the Creator who gave them to him. Through reasonable exercise he trained his physical powers. It is well known that he was a mountain climber who demonstrated his fearlessness and intrepidity on several steep ascents. Towards the more important faculty, the mind, he bestowed, of course, much greater solicitude. In fact he never ceased to be a scholar. Entering school at the usual period in infancy, he plodded for twenty years without a break, his studies earning for him at the end of that time the degrees of Doctor of Canon Law and of Philosophy. Then for five years he continued to learn in a better way, that of teaching. For it is a truism that one never knows a subject thoroughly until he has taught it. He was professor of Sacred Eloquence and Theology. The next twenty-four years of his life he spent in the Ambrosian Library, examining books and manuscripts, and communicating with students from all parts of the world who were specializing in particular fields of research. This work, it seems, made him a specialist in various fields. He crowned this quarter century of service with six additional years in the Vatican Library, where he was Prefect in charge. *Fifty-five years spent in studying, teaching, and in re-*

search work! There lies the secret of his vast store of knowledge! But that is only a partial explanation. It must be pointed out that side by side with his intellectual training, he developed his moral character. For while he was increasing his fund of knowledge, he was, during his entire life, either preparing himself for the priesthood, or performing the duties of a priest. Pius XI was wonderfully successful because he was wonderfully prepared. This is the natural explanation; there is above this the supernatural side. The Creator of the world never disappoints those who trust in Him and keep His precepts. If one reviews the writings of the late Pope, he will come across the explanation "after deliberation and prayer" many times. Therefore, while Pius XI used his natural powers to the fullest, he also sought aid from God and received it plentifully.

The crowning glory of a Christian is to yield his soul to God in a good condition: to return with interest the gifts which the Creator conferred upon him. Pope Pius XI has already been judged by God. There is no doubt in our minds that the judgment passed upon him was this; "Well done thou good and faithful servant, because thou hast been faithful over a few things, I will place thee over many things. Enter thou into the joy of the Lord."

10. The New Pope: Pius XII

March 8, 1939

Our broadcast this afternoon takes on the nature of a service of thanksgiving to Almighty God for the gift of a new Holy Father, for the good God did not leave us long fatherless, but has sent us a glorious successor to Pope Pius XI, in the person of Pope Pius XII.

According to the prophesy of Malachy, he is the Pastor Angelicus, the Angelic Shepherd, and there is much in his life and brilliant career as a churchman until now to justify this title. Two weeks ago in our broadcast, we referred to a certain Monk of Padua, who had gone one better than Malachy in naming ahead of time the Roman Pontiffs of the past two hundred years, but I am sorry to confess that he missed it this time;

for instead of taking the name of Gregory XVII, as the Monk of Padua prophesied he would, Eugenio Pacelli, walking in the footsteps of his predecessor, has assumed the name of Pius XII.

According to the Paduan Monk, the present Pope will travel widely among his people, studying their needs, conquering all his enemies. Certainly before his elevation to the Chair of Peter, His Holiness did travel extensively, not only in the Western World, but also he is the first Pope who ever has set foot in America; and when he did in 1936, he certainly did some traveling. Motor cars and express trains were too slow for him. He took to the air and flew to the Pacific Coast and back again. Neither was it the first time. He had flown much in Europe. While making his American tour, he carried a portable typewriter with him on the train and prepared speeches and wrote letters while flying long distances.

The Monk of Padua speaks of him as the "Pope of Unity". During his administration, the Greek Orthodox will return to union with Rome. We hope this proves true. (Our new Holy Father speaks nine languages and among them English quite fluently. We listened to a fine sermon which he preached at St. Ignatius Church while in New York.)

One satisfaction we have at Graymoor is that the Society of the Atonement will not have to be introduced to him because he knows about it already. It was on the 30th day of last December that we received from His Eminence, the Cardinal Secretary of State, as he was then, the following letter:

Very Reverend Father: I am charged by the Holy Father to convey to your Reverence the expression of his deep gratitude for the generous offering of St. Peter's Pence which you laid at his feet as a testimonial of the loving devotion of the Franciscan Friars of the Atonement. This gift and the noble sentiments of attachment from which it springs are very precious to His Holiness and He has commanded me to tell you that His appreciation will take the form of prayer that the grace of God in superabundant measure may be poured out upon you and upon your Community during the New Year. As a further mark of pleasure and benevolence, He sends to you and to them His paternal Apostolic Benediction. In accordance with your request,

66

the Holy Father will celebrate the Holy Sacrifice on the Feast of the Chair of St. Peter for the union of all men in the One True Fold.

With sentiments of great esteem and regard, I am, Very Reverend dear Father,

Devotedly yours in Christ,
E. Cardinal Pacelli

As far back as 1912, he was appointed by Pope Pius X, Under Secretary of State to Cardinal Merry del Val and through correspondence which we had at that time with the Vatican, he first learned of the Society of the Atonement and our Church Unity Vocation. It was probably while serving in the same capacity under Cardinal Gasparri, Secretary of State, during the Pontificate of Pope Benedict XV, that he may have had something to do with drafting the Papal Brief through which the Pope of the war period extended the observance of the Church Unity Octave to the Universal Church.

The first two syllables of the name of the new Holy Father in the Italian language mean peace (pace), and the vocation of a peacemaker has signalized his public career until now. I regret that the time allotted to me does not permit me to go into details, but the very first message to the world which he telephoned over the radio the day after his election dwelt upon the question of peace, and already he has summoned the four Cardinals of the German Reich to Rome to consult with him to end the persecution of Catholics in Germany-Austria and to bring about a new Concordat more satisfactory, more persevering than were those which Cardinal Pacelli made in the earlier days of the Hitler regime.

May he prove as Sovereign Pontiff the great peace Pope of the Twentieth Century, answering the dying prayer of Pius XI for peace.

11. Prince of the Apostles

First Edition, 1907

Written jointly by the Rev. Spencer Jones, M.A. a Church of
England Rector, and the Reverend Paul James Francis, S.A.
(The excerpts here presented are those from Fr. Paul's contribu-
tion. Revised 1923.)

Unity and The Rock of Peter

Since the First Edition of The Prince of the Apostles was
published in 1908, changes in the world undreamed of by the
men of fifteen years ago have taken place. When at that time
we called our Essay towards Unity—"A Study" probably the
majority of our leaders regarded it as such with languid interest,
and as purely academic.

The study of the papal claims now, however, has assumed
a far more serious and desperate aspect. At a certain critical
time in the gospel ministry of Christ, when He had proclaimed
in the synagogue at Capharnaum that it was necessary for mankind to eat His Flesh and drink His Blood in order that they
might have eternal life, St. John tells us that many of His disciples
"walked no more with Him," and the defection was so serious
that Our Blessed Lord turned to the disciples around Him and
put to them the question: "Will ye also go away?" And Peter
answered: "Lord, to whom shall we go? Thou hast the words of
eternal life." It was the same as though he had said: "Lord it is
You or Nobody; if You are not the Savior of the world, then
there is no Savior; upon the truth of your claim to be the Son
of God and the Messiah that should come stands or falls all
future hope for us."

At the present time we can use somewhat the same lan-
gauge in regard to the papacy in relation to the whole question
of Church or Christian Unity. The more the question of Unity
is a life or death one for Christianity at the present time the
more are all Christian men constrained to examine seriously the
claims of the Roman Papacy to be the divinely constituted center
of ecclesiastical Unity. The more the leaders of Orthodox, Anglican and Protestant thought are driven by the exigencies of
Christian civilization in these dreadfully perilous times to look
about and agree upon some central personage who can represent

68

in an organic way the Supreme Authority in worship, faith, and government the more are they constrained to address the Roman successor of St. Peter himself: "Holy Father, to whom shall we go; either thou art the One Shepherd of the One Fold to whose voice we must all hearken as the Vicar of Christ or else there is no Universal Shepherd nor can there ever be one Fold encircling within its walls the whole body of those who confess Jesus to be their Lord and their God."

There is no need for us to address to our readers an elaborate argument to prove the paramount need of Unity among Christians at the present time. Voices have been raised in every denomination of Christians throughout the world affirming this necessity. It is a crying need that has been voiced in conventions, and conferences and synods, in every part of Christendom.

In the four Gospels the name of St. Peter is mentioned as often as ninety-one times, whereas St. John's name, which comes next to his, is mentioned only thirty-eight times throughout the entire New Testament. This requires explanation, and the explanation is that St. Peter was recognized as first in importance and dignity. But, this is not the whole explanation; for it is plain that Our Lord was responsible for having first called him and placed him in a position of singular pre-eminence. For example, it is Jesus Christ who speaks: "Thou art Simon; thou shalt be called Peter." "Thou art Peter, and upon this Rock I will build My Church, and the gates of hell shall not prevail against it."

It is thus repeatedly, either by the words of Christ addressed to Simon and his companions, or by the words addressed by the Fisherman, Bar-Jona, to his Master, that Peter appears on the front of the stage as Prince of the Apostles, while the rest of the apostles occupy the background and when we ask the reason why, the answer is because Our Lord distinguished him from the rest and placed him in a position of superiority as His lieutenant now and His vicar in command after His ascension into heaven.

It would be unreasonable, of course, to expect this pre-eminence of St. Peter over the other apostles to be dogmatically stated in the Holy Gospels because the four Gospels are not theological treatises; they are narratives written by the evangelists, descriptive of the life of Christ, for the benefit of those who already believed, or should in after ages become Christians. The Church, as an organic, visible society, with its ministry, and sacraments, order of worship, creed and discipline was in existence for years before a single line of either the Gospels or the Acts were written.

The question is not whether we are compelled to believe in St. Peter's privilege by what we read in the Gospel, but whether the allusions to St. Peter in the Gospel's narrative are consistent with the dogmatic statements about him which the great majority of Christians have in all ages received and held. The pre-eminence of St. Peter and his Roman See are alleged as facts in possession. The question is: Do the sacred writings bear out this position or do they contradict it? That the Gospels so far from contradicting, strongly support St. Peter's primacy, every one that hath an eye, unobscured by the cataract of anti-papal prejudice, can very plainly see.

The Fisherman and His Boat

A study of St. Peter, as he appears in the Gospels, would be essentially incomplete did it ignore what may be called the dramatic teaching of our Lord as to the part He had predestined St. Peter to play in His Church. We know that the favorite method employed by Christ to instruct His disciples in the things of the Kingdom of God was by parables and that these parables were usually dramatic sketches, where a sower would go forth to sow his seed, or a rich man would "fare sumptuously," while a poor beggar starved at his gates. But Christ taught not by word of mouth alone, using imaginary characters to convey the lessons He desired to impress upon the minds of man, for all Judea and Galilee was a stage upon which He and His disciples performed many "miracle plays," acted out many dramas and every one of these Gospel scenes were meant to be a revelation of Divine truth. Next to our Lord, St. Peter is confessedly the chief actor and his role must be carefully studied, if, as we have already said, his place in the Church of God is to be adequately appreciated.

Not to unduly prolong the present chapter, one scene as sketched by St. Luke must suffice for this special department of our study of St. Peter in the Gospels.

"And it came to pass, that, as the people pressed upon Him to hear the word of God, He stood by the Lake of Genesaret and saw two ships standing by the lake; but the fishermen were gone out of them and were mending their nets. And He

70

entered into one of the ships, which was Simon's and prayed him that he would thrust out a little from the land. And He sat down and taught the people out of the ship. Now when He had left speaking He said unto Simon, 'Launch out into the deep and let down our nets for a draught.' And Simon answering said unto Him, 'Master, we have toiled all the night, and have taken nothing; nevertheless at Thy word I will let down the net.' And when they had this done they enclosed a great multitude of fishes, and their net broke . . . And Jesus said unto Simon, 'Fear not, from henceforth thou shalt catch men.' " (St. Luke 5:1-2.)

That our Lord meant the scene to be didactic is evident from what He said to St. Peter: "Fear not, Simon, henceforth thou shalt catch men." The sense is clear, the Galilean fisherman is to become a fisher of men. We know also that this name has clung to St. Peter, and to his successors in the Apostolic See, all along through the Christian centuries. St. Peter was not the only fisherman Jesus called to follow Him, neither is the Bishop of Rome the only one in the Apostolic sense to whom has been transmitted the office of catching men. But as a simple matter of fact, the title of "The Fisherman" has at some time or some how come to be associated exclusively with the Prince of the Apostles and the throne of his Primacy at Rome.

If any student of Christian literature, be he Roman or Anglican or Eastern, be he Catholic or Protestant, or even atheist or pagan, should encounter in his reading the expression, "the throne of the fisherman," or "the fisherman's ring" he would without any question know that the expression referred to the Roman Chair and signet of him to whom Christ originally said: "Henceforth thou shalt catch men."

It is Peter's ship into which our Lord chose to enter. A ship has always served as the type of the Church. The place assigned to the faithful in a church building is called the nave, from navis, a ship. Therefore in entering Peter's ship and teaching the people out of it, Christ gave an object lesson which all generations of Catholic believers have readily understood. By common consent "Peter's ship" ages ago became a synonym for the Catholic Church and of that ship, in the popular understanding of the phrase, St. Peter's successor at Rome still remains in full command.

What I have said above about the accepted meaning in Christian literature of "the fisherman's ring" and the "fisherman's throne" is equally true of the expression, "Peter's Ship," or "Peter's Boat." And in this connection, because out of Peter's ship Christ taught the multitudes, whether men accept Papal Infallibility or not, all Christians by the sheer force of association think of the Divine Teacher in Peter's boat when, as in 1854 and in 1870, the Pope speaks *ex cathedra.*

Studied with a fair and open mind, in the light of nineteen hundred years of Church History and the actual conditions of the Christian world to-day, there is no evidence more powerful for the universal headship of St. Peter and his successors in office than the Gospel record of our Lord's own words to Simon Peter.

That our readers may have before them a condensed presentment of this evidence in its vividness and strength we have collected, out of the Gospels, the principal Petrine texts in their order with the briefest possible commentary taken from the highest sources.

a. Not only is St. Peter's name always put at the head of the list, as was noted above, whenever the Twelve Apostles are enumerated in the New Testament, but St. Matthew expressly calls him, "The First," i.e., the Primate or Chief one (St. Matthew 10:2.)

b. Simon is brought to Jesus by his brother Andrew, "and when Jesus beheld him He said, Thou art Simon the son of Jona, thou shalt be called Cephas, which is by interpretation a stone." (St. John 1:42.) Thus, at their first meeting, Jesus promises a special name to Simon, which at once reveals an intention on the part of the "Rock of Ages" of associating this man peculiarly with Himself.

c. The name thus significantly promised is actually given when Christ chooses and sets apart the Twelve Apostles. Of so much importance is this conferring a new name on the Galilean fisherman, that three of the Evangelists make mention of it. Says St. Mark, "To Simon He gave the name of Peter"; St. Luke records, "Simon, who is called Peter"; St. Matthew, "Simon who is named Peter." Thus all four Evangelists (note the quotation from St. John above) tell us about this new name of Bar-Jona. This is the more extraordinary when we consider that only three of them mentioned the institution of the Blessed Sacrament (the fourth account being supplied by Saint Paul).

d. The explanation of this extraordinary attention paid to

the surnaming of Simon is given in the sixteenth chapter of St. Matthew. "When Jesus came unto the coasts of Caesarea Phillippi, He asked His disciples saying, Whom do men say that I the Son of man am? . . . And Simon Peter answered and said, Thou art the Christ, the Son of the Living God. And Jesus answered and said unto him, Blessed art thou, Simon Bar-Jona; for flesh and blood hath not revealed it unto thee, but My Father which is in heaven, and I say also unto thee, that thou art Peter, and upon this rock I will build My Church and the gates of hell shall not prevail against it." Could words be plainer? Surely the simplest and most obvious understanding of them is the right one.

Until it became the interest of those separated from the Unity of the Church, to read into them some other interpretation, they were commonly understood to mean just what they say, viz., that our Lord had called Simon from the beginning, Peter, because He intended to make him the Rock on which, after Himself, He would build His Church. It is because this interpretation of the text was the generally accepted one by the ancients, that among the many titles given to the First of the Apostles by the Fathers, Councils, and Liturgies of the Primitive Church, the greatest number have reference to him as the rock-foundation of the Catholic Church. Here are a few of them: "The rock of the Church" (Hilary of Poitiers): "the rock of the Church that was to be built" (Tertullian): "Receiving on himself the building of the Church" (Basil): "The immovable rock" (Epiphanius): "The most solid rock" (Theodoret): "The rock which the proud gates of hell prevail not against" (Augustine): "The foundation second from Christ" (Gregory Nazianzen): "The great foundation of the Church" (Origen): "The support of the Church" (Gallican Sacramentary): "The rock and foundation of the Catholic Church and the basis of the orthodox faith" (Council of Chalcedon). St. Leo, the Great, has paraphrased the passage as follows: "For thou art Peter, that is, whereas I am inviolable Rock, I the corner stone who made both one, I the foundation besides which no man can lay another: yet thou art also a Rock because thou art consolidated by My might, that what things alone are Mine, by My power may become common to thee by participation with Me."

e. Immense as the foregoing is, it is not all. Our Lord continues: "And I will give unto thee the keys of the Kingdom of

Heaven; and whatsoever thou shalt bind on earth shall be bound in heaven and whatsoever thou shalt loose on earth shall be loosed in heaven." Granted, that Christ intended to give to St. Peter all that the saints and doctors of the Church have ever claimed that He did, could He have used stronger language, in expressing that intention, than is here set down? As Christ is the Rock foundation of the Church and yet shares this with St. Peter, so by a change of figure, He promises that He will give him government and jurisdiction over His Church. Whatever may be said about His afterwards conveying the power of binding and loosing to all the Apostles (on which fact no one insists more than the Church of Rome), yet it remains that alone to St. Peter did He say "I will give unto thee the keys of the Kingdom of Heaven." The giving of keys has been by all ritual usage, whether sacred or profane, the outward and visible sign of investiture, possession and authority, and both the Old and New Testament afford us striking illustrations. God by the mouth of the Prophet Isaias says: "I will call My servant Eliacim ... and I will clothe him with My robe, and I will commit thy government into his hand: and he shall be a father to the inhabitants of Jerusalem, and to the house of Judah. And the key of the house of David will I lay upon his shoulders; so he shall open and none shall shut; and he shall shut and none shall open." (Isaias 22:20-22). Christ's supreme dominion over His Church is expressed by exactly the same figure in Apoc. 3:7: "These things saith He that hath the key of David, He that openeth and no man shutteth and shutteth and no man openeth."

f. In the very next chapter of St. Matthew's gospel is recorded a striking proof in practice as to our Lord's intention of making St. Peter His Vicar. "And when they were come to Capharnaum, they that received tribute money came to Peter and said, 'doth not your Master pay tribute?' He saith, 'Yes.' And when he was come into the house, Jesus prevented him, saying, 'What thinkest thou, Simon, of whom do the kings of the earth take custom and tribute, of their own children or of strangers?' Peter saith unto Him, 'From strangers.' Jesus said to him, 'Then are the children free. Notwithstanding, lest we should offend them, go thou to the sea, and cast an hook, and take up the fish that first cometh up; and when thou hast opened his mouth, thou shalt find a piece of money; that take and give unto them for Me and thee'." St. Matt. 17:24-6). Not only do

74

the taxgatherers come to St. Peter as the one, whom they evidently understood to be authorized to speak for the Master, and not only does St. Peter give them an authoritative answer, but the Master in telling him how to make good that answer, uses the extraordinary words "For Me and thee." It must be evident to every one that as Levi and all the children of Israel "paid tithes in Abraham, when Melchisedech met him" (Hebrews 7:9) so the whole Catholic Church of the future was involved in this question of Christ and St. Peter paying tribute. Without forcing the text in the least it is easy and natural to understand our Lord as saying in substance to the First of the Apostles: "A matter of principle is involved in this transaction and I wish to establish a precedent for all time in My Church and Kingdom. You will remember how a few days ago I promised to you the keys of authority in this kingdom, now therefore go and do as I tell you for Me and thee, and since you are My Vicar, you will understand that you are paying tribute not only for us, but those who are and shall be one of us."

g. At the Last Supper, in order to give the future rulers of His kingdom an object lesson of how they should discharge their office, Jesus rises from the table and girding Himself with a towel proceeds to wash the feet of His disciples and also tells them, "he that is greatest among you, let him be as the younger, and he that is chief, as he that doth serve." Remembering this admonition the Bishop of Rome, from the earliest times, has signed himself "the servant of the servants of God." Then having assured them all that He "appointed them a kingdom" and that they should "sit on thrones judging the twelve tribes of Israel," He turns and addresses Himself directly to St. Peter: "Simon, Simon, Satan hath desired to have you (plural), that he may sift you as wheat" (St. Luke 22:31). Take note that although Simon is addressed individually it is as the representative or head of the whole body. "Satan hath desired to sift you," i.e., St. Peter and "those who were with him," the entire body of the Apostles. Next, mark the counter move of Christ to checkmate His adversary. The Vatican Definition of 1870 quotes the words which follow as containing in them the divine promise of Papal Infallibility, and they reveal the sure basis of Church Unity. "But I have prayed for thee, that thy faith fail not, and when thou art converted, strengthen thy brethren." What is *infallibility*, but a faith that fails not, and what unity there be, save round one central figure, strong enough to impart solidity to all who are united with him? The infallibility and solidarity of His Church are the two things which our Lord prayed, might be preserved in St. Peter and if the prayer is not fulfilled in St. Peter's successor at Rome today, then where on earth is it fulfilled?

Take a look back at this point and note how consistent all the speeches and acts of our Lord to St. Peter have been so far. He first promises him a name which means stability and strength, then He actually confers it, then awhile after He explains its significance "thou art Peter and on this rock I will build My Church." He further promises him the keys of His kingdom, when we find Christ commissioning him to act as His Vicar, to pay tribute and saying "Do this for Me and thee." Forecasting the future of His Church and the malicious designs of Satan against it, He reveals what He has done and will do to circumvent the old dragon by telling St. Peter, in the presence of the others, that He has prayed for him that his faith would never fail and that his office should be to strengthen his brethren. Then comes the crucifixion and the resurrection and still our Lord's words and actions towards St. Peter show that He has undergone no change of mind concerning him. He appears to him first, before He does to the other disciples, after the resurrection. St. Peter is still in the foreground just as formerly. But it is St. John who sketches the crowning scene of all, that scene where the great Master Builder completes the constitution of His Church by lifting into place the key-stone of the arch, binding the whole into one.

"When, therefore, they had dined, Jesus said to Simon Peter, Simon, son of Jonas, lovest thou Me more than these? He saith unto Him, Yea, Lord, Thou knowest that I love Thee. He saith unto him, Feed My lambs.

"He saith to him again the second time, 'Simon, son of Jonas, lovest thou Me?' He saith unto Him, 'Yea Lord, Thou knowest that I love Thee.' He saith unto him, 'Feed My lambs.'

"He saith unto him the third time, 'Simon, son of Jonas, lovest thou Me?' Peter was grieved because He said unto him the third time, 'Lovest thou Me?' And he said unto Him 'Lord Thou knowest all things, Thou knowest that I love Thee.' Jesus saith unto him, 'Feed My sheep'." (St. John 21:15-17)

Some have said that no jurisdiction over all the sheep of

Christ was given to St. Peter in these three sentences; that all the passage means, is that as St. Peter had denied his Lord three times he was reinstated as a shepherd along with the other Apostles, by a thrice repeated sentence of forgiveness and restoration.

There is very little doubt that Jesus had the threefold denial in mind, but if St. Peter is henceforth to be a shepherd of the lambs and sheep in no more exalted sense than the other Apostles, why did Christ not include them also in His speech? "They all forsook him and fled" (St. Matt. 26:56) and with the exception of St. John, who among them, behaved any better than did St. Peter? If he needed a re-instatement, they needed it too. In fact, Jesus did afterwards invest them all with a world wide commission and endowed them as a united college with the plenitude of His own Divine mission, but as He said to Peter alone: "Thou art the rock; I will give unto thee the keys; I have prayed for thee that thy faith fail not; strengthen thy brethren." So to put the key-stone more firmly into the arch of Catholic Unity, He said three times to him, who was to represent pre-eminently the Good Shepherd, "Feed My lambs, feed My lambs, feed My sheep."

III

The Chair of Unity Octave

IN THIS SECTION *of our work we will show the beginning and development of the Chair of Unity Octave, probably Fr. Paul's greatest achievement, next to the foundation of the Society of the Atonement.*

He first conceived the movement on November 30, 1907, and thus wrote to Rev. Spencer Jones, in England, of his intention to inaugurate "a Church Unity Octave," as he then called it. The initial success in 1908 was so encouraging that he decided to promote it annually. He regarded the Octave as one of the special means which brought him and his community into the Church on October 30, 1909.

At first the movement was called the Church Unity Octave; in 1926, through the suggestion of Cardinal Bourne of Westminster, an alternate title was conceived. The new title, Chair of Unity Octave, became the official title of the movement in 1949. A few selections will show how well Fr. Paul liked this second name.

In connection with this title, may we cite the following quotation from Archbishop Francis Kenrick of Baltimore, who wrote in his book on the papacy: "By a moral miracle, which is the most splendid proof of the divine origin of Christianity, Peter still lives and teaches in his successors, and the voice of truth, coming forth from the Chair of Unity, reaches to the extremities of the world and is re-echoed by countless millions."

These selections will not treat of the various intentions for each day of the Unity Octave; they will be considered later under the section on "Our Separated Brethren." These latter parts present the ideas of Fr. Paul in regard to the origin and purpose of the Octave and the means of observing it. We have also included a copy of the petition which Fr. Paul circulated in an effort to have the Octave observed universally in the Church.

Though his hope was not fulfilled, his action shows how important he considered this crusade of prayer for Unity.

The Unity Octave is probably the only devotion in the Catholic Church which began outside the Fold of Peter. St. Pius X blessed it on December 27, 1909, two months after the Society of the Atonement had entered the Church. Other Popes have given it their blessing, especially Pope Benedict, who granted indulgences to it in 1916, Pope Pius XII who renewed them in 1946, and Pope John XXIII who urged its observance more widely throughout the Catholic world. Pope Paul VI promoted it widely in the Archdiocese of Milan.

Due to the revision of the Church calendar the Octave no longer begins on the feast of the Chair of St. Peter at Rome but the emphasis is still papal and St. Peter is considered the special patron of the holy enterprise. The papacy is the voice of Peter speaking in the name of Christ to the modern world.

Fr. Paul considered the Octave as the greatest project which came from Graymoor, in the sense that it became a devotion for the entire Church. He rejoiced, too, that others separated from the Church, such as the Orthodox and the Protestants, faithfully observe the January period as a time of prayer for Unity. Even though their concept of Unity differs from that of the Church, it is significant that they pray that God may grant them the religious unity they so ardently seek.

1. The Church Unity Octave

The Lamp, January, 1909

Last year there was inaugurated the observance of a Church Unity Octave beginning on the Feast of the Chair of St. Peter at Rome, January 18, and ending on St. Paul's Day, January 25. It was taken up with considerable zest and participated in by several thousand of the clergy, religious and lay people in the Roman Catholic and Anglican Churches. Under the fostering care of God, the Holy Spirit, we trust the present year will mark a still further growth and development of the observance. There is a peculiar fitness in this particular octave which at once appeals to everyone who recognizes the Apostolic See of Rome as the historic and providential point of a reunited Christendom. From the first ages of Church history Rome has been called the Apostolic See because it was jointly founded by the glorious Apostles, Peter and Paul, whose relics to this day repose within the great Roman basilica, the largest and most famous Church in the whole world.

A Church Unity Octave, therefore, which begins with the festival of St. Peter's Chair and ends with the Feast of the Conversion of St. Paul, brings us at once into touch with the foundation principles of Catholic Unity and lifts the whole subject on to the solid rock of Divine institution, scriptural and apostolic tradition. We ask every reader of *The Lamp* to take a zealous part this year in the observance of the Unity Octave, not being content with an individual participation merely, but acting as a promoter and extender of the observance by getting as many others as possible to also keep the Unity Octave. Speak to your lay and clerical acquaintances about it, write to those at a distance, ask for prayers far and near, secure as many Masses, Our Fathers and Hail Marys with intention as you can and we will be grateful, if you will report the results to *The Lamp* as we can form a better record of any increases on last year's observance. The following ways, according to opportunity or privilege, are recommended for the observance of Church Unity Octave:

1. Prayers, private and public.

2. Masses celebrated and communions received with intention for the return of all Christians to communion with the Apostolic See.
3. Sermons and instructions on the subject.
4. Church Unity Conferences, public or private, in churches, halls, houses, on the street, anywhere and everywhere as time or occasion shall make them wise and expedient.
5. Judicious dissemination of Church Unity literature.

2. The Unity Octave (1910)

The Lamp, December, 1909

In the twentieth century there is going on before our eyes, a titanic struggle between a clique of French politicians and the Vatican for the corporate control of the Church in France and upon the issue of that struggle depends the destinies of Gallican Christianity. So far, the balance of success has been with the Vatican, for the simple reason that the corporate solidarity of the French Church, resting upon the Rock of Peter, has remained unbroken.

If the present rate of individual conversions to the Catholic Church, say in the United States, were maintained for the next five hundred years, how much nearer would America come to being solidly Catholic than it is at the present time? It is true that the ratio of Catholic increase is tremendous, but, as every one knows, it is largely due to two prolific causes: (1) immigration from Catholic countries across seas and (2) the annual excess of Catholic births over Catholic deaths. Large as the number of individual conversions to Catholicism is, they are nearly neutralized, we fear, by leakages from the faith.

Wherein then lies the hope of the future for the Catholic Church in recovering to her sway the scores of millions of non-Catholics, who constitute at present three quarters of the population? Does not the hope lie in the supernatural wisdom, which will be given to the Catholic Church, to take advantage of that phenomenal movement towards unity everywhere forcing itself to the fore in Protestant conclaves and assemblies, so that at the hour ordained by God, the genius of Rome may seize and direct it into channels, which will eventuate in a series of corporate receptions that will leave to Protestantism nothing but the dregs of agnosticism.

Shutting their eyes to Rome's employment of the corporate method of conversion in treating with the uniate bodies of the East, men have persistently said that the Holy See would lend her support to no other but the individual process of submission to her jurisdiction, as far as Anglican and other non-Papal bodies in the west were concerned. *The Lamp* is now in a position to assert the contrary. A *"pusillus grex,"* a society of Anglicans numbering but a score of souls, has asked for the privilege of a corporate submission and reception, and received from the Holy See an affirmative answer. Though this little cloud on the horizon be but the size of a man's hand, it is the prophecy of an abundance of rain and an index of what Rome will do, when the corporate movement towards the center of Catholic Unity has gathered momentum and brought not a score but scores of thousands to assemble about the door and knock for admission to the Catholic Church.

Henceforward, no body of Christians who aspires to union with the Apostolic See need despair of ultimate success. Corporate submission is not "an iridescent dream." What Rome has done for the Society of the Atonement, she will do for other like bodies of Anglicans and their congregations. Rather than sacrifice Catholic essentials for the sake of federation with Protestant dissent, should they feel themselves compelled to separate from the Anglican fellowship, instead of imitating the English non-Jurors, let them know that the Holy See has but to be appealed to and the Holy Father will give them without stint the choicest graces and favors of the Catholic Church.

❊ ❊ ❊

The Lamp, January, 1910

When *The Lamp* in 1908 inaugurated the observance of a Church Unity Octave from the Feast of St. Peter's Chair at Rome, January 18, to the Conversion of St. Paul, January 25, it met with such a cordial response that we were encouraged to repeat the experiment in 1909, and we were pleased and astonished by the sanction and co-operation given to the proposal by certain members of the Catholic Hierarchy, by many priests and religious and by such influential papers as the *Ave Maria* and the New York *Freeman's Journal.* Nor was the observance confined to America, it extended to England, France and Belgium and even to Rome. What, therefore, may we not reasonably expect now that *The Lamp* has become an officially recognized Catholic magazine? Our appeal for Masses and prayers has received the blessing and warm approval of His Grace, the Most Reverend Archbishop of New York, and His Excellency, the Most Reverend Msgr. Falconio, the Apostolic Delegate. Their letters, printed on another page, cannot fail to inspire every Catholic who reads them, with a determination to participate personally in the observance of the Octave and to persuade others to do the same.

As for *The Lamp's* Anglican constituency, if they who comprise it did not share with us, to some degree at least, our longing to see the entire body of English-speaking Christians gathered into the one fold of St. Peter, there would be little reason why they should continue to read *The Lamp,* but the fact that they do so continue, affords us very good ground for hoping that they too will observe the Octave, as they did last year and the year before.

When Dr. Pusey learned that a great number of religious on the continent were praying for the conversion of Newman, he is reported to have expressed the belief that the event would soon follow.

During the years of waiting, which preceded our own corporate reception into the Catholic Church, it was an immense consolation to the members of the Society of the Atonement to know that not only hundreds, but many thousands of Catholics, religious and secular, clerical and lay, were constantly praying for us and for our union with the Vicar of Christ.

Surely then, our Catholic-minded brethren in the Anglican Communion, who are suffering intensely from the Protestant anomalies which enfold them, as with a mantle of thorns, will be glad to unite their prayers with ours that the baneful influence of those arch-schismatics, Henry and Elizabeth Tudor, may soon be utterly dissipated and all England be brought again into communion with Rome and firmly united with the Catholic world under the Apostolic rule of the Holy See.

Our exchanges can greatly aid in the general observance of the Octave, by recommending it editorially to their readers and for the love of God and the peace of Jerusalem, we ask them and all of our readers to secure for the intention all the prayers and Masses possible.

This last request is addressed in particular to members of Religious Congregations, Pious Confraternities and such associations as make a specialty of intercessory prayer, e.g., The League of the Sacred Heart, the Pious Association of San Marcello, Rome, the English Society of Ransom, the French Arch Confraternity of our Lady of Compassion and the Apostolic Mission Houses of Washington, New York and elsewhere.

3. The Church Unity Octave (1911)

The Lamp, December, 1910

It is time to remind our readers of the coming *Octave of Prayers* for the fulfillment of Our Lord's petition to His heavenly Father *"That all may be One."* You will remember that the Octave begins with the Feast of St. Peter's Chair at Rome, January 18, and ends with the Feast of the Conversion of St. Paul, January 25. The linking of these two festivals together by intercessions for the reunion of a divided Christendom and for the conversion of all who are not Catholics to the obedience of the one faith and the one Church is, in itself, an eloquent sermon, setting forth the very essence of Catholic Unity, its foundation and its method of construction. By the will and decree of Jesus Christ, has not the Chair of Peter been made for all time, the test of Catholic Unity and does not the conversion of the great apostle to the Gentiles epitomize that agelong work of the Holy Ghost in the extension of Christ's Kingdom until by missionary conquest at home and abroad the number of the elect is complete and all the dispersed sheep shall be gathered into the One Fold under the rule of the One Shepherd? The two cardinal things, therefore, to be prayed for during the Octave are first, that all Christians may become one by union with the Chair of Peter and second, that the whole body of the faithful may be so filled with the missionary spirit of the Apostle Paul that the kingdoms of the entire world will soon be merged in the one empire of Jesus Christ.

Last January was the third anniversary of the inauguration of this Prayer-Octave and it was signalized by receiving the approbation, first of the Most Reverend Archbishop of New York, then of his excellency, Msgr. Falconio, the Apostolic Delegate for the United States, and finally of His Holiness, Pope Pius, the reigning occupant of St. Peter's Chair. Its observance, so far from being confined to the United States, was kept with enthusiasm by devoted religious and other of the pious faithful in England, France, Belgium, Spain and at Rome. Under the fostering care of the Holy Spirit we hope it will be more widely observed than ever in 1911.

On our own part let us do what we can to bring this about. There are now over one thousand priests on the subscription list of *The Lamp;* if all these will tell the souls under their charge about the Octave and secure their co-operation, what a tremendous impetus will thus be given to the observance and what graces and blessings will be brought down from heaven, in answer to so many prayers, seasoned with acts of charity and self-mortification. Then again *The Lamp* numbers among its exchanges some eighty Catholic magazines, reaching through their columns hundreds of thousands of Catholics in all parts of the world. If these would, with one consent, recommend the observance of the Octave to their readers the good results could hardly be computed. We know the general disposition of faithful Catholics to pray; and to pray in particular from the feast of St. Peter's Chair until St. Paul's Day, first for the reunion of Christendom and then for the conversion of the whole world to Catholicism. Who could or would refuse such an appeal? Last winter editors wrote us that they would gladly have recommended the observance of the Church Unity Octave, but the notice came too late. This year to avoid this we are making our appeal for co-operation in plenty of time. God speed the observance and bless it beyond all our hopes and expectations.

4. Prepare For the Church Unity Octave (1912)

The Lamp, December, 1911

It is time to begin our preparation for the observance of the Church Unity Octave, from the Feast of the Chair of St. Peter at Rome, January 18, to the Feast of the Conversion of St. Paul, January 25, 1912.

On another page we give a short history of the Church Unity Octave, our purpose being to encourage all readers to help make the fifth anniversary of the inauguration of the Octave truly memorable. There were four features of the observance last January, which we devoutly pray may become more and more general year after year.

The first feature was the extensive notice given to the Octave by the Catholic press in the United States, Canada and England. We now have on our exchange list, a hundred Catholic periodicals, published in all parts of the world, and reaching hundreds of thousands of Catholics of every rank, ecclesiastical and secular. Every one of these we invite to publish in advance some notice of the Church Unity Octave for 1912.

The second notable feature of the observance in 1911, was the Mission to non-Catholics conducted by the Paulist Fathers, in Chicago, during the Octave. Why might not such missions be conducted in hundreds of parish churches in all parts of the country?

If it is objected that it would be impossible to engage special preachers to conduct such Missions simultaneously, the answer is a very simple one. Special Missioners need not be introduced for the occasion; the parochial clergy themselves can conduct their own Missions for non-Catholics. This is what the Paulist Fathers do every winter, both in New York and Chicago, and hundreds of Protestants, who never cross the threshold of a Catholic church at any other time, flock to these special services and fill the question box with their queries. We see no reason why the parochial clergy could not rival the Paulist Fathers in what has been, heretofore, a Paulist specialty. We hope that many of the Catholic pastors, among our readers, will be inspired to institute for their several parishes the custom of a Mission, for non-Catholics, during the Church Unity Octave every year, until it will be looked forward to, as the annual New Year event, by the entire population of the parish, who will speak of it, before and afterwards, as Father So-and-So's Mission to non-Catholics. At any rate, the experiment is well worth trying and we very much wish to see it made.

Corporate Communion of Converts on St. Paul's Day

The third feature and one worthy of the widest and most general extension had its origin in St. Paul's Cathedral, Pittsburgh, on St. Paul's Day, and consisted of a corporate communion made by Catholic Converts. Mr. Carlton Strong, former President of the Anglo-Roman Union, thus described it in a letter which was printed in *The Lamp* last March:

> What is believed to be the first local observance of the Church Unity Octave met at St. Paul's Cathedral on the Feast of St. Paul. It was a wholly spontaneous affair on the part of the eight or nine persons who were moved to make a general act of Communion with the common intention on that morning. The Mass which the Rev. Rector had kindly set aside for that purpose was celebrated at 7:30 o'clock at the High Altar by the Rev. Dr. Coakley of the Cathedral parish. Some regret was expressed afterward that more persons were not advised of the proposed observance but the whole thing came about on short notice without plan or direction.

As Mr. Strong added, it is very often that in this small, seemingly spontaneous way, things have their providential beginning which later take on wide and large proportions. A general recognition of St. Paul, as the apostolic patron of converts, and the adoption of the feast of his own miraculous conversion as the occasion of assembling in the Cathedral, or some well-known church, of as many of the converts of our large cities as could be gotten together at Mass, or at a popular evening service, would be productive of much good and give an added impulse each year to the home-missionary movement, now so happily expanding.

The fourth advance made last year, was the increase of religious communities offering their prayers and good works for the reunion of Christendom and missionary extension during the Octave. Concerted prayer for unity of Christians and the conversion of the world by thousands of religious from the feast of Peter's Chair to St. Paul's Conversion cannot fail in immense results and we ask the good sisters, the lay brothers, and the priest-religious everywhere to observe the Octave this year. "The prayer of the just availeth much." (St. James)

88

5. The Church Unity Octave (1913)

Now, for the sixth time, *The Lamp* issues its call for the observance of the Church Unity Octave, from the Feast of St. Peter's Chair at Rome, January 18, to the Feast of the Conversion of St. Paul, January 25. Every year the importance of observing this Octave increases because every year it becomes more imperative that all Christians should clearly recognize the Chair of Peter, as the divinely constituted center of Unity, and that the separatists of the East as well as the Protestants of the West, instead of any longer fighting against God by opposing the papacy, should return to communion with the Apostolic See and thereby give such a demonstration of Catholic Unity that the whole world would believe and, prostrate at the feet of Christ, cry aloud with St. Thomas, "My Lord and my God."

By way of preparation, we beg all who shall read these lines to resolve here and now to enter heart and soul into the observance of the Octave for 1913, and to enlist the sympathy and co-operation of others, both Catholic and non-Catholic, as far as possible.

Ways in Which the Octave May Be Observed

1. By prayer and daily or frequent Holy Communion on the part of the faithful generally. All Communions, hearing of Mass, prayers, stations of the cross, penances and alms during the Octave can be offered to the Sacred Heart for the fulfillment of His prayer, "that all may be one."

2. The same method of observance is recommended to the members of Religious Communities and the pupils, orphans, sick and aged under their care.

3. Priests are asked to recommend its observance to their people, both by private prayers and public devotions.

4. Sermons every night during the Octave on the Papacy and Church extension at home and abroad, calculated to strengthen the devotion of the people to the Apostolic See and to stimulate their zeal for missions, or a course of lectures specially addressed to non-Catholics.

5. A Corporate Communion for converts on the feast of St. Paul's Conversion with a popular service to close the Octave at night.

6. Distribution of tracts and books on the Papacy and the Authority of the Church among non-Catholics.

7. The Editor of *The Lamp* will be very grateful for any alms sent to *The Lamp* office to be used in printing and circulating literature relating to the Octave.

6. The Church Unity Octave (1914)

The Lamp, January, 1914

Make It a Real Week of Prayer

The January issue of *The Lamp* should reach our readers on the eve of the Church Unity Octave, and we cannot too earnestly urge you to observe this Octave in a real and serious spirit of piety and prayer.

Prayer, in its energy and power, may be likened to that invisible something in the material world which we call electricity; like the wind, we see its visible effects but the secret of its tremendous influence cannot be fathomed. By prayer we are permitted, in the Providence of God, to unite ourselves with the great dynamo of divine energy, which issues from the mind and will of the Author of all, those events that we designate by the term Divine Providence.

It follows, therefore, that a mighty concert of human wills and hearts attuning themselves to the prayer of the Redeemer of the World, *"Ut omnes unum sint"* (That they all may be one), and sustaining their concerted intercession through a period of eight days, must of necessity produce a result in the moral and spiritual sphere, commensurate with what we see in the physical world when a multitude of single wires converge their electric currents to a given center, there to be directed by a wise intelligence, toward some pre-determined end.

The prayers of a great number of individuals, offered to God, during the Church Unity Octave for the restoration of Catholic Unity to a disordered and divided Christendom, with the end view of the conversion of the world, consequent upon that Unity, cannot fail to produce, in the Divine Providence, results of the greatest value in the extension of the Kingdom of God and the salvation of souls.

Animated, therefore, with this confidence, let all our readers betake themselves to prayer during this octave and season their horizons with some degree of abstinence or self-denial, attending Mass and receiving Holy Communion as often as possible, in accordance with the intentions of the Octave, and the results cannot fail to be permanently satisfactory, both to the Sacred Heart of Our Lord and to us, who are the members of His Mystical Body.

7. The Church Unity Octave (1915)

The Lamp, November, 1914

We make our first editorial announcement of the coming Church Unity Octave one month ahead of schedule this year, because world conditions at the present moment summon us imperiously to pray, for the Peace of Jerusalem, as the exigencies of Church and State have never quite so appealingly called us to our knees before.

One of the most appalling aspects of the colossal conflict, is the impotency of the five hundred million disciples of Jesus Christ to stop the inhuman butchery, surpassing in its carnage the bloodiest war ever waged by uncivilized savages.

Never since the foundation of the world were so many millions of men under arms engaged in a single war. In comparison with the present European armaments, the army of Xerxes dwindles to the dimension of a single battle front, of one of the nine great nations, now battling for mastery. Yet with the exception of the pagan Japanese, all the combatants are Christians, and some fifty thousand of them have been constrained, to lay aside the vestments of the altar and the habit of Holy Religion, to don the uniform of civil soldier.

What is the explanation? How explain this impotency of the disciples of Christ to sheath the bloody sword and stay their hand from acting the part of Cain, the first of mankind to slay his brother? Why should even the voice of Peter have fallen unheeded upon the ears of these earthly potentates, whose diplomatic ultimatums are responsible for loosing the hellish dogs of war and rushing millions of peace-loving men from the mill, the farm, the market place, to be slaughtered like sheep in the battle trenches, above which devils dance and hold their fiendish carnival in defiance of the angels of God, who sang when the Prince of Peace was born, "Glory to God in the highest and on earth peace to men of good will?" For the first time in the history of the Roman Empire, the temple of Janus was closed, and universal peace reigned in all the world when the Word of God was made flesh and first came to dwell among us, but now the Prince of this world sits enthroned upon the altar, in a military Cathedral, whose mighty towers are builded of cannons, howitzers and siege guns, while with devilish glee he shouts, "Bravo" amid the din of death-dealing artillery and mocks at the Prince of Peace.

Why, O Catholics, O Orthodox, O Anglicans, O Protestants, are we, in union with our Divine Head, thus rudely jeered at by the denizens of hell? How is it that we are forced to be the spectators while our fellow-Christians, like savage, brute beasts, are killing each other, not by the thousands or the tens of thousands, but by the millions, in the amphitheatre of continental Europe? How is it that we are utterly helpless to stop this wholesale murder of Christians by Christians?

Be not so short-sighted as to lay the blame at the door of commercialism, the mere greed for gold, accursed though it be; charge it not to militarism, unless you are going to confound the effect with its cause; blame not the aged Emperor of Austria, or the Kaiser of Germany, the Czar of Russia, the King of England, the President of the French Republic, or even the original cause or pretext, the regicide of Serbia. Trace more deeply into the soil of Europe, the great taproot of this colossal tree, whose branches are laden with the golden fruits of commerce, the blood of the slain. The hand that planted the sapling, from which this mighty tree has grown, was Martin Luther, and the principles of the Protestant Reformation are the rich fertilizers on which it has thrived. The tree began to bear fruit, after its kind, while Luther yet lived, as the thirty-year war in Germany and all the other Reformation wars, which broke out all over northern Europe abundantly bear witness.

Ut Omnes Unum Sint. On the night in which He breathed His never-to-be-forgotten-prayer for the Unity of His Disciples, *Ut Omnes Unum Sint*, the Divine Founder of Christianity also provided the Bond of Unity and a visible touchstone of Catholic Fellowship, when, turning to Peter, the Prince and Head of the Apostles, He said to Him: "I have prayed for thee, Peter, that thy faith fail not, and when thou art converted, confirm (strengthen) thy brethren;" and after His Resurrection, He made His Divine will yet more manifest, by thrice addressing the Rockman, on whom He had said He would build His Church, "Feed My lambs, feed My sheep, shepherd My flock."

It is only when all the Christians, in all the world, clearly recognize the Supreme Authority of the Apostolic See, and the unerring orthodoxy of the voice of Peter, that all believers in Christ will be one again, as on the day of Pentecost, and the whole world, bending low beneath the outward witness of Christ's Sovereign Authority reigning among men, will indeed accept His Messiahship, and "the lion will lie down with the lamb," and all the world shall rejoice in a universal peace.

This is the message of paramount importance, which a sect-ridden Christianity and a civilized world, staggering under its load of militarism, needs at this hour, chastened by the terrible suffering entailed upon all mankind, by the savage mania for war, now sweeping so many nations in its vortex, it may be that Protestants and Orthodox alike will give reverent heed to the Vicar of Christ, and for this, fellow Catholics we have need to pray, and to season our prayers with fastings, vigils and penitential exercises. Therefore, we plead with our readers to make themselves, and others, ready to observe as never before the coming Church Unity Octave, from the Feast of the Chair of Peter at Rome, to the Festival of the Conversion of St. Paul, the great Catholic Doctor and Apostle of the Gentiles, i.e., from January 18 to January 25.

8. The Church Unity Octave (1916)

The Lamp, January, 1916

Only a few days after this issue of *The Lamp* reaches you, the Octave of prayer will begin. With one accord, we trust that you resolve to observe it. We estimate that at least one hundred thousand Catholics will read these lines. What an avalanche of prayers you can precipitate towards the throne of grace if you will, between the feast of the Chair of St. Peter at Rome, January 18th, and the Conversion of St. Paul, January 25th, observe this Octave. Consider the tremendous importance of the two grand objects for which your prayers are asked:

First, the Reunion of Christendom, so absolutely essential for the fulfillment of Our Lord's own prayer—that all who believe in Him might be one; and *secondly, the missionary extension of the Catholic Church into all lands until the whole world shall be converted to Christ.* You could not possibly select two themes on which to concentrate your prayers for eight days, that would be more agreeable to the Sacred Heart of Jesus and the Immaculate Heart of Mary, than those two, which constitute the substance of the Octave, we are asking you to take part in, and we cannot believe that we shall ask in vain.

Now for the practical way of putting this observance into effect:

1. There is nothing better than the use of the Rosary with intention. You all have your beads. Use them daily during the Octave, with intention for the return of all Christians, to obedience to the Vicar of Christ and for the multiplication of Catholic missionaries until the whole world believes for its salvation in Jesus Christ.

2. Enclosed in your *Lamp* you will find the form of prayer, specially set forth for use during the Octave. Please say the antiphon and prayer at least once daily and take note of the special intention for each day of the Octave.

3. *Go to Holy Communion without fail on the Sunday within the Octave,* i.e., on the third Sunday after Epiphany, January 23rd. If it is possible, go to Mass and receive Holy Communion every day. Remember that this Octave of Prayer was especially blessed by the late Holy Father, Pope Pius of holy memory, and that many Cardinals, Archbishops and Bishops in America, Canada, England, Ireland and other parts of the world have also approved of it and recommended its observance to the clergy and faithful under their spiritual care.

9. Letter to Anglican Bishops, 1916

Ut Omnes Unum Sint

To the Rt. Rev. Bishops of the Episcopal Church in the United States of America:

We, your little Franciscan Brothers, the Friars of the Atonement (Third Order Regular of St. Francis), ventured to address to you, two years ago, an invitation to join with many of the Roman Catholic Hierarchy, clergy and faithful, in observing the Church Unity Octave of Prayer, from January 18th to 25th, for the fulfillment of our Divine Lord's prayers that we, His followers, might all be One.

Of your Reverend Body several courteously accepted this invitation, the rest made no answer.

Encouraged by the interchange of correspondence which has occurred since then, between your distinguished Commission to prepare for a World's Conference on Faith and Order, and His Eminence, Cardinal Gasparri, Secretary of State to His Holiness, Pope Benedict XV, and by the fact that the Supreme Pontiff of the Catholic Church has confirmed the observance of the Church Unity Octave by a papal brief, a copy of which we are sending you, we are again inviting you and your clergy to unite with us, your Roman Catholic brethren, in praying during this Octave with special fervor for the reunion of Christendom.

None of us can be ignorant of the immense difficulties which lie in the way of a return to Unity, not least among which, is the deep gulf of separation, which rolls between us on the score of the papacy; but all the more on this account, ought we not to pray that God would remove, as a stumbling block out of the way of reunion, every false belief concerning the See of Rome, in order that all Christians may come to recognize either that it is the divinely ordained center of Catholic Unity, or that such a center must be looked for in some other direction?

Surely, if we are to unite later in a World's Conference on Faith and Order, we ought to gladly consent in the meantime to pray in concert during an agreed time that all who believe in Jesus Christ may be one.

Kneeling with you, as men of peace and good will, at the feet of our common Lord and Savior, the Word made flesh, we entreat you to accept this letter in the spirit of Christian charity and brotherhood in which it has been written.

The Friars of the Atonement

The Feast of the Lord's Nativity
December 25, 1916

10. Letter to English Church Union, 1917

Ut Omnes Unum Sint

To the Reverend Clergy and Lay-Officers of the English Church Union:

We, the Friars of the Atonement, your little Franciscan Brothers, stretch out our hands to you across the gulf of separation created by the Sixteenth Century Breach between England and the Holy See, and ask you to unite with us in the observance of the Church Unity Octave of Prayer.

It is not the first time that we have extended to you this invitation. Last year some of your number wrote us a cordial reply. No doubt, many others prayed in concert with us, without sending us any answer. A few wrote bitter things in reply concerning the Papacy and the Church of Rome.

We realize keenly the almost endless difficulties which will have to be overcome before intercommunion can be reestablished between Canterbury and Rome; not the least of which is the lack of unity in belief among Christians, concerning the Apostolic See and the claim of the Roman Pontiff to be the infallible and universal Shepherd over the Flock of Christ. But does not the existence of these difficulties, and the almost infinite variety of opinions and beliefs regarding the Papacy, which now divide Christendom, make it all the more a desirable thing that we should pray in concert during a given period, that God would take away from our eyes all false conceptions and erroneous opinions, and make us see, eye to eye, with the true vision of the Holy Spirit, concerning the Roman Pontiff, whether indeed he constitutes in his office, as the Successor of St. Peter, the divinely constituted Center of a reunited Christendom, or whether we must look for the Center of Catholic Unity elsewhere?

We are all conscious that God the Holy Spirit, at this time is brooding over the separation and almost chaotic fragments of a sundered Christianity and is moving us with a common desire, each to contribute our share towards the fulfillment of Our Lord's own prayer, that we might all be one.

Trusting that many, if not all, who receive this invitation will find it possible to join with us, from January 18th to the 25th, in sincere, fervent prayer for the Reunion of Christendom, we remain, in the bonds of Christian charity. . . .

11. The Church Unity Octave (1921)

The Lamp, December, 1920

Cablegram from Rome

On Friday, November 26th, the Editor of *The Lamp* received the following cablegram from Rome: "The Holy Father will celebrate Mass on January 18th for your Association." (Signed Papadopoulos)

The Association referred to are those who will associate themselves together during the approaching Church Unity Octave, from the Feast of St. Peter's Chair at Rome, January 18th, to that of the Conversion of St. Paul, January 25th, in praying in union with the Church's Divine Head, that all his Disciples may be one, even as He and the Father are One, also for the fulfillment of Our Lord's prophecy: "Other sheep I have, which are not of this Fold; them also I must bring and they will hear My Voice, and there shall be One Fold and One Shepherd."

"Papadopoulos": As the signature signified, the cablegram was sent by Monsignor Isaias Papadopoulos, Assessor of the Sacred Congregation which administers the affairs of the Oriental Churches. Monsignor Papadopoulos was consecrated by Pope Pius X, of holy memory, as the first Catholic Bishop of Constantinople since the great schism a thousand years ago. As announced in *The Lamp* last month, Monsignor Papadopoulos has been succeeded in his position of Greek Catholic Bishop of Constantinople, by Right Rev. George Calavassy, in order that the former may devote all his time to the affairs of the Sacred Congregation over which he presides.

It is to be noted that the Holy Father has selected January 18, which is the feast of the Chair of St. Peter, at Rome, on which to celebrate Mass for the intentions of the Church Unity Octave. Thus does the Vicar of Christ emphasize the definitely revealed truth that the Chair of Peter is the center of Catholic Unity and there can be no other.

Surely now that the Great Shepherd takes the lead of the universal flock in the observance of the Church Unity Octave, all the faithful, everywhere, will be the more strongly moved to follow the example of the Vicar of Christ and pray in union with him and the Sacred Heart of Our Lord Jesus Christ, *Ut omnes unum sint* (That all may be one).

In honor of this cablegram from Rome, we are making the present issue of *The Lamp* a Church Unity Octave Number, and we fervently hope and pray that the entire Army of *The Lamp* readers will be inspired by the example of our Holy Father to observe the Octave with conscientious faithfulness and strong confidence that our prayers, so agreeable to the mind of Christ and the desires of the Sacred Heart, will obtain a wonderful answer from God, the Father Almighty.

This the second time that the Holy Father has shown his approval of the Church Unity Octave; for in February 1916 he issued an apostolic brief extending its observance to the universal Church and enriching it with plenary and partial Indulgences.

When St. Francis was a young salesman in the store of his Father, Peter Bernadone, a beggar asked him alms for the love of God. Being very busy with a customer he rebuffed him. A moment later, when the beggar had turned towards the door, he repented, and running after him, put a piece of gold in the hands of the astonished mendicant. At the same time, he registered an oath that in the future whoever should ask him anything, for the love of God, he would do it to the utmost of his ability.

Now, dear readers, for the love of God, we are going to ask you everyone to observe next month, the Church Unity Octave, which will begin on the Feast of the Chair of St. Peter at Rome, January 18th, and end on the Feast of the Conversion of St. Paul, January 25th.

Never did the world since the dawn of Christianity need peace so desperately as it does at the present time, and the hope of a real and enduring peace lies in the return of the disciples of Christ to Unity and we who have the fulness of divine revelation and Truth know that such Unity can only be realized in the return of all Christians to communion with and loving obedience to the great White Shepherd of Christendom, the occupant of the Chair of Peter at Rome. This is what this Church Unity Octave emphasizes, and since February 1916 it has been the voice of the Successor of Peter which has called the whole Catholic world to its observance, rewarding those who shall heed the call with indulgences, partial and plenary.

First and foremost we appeal to the Hierarchy to make the Church Unity Octave in their several dioceses to be more generally observed in 1921 than ever before. The Cardinals of America, Canada, England and Ireland, the Archbishops and the Bishops, have always been the friends of the Church Unity Octave and some have been its greatest promoters. Time and space forbid us to tell, even briefly, what the Bishops have from the outset done to popularize the observance of the Octave among the faithful. Through the united action of the Hierarchy we hope to see the observance of the Church Unity Octave become as universal as the rosary devotions in the months of May and October.

It was, of course, to be expected that the religious trained as they are to a life of prayer, would be the first to observe in their many monasteries, convents and institutions the Church Unity Octave, and this expectation has been abundantly realized. While thanking our fellow religious, fathers, brothers, and sisters for the splendid service they have rendered the cause of Unity through the faithful observance of the Octave heretofore, the Friars of the Atonement humbly beg all the communities of religious everywhere throughout the Catholic world in the whole world to unite with one consent from January 18 to 25 in praying our Lord to hasten the blessed day when Catholic Unity will triumph over heresy and schism and the united hosts of Christ shall subdue all nations to the scepter of the cross and herald the universal reign of the Lord's anointed over the entire world.

It is our ambition to see the Church Unity Octave observed, not alone within cloistered walls, but by the multitude of the faithful in every church, in Christendom, and at the family altar in every Catholic home. Will not the one hundred and fifty thousand subscribers to *The Lamp* and all others, who scan its pages, share with us this noble ambition and do your utmost to propagate the observance of the Octave among the rank and file of the people?

12. The Church Unity Octave (1923)

The Lamp, December, 1922

When this issue of *The Lamp* reaches our Readers only one month will remain before the observance of the Church Unity Octave will be upon us—the eight day period of prayer, for the reunion of Christendom, which begins every year on the Feast of the Chair of Peter at Rome, January 18th, and ends on the Feast of the Conversion of St. Paul, January 25th.

Our readers will instantly recall that, at the meeting of the Hierarchy in Washington in September, 1921, a resolution was passed by the Archbishops and Bishops of America, that everywhere in the United States, this Church Unity Octave would be observed, not merely for 1922, but annually thereafter.

Since that important resolution was passed, the keeping of the Octave has spread increasingly and more universally in other parts of the Western Hemisphere, and throughout Europe, Asia, Africa, and the Islands of the Sea. In a letter recently received from Monsignor Calavassy, bishop of the Greek Catholics of Constantinople, the following statement was made with regard to the Church Unity Octave:

I am circulating a petition which I will send to the Holy Father after it will be signed by the Patriarchs and some Oriental Bishops, in which I ask him to make the Octave obligatory in the whole Church.

This important communication from the Bishop of the Greek Catholics in Constantinople, is evidence of how deeply rooted the Church Unity Octave has become in other parts of the world and we have been informed that similar petitions to the Father of Christendom will be addressed to His Holiness from Occidental Europe, where Cardinals, Archbishops and Bishops are supporting and furthering its observance.

We hope that this prayer from the Orient, where schism has been rampant with all its dreadful consequences for more than a thousand years, will be taken up and echoed in all parts of the Western Church, which also has suffered unspeakably from the heresies and schisms that starting in Germany, where the Protestant Reformation took its rise, has since the sixteenth century spread to all parts of the world, bearing increasingly its baneful harvest of immeasurable evil to the souls of men.

Our forefathers sowed the wind of heresy and schism long ago, and we, their children, are now reaping the whirlwind of dreadful wars which threaten the utter ruin, one may almost say the total annihilation, of the human race, unless those who bear the name of Christian can forget their religious differences and stand together as one man to oppose the reign of anti-Christ which is coming fast upon the earth in the form of Bolshevism, anarchism and all the other frightful isms which are a denial of the very existence of God and His moral and Spiritual reign over the consciences and the lives of men.

Increasingly, therefore, is it incumbent upon us, from year to year, to echo from our hearts the prayer which Jesus Christ, our Great High Priest Himself, voiced to God, the Father, on the night of His betrayal, with His sacrifice, for the sins of the world imminent upon Calvary's Cross: "Ut omnes unum sint"; "Not for them only (My disciples) do I pray, but for them also who through their word shall believe in Me, that they all may be one, as Thou, Father, in Me, and I in Thee; that they also may be one in Us, that the world may believe that Thou hast sent me." (St. John, 17:20-21.)

13. Church Unity Octave (1925)

Letter to the American Hierarchy

Right Reverend and dear Bishop:

Ever since I was first requested by Bishop O'Connell, of Richmond, to send out in December a reminder to the Members of the American Hierarchy of the resolution passed by the Bishops at Washington on Sept, 22, 1921, that "The Unity Octave to be held throughout all the diocese of the United States," I have continued to do so annually, about one month before the recurrence of the Church Unity Octave, between the Feast of St. Peter's Chair at Rome, January 18th, and St. Paul's Conversion, January 25th.

Owing to 1925 being the Holy Year, a special endeavor is on foot to make the Church Unity Octave more generally and fervently observed than ever before in its history, and I beg Your Lordship so to urge its observance by the faithful of your flock. It is to be noted that in his Encyclical of August 9th, concerning the Holy Year observance. His Holiness lays extraordinary stress on the Reunion of Christendom around the Chair of Peter. He says:

> "It is our earnest prayer that *the Churches which held apart from the Church of Rome by age-long and unhappy dissidences, may join with us.* Nothing could touch our hearts so much, than *that many from among them, if not all*

101

collectively, should pass into the One Fold of Christ, so that we may, on the occasion of this Great Jubilee, embrace them with special affection and write them down in the number of children most dear to us."

In exhorting the faithful as to what they shall pray for, when they go to Rome in pilgrimage, he continues:

"And further, our intention is that all who live in Rome, or come to Rome to gain the privileges of the Jubilee, should offer in unfailing prayer to the goodness of Almighty God another matter which is a source of thought and prayer to us, and of *great import for Religion* and that is, that *all non-Catholics may seek refuge in the True Church of Jesus Christ.*"

So general has become the observance of the Church Unity Octave in all parts of the Catholic world, that the time now seems opportune for an approach to the Holy Father, humbly petitioning the Successor of St. Peter to supplement the action of Pope Benedict XV, who extended the observance *Laudabiliter* to the Universal Church, by making the Unity Octave of holy obligation by the faithful everywhere, in the same manner as are the prescribed devotions to the Blessed Virgin during the months of May and October.

Through the zealous propagation of the Church Unity Octave, by certain of its promoters in Europe, petitions have been widely circulated to the above effect, and these are now arriving at the central office by every transatlantic mail from Cardinals, Archbishops, and Bishops in England, Ireland, Scotland, France, Belgium, Holland, Germany, Austria, Spain, Portugal, Italy, and from Rome itself. One of these was signed by Cardinal Logue the day before his death. I have no doubt that the American Hierarchy in passing the resolution for the general observance throughout the United States, together with the same action of the Canadian Bishops of the Toronto Province, have inspired, by the force of holy example, this widespread request on the part of the Bishops of Europe.

I would be most grateful for any counsel and help Your Lordship could give me, as to the best mode of approaching His Holiness, when a sufficient number of the bishops of the world, priests, religious, and faithful, have subscribed to the petition to make it worthy of the Holy Father's attention.

14. Last Call to Observe the Octave

The Antidote, January, 1925

We repeat the invitation extended to all readers of *The Antidote* last month, to unite in the observance of the Church Unity Octave, an eight day period of prayer for the Reunion of Christendom, beginning on the Feast of the Chair of St. Peter at Rome, January 18th, and ending on the Feast of the Conversion of St. Paul, January 25th.

As far as the Catholic Church is concerned, the observance of the Church Unity Octave is, more or less, universal in every part of the world. To make it more effective, we cordially invite our non-Catholic brethren to unite with us at this time, in repeating the prayer of Jesus Christ Himself which He addressed to God, the Father, at the Last Supper, asking that all His disciples might be one, even as He and the Father were one, in order that the world might believe and accept Him as its Divine Savior and King.

A non-Catholic might object to uniting with Roman Catholics in praying for Unity at this particular period, because he is not prepared to accept Papal Supremacy and Infallibility. But surely all non-Catholics must recognize that there cannot be a reunited Christendom with the Roman Catholic Church left outside! A Reunion that embraced only a minority could never be a reunion of the whole.

If all Christians became one in a fellowship and Communion, there would have to be a visible Center of Unity; and even if our Christian brethren outside the Catholic Fold are not prepared to recognize the Chair of Peter at Rome, as the divinely constituted Center of a Reunited Christendom, they ought to be liberal enough at least to concede to that most ancient and venerable of Apostolic Sees, a primacy of honor and ecclesiastical precedence, for the sake of Christian Unity.

This being so, liberal-minded non-Catholics ought to be able to unite with Catholics on the observance of this particular Octave. If you believe we are wrong, in claiming a *de jure divino* Primacy for the Bishop of Rome, then during the Octave pray for our disillusionment, permitting us at the same time to pray that the "Other Sheep" may come to see eye to eye with those within the Papal Communion, in order that all may hear the voice of Divine Authority, and constitute One Fold under One Shepherd.

15. The Name of the Octave

Letter to Cardinal Bourne of Westminster

St. Paul's Friary (Graymoor)
Garrison, N.Y., May 29, 1926

Your Eminence:

Mr. Wm. d'Andria, S.J. acting Secretary of the Church Unity Octave in England, has written me recently of the interview he had with Your Eminence prior to the meeting in April of the English Hierarchy, in the hope of obtaining unanimous approval of the Octave, similar to that granted to it some years ago, by the bishops of the United States and of the provinces of Kingston and Toronto, Canada.

He further states in his letter, that subsequent to the meeting, Your Eminence wrote him that the Bishops of England preferred not to act collectively but each would act in accordance with the needs of his own diocese and Your Eminence added: "If you can find an alternative title it will help the movement very greatly."

We have no situation in this country similar to that which exists in England and, consequently, the present name has served very well over here in America, no single Bishop ever having suggested a change of title.

The criticism of the existing name, which for some time occupied correspondence columns of the *Catholic Universe* interested me deeply and first aroused me to the possibility of misunderstanding. Since receiving Mr. d'Andria's letter, I have given the matter all the more prayerful consideration in order to offer Your Eminence an alternate title.

I think the solution of the problem, however, has been granted to the Mother Foundress of the Sisters of the Atonement, Rev. Mother Lurana Mary Francis, S.A. after specially invoking the Holy Ghost during the Whitsuntide Octave. She received it on yesterday, St. Augustine's Day, the Apostle of England, and the first Archbishop of Canterbury, an answer to her prayer which I trust, Your Eminence, will approve of, for it does

104

seem to me, personally, like a real inspiration of the Holy Ghost, namely, to substitute for the words "Church Unity Octave", a title which no one could misunderstand.

The only reason for having an eight day season of prayer, beginning on the Feast of the Chair of St. Peter at Rome, is because the Holy Roman See is the divinely constituted center of a re-united Christendom and that, above everything else, is the thing to be emphasized and borne witness to in this present time when, by the impulse of the Holy Spirit, no doubt, the minds of all Christians in every part of the world are being more or less exercised over the question of Unity.

Would not the adoption of this name add peculiar force to the petition to the Holy See, concerning which I spoke to Your Eminence in Rome, that the dignity of the feast of the Chair of St. Peter should be elevated throughout the Catholic world to the same rank as it enjoys in St. Peter's in Rome, with a special pronouncement on the subject from the Holy Father himself, once more reiterating what his predecessors have always said from the beginning—that the test of Catholicity and the center of Catholic Unity is none other than the Chair which St. Peter established in Rome, from which his successors, to this day, rule the Catholic Church throughout the world?

I sincerely hope the ultimate adoption of this alternative title, for what has become known as the Church Unity Octave, will solve the difficulty as far as Your Eminence and the English Hierarchy are concerned and that we shall have at last your full, hearty, and strong support for the Octave.

While interested in the return of all dissident Christians to communion with the Apostolic See, my first thought and prayer has always been for England.

Although I may be repeating what I said to you in Rome, may I be permitted to add, that I am by descent Welsh on the paternal side, English and Scotch on my mother's side. My grandmother was a Richmond. An enthusiastic antiquarian, of the family, has compiled a book tracing the descent back to the time of Edward the Confessor. It has, therefore, been a source of keen disappointment to me that this part of the world, seemingly thus bound up with the Unity vocation of the Society of the Atonement, should have been, until now, the most backward in espousing the observance of the Octave.

I am happy to report to Your Eminence that, as I am informed, many Bishops of the world have now signed the petition to the Holy Father to make the observance of the Octave universal as in the same manner petitioned to the Holy See to establish the Feast of the Kingship of Christ, not including the Hierarchy of the United States and Canada, which I have purposely held in reserve, until such time as the majority of the Bishops of the rest of the world justify us in asking the American Hierarchy to once more take corporate action in support of the Octave.

With the most pleasant recollections of the interview I had with Your Eminence in Rome about this time last year, and kneeling for Your Blessing, I am,

Your Eminence's humble and devoted servant in Christ,
Fr. Paul James Francis, S.A.

16. Letter to "Universe" (London)

March 26, 1926

Sir:

I note that considerable discussion has of late appeared in the *Universe* concerning the nomenclature of the Octave of Prayer held each year throughout the Catholic Church from the feast of the Chair of St. Peter at Rome, January 18, to that of the Conversion of St. Paul, January 25, for the return of all dissident Christians to the Unity of the One Fold under the One Shepherd.

A correspondent signing himself "Cyrillus" in your issue of February 12, writes as follows: "With regard to the Church Unity Octave, as the secretary points out in last week's *Universe*, it is of course clear to Catholics that we are praying for Oneness of Faith. Therefore, it is a pity that this title was not substituted for the totally misleading one, of Church Unity, which originated in a Protestant community (since then converted), and is seized upon by Protestants, to confirm their theory that there are several Churches. It is unlikely that the American translation conveys the term used by the Head of Christ's One Church, in the Latin Brief, approving the excellent object of this week of prayer."

As the editor of *The Lamp*, the magazine in which the Octave originated, will you permit me to state that we used the two words, Church-Unity, to describe the character of the

Prayer Octave, and primarily to distinguish it from the so-called, Christian Unity, widely exploited by the Federation of Protestant and other non-Catholic unitive enterprises.

The purpose of the Church Unity Octave was defined, from the very first, in the columns of *The Lamp,* as a period of eight days of prayer: "For the return of all Christians with the Apostolic See." The words quoted appear in the first published mention made of the Octave.

The reason we chose the Feast of the Chair of St. Peter at Rome, upon which to begin the Church Unity Octave was, of course, to emphasize what had been from the first issue of *The Lamp* its *raison d'etre*. This initial number lies before me as I write, and the purpose of its publication is summed up in one paragraph as follows: "No apology is needed for the publication of a monthly organ devoted to the eternal principles of Church Unity, which the Master Builder of the Catholic Church laid as the Foundation Stone of the mighty Superstructure, saying: "Thou art Peter and on this Rock I will build My Church, and the gates of hell shall not prevail against it."

As defined by the magazine that originated it, the "Church Unity Octave" means simply an eight-day period of prayer for the return of all separated Christians to the Unity of the Catholic Church. If anyone can provide a substitute title conveying the same thing in as brief a compass and impossible of misinterpretation, perhaps the Holy Father will accept it in place of the present title, which His Holiness has approved.

We think that "Cyrillus" has uncovered the root of the prejudice, that lies beneath the adverse criticisms of the Octave in your correspondence columns, when he states that "it originated in a Protestant Comunity—since then converted," the inference apparently being that, consequently, the Octave must have been conceived in heresy and brought forth in error.

In other words, that as originally established, the type of Church Unity prayed for was nothing, more or less, than the happy functioning of the Anglican "Branch Theory". Now ordinarily, all things might have been true, but in the particular case of the Church Unity Octave, nothing could be further from the facts. The editorial in the initial number, above mentioned, of *The Lamp,* February 1903, made the following profession of Faith: "We believe all that the Catholic Episcopate, in communion with the Apostolic See of Rome, believes, the dogmas of the Immaculate Conception and Papal Infallibility not excepted." We then knew, as we know now, that there is but one Holy, Catholic, Apostolic, and Roman Church, and that all who do not break bread in the House of Peter are outside the One True Fold.

"Cyrillus" concludes his criticism of the Church Unity Octave by saying: "It is unlikely that the American translation conveys the term used by the Head of Christ's One Church, in the Latin Brief, approving the excellent object of this week of prayer." In reply to the above it will be sufficient to quote the following translation of the Latin Brief, of Pope Benedict XV: "The prayers, however, which are to be recited for the Unity of the Church during the Octave, we have ordained, as above, are to be as follows, and, lest any changes might creep into them, we have directed that a copy of them is to be kept in the archives of the apostolic briefs."

Be so good as to note that the Sovereign Pontiff himself, prescribes certain prayers to be said "for the Unity of the Church during the Octave." This being so, it is difficult for some of us to understand why any Catholic could criticize adversely, the calling of such a period of prayer, a Church Unity Octave.

As one who has been marvellously led with certain companions, out of the "far country" of Anglicanism, into the fold of St. Peter and Catholic Unity, I hope it will not be taken amiss if I use the present occasion to deplore the tone of almost hostile criticism that certain of your writers have displayed, toward Lord Halifax and men of like mind, in the Anglican body. It seems to me, as an unworthy son of Saint Francis of Assisi, that, along with Oneness of faith, hope and charity have also their important offices in assisting to its consumation, the fulfillment, of Our Lord's prophecy: "Other Sheep I have that are not of this fold; them also I must bring that they will hear My voice and there shall be One Fold and One Shepherd." If our separated brethren, whether of the East or the West, are to be irresistibly drawn by the voice of the Good Shepherd back into the One Fold, from which their ancestors departed many generations ago, it will no doubt be because the charity of the Sacred Heart will find its human medium of expression, in not alone the Vicar of Christ and the chief shepherds united with Him, but also, in great body of the Catholic faithful.

17. The Church Unity Octave (1927)

The Lamp, December, 1926

The Church Unity Octave observance for 1927 is now fast approaching and although, in the meantime, the minds of our readers will be much taken up with the celebration of Christmas, we are constrained to interject a word of reminder about the Octave in the December *Lamp,* because the January issue will reach its readers only two or three days before the Feast of the Chair of Peter at Rome, January 18th, when the Octave begins.

Our readers are aware that a movement has been on foot for some years, gathering momentum all the while, having for its object the Universal Observance of the Octave by the Catholic Faithful of the whole world, in the same way that the special devotions to our Blessed Mother have become universal during the months of May and October. This, however, can come to pass only with the authoritative command of the Holy Father. As you all know Pope Benedict XV, by a Papal Brief, enriched the observance of the Octave with a plenary and partial indulgence and recommended it to Catholics everywhere, but he did not enjoin it as of obligation.

The first petition to this effect was presented to Pope Pius XI, our present Sovereign Pontiff by the Hierarchy of the Eastern Church, in communion with Rome, as far back as October, 1922. Three years later, in May, 1925, the Holy Year, the editor of *The Lamp,* for the second time presented a similar petition, this time signed by two hundred Cardinals, Archbishops, Bishops and Vicars-Apostolic of both the Latin and Greek rites, and representing the whole world. The day was an exceedingly busy one for His Holiness, being the Friday before the canonization of the Little Flower; one hundred thousand pilgrims were in Rome and one hundred and fifty Bishops. In that five minute interview the Holy Father might have denied the petition, instead, His Holiness chose what seemed to be the only alternative; he referred the petition to Cardinal Gasparri, Secretary of State where it still awaits the Holy Father's consideration.

Meantime, petitions, signed by the Catholic bishops of the world, have continued to accumulate in our hands so that now they number over four hundred and sixty, much more than twice the number placed in the hands of Cardinal Gasparri eighteen months ago.

If God wills, we will go to Rome again next October, and once again petition the successor of St. Peter, to confirm and supplement the brief of His predecessor by a decree providing for the daily recitation of the prayers of the Church Unity Octave, from the feast of the Chair of Peter at Rome, to the Conversion of St. Paul, in every Church and Oratory in Christendom. By that time we confidently hope to have a majority of the Bishops of the world supporting the petition.

We ask our readers of *The Lamp,* when they observe the Church Unity Octave this year, to especially pray that our Holy Father, Pope Pius XI will not only see fit to grant the petition thus supported by so great a number of the Catholic Hierarchy, but that through the Sacred Congregation of Rites, he will exalt the dignity of the feast of the Chair of Peter at Rome, to the same liturgical rank that it enjoys in the Vatican Basilica. By this action the whole world may come speedily to recognize that the divinely constituted Center of a reunited Christendom is none other than the Chair of Peter, in the Eternal City, where more than a thousand years ago the throne of the Fisherman supplanted that of the Caesars.

18. Church Unity Octave (1927)
and the
Feast of the Kingship of Christ

This year for the first time, on the last Sunday in October, the Faithful throughout the Catholic World will be celebrating the Feast of the Kingship of Christ, instituted by Our Holy Father, at the close of the Jubilee Year 1925. The creation of this feast, by the Vicar of Christ, in response to a strong appeal addressed to him by something like five hundred Bishops, besides many of the secular and religious clergy and large numbers of lay-folk, encourages us in our desire to see by the same Supreme Authority the observance of the Church Unity Octave from the feast of the Chair of St. Peter at Rome, January 18th, to the feast of the Conversion of St. Paul, January 25th, firmly established in every part of the Catholic Church.

The papal brief of Pope Benedict XV recommending its

observance as *laudabiliter* (i.e., praiseworthy) has had the effect of extending the voluntary observance of the Octave into all parts of the Church, both East and West. But of such paramount importance is the object of the Octave that already as many as 450 bishops, not including the hierarchies of the United States and Canada, have signed a petition to Pope Pius XI to still further confirm the Brief of his Predecessor by making this season of prayer for the return of all dissident Christians to the unity of the One Fold under One Shepherd of holy obligation in the same way that May and October devotions are decreed to be observed in all the churches and oratories of Catholic Christendom. The reason why we do not include any of the American or Canadian bishops who have added their names to this long list is because we believe, when the majority of the other bishops of the world have signed the petition, the hierarchy of America and Canada will take corporate action to the same effect, and this confidence is founded on the well known fact that several years ago, the Provinces of Kingston and Ontario and the entire episcopate of the United States at their Washington meeting, passed resolutions adopting the observance of the Octave in all their dioceses. Add the hierarchies of the United States and Canada, and we would have nearly six hundred prelates, a much larger number than, as we understand, signed the petition to the Holy Father asking for the institution of the feast of the Kingship of Christ.

It seems to us that the observance, by the whole Catholic Church, of the Church Unity Octave is the *logical consequence* of the institution of this feast of St. Peter which Feast we have just named, for the reason that Christ Himself in the prayer which He addressed to His Father, on the night of His betrayal, clearly indicated that before the whole world would hail Him as King and Master, it was needful that those who would believe on Him might become one, even as He and the Father were one. As the Good Shepherd, He declared that He had "other sheep" not of the Catholic Fold whom He was under constraint to bring and who would ultimately hear His voice and there would be "one fold and one shepherd". In Church history, as gradually the Kingdom of Christ has been extended more and more throughout the world, every century has been signalized by some particular issue. That which seems to stand out in our day with increasing prominence, and is everywhere recognized as the matter of prime necessity, is the unification of the forces which make for the reign of Christ among men. Not only Catholics, but Protestants of all descriptions and the millions of the Orthodox East, are praying for Christian Unity, holding conferences and synods, seeking some solution to the knotty problem. Now more than ever before, it is necessary for all disciples of Christ to believe and confess that the divinely constituted center of a re-united Christendom is the Chair of Peter at Rome. But as it is the Holy Ghost, who maketh men to be of one mind in a house, no one less Omnipotent than He can cause the scales to fall from the eyes of our separated brethren, so that with us who already accept it as an article of faith, they may recognize the Universal Jurisdiction and Supreme Authority of the successor of St. Peter and submit themselves for the sake of Catholic Unity, to the rule of the one Supreme Shepherd, over the one Universal Flock.

The only objection set up in opposition to the petition addressed to the Holy Father asking him to make the observance of the Octave universal by a papal decree, is the great number of obligatory devotions already in existence. But whatever weight there is in this objection, it is not sufficient to effect the paramount importance and we truly say the sacred obligation, under which all the faithful labor to echo Christ's own High-Priestly Prayer—*Ut omnes unum sint*—and surely there could not be devised a more appropriate and fitting time to unite the Catholics of the whole world in the discharge of their solemn obligation, than during the Octave, which begins with the feast of the Chair of St. Peter at Rome and ends with that of the Conversion of St. Paul, the Great Apostle to the Gentiles.

To further emphasize and exalt before the eyes of all Christians that Chair of Unity, which the *fiat* of the Almighty has established in the "Eternal City", it is proposed, in connection with the petition to the Holy Father, to ask the Sacred Congregation of Rites to elevate the feast of St. Peter's Chair at Rome, from its present status of a major-double, to that of a double of the first class, so that it may enjoy the same dignity everywhere throughout Christendom that it now possesses in the Basilica of St. Peter. A decree to this effect, coming from the Supreme Head of the Catholic Church with an appeal to all who call themselves Christians, to recognize the occupant of that Chair, the voice of Christ, Himself, calling his wandering sheep back to Catholic Communion, could not fail to produce an enormous effect, supported and sanctioned, as it would be, by the Blessed Paraclete whose office it is to guide the elect of God into all truth.

19. Letter on Unity Octave

Jan. 26, 1931

Yesterday, St. Paul's Day, at the 11:00 o'clock Mass, in the Church of the Immaculate Conception, Washington, D.C., I spoke of the Society of the Atonement and its special mission of Unity—*At-one-ment*, how it began outside the Fold of Peter and its corporate reception. I illustrated the penalty we had to pay for bearing witness to the Pope, by the Long Island incident. Father Hurney assured me, and so did others, that the people were greatly interested.

I had written out three-fourths of my radio sermon. I had no trouble at all in preaching. My only difficulty was to get into the compass of a half hour what I *had* to say to round out the argument.

I began with a brief statement regarding the origin and development of the Octave; its first fruits in the corporate reception of the Society of the Atonement within two years' time, followed a short time later by the submission of the Calday Benedictine monks and the Milford Haven nuns.

I related how the Octave's center in Rome was in the Church of Santa Paolo alla Regula, wherein is preserved, as an oratory, the very room occupied by Saint Paul during the first year of his imprisonment. I also said that at the very time I was speaking, Cardinal Van Rossum was giving Benediction of the Blessed Sacrament at the conclusion of the Octave's observance in Rome, for it was then about 8:30 or 9:00 P.M. in Italy.

I then proceeded to quote Our Lord's prayer *Ut Omnes Sint*, etc., showing how He revealed that Unity among Christians was an essential prerequisite to the conversion of the world, hence its tremendous importance. I then pointed out how Our Lord provided a center, or Chair of Unity, for all time in Saint Peter and his successors, in the Apostolic See of Rome.

113

The method established by Our Lord to extend His kingdom throughout the world was preaching and missionary propaganda. I quoted His command to the Apostles, "Go ye into all the world, etc.," and I cited His appearance years later to Saint Paul on the way to Damascus, thus changing him from a persecutor of Christians to the great apostle to the Gentiles.

Fallen Lucifer was then introduced as carrying on an age-long opposition to the Church, and I used the Church in the East, as illustrating the way he carried on his campaign, and the measure of success attending his efforts.

Raising up a series of heretics, beginning with Arius, after Constantine changed Byzantium into Constantinople, the imperial city, how politics took a hand and culminated in the rejection of the Vicar of Christ, by the East, and the acceptance of Caesar (in the person of the emperor) in his place. Then the punishment of the East at the hands of Mohammed and the Turk.

I next reviewed the conversion of the Slavs, first by the Papal Missionaries and Methodius, followed by the alliance with Constantinople of the Russian Czars and the setting up of a mighty church of all Russia and Siberia with *Saint Peters*burg as a substitute for Rome, the White Czar for the Great White Shepherd of the true Church, the house of Romanoff for the house of Peter, and then suddenly, in the heyday of its power, intolerance and pride, the sudden crash and falling of the mighty fabric, and the rising upon its ruins of the throne of anti-Christ in the present terrifying Soviet regime, with its brazen manifestation of the man of sin proposing to abolish God altogether. I pointed out the well known fact that this peril threatens all Christendom, America included.

Finally, an appeal was made to all who love Our Lord in sincerity and call Him "Lord and Master", to search the Scriptures, to study the Church's history and when they discover the truth about the Papacy as *jure divino*, to accept the rule of the Universal Shepherd. If obstacles seemingly unsurmountable prevent their entering at once into Catholic communion, at least they should hail the Vicar of Christ in their hearts, hear his voice when he speaks, as he has just done in the Encyclical on Marriage, and cooperate with the Catholic Church in the great struggle before it, to save Christian civilization from perishing under the assaults of Communism and infidelity, and to assist

in carrying on the missionary conquest of Asia and Africa until
the proclamation of the Angel of Apocalypse has come to pass
—"*until the kingdoms of this world have become the kingdoms
of the Lord's Anointed.*"

20. The Chair of Unity Octave

Catholic University, Washington, D.C.
January 18, 1934

By way of introduction let me say a word about the Church
Unity Octave hymn. This hymn, used in connection with this
observance, has been provided by Divine Providence. The history in back of it is this. Thirty-one years ago, when *The Lamp*
came out with its message to the other churches, that the center
of Catholic Unity was the See of Peter and there could be none
other, a copy of *The Lamp* fell in the hands of the Rev. J.A.M.
Ritchie, an Episcopalian clergyman. He was also an editor and
had a parish paper. His ire was aroused, so we received a letter
from him and he said that *The Lamp* was kindled from the
fire of eternal punishment. *The Lamp,* however, continued to
burn and his paper went out of existence. He later went to
California, and, at Los Angeles, he started a more ambitious
paper. Finally, *The Lamp* light became too brilliant and lighted
the way for his entrance into the Catholic Church.

He was received into the Church at St. Louis, and entered
the seminary to study. But as he had a family to take care of,
he thought it his duty to go out and earn a living. In the course
of time we invited him to Graymoor and he became managing
editor of *The Lamp.*

He always had a great devotion to the Church Unity Octave. He composed the hymn. Recently I went out to the Pacific Coast and was entertained by Fr. Ritchie, who had been
recently ordained. We had a very lovely five days together.
Since my return East, he became ill, and died January 4th.
This hymn, now that he has gone to his reward, will endear him
to us more and more.

It is a great pleasure to me to be here in this national
shrine of Our Lady at the Catholic University of America in the
nation's capital, and it brings me back twenty-six years to the

modest beginning of this Octave which was heralded by *The Lamp*. Even in those days there were many priests and bishops that read *The Lamp* and among the very first to observe the Octave was the present Archbishop of Boston. That was in 1908. The first practical result of the observance of the Church Unity Octave was the submission and the corporate reception of the Society of the Atonement into the Catholic Church about two years later. In December, 1909, the Octave received the sanction and blessing of Pope Pius X.

This brings us to the beginning of my sermon, to the promise our Lord made as the Good Shepherd . . . as recorded in the gospel of St. John: "Other sheep I have which are not of this fold; them also I must bring in and they shall hear My voice and there shall be one fold and one Shepherd."

The extraordinary development of the Church Unity Octave, now having the sanction of the Holy See, extended throughout the Catholic world by the papal brief of Benedict XV. It is observed magnificently in Rome itself. It has received the sanction of the American Hierarchy, the Canadian Hierarchy, the Polish Hierarchy, and all the hierarchies of the eastern churches in communion with Rome; and it is being observed everywhere more and more. This would indicate that it was something which the Holy Spirit had inspired originally and that it was the will and wish of God that we should take up the original prayer of Christ on the night of His betrayal: "that they all may be one, that the world may believe that Thou has sent Me to be the Messias." And if God wills that we pray He wills that the prayers be answered. Therefore He inspired us with hope, confidence and expectation for a realization of those words of His.

In what nature shall we expect the prayers to be answered? I know that some Catholics think of conversions as individual affairs, that we are going to bring about the answer of our Lord's prayer upon making a conversion here and there of an individual woman, and herald it throughout the world, especially if they be distinguished persons, as some have. But our Lord speaks of sheep; and sheep, you know, are gregarious; they go about in flocks and they move under the impulse of a leader.

Last October, I was touring through Idaho and, as the evening shadows began to fall, we met on the highway a vast flock of sheep. The owner of the flock said that there were twenty-five hundred in the flock. They were crossing a trail, densely massed together. As they passed over the bridge, to the left a pasture field showed itself protected by a fence. Below the fence two strands of wire were loose. The leader of the flock saw this opening and went for the hole; all the sheep followed him pell-mell and soon the road was clear of sheep ... they had entered the pasture for the night.

The wires were left opened on purpose by the owner. And so our Lord will provide an opening and will, Himself, direct the sheep when the time comes; they will move in ranks and there will be corporate reunions, and not just individual conversions.

Take for example the 150,000,000 orthodox Christians of the East. How did they become separated from the fold of Peter? Was it by individual lapses and fallings-away from unity? Not at all. You know the history. You know about the different leaders, the different patriarchs of Constantinople. What did the individual sheep have to do about it? They were cut off by corporate action.

Take the West. During the 16th century we had whole nations cut off and separated from the Chair of Unity. To what extent was it the action of the individual sheep? Were they not herded together? Did not their leaders lead them astray? We see that as we look into the history of today. Take the cantons of Switzerland. You will find one solidly Catholic and right alongside of it one solidly Protestant. How did this happen? By the corporate action of their leaders and not by individuals.

Prussia is today almost all Protestant. Bavaria is almost all Catholic and it is right next to Prussia. You will find that this happened because of the princes of the countries, Norway and Sweden ... Did the people leave by their own volition? You have heard of Gustavus Adolphus. He established a Lutheran hierarchy and branded the people with Protestantism. In a generation they forgot all about the Catholic Church.

As for England, we know all about Henry VIII and Queen Elizabeth. Here was a magnificent Catholic people, a flourishing people, loyal and devoted to the Holy See. They were cut off, not by their own action, but by an upstart who set himself up as sovereign head of the Church.

Now, if the princes of this world can sweep all nations into schisms and separations from the Holy See, it would be heresy to say that Almighty God was less capable than they, if He could not sound His voice and lead His sheep back into unity.

There are indications and movements of the present day which would indicate that our prayers are going to be answered in the near future.

Take Graymoor, where the Church Unity Octave began. In less than two years after, the Society of the Atonement was corporately received by the action of the Holy See. Among those who observed the Church Unity Octave in England were the Benedictine monks of Caldey and the Benedictine nuns of Milford Haven ... and three years after us, they too were corporately received into the fold.

Now we read a great deal about prominent Anglican clergymen and layfolk returning to the fold, but if that is the process by which all are going to return, we would like to know just how long it is going to take.

As far as America is concerned, how long is it going to take her to become Catholic? According to the Catholic directory, there were a large number of converts, but only half as many as those who fell away. At that rate how long will it take? There is a movement of Anglicans today which is not appreciated and not understood by the generality of the Catholics in this country. That is, the movement within the Church of England towards the Holy See.

Under Henry VIII the Church of England separated from the Holy See. When Mary, the Catholic, came to the throne, she, aided by Cardinal Pole, reestablished Catholicism in England; the schism was halted just as it was halted in the east by Photius. Then came the long estrangement of the Church of England through the machinations of Queen Elizabeth and her council. Will there ever come another Mary to bring back England to her ancient allegiance? Let us believe that something like that will happen. Long centuries ago, Edward the Confessor, who was gifted with prophecy, had a vision of the Church of England, and he saw in the distant picture a barren tree carried on for three furlongs and later brought back to her common stock. And if we take the three furlongs to be three centuries ... remember that it was in 1533 that Henry VIII declared that the Church of England was the Vicar of Christ.

There was a movement on foot sometime ago which led John Henry Newman into the fold, and who later became a Roman cardinal. And that movement has gone on and her leader today is seeking for a corporate return of the Church of England to the Holy See.

You shall say that the difficulties in the way are insurmountable and that this thing cannot be accomplished. But when we look into the East we see that the prayers are being answered. In the last few years we have had the Jacobites making a corporate return, their Hierarchy has been set up and the pillium conferred upon it by the Holy Father. Today there is a remarkable number in Russia, leaning towards reunion. In this country, fourteen orthodox Russian priests have made application to the Holy See for admittance, and the Holy Father thought it sufficient to send a Russian bishop to this country to take charge of them. It is true that at the time being the Soviet anti-Christians are in control, but that doesn't mean that it is always going to be in control. It is quite possible that the ancient Russians, who were once loyal to the Holy See, might return again. A Russian prince, George, cousin of the former Czar, was recently entertained at Graymoor. It is quite possible that some day this young prince George might be Czar of Russia. He is delighted with this movement and says it is the greatest thing that has happened to Russia in a century, and it might bring back the whole of Russia to communion with the Holy See.

Therefore, let us have faith, let us pray, let us believe that the omnipotent power of God will cause to be fulfilled those words of our Lord: "Other sheep I have that are not of this fold; them also I must bring and they shall hear my voice and there shall be one fold and one Shepherd."

21. A Crusade of Prayer

The Lamp, December, 1934

This issue of *The Lamp* teems with the theme of Mexico and the war on the Church to the death now raging in that unhappy country, which has been victimized by the emissaries of Antichrist. If you have not already read the address to our Lamp Army soldiers on page 357 by all means do so. Therein you will find the appeal of the Bishops, our American Hierarchy, to the faithful to carry on a Crusade of Prayer, that this persecution of the Church may be free to worship God according to their conscience, and the Church herself have liberty to exercise her functions, which of course she cannot do with her Bishops and her priests banished from the realm, and the children forced into secular schools to be taught atheistic doctrines.

We ask our Rosarians to use their rosaries most diligently in this crusade of Prayer, being mindful of Mexico when they recite the beads every day. In great crises of history, wonderful triumphs have been accomplished by the use of the Rosary on the part of the faithful. For example, when the Turks were threatening the subjugation of all Europe and were victorious upon land and sea, the Pope on the eve of a great naval battle at Lepanto in the Mediterranean, called upon the faithful, everywhere, to use their rosaries, which they did, and the result was a crushing victory over the Turkish navy by the Christians—a victory which was accomplished by the putting forth of Divine Power, undoubtedly at the intercession of Our Lady, responding to the appeal of her children on the earth. At first, the wind was in favor of the Turks, and they were pressing the Christians hard; but a sudden change in the wind drove the smoke of battle into their faces and discomforted them to such a degree that the tide of victory changed and the Christians triumphed so completely that never again did the Mohammedans secure the ascendancy.

Another instance was the invasion of Poland, by the Soviet army, some time after the conclusion of the World War. The red army of the Russians carried everything before it, the Bolsheviki could not be resisted. Once more, at the call of the Pope, the people assembled in their places of worship on the Feast of the Assumption, and there were processions and the rosary was recited. Then came a sudden change. This time it was the hosts of Poland and their French auxiliaries who swept everything before them, and drove the Red Army back into Russia, with such an overwhelming defeat that they have never ventured to repeat the experiment of invasion.

In 1928, when the murder of priests in Mexico was at its height a campaign of prayer was started in America, together with a vigorous protest on the part of the Catholic press against the outrages done to the Church in that unhappy land and, as a result, a temporary halt was made in the persecutions; through the good offices of Ambassador Morrow, a concordat was brought about and peace established between the anti-clerical Government of Mexico and the Church in that country.

Now that there is another outbreak of persecution, let us have recourse to prayer with confidence, that once again we shall bring victory to the Church's cause; and let us hope that this time it will be a crushing defeat and a complete overthrow of the reign of Antichrist in Mexico.

In conclusion I wish you, dear sons and daughters of the Atonement, a deeply happy and blessed Christmas.

22. An Announcement Before the Octave

Tomorrow is the feast of the Chair of St. Peter at Rome, the inauguration of the Church Unity Octave, a Graymoor product. Reverend Spencer Jones, M.A., the author of an extraordinary book called "England and the Holy See", with a preface by Lord Halifax, is the first real effort on the part of an Anglican clergyman to argue out the point of the return of England to her ancient allegiance to the See of Peter.

I say the first, but that is not exactly true, because Doctor Lee wrote a very powerful book, on Queen Elizabeth, about a generation previous to that, following on the same lines, but Reverend Spencer Jones, in a letter to me, suggested that it would be a good idea (this was in the old Anglican days) that a sermon be preached on the feast of St. Peter each year, advocating and setting forth the claims of the papacy as the center of a reunited Christendom. I modified that suggestion by saying to him that I thought, as a substitute, or at least accessory to his idea, would be that of a Church Unity Octave beginning on the feast of the Chair of St. Peter at Rome and ending on the feast of St. Paul, thus setting forth the idea of the prayer of our Blessed Lord, on the night He was betrayed, that the world might believe in His Messiaship. And consequently, this Church Unity Octave was inaugurated and has since been recognized by Supreme Authority and the Sovereign Pontiff and observed by the faithful throughout the world. At the same time we are working, to the end of advancing the work of universal observance, by asking the Holy Father to put forth a decree in the same way that the devotion to the Blessed Virgin and the recitation of the Rosary in May and October are now practically universal.

And so, year by year, we would note that the millions of Christendom were praying for the unity of Christians. It is very gratifying to know that the Octave is still observed in the Anglican Church, to a greater or less degree. I have just received a tract or paper put out in England, with a long list of distinguished clergymen, Lord Halifax, Lord Shaftsbury and some other leading nobles of England, endorsing it and calling upon the faithful to unite with Catholics, using the same prayers and praying for the same intention.

Now the Holy Father, as I said, sometime ago instituted a new feast for the Kingship of Christ, and this ought to emphasize the Octave all the more, because in order that the kingdoms of this world may become the Kingdoms of Christ, that He may be universally recognized as the Lord and Master of the world, this unity of His disciples is a prerequisite, according to His own mind, in His prayer, that I have just alluded to. And, as Graymoor is the home of the Church Unity Octave, the faithful here ought to excel in its observance.

23. The Missionary Conquest of the World for Christ

Shrine of the Immaculate Conception
Washington, D.C.
January 25, 1938

"That they all may be one that the
world may believe Thou hast sent me."

It must be obvious to you all why this particular time should have been chosen for a crusade of prayer for Church Unity, a period of eight days beginning on the Feast of St. Peter's Chair at Rome, and ending on the Feast of the Conversion of St. Paul, the great Apostle of the Gentiles. Threatened with powerful revolutionary forces which seek the destruction of all, Christians of all denominations have been driven to confer with each other how the re-union of Christendom can be brought to pass. World conferences have been held repeatedly of late years attended by representatives of the Protestant, Anglican, and Orthodox confessions and they have conferred together with earnest prayer and searching of hearts how they can get together, their divisions cease, and real Christian unity be established. The Church Unity Octave gives a definite and explicit answer to their queries.

There can be no Church Unity agreeable to the Divine Will built upon any other foundation than that which Christ Himself has laid.

The Octave proclaims at the very outset that the divinely constituted center of ecclesiastical Christian Unity is the Chair of St. Peter at Rome; that and that alone is the final test of Catholic communion. Every one who observes the Church Unity Octave prays definitely and explicitly for the return of all separated Christians to communion with the Apostolic See. The Octave fittingly ends with the Feast of the Conversion of St. Paul, because the end and fruit of Church Unity regained in answer to our prayers, is the conversion of the world for Christ. Our Lord prayed for the unity of His disciples in order that the world might believe in His Messiaship, that the kingdoms of the entire globe might become the kingdom of the Lord's anointed, symbolized by the conversion of St. Paul, the glorious apostle of the Gentiles.

The Church Unity Octave began in 1908 and so it has now been observed for a period of thirty years and we might take an inventory of what has been accomplished as the result of our praying and what the prospects are of larger fruitage in the next thirty years.

The first fruits produced by the Octave was the corporate reception of the Society of the Atonement, itself, into the One Fold of the Catholic Church under the One Supreme Shepherd, the Successor of St. Peter. It was only twenty-one months after the first observance when the reception of the Society took place. Three years later, two religious communities in England followed Graymoor's example, the Benedictine Monks on Caldey Island, off the coast of Wales, and the Benedictine Nuns of St. Bride's, Milford Haven, South Wales. Both communities were observing the Church Unity Octave when simultaneously, no doubt moved by the Holy Spirit, they resolved to imitate the Society of the Atonement. Last year, two other Anglican communities did the same thing—the Brotherhood of Christ the King in England and the Society of the Love of Jesus, an Anglican Sisterhood in Vancouver, British Columbia. It was during the observance of the Church Unity Octave, one year ago, that the Anglican Sisters in Vancouver invited the Archbishop to visit them and made known to His Grace their desire to be received into Peter's Fold. Some years ago a large group of Jacobite Christians in India of the Syrian Rite, were corporately received under the leadership of Mar Ivanios, and Mar Theophilus and only a few weeks ago, another Jacobite prelate in India, has submitted to Rome to be followed by many of his priests and people. But these first fruits of the Octave of Prayer are only preliminary to much larger corporate submissions in the future.

The most outstanding result of the Octave has been the evolution, of the so-called Oxford Movement in the Church of England into a Papal Movement, which is gathering increased momentum every year. To appreciate this let us go back thirty-five years to the time when *The Lamp* was first issued at Graymoor, to bear witness to the Chair of Peter, as the divinely constituted center of a re-united Christendom. Immediately after its first issue *The Living Church,* the leading weekly of the Episcopal Church in America, hastened to reassure its readers not to be alarmed at the Papistical teachings of the Graymoor luminary. The editor assured his readers that Father Paul was an erratic monk and stood absolutely alone in his papal views. Then when Spencer Jones, author of *England and the Holy See,* and the Rev. Arthur Lloyd of the Episcopal Church in Japan began to write for *The Lamp, The Living Church* called it a triumvirate and reassured its readers there was absolutely no cause for alarm.

It is really almost incredible when one looks back to the commencement of the Octave, thirty years ago, that last year as many as fifteen hundred, of the Church of England clergy, observed the Church Unity Octave and as many as forty religious communities of men and women. And they prayed for the same intentions as we Catholics do, among them that the Anglicans return to their pre-Reformation allegiance to the Holy See. One thousand members of the Church of England signed a profession of faith put forth by the Council of the Church Unity Octave, embracing the entire dogmatic creed of the Holy Roman Church. Meanwhile the papal leaven is spreading rapidly among the rank and file of the Anglican Communion. That something vast and far-reaching in the way of Papal submission is certain to follow in the next thirty years seems to me inevitable, the powers of hell, on the contrary, not withstanding. But the special thing we pray for on this concluding day of the Octave, is the conversion of the entire world to Christ. What about that—what is the present outlook?

About one hundred years ago, Macaulay, the English Historian, wrote that famous tribute of his to the Catholic Church, when he described some day in the far distant future some New Zealander standing on London Bridge would contemplate the ruins of Westminster Abbey and behold about him the evidences of the revival in England of the glories of the Catholic Church. In that flight of oratory he declared the Catholic Church as having one hundred and fifty million adherents at the time. If his statistics were correct, then the Catholic Church has more than doubled her membership in the past hundred years, and in spite of all the persecutions that have been going on of late. Undoubtedly the Church is making great strides, especially in the field afar at the present time. The illustrious pontificate of our present Holy Father has been characterized by nothing more glorious than his promotion of missionary propaganda in Asia, Africa, and the Islands of the Sea.

24. Before the Unity Octave

Radio Broadcast
Graymoor, January 15, 1939

We are now within three days of the Commencement of the Church Unity Octave for the year of grace 1939. The Octave begins on next Wednesday, January 18th, which is the Feast of the Chair of Peter at Rome. It must be obvious to everybody the reason why, in founding the Octave through the medium of Graymoor's monthly magazine, The Lamp, some twenty-one years ago, we selected this particular feast.

If Church Unity is ever to be realized among Christians, it must be by every Christian in the world getting into communion with the occupant of St. Peter's Chair at Rome; for that, by the changeless decree of Almighty God Himself is the center of Church Unity.

The big majority of all Christians in the world at the present time call themselves Catholics, not only Roman Catholics, but

Orthodox Christians of the East and High Church Anglicans. Yet—the infallible test of Catholicity is communion with the Apostolic See at Rome. Hence, we begin this Octave of prayer on January 18th, the Feast of St. Peter's Chair at Rome. It carries an alternative title, viz., Chair of Unity Octave. The reason why we call it an Octave instead of a novena, is that it ends on the feast of the Conversion of St. Paul, January 25th, which is the Octave of the Chair of Peter Feast.

We behold in our own day all over Christendom, the sad and disastrous results of a lack of unity among the professed disciples of Christ. See what has happened in Germany as the fruit of Christian dis-unity and division. The Nazi leader, Adolph Hitler, is not only persecuting and hounding out of the country the Jews, but is developing into a persecutor of Christians, both Catholic and Protestant. Hitler's rise to power is one of the direct results of the division of the Christians of Germany into hostile camps, Catholic and Protestant. He would never have risen to power save by the vote of non-Catholic Christians. The Catholic Center Party always opposed the Nazi dictator. It was his Protestant supporters who gave Hitler his first majorities and led to his dictatorship.

We have the spectacle in Mexico of the triumph of Communism—a government intensely anti-clerical, killing priests, and murdering nuns in its earlier stages, and in its later development, not only banning priests from the exercise of their ministry, but actually teaching Catholic children in the schools to become atheists.

No man can deny that our government in Washington, from the days of Woodrow Wilson until now has aided and abetted the succession of revolutionary masters of Mexico, the notorious Elias Calles among them, who have carried on a deadly persecution of the Catholic Church in this country. And there is no doubt that our government in doing so has had the sympathetic approval of a majority, at least, of the non-Catholic Christians in America, just as they have revealed their sympathy with the Red Government in Spain rather than the Catholic Nationalists under Franco's leadership, who are battling not alone for their nation's preservation, but for the preservation of Catholic civilization against Christianity's deadly foe, anti-Christian Communism.

What a sad departure from that new precept of charity

which Christ imposed upon His disciples in the institution of the Blessed Sacrament, saying, "A new commandment I give unto you, that ye love one another even as I have loved you." Foreseeing all this, no wonder He prayed to His Father, asking "That they might all be one in Us."

If Communism ever gets the mastery in our own beloved country, it will only be because of the division existing between the Catholic and non-Catholic Christians of our nation, who by reason of this division have failed to present a united front against the common enemy. In a word, Christendom is in danger of being subjected to the rule of anti-Christ because the Christians of Christendom constitute a house divided against itself.

25. A Call to Prayer for Christian Unity

The Lamp, January, 1940

My New Year's wish for you all is an abundant increase of holiness and happiness as your portion from the Lord during the year of grace 1940. When this letter reaches you the Church Unity Octave will either be about to begin, or else already be in progress. To whom can I appeal for its faithful observance with greater certainty of success than to the members of the Rosary League of Our Lady of the Atonement? Prayer is the very object of the League's existence and none more than you are likely to appreciate the real value and importance of an eight day period of concerted prayer for the reunion of Christendom.

The Lamp has done many great things and I trust will do many more in the future for the greater glory of God and the salvation of souls. But the greatest thing *The Lamp* ever did do, and probably ever will do, was to inaugurate the Church Unity Octave. This statement may surprise some of our readers and yet upon reflection, I believe you will unanimously agree with me that what I have said is absolutely true. I need not labor to prove to Catholics that prayer is the greatest instrument a benevolent Providence has placed in the hands of man.

Picture to yourself a Commander-in-Chief, seated in his private office at Army headquarters. He holds in his hands a telephone by means of which he communicates with the generals of his staff posted at various points of observation on the battle front. Thereby he is informed as to the varying fortunes of the battle and through it he sends for the word of command at which a thousand guns roar in deafening concert and a million men move forward to engage the enemy. Prayer is the telephone which divine omnipotence has placed in the hands of His creatures on the earth. It is a long distance telephone by which we reach the ear of the Almighty at the Center of the Universe. The creature who holds within his hands the telephone may not command the Almighty, but by the benevolence of Our Father in Heaven, he is permitted to make known his request; and as we ask, so it is done by the Lord of Heaven and earth. This we have upon the word of God Himself: "Ask and it shall be given unto you ... Whatever you shall ask the Father in My Name, He will give it to you."

We are taught by our religion that it is necessary to salvation for a man to pray, for if a man will not ask for eternal life it will not be given him. Since, therefore, the Almighty has willed to act in human affairs subject to the prayers which are addressed to Him from the earth, which is His footstool, we can hardly fail to recognize the enormous possibilities of the Church Unity Octave. Once we make its observance *universal*, not only among Catholics in all parts of the world, but among the "Other Sheep" now unhappily cut off from communion with the Apostolic See, and as a result of this universal repetition on the part of the Christian believers of the original prayer of Our Blessed Lord, "That all His disciples may be One," what else could we expect but a corresponding answer from the Almighty and the speedy fulfillment of Our Lord's own prophecy: "Other Sheep I have, which are not of this Fold; them also I must bring and they will hear My voice and there shall be One Fold and One Shepherd."

26. The Chair of Unity Octave

Meditation, January 25, 1940

We come to the conclusion of the Octave today, the Feast of the Conversion of St. Paul, the great apostle of the Gentiles. This feast ought to mean a great deal to us because primarily we are a Pauline institute. We have Atonement progenitors by family descent. We call St. Francis our Father, the Patriarch of Assisi, but before Francis there were other Atonement ancestors from whom we derived our inheritance. The Children of Judah hark back to Abraham, although they hark back to him through Jacob and Isaac. St. Francis is the Isaac, our Isaac, St. Paul is our Abraham.

The first intimation of the vocation received by the Father Founder was not Franciscan. It was Pauline: "This is what you will do some day, found a preaching order like the Paulists." During the first life of St. Francis we discovered the devotion to St. Paul. We ought to be started with the Pauline Christology and his teaching. Then strive to walk in his footsteps proving ourselves worthy sons of the great apostle to the Gentiles.

Yesterday we celebrated the feast of Timothy, one of the sons of St. Paul, to whom he was very devoted, and he acquitted himself magnificently until he won the martyr's crown gloriously.

In the Old Testament we have the great prophet Elias who, beyond all the rest, worked miracles even to the raising of the dead. Another son rivalled his spiritual Father, Eliseus. God honored Elias by taking him up into heaven without his undergoing the process of death, and as they were journeying on together Elias intimated to Eliseus that his end was near. Eliseus asked that a double portion of his spirit might descend upon him. Elias said it will be so and his mantle fell upon him when he discarded it, and they came to Jordan. Elias performed a miracle which has been repeated in substance a number of times by great Franciscan preachers. He put his mantle on the River Jordan. It parted and they passed through on dry ground. Sure enough his mantle fell from him. Eliseus picked it up and certainly a double portion of his master fell upon him. He repeated and rivalled the miracles of his father in a splendid record for himself in the history of his regime. Let us pray, that upon the Friars of the Atonement, missionaries and priests, may descend a double portion of the spirit of St. Paul. That spirit must act within us that there may happen in us what happened to St. Paul. The Christology of the great apostle which has impressed itself so much upon the mind of the Church, perhaps in no age more than at the present time, is that of the Mystical Body of Christ, a teaching which we emphasize and set forth, particularly in our doctrine of the Atonement, of our being children of the new Adam. In virtue of our new birth and our becoming thereby, by putting on Christ, partakers of the divine nature. St. Paul said, "It is no longer I that live, but Christ that liveth in me." Whatsoever I do, wheresoever I live, "I live by the power of the Son of God, who gave Himself for me. I can do all things through Christ who strengtheneth me. I will glory in my infirmities that the grace of God may more abound."

The spirit of humility consists in recognizing our natural weaknesses, our infirmities and our poor capacity of fulfilling the great commandment, to love the Lord thy God with all thy heart, mind, soul and strength, and my neighbor as myself. We cry out with Elias on Mt. Carmel, or with St. Francis with his arms stretched out: *Deus meus et omnia.* We call down the fire of Divine love from heaven, calling upon Jesus Christ to possess us more fully, inflaming our whole hearts with the Divine Love in union with His own Sacred Heart, as the gold or iron is plunged into the furnace until it too takes on the nature of the fire and burns, red with heat, then white with the intensity of it. We must remember how St. Paul gloried in the cross: "God, forbid that I should glory save in the cross of Our Lord, Jesus Christ, by whom the world is crucified unto me and I unto the world."

When Christ comes and incorporates us into Himself, He wills that we do as He did, going about doing good, spending and being spent for the souls of men, and with the eye always on the summit of Mt. Calvary, to find our lives by the death of the cross, not waiting till perhaps an opportunity might be given to us to be martyred even against our own will, as Communists coming along to shoot us. We die daily by the process of mortification, that man with his corrupt tendencies, his weaknesses and infirmities. Our Lord will conquer them by self-denial, by mortification of our appetites, giving to the body what it needs for strength to work for God. We must cut out the luxuries and those indulgences that cause man so much to sin.

Let us realize that we have to work this out for ourselves as individuals, for everyone must stand alone before the judgment seat of Christ to give an account of his stewardship. The records will be there in the Lamb's book of life, all the weaknesses, all the wrong words, all the indulgences, all the failures to embrace the opportunity when it came, and cast it away.

There ought to be a keen examination of our own part

every day in anticipation of our judgment, check up day by day the falls, failures to keep our rule, failures to make the best use of the time given us today, which, if we lose, is lost forever.

Let us in our Communion this morning address to Our Lord a request that the double portion of the spirit of St. Paul may descend upon us, and we may walk in his footsteps in the matter of his Christology, surrendering ourselves so completely to our Divine Lord, Himself, that He may reign in us from the crown of our head to the soles of our feet, so we may become vessels fit for the Master's use, so we may be able to say with St. Paul: "it is no longer I that live, but Christ that liveth in me. I glory in the cross of Our Lord Jesus Christ, by whom the world is crucified unto me and I unto the world."

* * *

Petition for Universal Observance of Octave

(1923-30)

Most Holy Father:

Inasmuch as Pope Pius X, of holy memory, blessed the Church Unity Octave, originated by the Friars of the Atonement at Graymoor, Garrison, New York, prior to their corporate reception into the Fold of Peter; and inasmuch as Pope Benedict XV by papal brief extended the observance to the universal Church; and since it is now observed practically in all parts of the Catholic world with increasing devotion year by year, prostrate at the feet of your Holiness who has revealed the solicitude of your heart as the Shepherd of Christ's Flock for the return of the Other Sheep in so many striking ways, we, the undersigned, humbly entreat that you will still further confirm the Brief of your illustrious predecessors, and through an Apostolic Letter to make the Octave of holy obligation by the faithful everywhere, in the same manner as are the prescribed devotions to the Blessed Virgin during the months of May and October.

IV

Our Separated Brethren

IN THE WORLD TODAY *there are more than three billion people. Of this number, about 600 million are Catholics. Those who are followers of Christ, but not members of the Catholic Church, constitute about 400 million, comprised chiefly of Protestant communions in Europe and America and the Orthodox in the Near and Middle East, as well as in Russia and other Communist dominated lands.*

"Our Separated Brethren" is taken from the sermons and writings of Fr. Paul dealing with the intentions of the Chair of Unity Octave. He wanted the faithful to pray for unity during this providential time and he sought to enlist their interest and fervor. Fr. Paul had a special appreciation for the Orthodox, who have retained so much of Catholic belief and practice, despite their opposition to the Holy Father. He had a particular understanding of the mentality and the position of Protestants, especially of the Anglicans, and he wanted all of them to gain what he had found in the Church of the Savior.

Those outside the Church are separated, but they are brethren of the same heavenly Father and redeemed by the Divine Son. Mary, too, is their Mother, even though they may not enjoy full membership in the Church.

Everywhere there is a religious ferment alive in the world: the ecumenical movement of the present day, has grown into a federation of most Protestant religions, known as the World Council of Churches; the Pan-Orthodox Meeting, took place at the Island of Rhodes in September, 1961; the Vatican Council, convened on October 11, 1962 are so many indications of the prominence of Unity in the world today. Pope Paul VI has asserted that he will continue the policy and program of Pope John in working for the renewal of the gospel and the adaptation of the Church to the modern world. In regard to our separ-

ated brethren, his arms and his heart are wide open to welcome them to the full unity of the one and only Fold.

If the intellect does not know, the will will not be enkindled by love. And so it is important that Catholics are aware of some of the problems which their non-Catholic brethren face, so that they may be apostles according to opportunity, talent and grace, in bringing the separated brethren to the One Fold.

In our selection presented here we have followed the listing of intentions of the Chair of Unity Octave, e.g., Unity in general, the Separated Brethren of the East, the Anglicans, and so on.

As Fr. Paul said, the faithful must have the spirit of the Good Shepherd. They too must seek for the wandering and the straying; they must go to them. And so as Fr. Paul acted during his lifetime, so would he urge us to do at the present day.

1. The Chair of Peter

St. John's Church, Graymoor,
January 18, 1925

Probably the fact which has impressed upon the world at large the name of Graymoor more than anything else is that the Church Unity Octave should have originated here. Therefore, we should have a special zeal in our observance of the Octave not because of the reputation, but because, in the providence of Almighty God, so small an instrumentality should have been selected to originate a movement so vital to the well-being of humanity at large. It springs from the very Heart of Jesus Himself, and on the night of His betrayal, looking forward into the future He prayed that His disciples might be "one" and the world might believe in the Messiahship, recognizing that the unity of the world is conquest of souls.

It is the way of divine providence at various stages of the history and development of the Church to raise up certain societies of men and women to accomplish great purposes. For example, when the great apostascy of the sixteenth century took place, as far as the Church of Rome is concerned, when the standard of rebellion was raised by Martin Luther, not only individuals and congregations, but even whole nations fell away from the unity of the Rock of Peter. When almost the entire northern part of Europe was in revolt against the Vicar of Christ and there seemed to be no way of stopping this constant falling away from the unity of the Church, it carried along vast multitudes of souls, spreading from city to city and from state to state. God raised up a special Society whose office it would be to stem the tide of this defection. A great man was chosen, named Ignatius Loyola, a soldier by training and profession, and he organized under the inspiration and guidance of the Holy Ghost, a powerful company of militant soldiers of the army of Christ, who were destined to accomplish a wonderful achievement, and that organization was the Society of Jesus.

The hatred of the devil toward that Society has been very intense because it frustrated and defeated in a large measure his purposes, and he has never ceased to put out from his vile

135

mouth all kinds of imputations and charges against this same Society of Jesus. In the eyes of some people today the Jesuit is the sum and substance of all craftiness and iniquity and anything that happens in the Catholic Church that they can put their hand on, and think about as mischievous and evil, they lay to the door of the Jesuit. Nevertheless, that wonderful body of men achieved their purpose and stayed the tide of Reformation so that ten years after it was started, it was checked in its immense spread of power and influence and has gradually declined ever since.

At the present time it is evident in the operations of the Holy Ghost upon the minds of men that God wills and desires that unity should prevail. Those terrible divisions and detractions that have resulted in Christianity by reason of the breaking up of those who called themselves Christians with so many differences and divisions without end, these should give birth to a new order that should aid the forces of the Church in its great struggle against the powers of hell.

This is manifest in the Protestant bodies very largely because, whereas the tendency of Protestantism is itself in its influence on the individual conscience, the individual judgment of the things that concerned himself as to his salvation and their loyalty to Christ—the tendency of it was to produce division and subdivision, and endless differences of opinions and beliefs. This was evidenced by a certain Scotchman as I sat beside him, who declared that in the kirk to which he belonged, he and his wife were the only orthodox ones and that sometimes he even questioned the orthodoxy of his wife. Now we see at the present time a very marked effort being made among the Protestants towards unity among themselves. For instance, someone in Canada sent me a clipping from one of the city papers which said that the Methodists, the Presbyterians, and Congregationalists of Canada had arrived at an arrangement by which they were going to be unified and federated, and that there were some individuals, more patricularly among the pastors of the Presbyterian Church who were making a fight against those bodies, but it has gone so far as to have recognition in their civil courts and confirmation was practically a fact.

We have in the United States a federation among the Protestant bodies which aims to advance unity among them in trying to eliminate the waste of energy in having a multiplicity of churches and sects, particularly in the towns of the West. For example, a priest in a town in Iowa wrote to me in regard to the observance of Church Unity Octave and said that there were fifteen churches in his town, a town of twenty-five hundred people. So we recognized that they are making great headway towards federation among themselves and the Episcopal Church is very much concerned and interested in the matter, so they have made preparations for a world conference of Faith and Order and are making overtures in various directions among the Protestant people and denominations towards Unity.

Now we are to recognize in these events a sort of movement of the Holy Ghost in bringing back to some kind of unity those who have been broken up into such enormous amount of divisions, but they need to learn and to recognize, all our separated brethren, that all plans for unity among those who profess to be His disciples until His own words, as the Good Shepherd, are fulfilled: "Other sheep have I which are not of this fold; them also must I bring and they will hear my voice and there shall be one fold and one shepherd." And that "one fold" must be the Catholic Church, and the "one Shepherd" the successor of St. Peter to whom Our Lord originally gave jurisdiction of the Universal Church: "Thou art Peter (rock) and upon this rock I will build My Church and the gates of hell shall not prevail against her."

Now, then, at this stage of development in the trend toward unity, it is very essential that Protestants, as well as the Eastern brethren who had broken with Rome a thousand years ago, should have impressed upon their minds that all their efforts for unity will be in vain, unless they recognized the divinely constituted Chair of Peter ot Rome as the center of a reunited Christendom and we might bear witness to that fact insomuch as the Church recognizes it fully and has recognized it for nineteen hundred years as to those who were separated from that unity.

We understand why God raised up the Society of the Atonement, for the very word—Atonement—which is an English word, applied to the Sacrifice of Christ on Calvary means unity in its etymology; Atonement means At-one-ment. The idea is that man being separated from God by the rebellion of man, Christ, the Son of God, came down to earth to redeem mankind by taking into union with the Divine Nature our human nature. Then He lay down His life to reconcile those sinners who had been separated from Him and cut off from unity with Him so that, by His Sacrifice, the wall of division, as St. Paul says, has been taken away, and man and God are united again. Thus the purpose of the sacrifice was to make it possible for man and God to be "at one". And so the word Atonement signifies unity. And since Satan through his efforts at division and strife, playing on human nature through pride and jealousy, with its racial distinctions, its political influences, etc., has caused all those divisions among the disciples of Christ, it is the work of the Holy Ghost to bring them back into unity. It is the work of our Society, not only to pray for unity, but also, under the power of God, to bend our efforts to convince our separated brethren that their opposition is based upon falsehood and error in interpreting the Scriptures, that they are simply like St. Paul "breathing out threatenings and slaughter" to whom Our Lord said: "It is hard for thee to kick against the goad."

It is not necessary for me to stand here and belabor an argument from the Scriptures to prove and convince this congregation that the Church is a divine institution. We all believe that, and therefore, it would be a waste of words, but it is for us to realize our vocation, in season, to bear witness to those things towards our separated brethren. We have seen in the last few years a wonderful turn of the kaleidoscope of political events which have toppled the great throne of the Czars in Russia and another fine little scheme of the devil has been knocked to pieces, for the devil sought to build a bogus holy Roman Empire in the East. He substituted for St. Peter's successor at Rome the Czar; he dressed him up in a white robe to represent the Holy Father, or rather made him father of the Holy Empire so that the Russians were taught in their books of theology that the primacy had passed from Rome to Constantinople, and from Constantinople to St. Petersburg, and that the real successor of St. Peter was the holy Czar and had combined jurisdiction over the souls of men as well as over the state, so that he was master over both souls and state.

And this great Russian Empire increasing in power, rose up as a menace to Europe and had its eye on the capital of Constantinople and on Rome, it was antagonistic to the exercise of the Catholic religion within the borders of the Roman Empire and the Poles were dreadfully persecuted. And now the Eastern proletariats are foundering around and beginning to recognize that, after all, the Pope of Rome is not only the Patriarch of the West, but has jurisdiction over all the sheep. So that there is in that direction a movement towards Rome and Providence has taken this little Society of the Atonement as the instrument, as the Bishop of Constantinople and Greece declared to us repeatedly in his letters that the Union-That-Nothing-Be-Lost is the main standby in his work through the financial assistance we have rendered him. It is a very great and tremendous vocation which rests upon the Society of the Atonement, and we should throw ourselves into it with a great amount of enthusiasm and be ready to lay down our lives in witness of what is called the Catholic Papacy, namely, the Chair of St. Peter at Rome.

We have still much to do, to make the observance of the Church Unity Octave of obligation throughout the entire length and breadth of the Catholic Church. The latest development is a movement to petition the Holy Father to make the observance universal by some act, as for instance, our own Archbishop makes it universal, in his archdiocese, by sending out directions to all the clergy that they must observe this Octave, that they must say the prayer for the healing of schism throughout the diocese, that the Sisters must tell the children to recite one decade of the Rosary for the unity of the Church, and thus it becomes practically of obligation.

Now, what we hope to have the Holy Father do, when he finds he is justified, is to make a decree so that the observance of the Octave shall be universal, just as the devotion to the Blessed Virgin in October is universal. Another desire is that the feast of the Chair of St. Peter at Rome shall be exalted from its present status to the same rank as the feast of the Apostles and also, that the feast of the Conversion of St. Paul shall be raised to the same rank, so that by that act there will be the more emphasized by the whole Catholic body the importance of this petition to bring into unity with the Chair of Peter so that there should be one fold and one shepherd and there is absolutely no other way of accomplishing that, whether they be Protestant Christians or whether they be Orthodox Christians, or whatever kind of Christians they are. They must recognize the fact that the living rock on which the dogma of the faith of Christ is built is unity with the successor Peter, the Pope at Rome.

2. The Unity of God

Convent Chapel, Graymoor
January 18, 1929

During the course of the Church Unity Octave I propose to give you a brief conference at Mass each morning on the subject which is uppermost in our mind at this time, and that is, the unity of the disciples of Christ in the communion of the Holy Church which He founded.

Unity is one of the essential attributes of the Divine Being. God has been revealed to us not only as one, but also as three in one. There is the Father, the Son, and the Holy Ghost, three distinct Persons, and yet, such is their unity that they constitute one God. That is part of divine revelation. In the Old Testament the unity of God was revealed and the Jews worshipped Him as one God. It was only when the Son came into the world to show and reveal to us the Father that we have the manifestation of the three-fold personality of the Godhead. It was revealed at the Baptism of Christ on the bank of the Jordan by St. John the Baptist, for when He was baptized, the heavens opened, the Holy Ghost descended from Heaven in the form of a dove, and the voice of God, the Father, speaking from Heaven proclaimed: "This is my beloved Son in whom I am well pleased. Hear ye Him." Thus we have the revelation of the Divine Trinity, and so it is set forth in the very Person of God. Plurality and yet oneness in that plurality, so perfect is the unity of God, perfect harmony of the will of the Father, the will of the Son, and the will of the Holy Ghost; such perfect correspondence in all their actions that they constitute absolute proof of one God, so that in the very Person of the Godhead is manifested to us this element of unity.

When our Lord Jesus Christ, came into the world to make unto Himself a new people, those that should be regenerated and become members of His mystical body, He set forth the divine will that they should constitute in themselves a unity. On the night of His betrayal after He had instituted the Blessed Sacrament which is the sacrament of Unity, He addressed His Father in a wonderful prayer, in which He prayed particularly for the unity of those who believed in Him and He used very strong language: "As Thou Father in Me and I in Thee, that they may be one in Us."

140

The unity that exists between God the Father and God the Son is a most intimate one, and yet our Lord desires that the same unity might be manifested and set forth in the members of His Mystical Body, in His elect, those whom He shall redeem or has redeemed, by His Precious Blood, and whom He shall present without spot or wrinkle, or any such thing, glorious before His Father in heaven. In them, He desires that there should be manifested a unity akin to that which exists between Himself and His Father. Now this is a unity of love and also, unity of will. He was asking of the Father a tremendous blessing but owing to the infirmities of men and their imperfection by reason of their fallen nature, the prayer has only been answered in a very limited degree on the earth.

It will be perfectly answered in the final consummation of all things when all the members of His body have been perfected in sanctity and when they attain the Beatific Vision. There will prevail around the throne of God a unity among the faithful that will be the reflection of unity that exists before and in the Person of God Himself. Meantime, on the earth, knowing the will of God, we should strive to realize in ourselves that unity; unity of will, by having no other will, but the will of God the Father, even as Our Lord Jesus Chirst, came to do the will of Him that sent Him. Then unity of charity, being bound together in that wonderful intimacy which can only be brought about by love, and while we strive by correspondence to grace to realize this unity among ourselves and in unity with God, we are at the same time beholden to take up the prayer which Christ Himself presented to the Father and pray it not only for ourselves, but for all the faithful, for all that have been regenerated and all that have been redeemed by the Precious Blood of Christ, that they may realize in themselves and in unity with God the answer to that prayer of Christ addressed to His Father: *Ut omnes unum sint.*

3. United to the Holy Father

Radio Broadcast
January 21, 1938

In more recent years several world conventions have been held by non-Catholic religious bodies, or denominations, to consider the subject of Christian Unity. Everybody recognized the necessity of Christians getting together in some kind of unity for their self preservation against the anti-Christian forces of the world which are threatening the destruction of Christianity altogether.

But there is no other unity possible in the Divine economy save that which is built upon the same foundation as the one on which Christ Jesus, the Lord and Master, founded His Church, and you know what that foundation is, for it is clearly written in the Holy Gospel according to St. Matthew, who tells us how, when Our Lord with His disciples was at Caesaria, Philippi, Christ asked them: "Who do men say that I the Son of Man is?" And they made answer: "Some say that Thou art Elias, and others Jeremias, or one of the Prophets." Then Jesus said to them: "But whom do you say that I am?" And Simon Peter, speaking up, made answer: "Thou art Christ, the Son of the Living God." And Jesus answering, said to him "Blessed art thou, Simon, son of Jonas, because flesh and blood hath not revealed it to thee, but My Father who is in Heaven. And I say to thee that thou art Peter, and upon this Rock, I will build My Church, and the gates of hell shall not prevail against it. And I will give to thee the keys of the Kingdom of Heaven (by which He meant His Church) and whatsoever thou shalt bind upon earth, it shall be bound also in Heaven, and whatsoever thou shalt loose upon earth shall be loosed also in Heaven." In other words, He promised to give him supreme power and jurisdiction over His Church.

After His resurrection from the dead, Jesus said to Peter three times: "Feed My lambs; feed My lambs; feed My sheep." By so doing He fulfilled the promise He had made at Caesaria Philippi, because He gave him, as the Universal Shepherd, jurisdiction over His sheep and it was not to Peter alone, but to St. Peter's successors to the end of time that this jurisdiction and supreme power was given.

If you should read the history of the great divisions that have taken place among Christians since the very days of the Apostles, you will find that these divisions were created by the departure from the unity of the Catholic Church, that is to say, from communion with the Apostolic See of Rome, of certain members, groups, or national parts, of the Universal Church. For example, in the tenth century, under the instigation and leadership of the Emperor and Archbishop of Constantinople well nigh all the churches of the East separated from communion with Rome, or, in the sixteenth century, the Protestants of Germany, Switzerland, Holland, Norway, Sweden, Denmark and Scotland turned their back on the Great White Father of Christendom and set up a hundred and more of clashing creeds and denominations. Or again in the case of England, where King Henry VIII separated the nation from the Holy See, and Elizabeth, his daughter, confirmed the act of her father and established the state Church of England as a separate organization from the Church Catholic, everywhere and always in communion with the Apostolic See.

So—it is evident why the originators of this Octave, who were none other than the Graymoor Friars, chose the Chair of Peter at Rome as the first day of the Octave of Prayer for Church Unity. It is also evident why the feast of the Conversion of St. Paul should conclude the Octave. When Our Lord appealed, on the night of His betrayal, for the unity of Christians, He concluded the prayer with the words: "That they all may be one, that the world might believe that Thou, My Heavenly Father, has sent Me."

There must be unity first among Christians in order that the Church may triumph throughout the world and all nations might believe and accept Jesus Christ as their Savior, and the proclamation of the angel of the Apocalypse may be fulfilled and "The kingdoms of this world shall become the kingdoms of the Lord's anointed."

The reunion of Christendom around the See of Peter is a necessary preliminary to the conversion of the world, and that ought to increase the desire on the part of all the faithful that every Christian separated from the Holy See ought to return to communion with the Chair of Peter at Rome. Christ, the Good Shepherd, expressed His own desire for this when He said: "Other sheep I have which are not of this fold," that is to say, the Fold of Peter, "Them also I must bring and they will hear My voice and there shall be one fold and one shepherd."

When, therefore, you unite with us in the observance of the Unity Octave, it should be to pray specifically that this happy consummation may be brought to pass, and all those, who down through the centuries, have been separated from the Chair of Peter at Rome may return to Catholic Communion, that is to say, to communion with the Apostolic See, which in the Providence of God was set up by St. Peter himself in the capital of the Great Roman Empire, the City of the Seven Hills, sometimes called the "Eternal City"—Rome.

The divisions among Christians which now exist are extremely sad. They have had a destructive effect upon Christianity itself, for when Christians are so divided in their belief and hold doctrines that contradict and destroy each other, they are weakening Christianity as an institution in the world. And every year we see the number of these increasing among us that have rejected Christianity altogether.

The latest evolution that has taken place in Christendom, by reason of this division among the disciples of Christ, has been the rising up in every part of the world of a brand new sect that had little or no existence prior to the World War. I refer to Communism, which denies the very existence of God and is filled with a diabolical hatred of Christianity, so much so that it is sometimes called the manifestation of anti-Christ in the world. Wherever it gains the mastery, and it has gained complete control over some of the mightiest governments on earth today, its advocates and adherents thirst for the blood of Christians. Torrents of Christian blood have continued to flow in all parts of Soviet Russia, and anywhere from ten to twenty thousand priests and nuns have been put to death, by the Communists in Spain, during the past three years. The divisions among American Christians have opened the door for Communism to enter America, and this nation is being Sovietized at a rapid rate in consequence. The sense of self-preservation ought to spur us on to pray most fervently with the great High Priest of our profession that all His disciples may be One, that the world not only may be saved from anti-Christ, but Christ's Church may triumph everywhere and all nations unite in the confession of the One True Faith of the Holy Catholic Church of the centuries, and all united in the communion of the One Fold under the One Shepherd.

We beg you, therefore, during the few days of this Octave which are left, to pray in union, not only with the vast multitudes of the Catholic Church throughout the world, but with thousands of Anglicans, Orthodox, and other sects of various kinds.

144

4. Only One Unity

Radio Broadcast
January 21, 1940

On Thursday last, the feast of the Chair of Saint Peter at Rome, there began the observance throughout the world of what is commonly called the Church Unity Octave—a period of eight days of concerted prayer for unity among Christians. The observance was inaugurated by no less a personality than His Holiness, Pope Pius XII, successor of Saint Peter and present occupant of his chair, or *Cathedra,* in Rome. Following the example of his predecessors, Pope Pius XI, Pope Benedict XV, and Pope Pius X, the Holy Father celebrated his Mass on Thursday morning last, feast of the Chair of Peter at Rome, for the special intention of the return of all separated Christians to communion with the Apostolic See. This information was conveyed to me personally by His Eminence Cardinal Canali, who at the same time sent the Holy Father's blessing to the Friars at Graymoor, where the Unity Octave originated thirty-two years ago, and which has since spread not only throughout the Catholic world, but is widely observed throughout the Anglican communion, among the Orthodox of Europe and the Near East, and has more recently been participated in by the Protestants of France and the Christians of Scandinavia.

A letter from Athens under date of December 19th, written by the Most Reverend George Calavassy, Catholic Bishop of all Greece, received by me a couple of days ago, reads as follows: "Reverend and dear Father: It is a pleasure for me to be able to send you here inclosed a copy of the circular letter sent to all the Bishops in the East by His Eminence Cardinal Tisserant, Secretary of the Sacred Congregation for the Oriental Churches, in behalf of the observance of the Unity Octave of prayers.

"As you know, all over Greece and Turkey, everywhere there is a Catholic Church or Chapel, the Unity Octave is observed. This year we shall see that something more be done according to the Holy See's instructions. The present international situation imposes particularly these special prayers for Unity, since it is very probable that the ultimate fighting is going to be between Christianity and Communism. We hope, therefore, that all Christians will, more than ever before, realize their duty to do all they can for uniting the Christian forces in the unity of faith and morals."

The Confraternity of Unity, an organization having a Secretariat in the United States and Canada, as well as the British Isles and Dominions, but limited to the Anglican Communion, have addressed to the members and friends of the Confraternity, a letter, a copy of which I hold in my hand. This letter says "The unity of Christendom, the unity of the followers of Christ in His mystical body, the Church, must appear to all Christians in these days of bloodshed and strife to be of vital importance, not only for the peace of the world and the welfare of men on earth, but also for their eternal salvation."

We ask not only all Episcopalians who may be listening in to join with us in the observance of this Octave, but also all our non-Catholic friends who bear the name of Christ.

And now, in conclusion, I ask all my listeners who call yourselves Christians, whether Catholic or non-Catholic, to join with me in saying the Church Unity Prayer—"O Lord Jesus Christ, who saidst unto Thine Apostles: Peace I leave with thee, My Peace I give unto you, regard not our sins, but the faith of Thy Church, and grant unto her that peace and unity which are agreeable to Thy will. Who livest and reignest God, forever and ever. Amen."

5. Our Brethren of the East

The Lamp, October, 1926

No one who believes in the divine plan of One Fold and One Shepherd can fail to be intensely interested in all that concerns Russia and the Near East—the lands, in which live the greatest number of those Christians, who while they have retained their ecclesiastical organization and their faith, have been for nearly a thousand years separated from the Seat of Unity. The origin of the separation was in large part, political, and the present population of these lands are in no wise responsible for the condition in which they find themselves nor are they, in general, responsible for the material ill-being which has come to be their lot within the past decade or so.

The welfare of the Near East, in its broadest sense, has been, as is well known, a matter of the greatest concern to our Sovereign Pontiff, Pope Pius XI. Both through his scholarly research and through personal contact, especially with the Russian people, His Holiness has learned to know and appreciate their needs. Hence, on his ascending the throne of Peter, one of his first steps was to endeavor to ameliorate their lot, to show them the depth of his paternal charity to them.

When the Russian people were suffering from famine and want, the Pope at once organized a relief mission and sent as his personal representative the Rev. Edmund A. Walsh, S.J., regent of the School of Foreign Service and vice president of Georgetown University, to take charge of it. Father Walsh spent two years in Russia administering physical relief to the suffering. His was not a religious mission, in any sense, save in that its origin was inspired by the Christian law of charity. Catholic, Orthodox, Bolshevik, Jew, Mohammedan or atheist, if he were needy, could apply and would receive aid with no questions concerning his faith or lack of it asked.

Meantime, owing to the political, economic and religious changes in their own land, many Russians sought refuge abroad. Refugee colonies were to be found in almost all the larger European cities and many came to America also. In not a few cases, they had fled, leaving all behind them, and were in dire need. Wherever they went they found the Catholic clergy ready to lend a helping hand. Outstanding in their efforts in this direction have been Bishop O'Rourke in Danzig and Bishop Chaptal in Paris. But Russia and the Russian colonies were not the only places where little children were starving and where religion was oppressed. In many other regions of the Near East similar if not worse conditions prevailed.

During the war, among the Catholic clergy who were serving as chaplains with the Allied forces was Monsignor Richard Barry-Doyle. Monsignor Barry-Doyle saw a great deal of military service in the Near East and saw with his own eyes the sufferings and privations of the people of that much talked of country. He longed to bring bread to their famished bodies and the teachings of the Church to nourish their souls. The faces of these people haunted him and soon after the war he founded The Catholic Near East Welfare Association to accomplish these objects. The readers of *The Lamp* are very familiar with the

147

progress of this work and have always been ready to aid it with splendid generosity.

About this time a Benedictine priest, the Rev. Augustine von Galen, was residing in Vienna and he, impressed with needs of the Russian refugees in Austria, conceived the idea of forming a society to aid them, especially in the matter of trying to reunite them with the Catholic Church. He called his society "The Catholic Union" and with the permission of his superiors, began to organize his work in several centers.

Both Monsignor Barry-Doyle and Father Galen came to this country to seek the assistance of American Catholics but it early became evident that both of them were working for practically the same end and that two such societies, occupying the same field, might readily tend to overlap their efforts and produce confusion in the minds of the people. Hence the project of combining these two works was taken up and the case was submitted to the judgment of the Holy See. After a careful consideration of all phases of the matter, it was determined that the work should be enlarged in scope and be placed under the immediate direction of the Holy See and of the American Hierarchy. The Holy Father, mindful of the excellent work done by Father Walsh in Russia and his wide acquaintance with the problems involved, conferred upon him the honor and responsibility of being president of the new organization. At the same time, in an official letter His Holiness directed that "in view of the personal interest hitherto manifested in 'The Catholic Near East Welfare Association' by His Eminence Cardinal Hayes, it seemed well that he should be designated as Protector of the enlarged association for which" the same letter says, "the title Catholic Near East Welfare Association will be sufficient to express adequately the general purpose and scope to these two unified organizations," at the same time it being "declared that this title includes also the 'Catholic Union' and the purpose for which that Society has hitherto labored."

The interest of the Society of the Atonement in the work is well known to all. For years *The Lamp* has had a "Greek Page" in which it has chronicled matters of interest connected with this endeavor, and the Father Founder of the Society has accepted a place on the Executive Committee, to which he will gladly give as much of his time as he can spare from his other duties. The readers of *The Lamp* are all familiar with our heartfelt desire for the Unity of Christendom and they will rejoice to know that long cherished hopes for a "Catholic Near East Association" on an international scale has at last been fulfilled. We bespeak for the new "Catholic Near East Welfare Association" the heartiest cooperation and support of all our *Lamp* readers and trust that they will regard its appeals directed towards the accomplishments of the great aim of the Society of the Atonement: "That all my be One."

Pope Pius XI has stated that he wished his Pontificate to be known for his efforts at the beginning of the restoration to true Unity of all peoples who are outside the True Fold. This association will furnish, we believe, if it be properly supported, an answer to his prayer and to that of the Divine Lord.

6. The Return of the Orthodox

January 19, 1930

The special intention of this particular day in the Chair of Unity Octave is "The Return of all Oriental Separatists to communion with the Apostolic See".

"Other Sheep I have that are not of this fold, them also I must bring and they shall hear My voice, and there shall be One Fold and One Shepherd." (*Jn 10:16*)

The Church, as you know, started in the East; it began in the city of Jerusalem and finally St. Peter established the Apostolic See in Rome and the gospel was spread through the Roman Empire. After the persecutions were ended, the Church came out of the catacombs and the Christian emperors allowed churches to be built in the great cities of the Roman Empire, and fostered them and gave them large sums of money for the purpose of aiding the people.

Then came the heresies. These errors for the most part flourished in Oriental soil because the minds of the Greeks are very subtle; and in their study of various subjects of theology, particularly the character of Our Lord, they started the heresies. There was the heresy of Arius, which started very early in the time of the first Christian emperor, who denied the divinity of Christ. Finally there was a Council held at Nicea and Arius was condemned, but that was not the end of Arianism. Con-

149

stantius, the son of Constantine, himself became an Arian and the power of the Roman Emperors was thrown on the side of heresy. There was a time when it was said, "Athanasius against the world." But finally Arianism is now pretty well stamped out, except some of the modern Unitarian sects, which do not amount to very much.

But some of the heresies of the East have continued until the present time. For instance, there was Nestorius who tried to emphasize the divinity of Christ in contradiction to Arius. He did not keep the proper balance but divided the personality of Our Lord, saying that He had two persons, and that one of these persons was God, and the other man and the son of Mary; so that he denied that it was proper to call the Blessed Virgin the Mother of God. When he was condemned he was cast out of the Church, but his teaching produced a system, because it came from the region of Antioch and was held in high esteem. Many sided with him and the Syrians largely went into the schism, and the Nestorian schism has continued in the East until this very day.

Then there came the opposite of Nestorianism; the pendulum swung to the other extreme, and a certain theologian began to assert that Our Lord had only one nature. He was so divine that He had no human nature, and these were called the Monophysites, and they were condemned in the General Council. The followers of this teaching captured Egypt for their schism, and practically all Egyptians became Monophysites, largely due to the supremacy of the Egyptians over the Greeks, so that the racial element played its part, and Egypt became Monophysitic. When the time arose for the appearance of Mohammed, all Syria and Jerusalem were taken captive by the Arabs under the leadership of Mohammed. Egypt fell an easy prey to the Mohammedans for the very reason of this strife on account of Monophysism. As the Protestants today have an antagonism to the Catholic Church so the Monophysites took an antagonism to the Greeks and they actually preferred to be ruled by the Moslems than to be ruled from Constantinople; consequently Alexandria fell into the hands of the Mohammedans.

For a long time Constantinople held out, then came the clash between Constantinople and Rome in regard to politics, and the Greeks wanted to be supreme and claimed that Constantinople was superior to Rome, the most important city in the empire, and therefore, the Archbishop of Constantinople should be equal with the one in Rome. This led to jealousy and friction and finally gave excuses to the Easterns for finding fault with Rome, particularly under the introduction of the "Filioque" into the Creed and they said, "Oh well, Rome has fallen away from the Faith, we are the representatives of the Catholic Church," and they went into schism. This was due to Michael Caerularius (1054) leaning upon the arm of an earthly prince rather than upon the Vicar of Christ. They had their punishment because, rejecting the Holy Father and saying, "We will have no other king but Caesar," Constantine was put down by the inroads of the Mohammedans and the Oriental empire was set up in the East and an Oriental prince became the dominator of the Catholic Church. Nobody could be made Archbishop or put into any position of authority but by his sanction, and consequently, the church of Constantinople became weak and oppressed under the rule of the Saracens. Then in the course of time there grew up a great kingdom in Eastern Europe, now known as Russia and Siberia. Missionaries came to them with the blessings of the Apostolic See, and they achieved great success in their work, but finally the Czar of Russia preferred to unite himself with Constantinople rather than with Rome.

It was a case of political policies again, and all that great section went into schism. Thus the largest portion of the Oriental schismatics, or the Orthodox Church as it is called, is not around Constantinople, but in Russia and Asia, all the sections that were run over by the Mohammedans. They were weak in number, only vassals to the Mohammedan power, and a great kingdom rose up with Saint Petersburg as its center, and it would seem that Satan here tried to raise up a church that would ultimately triumph over the Church of Rome. The devil is a good imitator, so he imitated Rome; the Czar was the supreme master of the church, the head of it, and the "Great White Father", corresponding to the "Great White Father", the Shepherd of Christendom, the Pope of Rome. Russia was then already under the sway of St. Petersburg. The emperor of Russia being named Peter, the city was named after him, Saint Petersburg; so it was the Chair of Saint Petersburg, and it was thought by the Russian Church that there could be only one church and that the Bishop of Rome had fallen away from the Faith and had be-

151

come apostate and cast out, and that the successor Saint Peter was really the Czar and the bishops under his rule. They are bold in their claims that that was the church and the only Catholic, Apostolic Orthodox Church of Christendom. Even to the name of the dynasty you have the imitation perpetrated; it was the House of Romanoff which was the domination of this great church, and the ambition always of "Holy Russia" was to get down into Italy and subjugate Rome to the thralldom and the rule of czars, but all this was frustrated by the great world war and the fall of Russia. Then Satan comes out in the manifestation of himself in the great man of sin in this Soviet rule, which has thrown off the mask entirely and has come out straight for the destruction of all religion and is teaching the youths of that country to deny even the existence of God and to cultivate Communism as their particular political theory and philosophy of life.

Now it represents a problem today, of immense importance and immense interest, the efforts of the Holy See to win back again to their original allegiance to the vicar of Christ the separated multitudes of the East. For the most part they are Christians, Orthodox in faith; they eccepted the seven General Councils in the same way as the Protestants accept the Bible as their religion. The persecutions that they have endured on account of the Soviet regime has somewhat inclined the minds of the Easterns towards the Holy See, and the hopes, therefore, of a return of the Orthodox Christians of the East to their original allegiance to the Vicar of Christ are encouraging at the present time. When we pray today for the "Return of Oriental Separatists to Communion with the Apostolic See" it ought to be the prayer of faith. A thousand years have rolled by since the East broke communion wilfully with the Church of Rome, which is the capital of the whole Catholic world, where St. Peter established the chair of his authority. And we understand that to be a Catholic is to be in communion with the Apostolic See. When Our Lord spoke of the "other sheep" and then of the "one fold under one shepherd" he referred to the one shepherd as St. Peter, his successor, whom he placed over that Church. Because Our Lord said that those other sheep would hear His voice and there would be one fold and one shepherd, we must believe that sooner or later His own prayer will be answered because He is the Truth.

152

We offer our prayers and offer ourselves to Him to cooperate with Him in any way that He may see fit to be of some assistance in accomplishing this great work of the return of the other sheep to the Fold of Peter. Let us, therefore, continue our prayers with faith, manifesting towards them great charity and love as the Good Shepherd Himself does, and wait and look forward with confidence to the day when Our Lord's prophecy will be fulfilled and all these that have been alienated so long from the Catholic Center, may be once more restored to communion with the Apostolic See.

7. The Return of the Orientals

The special intention we are praying for today is "the Return of the Oriental Separatists to Communion with the Apostolic See".

The Oriental represents the most ancient of the schisms that took place during a series of heretical manifestations in the Church of God, and finally there was, for political reasons, a rivalry between old Rome and the new Rome, the city on the Tiber and the city on the Bosphorus, Constantinople. About a thousand years ago the East broke away from communion with the West, for a long time there was scarcely any representative of the Holy See left in Asia Minor, Persia, Egypt and that portion of Eastern Europe adjacent to Constantinople, and the great vast regions north of Constantinople, called Russia and Siberia. We will not go into the details of that schism just now, but as we are called to pray for the other sheep to return to unity, and such a very large number of them are Oriental sheep it is not surprising that besides praying, our holy Society should have some active part in the work of bringing back into unity the Oriental separated Christians.

A very important institute has been organized. It is now a papal society under the particular patronage of our Holy Father the Pope, and as it were, the apple of his eye, for he looks upon it with great interest and paternal consideration, a society that has been organized in the United States, called the Catholic Near East Welfare Association, which is really an outcome of Graymoor. Some years ago, at the close of the world war the Holy Father dispatched to this country Monsignor George Calavassy. He was a Greek, from the Island of Sira, a small island in the Mediterranean, which has a tradition away back of union with the Apostolic See; it is not a large island and the inhabitants are not very numerous, but it has always produced a fine number of priests and a devout people. Bishop Calavassy was a native of this island and was chosen by the Pope while he was a priest to go on a commission to the United States, and having arrived here he got into communication with Graymoor, came up to see us, and we cooperated with him all we could during the time that he was in this country. Finally he became interested in the Near East Relief, which is a Protestant association; then he conceived the idea that perhaps if someone got on their board who was a Catholic and he were delegated to get all the alms he could from Catholics in the United States, and if they got a board of that sort it would lead to an appropriation for work in Constantinople. Accordingly, we cooperated in that regard and Mr. George Walter Smith, at one time head of the bar association in Pennsylvania and a very prominent Catholic, was appointed on that board and actually went on that expedition to Constantinople with others, but as time went on we learned by experience that they did not propose to use any of their money for Catholic propaganda. They gave one excuse after another, with the result that not anything at all got out of the treasury of the Near East Relief into Catholic agencies.

Then we conceived the idea of forming in the Catholic Church something corresponding to the Near East Relief and to have our own Near East Relief. Later on, when Bishop Calavassy went back to Rome he was made a bishop and established over Constantinople and all Greece. He then met the chaplain of the British Army, who was stationed at Constantinople, Monsignor Barry-Doyle whom he sent to this country with a letter of introduction to the editor of *The Lamp*, because we had promised to keep alive the work of Bishop Calavassy in this country and the interest in his cause. We had set aside one of the departments of the Union-That-Nothing-Be-Lost, particularly for the East and established the Greek Page in *The Lamp*. We received Monsignor Barry-Doyle very cordially and did our utmost for him. He was a stranger in this country, and being a British chaplain, although an Irishman, he met with a good deal of difficulty in making headway, but we introduced him to a Converts League, secured lectures for him, and we had, in the meantime, secured the appointment of the Cardinal of Philadelphia on the board as Cardinal of the Sacred Congregation of the Oriental Church, which the Holy Father had established sometime previously. We, accordingly, wrote to the Cardinal, reminding him that he belonged to this Congregation, asking that Monsignor Barry-Doyle might be given an opportunity to lecture in Philadelphia. The Cardinal agreed and he took advantage of it. Then we said to Monsignor Barry-Doyle, "Now when a man lectures in this country he generally gets some secretary to manage things for him, you are more or less ignorant of American ways and that is what you need." So we began to look around and presently there came to the Mount of the Atonement one day Mr. Joseph Moore, who had been engaged in the circulation work of Church Extension and several others, and I approached him with the subject, for I saw instantly that he had the qualifications he needed for Monsignor Barry-Doyle. Consequently we proposed the matter and a meeting was held up on the Mount of the Atonement, made up of the three, Monsignor Barry-Doyle, Mr. Moore and myself, and we defined the way of the association, for now we could see our plans materializing of a Catholic Near East Welfare Association. Consequently it was organized and incorporated in the City of New York.

Not long after that came a prominent Benedictine from Europe to this country, Docton von Galen, who had been confessor to the Austrian Kaiser, Joseph Francis. He had his *Catholic Unio*, which was very much the same thing as the organization established by Monsignor Barry-Doyle; in fact, he developed something almost parallel, so much so, that they were in conflict with one another. We finally urged both parties together, and going to Rome in the Holy Year (1925) I was commissioned by them to negotiate with the Holy See, through the Sacred Congregation, for a consolidation of these two societies under Papal favor. We spent a great deal of time in Rome working on that proposition; we were assisted particularly by Father Paschal Robinson, O.F.M., who afterwards became Archbishop, ministering at Jerusalem. He is now the Papal Nuncio in Ireland, the first Nuncio from the Holy See to Ireland since the seventeenth century in the days of Cromwell. The result ultimately was that the other society was suppressed, the Catholic Near East Welfare Association and Doctor von Galen's society were consolidated, the Holy Father took it under his special protection, made it a papal society and appointed Father Edmund Walsh, S.J., as its first president.

8. The Reconcilation of Anglicans

January 20, 1937

The special intention to be prayed for during this—the third day of the Church Unity Octave—is the reconciliation of the Anglicans to the authority of the Vicar of Christ.

Just about this time twenty-eight years ago, a little while before the Society of the Atonement passed from the Anglican Communion into the Fold of Peter, I called one day upon His Eminence, Cardinal Gibbons of Baltimore, and during the conversation which followed, the greatly beloved prelate declared that, if the Anglicans returned to Catholic Unity, the Catholic Church would conquer the world for Christ. Addressing His Father on the night of His betrayal, Jesus prayed that His disciples might be one in order that the world might believe. He foresaw the sad effects of division in the Christian family and how necessary Unity among the members of His Church was for the extension of that church throughout the world, until by missionary conquest of the peoples of the earth, the kingdoms of this world should become the kingdom of the King of kings and Lord of lords. Cardinal Gibbons, I believe, spoke that day by inspiration. If all those Christians who constitute the so-called Anglican communion, reckoned at something like 30,000,000 were firmly united with Rome—as the Ecclesia Anglicana or Anglican Church was united with the Apostolic See before the 16th century schism, it would give a tremendous impetus to the missionary conquest of Asia and Africa on the part of the Catholic Church. Hence the great importance of the special intention for today, namely, the reconciliation of Anglicans to the authority of the Vicar of Christ.

It was an Anglican clergyman, the Rev. Spencer Jones, M.A., rector for forty-five years of Moreton-on-March, a small country parish in England who prepared the way, for the institution of the Church Unity Octave in 1907, by writing to the Editor of *The Lamp* at Graymoor and advocating the preaching of sermons on the feast of St. Peter in June of every year, pointing to the Holy See as the center of a reunited Christendom. To that letter the Editor of *The Lamp* replied, saying that it seemed to him it would be even better to observe an Octave of Prayer for Church Unity beginning on the feast of the Chair of St. Peter at Rome, January 18th, and ending with the feast of the Conversion of St. Paul, the great Apostle of the Gentiles, January 25th. These two feasts would link together the two portions of our Lord's prayer "That all may be one that the world may believe that Thou hast sent me." Unity of all Christians with the Chair of St. Peter at Rome must first be realized and the conversion of the Gentile world, begun by St. Paul, would soon be triumphantly completed.

Spencer Jones accepted the idea with enthusiasm and accordingly, in January of the following year, 1908, the Church Unity Octave began. For a long time its progress in England was slow because the prejudice against Rome was still strong among so-called Anglo-Catholics, but a tremendous change has taken place since the World War and now the members of the Church of England rival those of the Catholic Church in the observance of the Octave, and a great desire seems to be taking possession of the hearts and minds of hundreds upon hundreds of the Anglican pastors to lead their sheep back to the "one Fold" under the "one shepherd" from the far country of Anglican estrangement.

I made my first visit to England last May and met in the flesh Rev. Spencer Jones, M.A., for the first time—an octogenarian like our Holy Father, the Pope, but still possessed of great mental vigor and still the active president of the Church Unity Council. I was entertained at dinner in London by another leader of the Anglo-Roman Unity movement, who invited certain of his co-workers, notably the Lord Abbot of the Anglican Benedictine Abbey of Nashdom, to break bread together at his table. They gave me the best kind of evidence of how strong and deep there has taken root in the heart and mind of those Anglican leaders the desire to return not as individuals, but as shepherds with their flocks to the great white Shepherd of Christendom, the successor of St. Peter, to whom Our Lord gave the original commission: "Feed My lambs; rule and shepherd My sheep."

The literature published by these Anglican advocates of reunion has taken the place of the famous "Tracts for the Times", published by Cardinal Newman and others at the commencement of the Oxford Movement more than one hundred years ago. Some of the most scholarly and ablest expositions of the scriptural, doctrinal, conciliar, and historical arguments for the papal supremacy and infallibility ever written have been produced by these Anglican writers, and the volume of literature put forth by them in support of the *de juro divino* primacy of the Apostolic See of Rome, as the divinely established center of a reunited Christendom is constantly on the increase.

In a sermon on Church Unity some years ago the Catholic Bishop of Clifton, England, mentioned a prophecy made of King Edward the Confessor. The saintly king saw in a vision the Church of England as a stately tree cut from its roots and carried a distance of three furlongs. Then by no human power he beheld it brought back and take root again in its parent stock. Now there is nothing in the ecclesiastical history of England which corresponds to that description except the severing of the Church of England from her roots in the papacy begun by Henry VIII and consumated by his daughter Elizabeth. If we might measure the furlongs in time rather than in space and allow a century for a furlong, the coincidence is certainly remarkable, for it was by an act of Parliament in 1533 that the severance of the Church of England from the Holy See began and it was in 1833, just exactly three hundred years afterwards that the Oxford Movement was inaugurated. Cardinal Newman, the corypheus of that movement, sometime afterward made his personal submission to the Holy See and became a Cardinal of the Holy Roman Church, and he and others have declared the *terminus ad quem* or purpose of the Oxford Movement was the return of the English to their pre-Reformation allegiance to the Holy See.

It is our own personal belief that this reunion will be actually accomplished. History repeats itself and what has once happened can happen again. After the first severance of the Church of England from Rome, in the reign of Henry VIII, the breach was healed and communion with the Apostolic See was reestablished during the reign of Mary the Queen. Nothing so radical has happened since to make impossible another and final restoration of the Church of England to communion with Rome. It is for that we pray devoutly and we ask our listeners in to pray with us. Surely it is a consummation devoutly to be wished!

9. The Reconciliation of the Anglicans

Shrine of the Immaculate Conception
Catholic University, Washington, D. C.
January 20, 1940

"They that be of thee shall build up the old waste places. Thou shalt raise up the foundations of many generations and thou shalt be called the repairer of the breach, the restorer of paths to dwell in" (Is. 53:12).

I am very happy to be once again here at the Catholic University partaking with the students and those who have come together for the observance of this Octave, and particularly on this night which is devoted to prayer for the return of the Anglicans to communion with Rome. That is a very important prayer to make, and it will bring forth wonderful results in the line of the prayer which Our Lord uttered on the night of His betrayal when He addressed His Father: "That they all may be one as Thou Father in Me and I in Thee, that they also may be one in Us, that the world may believe that Thou hast sent Me." (Jn 17:21)

In the month of March, 1909, I expressed to His Eminence, Cardinal Gibbons, the desire of the Society of the Atonement of being corporately united with the Apostolic See and after I had stated my purpose in coming, the Cardinal said: "If we had the Anglicans with us we could conquer the world for Christ." I have always thought that the Cardinal was speaking somewhat by inspiration when he spoke these words. There is no more missionary people in the world today exercising such large influence over the English speaking people that has scattered itself all over the face of the earth from Great Britain, and if that missionary power of that English-speaking race that has sought the extension of the British Empire, were devoted to the extension of the Kingdom of Christ, I think that Cardinal Gibbon's prophecy would be fulfilled and that we could conquer the world for Christ.

So it is a very important prayer that we are making, and if we can bring back into union once more with the Catholic Church and in communion with St. Peter, this race that has fallen into schism and gone into the far country and has been separated from the Apostolic See, the results for the conversion of the world would be tremendous.

These words I select because they express, I think, one of the purposes of Almighty God in calling into being the Society of the Atonement. I can hardly understand any reason why God should have selected two Anglicans to found the Society unless He had some such purpose in view as expressed in these words. When Mother Lurana was praying for guidance as to whether she should accept the invitation extended to her to make her foundation in the lonely wilderness surrounding Graymoor, amid the highlands of the Hudson, this was the answer that she received, this very text: "Thou shalt be called the Repairer of the Breach . . ."—the breach was to mean the 16th century breach from Rome.

Let me tell you something of the development of the Institute on these lines. When 30 years old I felt a strong impulse, to carry out the vocation which had been given me in childhood, to found a preaching order like the Paulists. I did not know what to call it. I felt that it ought to have something to do with the Cross and Passion of Our Divine Redeemer, but the difficulty was to find a name which had not already been appropriated. So after thinking on the subject for many months, and praying for light at the same time, I one day read of an experience which St. Francis had when he was invited by the richest young man in Assisi to spend the night with him, and the next morning the young man proposed to imitate him, and to become as poor, as the poor son of the rich merchant of Assisi. St. Francis hesitated to say to this rich young man: "Follow my example, sell everything you have got, distribute to the poor, take up your cross, join me and follow the gospel." So they went together to the church and at the end of the Mass, St. Francis went up to the priest and asked him if he would open the missal three times, and the priest did so, and each time it was: "If thou wilt be perfect, go, sell what thou hast and give to the poor. Take nothing for the way. If any man will come

160

after Me, let him deny himself and take up His cross and follow Me." I said: "Why can't I do as St. Francis did?" Then I took the bible down from the pulpit, opened it three times and received three texts, and I saw these words in St. Paul's fifth chapter to the Romans: "And not only so, but we also joy in God through Our Lord Jesus Christ, by whom we have now received the Atonement." I said: "That is it—the Society of the Atonement."

Years after I read a book which referred to that same chapter of Romans in connection with Henry VIII. A little after the text I have quoted, come the words: "For as by the disobedience of one man, many were made sinners; so also by the obedience of one, many shall be made just." Then in the book which the King was supposed to have written, but which Cardinal Fisher wrote for him, this very text was used by Henry against Martin Luther. But Henry did the same thing in England because the Pope would not grant him a divorce from his lawful wife, Catherine of Aragon, so that he could marry Anne Boleyn who was already in the family way, and he was hoping for a son from his true wife—took the matter into his own hands, and broke England away from the Holy See.

About this same time I was reading a sermon by the Catholic Bishop of Clifton on the matter of Church Unity. And in this sermon the Bishop refers to a vision that was given to Edward the Confessor, who was raised to the altar as a saint. In this vision Edward saw the Church of England as a tree cut from its parent roots, and then carried the distance of three furlongs; after that by no human power was brought back, and taking root in its original stock again. Now there is nothing in the history of the Church of England to correspond with that up to the time of Henry VIII. Henry VIII cut the tree away from unity by an act of Parliament and began what was more fully confirmed by his bastard daughter, Elizabeth, by the establishment of what was called the Church of England. Now take the three furlongs measured in his time and apply three centuries, and we have a striking development. It was in 1533 that the Act of Parliament through the instigation of Henry VIII was passed, and England was torn from Communion with Rome. Three centuries afterwards exactly in the year 1833 saw the beginning of what was called the Oxford Movement, and the purpose of this movement was to prepare the way for the return of the Church of England to her pre-Reformation allegiance to the Apostolic See.

Now we spoke about the disobedience of one man. And the leading figure of the Oxford Movement was John Henry Newman, another Henry, but his first name was John, the name of that particular saint of the Atonement on the Cross to whom Our Lord uttered the words: "Son, behold thy Mother", meaning the Blessed Virgin, and to His Mother: "Mother, behold thy son".

And whereas the spirit of rebellion, of disobedience, was in the heart of the first Henry, it was the spirit of the New Man, Jesus Christ, that was in the heart and in the mind of John Henry Newman. So he was the beginning of the principal of the Atonement, reconciliation, bringing back to God those who had been separated by the sin of disobedience and dis-union. Christ came to save the world. He was to offset the disobedience of our first parents by the supreme test of the Passion. He was to become obedient unto death, even the death of the Cross. And it was through that supreme test that He was to become the Father of the world to come, the Atonement race, to distinguish them from the children of disobedience. So this principle of disobedience, rebellion, set forth by Henry VIII and the spirit of obedience which distinguished John Henry Newman, under the providence of God, was to be once more the reconcilation of the Church of England to the Holy See.

History repeats itself and what once has been can be again. Henry VIII first of all cut the Church away from unity with Rome, but in the reign of Mary, his true daughter of his true wife, the Church was restored to communion with Rome again. Then came Elizabeth, the product of that sinful marriage, and when she came to the throne she knew that she was declared a bastard by the Holy See and she had to choose between allegiance to the Vicar of Christ or to be the Queen of England. She chose the latter, and through her ministers once more England was torn away from unity with the Apostolic See.

Now when reading on the anniversary of the Oxford Movement about the visit of John Henry Newman to Rome, and how he was stricken down with a fever, he said to the servant: "I shall not die. God has given me work to do at home, back in England," and returning he composed the hymn: "Lead kindly light, amid the encircling gloom, lead thou me on." And I was curious to ascertain whether that same Sunday was the same Sunday that sixty years afterwards I received the name and text of our Institute. The sixth Sunday after Trinity after the Anglican reckoning; the Seventh Sunday after Pentecost by the Catholic calendar. And there, sure enough, when I looked it up I found that the sermon of John Keble was preached on the Seventh Sunday after Pentecost.

Now, seventy years after the beginning of the Oxford Movement in 1903 *The Lamp* came out from the Mount of the Atonement and proclaimed for reunion with Rome. I remember in October, 1901, saying to Mother Lurana that I was the only clergyman, so far as I knew, in the Anglican Church among thirty thousand that held the Papal views. And it was not long afterwards that the same thing was reiterated by *The Living Church,* the organ of the Episcopal Church in this country. *The Living Church* hastened to reassure the Anglicans who had been disturbed that "it was only an eccentric monk at Graymoor and that he was absolutely alone in such views."

Let me tell you of some of the difficulties we had when we started out to preach. A college chum of mine, with whom I had roomed for five years, had a parish down at the end of Long Island and he invited me to come down and preach a sermon before the Archdeacon. I notified him that I was willing to come down, but that I would preach on the subject of Church Unity. So he was alarmed and called the Archdeacon and said it will not do for him to come here and preach about the Pope. So they knew the train I was to travel on, and the Archdeacon got on the train, sat down beside me and said: "How do you do, Tommy?" Sometimes they called me "Tommy". And then the debate went on as to whether I should preach the sermon the Lord wanted me to preach or whether I should listen to the Archdeacon. And I said: "Well, now the Archdeacon represents authority and I should obey authority." The argument went along in my mind as to whether I should preach the sermon on the Pope or not until I got into the church. There was a large number of clergy present. They had a clergyman from the North of Ireland read out in a loud voice: "Son of man, arise and stand upon thy feet, and preach unto them, the words I have given thee," etc. I said I have to preach that sermon on the Pope. I got up and read out to them about Peter and John going up to the temple on the ninth hour, and so on.

And I went on to say that I was going to tell them why the Church of England and her daughter, the Episcopal Church in America, although the English had colonized America and the Church should be the leading Church in America. But as a matter of fact, it was only about one per cent of the population: though we have lots of millionaires and we spend lots of money on foreign missions, yet we do not seem to do very much.

Now I am going to give you the remedy. In the days when the Church of England was united with the holy Roman See, and her missionaries took their blessing and their orders from the successor of St. Peter, they, together with the missionaries from Ireland, converted all of northern and the central part of Europe, and if only once more we could get back into communion with Rome, and our missionaries should receive from the successors of St. Peter their missions, then again we could and would do much for the conversion of the world. As I went along these lines, the feeling in the congregation was becoming more and more tense. But this clergyman from the north of Ireland could stand it no longer. He went to the Archdeacon and said: "Stop him, stop him!" The Archdeacon looked as if he had been injured in an accident, so the north of Ireland clergyman turned around and shouted: "Let your light shine before men and glorify your Father Who is in Heaven." In the Episcopal Church that is the signal for the collection. The last words I said were "The Chair of Peter."

There was some consultation that night among the clergy. By the way, I was to have stayed that night at the home of two wealthy ladies, members of the congregation, but after the experience at the church I stayed at the local hotel. The next morning I came around and stood at the back of the Church, while the clergyman from the North of Ireland read a fiery resolution to the meeting, condemning me, fore and aft for my doctrines and proposing that it be published in all the church papers throughout the country. But even then I got a chance. Well, there was a tall, fine looking man who had once been a clergyman in England and while there was very zealous. He arose, "Well," he said, "we have a clergyman here in good standing in a neighboring diocese and he speaks about unity with the center of Christendom, I move that the resolution be put on the table." And put on the table it was. Nevertheless, it got into the papers and I did not get any more invitations to preach anywhere. So I had to preach on the steps of City Hall in New York or up in Newburgh, N.Y.

Now then, see the difference that has taken place in the Anglican Church since then. When I got back home I started the beacon light of *The Lamp* and it carried the message much further than if I had preached every night and about the Pope every time. Through the pages of *The Lamp* which had been started in 1903, the Church Unity Octave was started in 1908; and we had many readers among the Catholic clergy, and when I sent out an invitation to them to join the Octave one of the very first to reply was the Cardinal Archbishp of Boston: "We will be with you and I will ask my clergy to join with you in the Octave." And a bishop in California did the same.

Spencer Jones, the author of "England and the Holy See," joined with us in the observance of the Octave and promulgated it in England, and every year it has spread and extended in England. And *The Lamp* and Graymoor, nor even the Jesuits could hardly put forth anything stronger than this annual call of the Church Unity Octave gotten out by the Committee of the Anglican Church. Here are some points of what they say:

"1. The conversion of the world depends upon the visible unity of the Church of God for Our Lord, prayed, 'That they all may be one . . . that the world may believe.'

"2. He provided the means for the maintenance of this unity by the appointment of a visible head for the visible body: 'Thou art Peter and upon this rock I will build My Church.'

"History has shown what interpretation the Church has given to this text, for none other has ever been the Church's acknowledged head upon earth, than he who sits on Peter's throne. Separation from this center of Unity has always led the separated into further schisms, while acknowledgement of it by all must necessarily result in the healing of all divisions.

"In these days when the powers of anti-Christ are gathering to achieve the domination of the world, no words are needed to stress the necessity of unity in the hosts of Christendom. While the immediate duty for each is to apply his faith as he has received it to the strengthening of the spiritual forces of the kingdom of God, yet we must keep in mind the reconstruction of the world after war and prepare for a peace that the world through its own power cannot give; a peace that must be founded on the eternal law of God, of justice and charity and the acknowledgment of the sovereignty of Christ.

"But that the voice of the Holy Spirit speaking through His Kingdom on earth may be heeded and recognized as divine, the peoples must hear Christendom proclaiming the truth and the law, not through many voices of the Babel of today but with the assurance that springs and can spring only from the conscious possession of infallible authority. Such authority obviously cannot be shared by bodies that give contrary teaching. . . ."

Let us then recall the "Sentence" inscribed in the Acts of the Third General Council of Ephesus: "It is doubtful to no one but rather known to all ages that the holy and blessed Peter, the Prince and Head of the Apostles and pillar of the faith and the foundation of the Catholic Church, received from Our Lord, Jesus Christ, the Savior and Redeemer of the human race, the keys of the kingdom and that to him was given the power of loosing and binding sins, who up to this time and forever lives and exercises judgment in his successors."

Now I have said that in 1901, as far as I know, I was the only Anglican clergyman holding these views. Do you know that last year this same message was sent out by this Committee and, in sending it out, they asked them to indicate whether they were in full agreement or in general agreement. Full agreement meant that to take the same dogmatic stand as the Church of Rome and 750 out of 1700 expressed themselves in full agreement. And in addition there are over forty religious communities praying for this objective. One of the first fruits of the observance was the corporate reception of the Society of the Atonement. Three years later the Caldey monks, the Benedictines of the Isle of Wight and the Benedictine nuns of Milford Haven; since then these communities have grown and prospered in the Church.

A Catholic priest I met in London two years ago told me that he had visited much among the Anglican Church and he said it was pitiful to see their longing to throw themselves at the feet of Peter, and such is their zeal in observing the Church Unity Octave that it transcends even the zeal of the Friars of the Atonement and Graymoor. I was told of a community that was on their knees before the altar for eight days. Now, at Graymoor, the Sisters watch for 24 hours but even at Graymoor we do not pray like this.

166

So, let us hope that those Anglicans by their prayers, so much in harmony with the prayer of Our Lord, Jesus Christ, will one day lead to the submission of a large body of sheep under the leadership of their shepherds who will come stepping down into the One Fold with the One Shepherd.

10. The Conversion of America

January 22, 1939

We are now in the midst of the celebration of the Chair of Unity Octave, which always begins on January 18th, the feast of the Chair of St. Peter at Rome, the divinely constituted center of a reunited Christendom, and January 25th, the feast of the Conversion of St. Paul, the Apostle to the Gentiles.

On the night of His betrayal, the Great High Priest of our profession, addressing His Father in heaven, prayed that His disciples might all be one, that the world might believe in His Messiahship. This would indicate that unity among Christians must first be achieved before the world can be brought to believe in the Messiahship of Christ, and the kingdoms of this world become the kingdom of the King of kings.

The observance of this Octave, which was inaugurated at Graymoor through the medium of its monthly magazine, *The Lamp,* has spread far and wide throughout Catholic Christendom, and not only is it observed by Catholics, but many of the Orthodox among the Greeks and Russians observe it. As many as 1500 of the clergy of the Church of England with their congregations are observing it right now and as many as forty Anglican religious communities. It has also spread to some extent among the Protestants of France, Norway and Sweden. Many Episcopalians in America, likewise, observe it.

There is a special intention to be prayed for each day. The special intention for today, January 22nd, is Catholic Unity for American Christians.

Permit me to direct the attention of my listeners to the words uttered by Christ, as the Good Shepherd, "I am the Good Shepherd, and know My sheep and am known of mine. And I lay down My life for My sheep. Other sheep I have which are not of this fold. Them also I must bring and they will hear My voice and there shall be One Fold and One Shepherd."

167

The "One Fold" under the "One Shepherd" we under-stand to be all those members of the Catholic Church who are under the jurisdiction and rule of the Great White Shepherd of Christendom, the successor of St. Peter, the Chair of whose authority was established by St. Peter, himself, in the city of Rome, and has persevered there during the 1900 years that have elapsed since St. Peter was the bishop of the Holy Roman Church. When Our Lord, the Good Shepherd, speaks of the "Other Sheep" which are not of this fold He had in mind by prophetic vision all the professed Christians of the whole world in this day and generation who are not of this Fold, that is to say, the Catholic Church.

As far as America is concerned the "Other Sheep" are all the baptized Christians in the United States who are not in communion with the successor of St. Peter, to whom Our Lord gave jurisdiction over His sheep, saying: "Feed My lambs; feed My sheep; rule and govern My sheep."

When we pray today that all Christians in America may become one, we are praying in effect that all the "Other Sheep" of Christ in the United States, whether they be Presbyterians, or Baptists, or Methodists, or Russian Orthodox, or Episcopalians, should heed to the voice of the Good Shepherd and return to the unity of the One Fold over which He established St. Peter and his successors in the Holy Roman See as the One Supreme Shepherd by divine appointment.

The Good Shepherd, speaking of His sheep, declares He must bring them and He prophesies that they will hear His voice and hearing it, will return to the One Fold from which not they, themselves originally separated but their ancestors some 400 years ago, going into schism and wandering into the far country of separation from the Catholic Church of the ages, which always has been, and always will be, under the jurisdiction of St. Peter, the Great White Shepherd of Christen-dom and his successors, who occupy the Chair of Unity, which he, St. Peter, established in the city of Rome.

Permit me as one of the under-Shepherds, commissioned by the successor of St. Peter, Pope XI, to call you back to Unity. Jesus said you would hear and recognize my voice as speaking for the Good Shepherd Himself. You know that St. Paul, writing to the Corinthians says: "Now then, we are ambassadors for Christ as though God beseech you by us. We pray you in Christ's stead, be ye reconciled to God." And so, when St. Paul preached to the Gentiles in Christ's name, it was as though Christ Himself had spoken to them and invited them to be His sheep. Perhaps you know I was once a Shepherd of the "Other Sheep" outside the Fold of Peter. In other words, I was a Minister of the Episcopal Church, for a number of years Rector of St. John's Episcopal Church in Kingston, New York. And finally I came to Graymoor and established there the Society of the Atonement, which was, as it were, a little flock of sheep, of which I was the shepherd. But those words of the Good Shepherd impressed themselves upon my mind and heart and I recognized the call of the Good Shepherd and I led the little flock that God committed to my care, from the far country of Protestant Episcopalianism, into the One Fold under the one Shepherd.

Now I am an ambassador for Christ, fully constituted Pastor under the Great White Pastor or Shepherd at Rome. And when I call to the other sheep, still in the far country of separation from the Fold of Peter, it is really the Good Shepherd calling you, because He says: "I must bring those other sheep into the one Fold of Peter, My Vicar." It is with Christ a matter of necessity, of supreme desire. And then He says: "They will hear My voice." Is that true in your case? Will you hear the voice of the Good Shepherd calling you to come into the Fold of the Catholic Church under the one supreme Shepherd, the Great White Shepherd of Christendom, whom the 300 million sheep in every part of the world under His Rule, universally called by common consent, the Holy Father? Pray about the matter! You wish to hear and always obey the Voice of the Redeemer, the Savior of the world, the Good Shepherd, who gave his life for you! Be sure by doing so that the Good Shepherd will be greatly pleased because you will be gratifying the supreme desire of His Sacred Heart.

When in loving obedience you hear the Good Shepherd's voice, then follow where He calls! For: by so doing you will contribute your share to the fulfillment of the prayer that is now going up from many thousands of faithful sheep of Christ, that the Christians in America may become One in communion with the Chair of St. Peter. God speed the day when the Christians of America will constitute but One Fold under One Shepherd.

11. The Return of Lapsed Catholics

January 23, 1939

This intention covers a very large field—of those who fall away from the practice of religion, absolutely drawing away from the Church altogether. It is tremendous. Fr. John O'Brien wrote a book, including this part of it, in which he states that lapsed Catholics over the year amount to half a million. Perhaps that is a little too much, but there is some ground for his calculation. If all the Catholics who came by immigration to America and their children who were baptized into the Church had remained faithful, instead of having 22 million we probably would have three times that number.

When we made application to the Holy See to receive the Society of the Atonement into the Fold of Peter, we asked the Pope to take our holy Society under his particular protection that it might fulfill its vocation and purpose for which it was called into being by God. We mentioned that one of the three things we wished to do was to reconcile sinners unto God through the Sacrament of Penance and to bring back those who had fallen away from the altar rail, not receiving Holy Communion anymore. That must always be a very important part of our vocation.

This is a preaching order as was expressed by the intention of the Holy Spirit in the very early days of the Fr. Founder, and if we are to bring back the wandering sheep, gone into the far country with the prodigal son wasting his substance in riotous living separated from the father's house, it must be by preaching, not necessarily from the pulpit, but by individual contact. So while we pray with fervor that the lapsed may come back to God, we must be prepared to follow the example of the Good Shepherd, leaving the ninety-nine in the fold, and going out into the mountains and the far country to seek the wandering sheep, the ones that had lapsed and fallen away, and keep on seeking until we have found and brought back the last, even though it be on our own shoulders.

To exercise this ministry we must have the love of the Good Shepherd in our hearts for the wandering sheep. One of the stories that is told of St. John, the beloved disciple who leaned on the breast of the Divine Redeemer at the Last Supper, is that in his old age he had been some time away from Ephesus and returning, he missed in the congregation one of his disciples, a young man. He inquired of the shepherds what had become of him. They told him he had lapsed, gone away, joined a company of bandits. And he reproached them for having allowed such a thing as that to happen. He went out into the mountain vastness himself, infirm with age as he was, stayed until he encountered the young man, and with the display of the shepherd's heart he prevailed over him and brought him back to Confession and Holy Communion.

Let us pray, therefore, today, not just in a general way, for the return of the lapsed to the practice of their duties as Catholics. Let us pray to the Good Shepherd to infuse more of His own love of the sheep for which He laid down His life, that we may have more apostolic zeal to grasp every opportunity given us to seek until we find.

12. Lapsed Catholics

Meditation, January 23, 1940

The multitude of Catholics these days is very great, for one beholds churches filled with communicants every Sunday, and churches filled till high noon with congregations that crowd the building to capacity. For the most part, one might assume that in that part of the Lord's vineyard, at least, there were not many lapsed Catholics, but if one went out either as a priest or as a sister religious, visiting that very section one would soon be disabused as to the idea that there are few lapsed Catholics in our great cities. They are, in fact, numbered by thousands and tens of thousands. Take the parish of St. Cecelia, New York, where we happen to be familiar through its being a center for our Sisters. The pastor was requested by the Archbishop to take a census and ascertain how many Puerto Ricans there were in that section and so our Sisters set out to canvass that section. The report was that they had visited 2000 families, i.e., Puerto Ricans alone, to say nothing about the Italians or the Spanish.

Imagine those 10,000 Puerto Ricans attending Mass on Sunday. They would flow into the streets every Sunday, and not half of them would be able to get in. But with all the Irish that are left, and the Spanish and the Italians there is plenty of room. As far as attending Mass is concerned, and approaching the Sacraments there is no better showing in the Catholic world than in America, except Ireland, perhaps. As far as Italy is concerned, I was told there that 90% of the men do not practice their religion, the women do a little better, and the same is true of France. About 10% of the people are quite pious, 90% of them are indifferentists or lapsed. So Our Lord and Our Lady looking down from heaven, must have very great grief. Jesus wept over Jerusalem because He came unto His own, and His own received Him not.

That is the trouble with the world at the present time. Take the Apocalypse in the description of the vials of the wrath of God poured out in succession on the human family. The explanation given is that the people turned away from God. It is true that the people create themselves the condition that leads to war, working out their own destruction by reason of their turning away from God. As part of the Mystical Body of Christ, we should be all one mind and heart with Christ and with our Atonement Mother. Their hearts are filled with sorrow. They desire that we share their sorrow and longing for the lapsed by prayer and penance. Jesus our great High Priest who ever liveth through the prayer He made on the Cross. Not only does He make intercession in the Holy Sacrifice of Himself, but from His throne in heaven He intercedes for them: "Father, Father, forgive them, they know not what they do," and with the father at home, the father of the prodigal in the far country who wasted his substance with riotous living, his heart went out even when he came to himself and said, "I will arise and go home to my father." He didn't have to bang at the door, or ring the door bell repeatedly, and have some servant come and place the request: "Ask if my father in," and be told that his father is out. On the contrary the father went to meet him, fell upon his neck and kissed him. Our Lord expresses His attitude towards the wandering sheep: the good shepherd who left the 90 and nine to the risk of his life and he went to seek the sheep that was lost.

So this spirit should express itself instead of resting with the situation saying: "I cannot help it, it is too bad." We must have the spirit of prayer. First we pray, then put the prayer into action as opportunity is given to us. It may be that only one soul comes particularly to our attention, and in our labors and efforts we should exert ourselves, going out seeking that very soul.

Let us therefore embrace the opportunity and privilege of this day, to pray earnestly that God will have compassion on sinners, and by the power of the Holy Spirit operating particularly in the missionaries of the cross and in those members of the Mystical Body of Christ, that they become vessels of sanctification fit for the Master's use, so that through them Christ may still carry on His mission of seeking souls and accomplish, if not the full conversion of the world, the bringing back of the multitudes who have lapsed the Sacraments. We will accomplish much. We know how wonderfully successful St. Francis was in his day when he went out to preach.

Let us offer ourselves upon the altar of sacrifice and say, "Lord, here am I. I can do nothing of myself, but with You all things are possible; and I would help fulfill the desire and the longing of the lapsed to return to penance and their God. I am at your service." We must begin by each sharing the longing of the Sacred Heart to bring back the wanderers who have fallen away from God. It must express itself in prayer.

13. Shall We Try to Convert the Jews?

The Lamp, May, 1914

Long have we prayed and much have we thought about the conversion of the Jews, who have come in such vast numbers to our shores. In greater New York alone there are over one million Jews, and as far as we know, there exists not one Catholic mission, having as its specific object the conversion of the Hebrew people, nor in fact have we heard of such a mission existing in any part of the United States. The question is whether Our Lord's command, "Go ye into the whole world and preach the gospel to every creature" (*St. Mark 16:15*) is to be regarded as a dead letter as far as the Jew is concerned. The Holy Spirit found it a hard task at the first to convince St. Peter and the Apostolic College that Christ died for the Gentile nations as well as for the Jewish race. Shall we Gentile Catholics go to the opposite extreme and act as though Our Lord did not die for the Jew at all, but for the Gentile only?

A misinterpretation of St. Paul: There seems to be a general impression abroad that it has been divinely revealed through St. Paul that the Almighty has excluded Jews from salvation until the full conversion of the Gentile world is accomplished, after which the Hebrews who are still on the earth will have a chance to be grafted again into the olive tree from which they were broken off when they rejected the Messiah and crucified the Lord of Glory. Those who labor under this impression should read very carefully the eleventh chapter of St. Paul's Epistle to the Romans, in order to get a truer impression of what the great Apostle to the Gentiles actually does teach concerning the salvation of the Jews. He begins by asking, "Hath God cast away his people? God forbid. For I also am an Israelite of the seed of Abraham, of the tribe of Benjamin. God hath not cast away his people which He foreknew. Know you not what the Scripture saith of Elias; how he calleth on God against Israel? 'Lord, they have slain Thy prophets, they have dug down Thy altars and I am left alone and they seek my life.' "

"But what is God's reply to him? 'I have kept for myself seven thousand men who have not bowed the knee to Baal.' So too at the present time there is a remnant, chosen by grace...." (*Rom*, 11: 1-5)

Now this remnant of the elect Hebrews who have believed and been saved did not become extinct when the Apostles who were Jews died, but in every succeeeding generation there has been a considerable remnant of the Hebrew people who have accepted Christ and have been grafted as living branches into the vine of Christ's Apostolic Church. Scholars well versed in Semitic ethnology tell us that Christians of Jewish lineage, especially in the countries which border on the Mediterranean, are much more numerous than is generally supposed and we have little doubt that this is true. Certain it is, that there have been notable conversions to Christianity among the Jews in every generation.

A deep-rooted fallacy: The notion which has taken deep root in the minds of so many Catholics that it is a hopeless task to try to convert a Jew belongs to a class of pernicious fallacies, which ought to be buried in the same deep hole with the oft-repeated argument against the foreign missions that there are so many heathens at home. With so little zeal manifested in their behalf, it is really a wonder that Jewish conversions to Catholicism are as numerous as they are.

We are constantly meeting with Jewish converts, or hearing about them from other priests, wherever we go. Our solitary companion for years on the Mount of the Atonement was a Jew, and he stood loyally by us, when on account of our witness to papal supremacy and infallibility our most trusted friends abandoned us.

Shall the Protestants provoke us to jealousy? On the desk before us is a letter which we have received from a Protestant Jewish Minister, working among his own people in Brooklyn.

If these Protestant Evangelists can succeed as well as they do, the Catholic missionary ought to do much better. We were conversing the other day with a former member of the New York Apostolic Mission Band, who informed us that in conducting a mission to non-Catholics in some part of New York City where the Jewish population is particularly dense, the church would be filled largely with Jewish inquirers during the mission, and this suggests the question, if we have missions to *Gentile* non-Catholics, why not also make a specialty of missions to the *Jewish* non-Catholics?

For ten years now the conversion of the Jews has been daily prayed for by members of the Rosary League of Our Lady of the Atonement, and we trust the time is not far distant when we shall begin to see some visible results of so many prayers. Meanwhile we invite a discussion of the whole question in our correspondence columns, and we shall be very grateful to any of the clergy who will employ their pen in helping us foster a deeper and most hopeful interest in a subject of such vital importance to such a vast number of souls.

14. The Jewish People

The Antidote, February, 1922

Recently the editor of *The Antidote* had occasion to write to the editor of *The Jewish Criterion,* published in Pittsburgh, Pennsylvania. Our letter seems to have appealed to the editor of that up-to-date magazine, as under date of December 30th, we find in the *Criterion* the following editorial comment: "I like to receive letters such as came to me the other day from a Friar, who resides at St. Paul's Friary in Garrison, N. Y. He writes: 'I am sending you under separate cover a sample copy of our magazine which aims to bring about a more cordial relationship between Catholics, Jews, and Protestants.' But what impressed me more than anything else was the broad way in which he closed his letter: 'I remain on the broad platform of the Fatherhood of God and Brotherhood of Man, fraternally yours, etc.' No sectarianism about that. Just a big universal religious note is struck. Some day I am going to look up the author of that letter. He is a true man of God."

We sincerely hope the editor of *The Criterion* will carry his good intention into effect and some time arrive at Graymoor, where upon ascending the Mount of the Atonement, he will find the editor of *The Antidote* ready to welcome him with outstretched hand.

He will find that other Jews, not a few, have ascended our holy Mountain before him, but in order that his astonishment in this regard may be somewhat mitigated we tell him now that one of the Friars of the Atonement, whom it will give us the greatest pleasure to introduce to him is a Lay-Brother of our community by the name of Brother Anthony, who has worn the habit of a Friar of the Atonement for twenty-one years, and every drop of blood in his veins is Jewish.

At the request of another Jewish convert to the Catholic Faith, he recently wrote an account of his acceptance of Christ as the true Messiah who came to Israel nineteen centuries ago. We are printing that account in the hope that it will interest without causing any anger in the hearts of our Jewish readers.

While the editor of *The Antidote* is glad to stand with any of his fellow men on the broad platform of the "Fatherhood of God" and "Brotherhood of Man", he takes especial satisfaction when the brother man that rubs shoulders with him happens to be a Jew. Our ancestory is Welsh, and there are some who think the Celts of Wales and of Ireland belong to the lost tribes of Israel. Whether this be so or not must, we fear, remain a speculative question. But one thing Catholic Christians have no doubt whatsoever, their spiritual descent is from Jesus, the Son of Mary, of the house and lineage of David. To go still further back we are the spiritual children of Abraham to whom the covenant promises of God were originally made, and since the Jews are of natural descent from the same Abraham, we ought to be able to recognize in them a kinship more brotherly and closer than

176

that which we claim with some other branches in the human family.

We hope that this profession of brotherhood will be no less acceptable to the Jewish Readers of *The Antidote,* when the writer goes further in the way of personal introduction, claiming a yet stronger affection for the Jews by reason of his bearing in holy religion the name of Paul, a name which originated with one of the most illustrious Jews that ever left an indelible impression upon human history.

Saul of Tarsus, or St. Paul, as we Catholics call him, was not only a Jew, but if love of his own people entitles him to their love in return, few, if any, are deserving of so much esteem on the part of the Jews as St. Paul. We do not believe that any Hebrew, of ancient or modern times, went so far as the great Christian Jew of Tarsus in his willingness "to spend and be spent to the utmost" for the benefit of the Jewish people. He was not only ready at all times to lay down his life for them, but although having been carried up in spirit to the seventh heaven and realizing in consequence all the more keenly what the bliss of heaven through eternity would be, yet for the sake of his own people he declared that he was willing to be accursed from Christ and to spend Eternity in Hell, if by that personal sacrifice he could open the eyes of his own people to see in Jesus Christ of Nazareth their Savior and Redeemer. To prove this assertion we quote his exact words as he penned them to the Jews and Gentile Christians of Rome:

"I speak the truth in Christ, I lie not, my conscience bearing me witness in the Holy Ghost: That I have great sadness, and continual sorrow in my heart.

"For I wish myself to be accursed from Christ for the sake of my brethren who are my kinship according to the flesh. Who are Israelites, to whom pertaineth the adoption of sons, and the glory, and the covenant, and the giving of the law, and the services of God, and the promises:

"Whose are the fathers, and of whom is Christ, according to the flesh, who is over all things, God blessed for ever. Amen." (*Rom 9:1-5*)

However skeptical a Jew might be as to the correctness of St. Paul's conception and belief concerning the divinity of Christ, he can hardly fail to admire the love of his own people which would inspire sentiments such as we have just quoted from his writings.

But, what profit is there to a Jew of the twentieth century in assuming as a foregone conclusion that St. Paul's miraculous conversion from the attitude of a persecutor of the Christians to a position of leadership among the Apostles of Jesus Christ was the result of a mental abberation, and was not founded upon truth?

What if St. Paul were right! Would not the Jews of today be better off both in time and eternity by discovering that after all their prophets are true as to the Messiah He was promised by them, and that He has actually come. He is now reigning with those who accepted him, whether Jew or Gentile, in the Heavenly Jerusalem so graphically described by St. John, another Jew, in the Apocalypse, the last book of the Christian New Testament, separate and apart from which the most learned of the Talmudists and Jewish Rabbis will search in vain for a satisfactory interpretation of the Old Testament, as we Christians call the Hebrew scriptures.

It will be noted in the story of the young Jewish barber related below that in his quest for Israel's Messiah, that he prayed to God of his Fathers, even to God of Abraham, Isaac, and Jacob to show him whether He whom the Christian worshipped as their Savior and their God was in reality the Messiah whom his own people had looked for during so many centuries. At the same time he promised that if it was so shown to him, he would acknowledge and follow the Messiah no matter what the cost might be.

The Editor of *The Antidote* does not doubt for a moment that if the millions of Jews in the world today, who have not found the true Messiah would address to the God of their Fathers the same prayer, that Brother Anthony did over twenty years ago, they would receive the same answer that divine providence vouchsafed to give to him.

After his baptism and profession of the Christian Faith, Brother Anthony had to run the gauntlet of his people's displeasure, some of whom were ready to disown him altogether. But all this has long ago changed and his present relations with the members of his family are thoroughly cordial; not only do they welcome him as an honored guest when he visits their homes occasionally, but they come in large numbers to the Mount of the Atonement every summer to visit him in return and of course they are always heartily welcomed.

It is certainly true that many of the Hebrew people have been deterred from making any genuine effort to discover whether Christ was truly what He claimed to be by the thought of what it would cost them did they become Christians. But let the Jewish inquirer conquer and put behind him his fear of consequences, and determine to know the truth about Christ, at any price, then his quest will result in what it has always resulted on the part of those Jews, who like Nicodemus, have discovered that Jesus, the Son of Mary, was not only the Messiah foretold by David, Isaias and Daniel, but that He was much more than another King Solomon, being in fact nothing less than Emmanuel, "God with us." Or, as St. John in his Epistle describes him: "In the beginning was the Word; and the Word was with God, and the Word was God; and the Word was made flesh and dwelt among us and we saw His glory, the glory, as it were, of the only-Begotten of the Father, full of grace and truth."

As Isaias foretold concerning Him, Christ came as a suffering Messiah because as the Lamb of God, He was to fulfill the Jewish sacrifices and be offered upon the Cross to make an Atonement for the sins of the world.

It is also true that no one can follow Him who is not willing to bear, in some form or another, the reproach of the Cross, and to be to some degree a paschal victim in union with this same suffering crucified Messiah. But St. Paul reminds us that the sufferings we incur in the following of Christ, whether we be Jews or whether we be gentiles, is as nothing in comparison with the glorious rewards, both in time and eternity, that are the inheritance of all who confess Christ and follow Him faithfully.

Let no Jew, therefore, be afraid to investigate the claims of Christ as a fulfillment of all that the prophets of the Old Testament spoke and wrote concerning the Messiah; and in order that they may the more infallibly and certainly discover in Christ the Emmanuel that should come, let them, as Brother Anthony did, earnestly entreat the God of Abraham, Isaac, and Jacob, to show them whether Jesus Christ is the true Messiah of the Jews or not.

If the end of your investigation does not bring you to your knees before the Christian altar, with the words of St. Thomas' confession upon your lips: "My Lord and my God;" it will at least be a source of gratification to you that at least you had enough love of the truth and courage to make in all sincerity an honest investigation of the claims of Christ. But should your investigation turn out as Brother Anthony's did, your happiness and good fortune will pass all understanding and last for eternity.

15. The Conversion of the Jews

Radio Broadcast, January 7, 1940

You have just been listening to the story of my first companion on the Mount of the Atonement, and you will recall the prayer he composed as a young Jew addressed to the God of Abraham, Isaac and Jacob, asking for light as to that Great Central Personality of the centuries, Jesus of Nazareth.

I wonder how many of those who are listening in at this moment have addressed a similar prayer to the God of Abraham, Isaac and Jacob about the same Personality. Again I wonder how many take the same attitude towards this all important question of another young Jew whom I conversed with on the train sometime ago between Washington and New York. He said quite frankly, "Father, I do not want to pursue that question with a view of obtaining an affirmative answer. It would cost too much of sacrifice to confess Christ as the Messias and the Savior of the world."

But it is not only the Jews who may be, by chance, listening to me this afternoon who have not as yet found the Messias and with a greater or lesser degree of uncertainty are asking the question addressed by Brother Anthony to the God of our Fathers. There are Gentiles, plenty of them, who have not yet arrived at a saving faith in Jesus Christ as the Savior and Redeemer of the world.

Only a few days ago I received a letter from a New York gentile who wrote as follows: "I am a non-Catholic. I am not a member of any Church or denomination. I have been an orphan practically all my life, and I do not know that I was ever baptized. I have tried several doctrines and have never been satsified, and now I am asking Pilate's question, 'What is truth?' In your prayers will you please ask that I be given light?"

To such, the experience of Brother Anthony ought to serve as an inspiration to do as he did.

Moses, addressing the Israelites in the desert just before his withdrawal from them to go up to the lonely mountain to die alone said, "If thou shalt seek Him with all thy heart and with all thy soul." If that was true 3500 years ago, it is true today. "If thou shalt seek the Lord Jesus as God Incarnate, the Word made Flesh, who is the Lamb of God, who offered Himself on Calvary to take away our sins and opened to us the gates of everlasting life, you will surely find Him, for all the while He is seeking you," as Francis Thompson, the great English poet, declared in the "Hound of Heaven."

Upon one occasion Jesus preached on the Sabbath in the synagogue of Capharnaum. The day before, on the mountain side, he fed 5,000 men besides women and children with five barley loaves and two small fishes, which He had blessed, broken and given to His disciples who distributed them to the multitude. After this miracle the people wished to make Him a king, but He departed from their midst and now they had followed Him across the sea and crowded the synagogue to hear Him once again.

He said to them, "Labor not for the meat that perisheth. Your Fathers did eat manna in the wilderness and are dead. I am come to give you a meat, that he that eateth of, shall live forever." But when they cried out: "Evermore give us this bread," He declared that the bread He would give them would be His Flesh, which He would give for the life of the world. "Whosoever eateth My Flesh and drinketh My Blood hath eternal life and I will raise him up at the last day."

And the people cried out, "This is a hard saying. Who can receive it?" And many who had followed Him as the Messias walked after Him no more. Then He turned to His disciples and said: "Will ye also go away?" And Saint Peter, answering, said to Him: "Lord to whom shall we go, Thou hast the Words of Eternal Life."

If you, my brethren, seek the Messias, do not turn away from Christ. You will not find the Messias anywhere else, in the past, in the present, or in the future. Saint Peter spoke truly: "Thou hast the words of eternal life."

True also was the confession he made at Caesarea Philippi: "Thou art the Christ, the Son of the Living God."

16. Letter on the Missions

The Lamp, October, 1923

You will note in the Rosary League Intentions that the Special intention for October is the Conversion of Japan. This intention was inspired by the dreadful catastrophe of a month ago when the earth suddenly opened beneath the cities of Tokyo and Yokohama and swallowed up thousands of human victims, while floods and fire destroyed tens of thousands more. A greater catastrophe of its kind has never been experienced in human history and has elicited expressions of sympathy and help for the Japanese from all the nations of the world. Along with the material help which America in particular has extended towards the afflicted people of what they themselves call "The Kingdom of the Rising Sun", it is most fitting that we should pray through our Blessed Mother of the Atonement to Almighty God to convert the hearts and intellects of the Japanese so that their eyes being opened, they may recognize in this awful visitation the hand of divine chastisement and, forsaking their false gods, embrace the religion of salvation which, until now, they have been extremely slow to accept.

Although St. Francis Xavier met with some considerable success and many conversions followed his missionary labors in Japan, a dreadful persecution broke out not long afterwards and for three hundred years scarcely a vestige of the Catholic Faith was left in the Islands. The Chinese have shown great alacrity in accepting the teachings of our Catholic Missionaries so that Catholics at the present time in the Chinese Republic aggregate two million souls whereas the Catholics of Japan number less than 100,000. Undoubtedly, it has been the characteristic pride of the Japanese and their intense materialism which has rendered them so impervious to Catholic influences, so backward in bowing beneath the scepter of Jesus Christ and His religion whose foundation stone is humility.

17. Saint Paul and the Missionary Conquest Of the World for Christ

Radio Address,
Immaculate Conception Church,
Washington, D.C., January 25, 1931

I am very happy to be here this afternoon at the conclusion of the Church Unity Octave, the eight days of prayer, which originated at Graymoor, the purpose of which is to intercede for the gathering of all Christians not of the Fold of Saint Peter into Catholic fellowship and unity in that Church which Christ Himself established when He said:

Thou art Peter and upon this rock I will build My church, and the gates of hell shall not prevail against it. (*St. Matthew 16:18*).

Yes, *His* Church which He the Truth affirmed would endure throughout all ages unto the end of the world.

The Church Unity Octave, or Chair of Unity Octave (its alternate title), begins with the Feast of the Chair of Saint Peter at Rome, January 18, and ends with that of the Conversion of Saint Paul, January 25. At the beginning of this observance in 1908, the Society of the Atonement itself was outside the Fold of Peter, being made up entirely of members of the Episcopal, or Anglican Church, who were followers of St. Francis of Assisi and observers of the rule of life for both men and women, which he established. The very first fruit of this, our apostolate, was that within a period of less than two years the entire Graymoor Society, Friars, Sisters and Tertiaries, was corporately received into the Catholic Church, in October, 1909, over twenty-one years ago. Another notable result of this Octave of Prayer followed shortly afterwards: among those who observed it each year were the Benedictine monks of the Isle of Caldey, off the coast of South Wales and the Benedictine Nuns of Milford Haven, not far distant. These two flourishing communities were a source of pride and satisfaction to the entire High Church Party in the Church of England. By divine inspiration and wonderful unanimity both these communities made petition simultaneously to Pope Pius X, gloriously reigning in the Chair of Peter, to enter the Catholic Church and they, too, were corporately received, following the precedent es-

183

tablished by the earlier submission of the Society of the Atonement.

Since then the observance of this Octave of Prayer has spread for and wide. In 1916 Pope Benedict XV by an Apostolic Brief extended its observance to the entire Catholic world.

It is interesting to note that on this particular day, the feast of Saint Paul's Conversion, and at this very hour, at the chief center of the observance of the Octave in the City of Rome, i.e., in the church of Santo Paolo alla Regula, Benediction of the Blessed Sacrament is being given by His Eminence, Cardinal Van Rossum, Prefect of the Sacred Congregation of the Propagation of the Faith, as a conclusion there of the Octave's observance; just as the same Benediction of Our Lord in the Blessed Sacrament will be given in a few moments here in the Church of the Immaculate Conception in Washington, our great Nation's capital city. It will interest you to know that this Church of San Paolo contains, in the form of a beautiful chapel, the very room which, as mentioned in the Acts of the Apostles, Saint Paul occupied for two years during his imprisonment prior to his martyrdom. In this Church on each day of the Octave different Cardinals and other distinguished prelates of Rome have given Benediction or preached.

It must be evident to all why this particular Octave was selected for united prayers for the Unity of Christian believers and the conquest of the entire world for Christ.

We recall to mind the prayer which Our Lord Jesus Christ Himself uttered in the Garden of Gethsemane after He had instituted the Blessed Sacrament in the upper room of Jerusalem on the night on which He was betrayed:

Holy Father, keep them in Thy name whom thou hast given Me; that they may be one, as We also are.

While I was with them, I kept them in thy name. Those whom thou gavest Me have I kept; and one of them is lost, but the son of perdition, that the scripture may be fulfilled.

And now I come to Thee; and these things I speak in the world, that they may have My joy filled in themselves.

I have given them Thy word, and the world hath hated them, because they are not of the world; as I also am not of the world.

I pray not that thou shouldst take them out of the world, but that thou shouldst keep them from evil.

They are not of the world, as I also am not of the world. Sanctify them in truth. Thy word is truth.

As Thou has sent Me into the world, I also have sent them into the world.

And for them do I sanctify Myself, that they also may be sanctified in truth.

And not for them only do I pray, but for them also who through their word shall believe in Me; that they all may be one, as thou, Father, in Me, and I in Thee, that they also may be one in Us; that the world may believe that thou hast sent Me. (*St. John 17:11-21*)

In this prayer of the Divine Redeemer of the world we have it clearly revealed that Unity among Christian believers is not only most desirable in itself, but it is an essential and a necessary prerequisite to the full acceptance of Christ, by the entire world, as its Savior and King and of the resultant consummation of His universal reign over the nations of the world.

Anticipating the necessity of unity among His disciples, is it not most reasonable to expect that Jesus Christ would provide an imperishable center or Rock of Unity in that Kingdom or Church, which He Himself set up and established among men on earth? This kingdom is figured in the prophecy of Daniel as a stone cut by no human hand out of the mountainside and growing until it gradually filled with its presence and power the whole earth.

Yes, to all men endowed with the supernatural gift of the Catholic Faith, it is as obvious as the sun shining in the midst of a cloudless sky that Jesus Christ provided for His Church a center of Unity in the person of Saint Peter, His first Vicar, and ever afterwards in his successors, the Bishops of Rome.

The charter, or constitution of Christ's Church is clearly outlined in the Holy Gospels and even more particularly the headship and authority of Saint Peter. Very briefly let me recall to your mind the famous words of Christ to Saint Peter after he had confessed His divinity at Caesaria Phillippi:

Jesus answering said to him: Blessed art thou, Simon Bar-Jona; because flesh and blood hath not revealed it to thee, but My Father who is in heaven.

And I say to thee: That thou art Peter and upon this rock I will build My Church, and the gates of hell shall not prevail against it.

And I will give to thee the keys of the Kingdom of Heaven. And whatsoever thou shalt bind upon the earth, it shall be bound also in Heaven; and whatsoever thou shalt loose on earth, it shall be loosed in Heaven. (*St. Matt. 16: 17-19*)

In these words our Divine Lord gave to the head of His Church and his successors, the power of governing, controlling and directing His Kingdom, and just prior to His crucifixion promised to Saint Peter the divine assistance and special illumination of the Holy Ghost, in order that he might always know and declare the truth and so protect the Church from error. The last occasion was His discourse at the Paschal Supper, when He said to the Apostles: "Satan hath desired to have you, that he may sift you as wheat." Then fixing His gaze full upon Peter, he added: "But I have prayed for thee, that thy faith fail not; and thou, being once converted, confirm thy brethren." (*St. Luke 22: 31-32*)

Not in Peter alone, but for nineteen long centuries has this prayer been marvelously fulfilled in his successors the Roman Pontiffs. The faith is always being assailed, Satan is constantly seeking to sift the successors of the Apostles as wheat, but invariably it is the Roman Pontiffs who confirm and strengthen their brethren, the Catholic Bishops in communion with the Apostolic See.

"Feed My lambs, feed My lambs, feed My sheep." In these words Christ gave to Saint Peter universal jurisdiction to feed and rule both the lambs and sheep of his flock, not alone during his own lifetime, but until the end of time in the person of his successors.

Thus did our Lord provide for unity among His disciples and the touchstone of Catholic Unity has ever remained and ever will remain, *The Rock of Peter.* A hundred conflicting voices in this generation cry out to Christian men, each propounding a theory and doctrine concerning the divisions of Christendom, and each with a remedy for the healing thereof. But the Son of God, to whom the Father Almighty has given all authority and power in heaven and on earth has, as we have shown, Himself, established the center of Unity and that center

186

is none other than the Chair of Saint Peter at Rome. Against that mighty see the gates of hell have not ceased to lift themselves up in repeated assaults for well nigh on two thousand years, and still the words of Christ remain operative, for the Rock of Peter on which He built His Church in union with Himself is the Rock of Ages and it still stands like Gibraltar, for the gates of hell *have not prevailed.*

In our own day and generation we beheld the watchful Shepherd of Christ's flock strike at a new heresy, that of Modernism which, like a honeycomb of decay, was threatening to undermine the very foundations of the Church. But with the authority given him by Christ, the great Pope Pius X struck so effectively that the menace was swept completely out of the Catholic Church, and within her borders Modernism is dead.

Let no man, however, despise the power of Satan. Lucifer was hurled by Saint Michael from the battlements of heaven, but he fights on desperately still and the history of Christianity demonstrates his tremendous power and subtlety, fallen angel though he is.

After His resurrection from the dead, Jesus meets seven of His Apostles on the shores of the Sea of Galilee, provides them with food, eats with them in the early morning hour, and then elicits from Saint Peter a three-fold confession of love and fealty, thus offsetting his three-fold denial on the night before the Crucifixion. Then Our Lord restores them to divine favor and at the same time gives him the commission to rule and govern His flock in the words we quoted a moment ago: "Feed My lambs, feed My Lambs, feed My sheep."

It was the will of Jesus Christ that the Christian faith should be propagated through the world by missionary labors and preaching. Assembling His disciples around Him before His ascent into Heaven, He breathed on them saying:

Receive ye the Holy Ghost. (*St. John 20:22*)

Going therefore, teach ye all nations; baptizing them in the name of the Father, and of the Son, and of the Holy Ghost,

Teaching them to observe all things whatsoever I have commanded you; and behold I am with you all days, even to the consummation of the world. (*St. Matthew 28: 19-20*)

Greatest among the first apostolic missionaries was Saint

187

Paul, whom Our Lord converted by an apparition of Himself on the road to Damascus, which event changed him from a persecutor of the Christians to the foremost Apostle of the Gentiles.

This day is the annual festival commemorating that wonderful conversion and it fittingly concludes the Church Unity Octave—for did not Christ pray that His disciples might all be one "that the world might believe", that is, accept His Messiahship? The Chair of Saint Peter at Rome is the center of Unity and only through communion with the Apostolic See and under the blessing and power of Saint Peter's successors will the missionaries of the Cross of Christ, among whom Saint Paul still stands forth as the greatest, accomplish the tremendous commission of converting the entire world to Christ.

Let us glance backward for a moment to see how the great enemy of salvation has hindered and retarded the conversion of the world by creating divisions among Christians, thereby leading them into heresy and schism. However, the vastness of the subject and the brevity of time allotted, compel me to confine my survey to one part of the world, let it be the Near East. The first countries to be evangelized were Palestine, Syria, Northern Egypt and Greece, with such great cities as Jerusalem, Antioch, Alexandria, Ephesus, Athens and later, Constantinople. In the Book of the Apocalypse we read of "the seven Churches of Asia." The first Christian emperor, Constantine, upon his conversion changed the name of ancient Byzantium into that of Constantinople and made it the Eastern capital of the Roman Empire. Then Satan began at once his work of division by raising up a succession of heresiarchs there in the East, beginning with Arius, who denied the divinity of Christ. One after another these were dealt with by the successors of Saint Peter, the Popes of Rome, supported by a series of councils, general or provincial. As a result, heresies and their founders were continuously cast out from the Church, but each one represented a schism or sect that often persisted for many years, even centuries, and some remain in the East even to this very day.

Then politics also, especially Eastern ambition and jealousy of the West, ecclesiastical and material, played its part, backed up by the civil power of the Eastern Emperors, and finally with the Patriarch of Constantinople as its head, the entire East refused to any longer acknowledge the supreme jurisdiction of the

Successor of Saint Peter, and so lapsed into the Great Schism of the tenth century.

This was followed a few centuries later by a terrible disaster to Christianity in the East. The Mohammedan power rose up, finally captured Constantinople and subjugated the whole Christians East to one of the cruelest and most relentless persecutions to which any portion of Christendom has ever been subjected. In choosing Caesar rather than Christ's Vicar to rule over them, they chose Caesar's domination.

Later, came the missionary conquest of the Slavs, a people in Northern Europe occupying a territory of enormous extent stretching from the Balkans and Galicia, northward and eastward through Russia and Siberia to the Pacific Ocean. The first missionaries to the Slavs were Saints Cyril and Methodius. Both of them were in communion with Rome and received the blessing and sanction of Saint Peter's successor for their missionary labors. But ultimately the Czar, Peter the Great, and the succeeding Russian rulers chose to accept missionaries from the schismatic Patriarch of Constantinople, thus affiliating ecclesiastically their nation, if nation it could then be called, with the separated East, and the most gigantic schismatic Church of modern times was born! As was to be expected, the Russian Czars actually declared themselves head of this national Church and claimed the prerogatives of Saint Peter himself.

It is a curious analogy that the capital city of the Czars was named Saint Petersburg, the city of Saint Peter; the Czar himself was clothed in white, the color worn by the successor of Saint Peter at Rome, and he became to Holy Russia the "Great White Father" and Supreme head of its Church. This body called the Orthodox Church claims to be the only true Church of Christ and maintains that it has succeeded to the commission and jurisdiction originally conferred by Our Lord upon Saint Peter. To return to these strange analogies, let me say, last of them all, that the house of the reigning family bore the name of Romanoff.

But when this mighty church, which all through her existence relentlessly persecuted Catholics within her realm, was at the very acme of her pride and power, like a thunderbolt out of the sky, came the downfall of the Czar and the extinction of the Romanoff dynasty. But upon this ruin has risen up within the last fourteen years a most sinister and terrifying manifestation

189

of the power of evil; in fact it would seem as though the "man of sin," that mysterious personage mentioned by Saint Paul, and foretold in the Apocalypse, has all but become incarnate in these latter days. I refer to the Soviet administration, the communistic government which rules Russia at this time. Since the fall of the Czar, the great Russian people have suffered an agony and a torture of bloodshed similar to that of the first ten persecutions of the early Church.

Industrially, the present government of Russia is preying upon its own children; men are being forcibly drafted and sent to far distant mines and farms to labor and toil as slaves—for that is what it amounts to. It is only a question of a short time when the same drafting will take place for women, for the government propaganda is already preparing the minds of the people, and public opinion of other countries, for this terrible procedure.

I say that this is the greatest danger that has threatened civilized Christendom within its past of nineteen hundred years. In Russia God is defied, religion is declared to be the "dope of the people" and "atheism" their emancipation. Let us fear lest this red plague spread within our own borders.

It has been characteristic of every departure from the Catholic faith, that nations fall by degrees, they begin and then keep on denying the faith in increasing ration until that faith within their borders is dead. I trace back through Soviet propaganda to the Protestant Reformation as the former's cause. We are now beholding its culmination, an abyss! History has noted the cause's development through all the stages of a rationalism which rejected not only Catholicism, but the Bible which the reformers declared in the sixteenth century to be "The only basis of religion". I repeat the early apostacy of the so-called Reformation lies at the basis of Bolshevism and its embryo. But behind Sovietism, in the background of that terror is Satan himself, the great enemy of our salvation, Lucifer, fallen from heaven, but fighting desperately because he knows that his days are numbered upon earth.

The only hope of Christian civilization today is the Catholic Church with her three hundred million souls, (1931) united with the Apostolic See. There only, is the answer to, and fulfillment of Our Lord's Prayer that "they might be one", one in their faith, one in their charity, one in their hope of eternal life.

We send out an appeal to our separated brethren, who are Christians, and who love our Lord Jesus Christ as Lord and Master, to search their consciences and to study the scriptures and the history of Christianity throughout the ages in order that they may ascertain if it not be true that Christ founded a Church, provided it with His own vicar, gave him His own supreme authority over His flock, and told him to rule and govern them with love and fidelity through His successors unto the end of time.

So let me from this pulpit say to all, such as far as my voice will reach over this radio, *that our Lord, Jesus Christ Himself has revealed the center of unity* that He has set up in the Eternal City on the Seven Hills of Rome where the successors of Saint Peter, the Popes, have reigned over the universal church for nineteen hundred years. Our Lord's words will never fail: "Thou art Peter and upon this Rock I will build My Church, and the gates of hell shall not prevail against it."

It may not be possible for some of you, our separated brethren, to at once get back into visible communion with the Apostolic See, but you can have the desire and you can be loyal in your hearts to the voice of Christ's Vicar; you can cooperate with him, listen when he speaks, and pray for the day when all barriers being taken away, the words of Christ shall be fulfilled:

> And other sheep I have, that are not of this fold; them also I must bring, and they shall hear my voice, and there shall be one fold and one shepherd. (*St. John* 10:16)

And when that prophecy is fulfilled, then the hour of Christ's triumph shall have come and with it the consummation of all things.

There are a thousand million people neither Catholic nor non-Catholic in the great continents of Asia and Africa, and work was prospering in the missionary conquest of these countries; the Chinese had a desire to hear of Christ, and likewise the Indians, but the efforts of the power that is desperately struggling to rule China and striving to subjugate India, the Communism that issues from Russia has made it very evident that a death struggle is going on, and whether paganism or Christianity shall be dominant only God knows.

Oh, then let us, by our prayers, hasten that day when all who believe in Our Lord God shall be united with the Apostolic

See of Rome. Then only shall Christendom be strong enough to throw down, dissipate and scatter this last onslaught of the satanic power and hasten the day when all Asia and Africa, as well as Europe, America and the islands of the sea shall confess with one voice, Christ as their King, their Lord and their Redeemer!

18. Extending the Church

Sermon, October 24, 1937

When the Savior of the world was looking forward to His Passion and death on Mount Calvary, He exclaimed: "A grain of wheat, except it die, abideth alone, but if it die, it bringeth forth much fruit." When the late William Jennings Bryan visited the pyramids of Egypt, there was placed in his hands a few grains of wheat that had lain dormant beside an Egyptian mummy for two thousand years, and the great commoner expressed the thought that if those few grains of wheat had been cast into the soil and allowed to multiply themselves, first the blade, then the ear, then after that the full corn in the ear, and the process of sowing and reaping had continued year after year until this present time, then the offspring from those original grains of wheat would now be sufficient to feed the teeming millions of the earth.

Our Lord, Himself, is the grain of wheat, who died, and then reproduced Himself, first of all in the Apostles, and then through their missionary labors in an ever-increasing multitude of the Faithful, each of whom is a grain of wheat, sprung from the loins of the Christ, who died and rose again. The baptized constitute the Mystical Body of Christ. They are bone of His bone and flesh of His flesh, and as Christ, the Head of the Church, as a grain of wheat, fell into the ground that He might increase and multiply Himself in His elect, it is incumbent upon these same grains of wheat that sprung from Him to carry on the process of propagating the seed of God, the sons and daughters of the Atonement.

We know that before He ascended up into Heaven, Christ committed the missionary extension of His Church to His Apostles. "As the Father hath sent Me, so I send you. Go ye into

192

all the world. Make disciples of all nations, baptizing them in the name of the Father and of the Son and of the Holy Ghost." As Christ Himself was consumed after He had once become the Son of Man, taking humanity into union with the Godhead, so every member of His Mystical Body should be inflamed with this same desire and should be willing to make the same sacrifice of himself that Christ made. And as it cost Him His life to reproduce, increase and multiply the members of His Mystical Body, so it is incumbent upon His priests and the faithful to become missionaries and to be willing, in the process, to lay down their lives that through their deaths they may generate, multiply and increase the seed of the elect. When the mother of the sons of Zebedee asked for her two sons, James and John, that they might sit, one on His right hand and the other on His left hand in His Kingdom, Jesus said: "You know not what you ask. Can you drink of the cup that I shall drink and be baptized with the baptism that I am baptized with?" And they answered Him: "We are able." And He warned His disciples that they would be required to do the same thing, and with the exception of St. John, everyone died a martyr's death. And St. John went through the cauldron of burning oil, which to all intents and purposes ought to have made him a martyr, but God intervened and prolonging his life, because the infant Church needed his presence a longer time on earth.

The principal agency by which the laity do their part in the propagation of the faith and the increase and multiplication of the regenerate children of God is through marriage. And when a Catholic man and woman unite and join themselves together at the altar rail, they ought to understand that the chief purpose of their coming together is that they might jointly fulfill the divine command to increase and multiply the seed of the Atonement, the children of Israel into the promised land that they might increase and multiply and fill it with the seed of Abraham. So will God fulfill the covenant He made with the faithful that He would multiply their seed until they would become in numbers as the stars in Heaven or the sands of the seashore. And to the spiritual "Israel" each has a duty to contribute his share towards hastening the day when the proclamation of the Angel will be fulfilled and declared before the throne of God: "The kingdoms of this world have become the Kingdoms of Christ, the Lord's Anointed."

It is for this reason that the Catholic Church so strongly opposes the modern propaganda of race suicide, under the specious nomenclature of birth control. Of course, especially for the mothers, there is the principal sacrifice of laying down their lives for their offspring. We know that the process of childbirth is painful and sometimes fatal to the mother. I was in the office of a manufacturer in New York the other day and he showed me upon the wall a fine picture of his beautiful wife and a group of four children, and he knew as well as I that the bringing forth of those children had been too much for her weak heart and she had passed to the Lord two years previously. Our Savior says: "A woman, when she is in travail, hath sorrow, but, when she has been delivered, she remembereth no more the sorrow, for joy that a man is born into the world."

One of the arguments for small, restricted families, which prevails even among Catholics in our day, is that the cost of feeding, clothing and educating children is so great, that they are justified in restricting the number to two or three at the most. But Catholic parents, if they have the spirit of Christ and His desire to lay down His life that the redeemed may live, will willingly make the sacrifice which the production of a large family must impose on them.

But, whereas marriage is the principal agency through which the layfolk fulfill the divine command to increase and multiply the seed of the Atonement until the regenerate fill the land, they have not discharged their full duty by begetting sons and daughters unto God and having large families. They still must have some share in the evangelization of the world in carrying out Christ's Command: "Go ye into all the world, preach the gospel to every creature, and make disciples of all nations."

It is the special office of the priests and the religious men and women to become missionaries in all lands, but, when some of our American young men enroll themselves in a missionary society like that at Maryknoll, and the young women enroll in the Maryknoll Sisterhood, there is still the problem how they are going to be supported. When they go to China, Japan or Korea they will need money to build houses, churches, and hospitals. and they look back to the faithful at home and the faithful have their opportunity to share in the work of propagating the Faith by making a sacrifice of the money which they have earned, or which has come to them perhaps in meagre fashion, by contributing to the work. That is the divinely ordained economic way by which those that stay at home can still do their part in obedience to the divine command: "Go ye unto all the world, preach the Gospel to every creature."

In the great World War, when America sent 2,000,000 of her sons across the sea, there was plenty for the American citizens that remained behind to do in what was supposed to be a battle to make the world safe for democracy. The gospel of self-denial and saving was not only preached by Mr. Hoover, but it was practiced by the people. They had meatless days and restricted diet in order that they might contribute more to the support of the soldiers on the battle front. Liberty bonds were purchased by the millions that the money might finance the American armies abroad, and all was done with enthusiasm and gladness out of the spirit of patriotism. So the Catholic faithful ought to make the sacrifice gladly and endeavor like Christ to be the grain of wheat fallen into the ground that He might live in a multitude of grains of wheat, propagated through the process of death and sacrifice, we all ought, whether we are priests or whether we are layfolk, by cooperation with the Holy Ghost to be filled with apostolic zeal for the conversion of the world, even the point of laying down our lives.

A missionary in Alaska was telling me about the salmon that came in from the sea in the spring of every year to spawn and they seek, for the purpose, high waters near the source of the Yukon; filled with that great desire to propagate their kind, they go up the river impelled by the spirit of sacrifice. Sometimes they encounter a powerful and almost irresistible rapids or water falls, obstructing and opposing their further advance, but in their determination, throwing themselves against the tide, cutting their bodies upon the sharp rock and mingling their blood with the water of the river. So fierce is their eagerness to get to the place of spawning that they leap six feet into the air on the way up the river. Yet, perhaps they know by instinct that when they have delivered the spawn, the price at which they will multiply their own kind by tens and hundreds of thousands, even millions is that they will never go back to the ocean. They will die—but young salmon will rush down with the flow of waters into the sea, and multiplying their numbers ten thousand times ten thousand. That same spirit ought to actuate not only

195

the bishops, priests, and the religious, seeking to propagate the faith throughout the world, but the layfolk, particularly those who have not been called to the married state and therefore cannot propagate the faith by bringing forth children in matrimony. They ought to be moved by a great spirit of sacrifice, as for instance paying the ransom price of Chinese babies, rescuing them from the dunghill, having them baptized and brought into the Kingdom of God through the missionary fathers and sisters.

No doubt many, if not all of you, have heard of Matt Talbot, the Irish working man who lived a life of such frugality that, although his earnings were so limited, he practised such self-denial in his personal expenses that he actually contributed large sums of money to the missions through the Society of the Propagation of the Faith.

Perhaps you have never heard about John Reid, who was instrumental in building the preparatory college of St. John's on the Mount of the Atonement, whose parental home was a mere shack on the outskirts of Waterbury, Conn., and when he was a boy heard the first Mass celebrated in that city, which is perhaps the most Catholic city in the United States, having a Catholic population of 75 per cent. John Reid carried economy to such an extent that he never even purchased a box of paper at the stationers, but wrote his letters on yellow sheets torn out of an old ledger that had been in the family from his boyhood. On one occasion some friends called to see him in the evening. There was burning, upon the table, a kerosene lamp and while they were engaged in conversation he blew out the lamp and talked in the dark to save the kerosene. Such were his penurious practices that he had the reputation of being a miser and when he died and we sent one of our fathers and a brother over to arrange for the funeral, his fellow citizens of Waterbury, who carried his body to the grave, asked that they be paid what they would lose by being absent from their jobs; "For," said they, "this old miser doesn't deserve that we should lose a day's pay to carry him to the grave." Yet he had contributed thousands of dollars out of his savings to propagate the faith in India and China, as well as at home in the missions among the colored people and the Indians, and, as we said a moment ago, built St. John's College, on the Mount of the Atonement, for the education of young men for the priesthood.

When he came to make a visit to us he did not take a railroad train from Waterbury to New York, but he would travel all night by trolley and appear early in the morning in time for Mass, all to save the carfare, the trolley across the country being a more economical way of travel. One morning, having arrived in this manner, when we were sitting alone together, he thrust his hand into his inner coat pocket and pulled out a roll of money and passing it over to the Father General of the Society of the Atonement he said: "I have just sold part of my farm to an ice company and this is the price they paid for the land. Here it is. I have not kept a dollar for myself."

The foreign missions ought to appeal to us American Catholics with particular eloquence and forcefulness. When there was the great apostasy from the Church in the sixteenth century and millions fell away from the Catholic communion, going into the various sects and heresies, that loss was offset by the discovery of the Western hemisphere, and in a very short time Franciscans, Dominicans, and other missionaries sent out from Spain, Italy and Portugal, converted all of South America and Mexico. They were in the process of converting North America, covered by the United States and Canada, when the coming of the colonists from Protestant England interfered with that process of conversion as far, at least, as the United States was concerned. A single missionary in Mexico baptized as many as one hundred thousand of the native Indians and St. Francis Solano rivaled in his missionary labors the work of St. Francis Xavier in India—with this difference—that the conversion of India was only partly accomplished, whereas South America was almost entirely converted to the faith.

V

Our Lady and Unity

FATHER PAUL *wrote and spoke much about our Blessed Mother. He rejoiced on her feast days, such as the Annunciation, the Assumption, the Immaculate Conception, and the Mediatrix of All Graces. But the feast and devotion dearest to his heart was that which he began, together with Mother Lurana: Our Lady of the Atonement. It was on this theme that his tongue and pen found frequent and eloquent expression, as he urged the members of his religious families and, indeed, all Catholics, to a deeper appreciation of devotion to the Mother of God under her holy title of the Atonement.*

In this section we have chosen the words of Father Paul which deal chiefly with Mary as patroness of Unity. He stressed her role in the mystery of Calvary when she shared in the redemptive sacrifice of her beloved Son. But he also emphasized, and even more, the role of Mary in uniting souls to God. In both aspects of this spiritual motherhood, Mary is Our Lady of the Atonement. The Graymoor founder was fond of saying that Our Lady of the Atonement means Our Lady of Reconciliation and Unity—or Our Lady of the At-one-ment. She is the model of the soul's union with God. She is the Heavenly Patroness of Christian Unity through whom her separated children will come to true religious unity in the one true fold of the Good Shepherd.

The Friars and Sisters of the Atonement joyfully celebrate the feast of Our Lady of the Atonement on July 9th, the anniversary of that day in the life of Fr. Paul when he discovered the name Atonement. In 1893, in St. John's Church, Kingston, New York, he opened the New Testament and read this verse from St. Paul: "We joy in God through Our Lord Jesus Christ by whom we have now received the Atonement." (Rom. 5:11—King James Version)

The Graymoor Religious seek to promote and increase devotion to Our Lady under the Atonement title, by means of the Rosary League, founded in 1901 at Graymoor and directed by the Sisters, and through the League of Prayer for Unity, conducted by the Friars, which received papal approval in 1956. Both communities strive to fulfill the words of Fr. Paul in their personal lives and in their apostolate: "It has profoundly impressed us that our mission is not only to preach Christ Crucified, but also to promote and extend devotion to Our Lady of the Atonement ... until a vast number of the faithful shall be united with Our Lady, Our Mother in Heaven, in the work of prayer and intercession for the conversion of the whole world to Christ, so that the Passion and Atoning Sacrifice of our Divine Redeemer may be made effectual to the fullest extent in the salvation of souls and in the completion of the number of God's elect."

1. The First Writing on Our Lady of the Atonement

Rose Leaves, October, 1901

The Blessed Virgin is known among Catholics by many names and is invoked under many different titles. Among these are the following: Our Lady of Loretto, Our Lady of Lourdes, Our Lady of Grace and Our Lady of Mercy. In her wonderful condescension and love the Mother of God has been pleased to reveal herself to the Children of the Atonement under a new name, thus giving remarkable evidence that the honor, love and prayers addressed to her, as Our Lady of the Atonement, she is graciously pleased to accept.

We have every reason to believe that the Blessed Virgin specially loves this title—that links her name with that of Jesus in the glorious work of the Atonement wrought upon the cross. It must bring to her remembrance that blessed Atonement Day when she stood by the Cross of Jesus and heard Him say to her, "Woman, behold thy Son," and to the disciple whom He loved, "Behold thy Mother." Then too, Atonement speaks of reconciliation, pardon, peace, of the fulfillment of the prayer first breathed by her divine Son, so often repeated by herself, that all Christian believers might be one.

Can we invoke the Blessed Virgin with a title more apt to touch her maternal heart than the one which associates her with Calvary's sacrifice and proclaims her the compassionate Mother of us poor sinners, redeemed by the Precious Blood of Jesus?

Hail Mary of the Atonement, my Lord's Mother and mine, pray for me and all who thus invoke thee now and at the hour of our death. Amen.

2. Our Lady and Our Vocation

Retreat Notes, March, 1907

The Catholic Church, with an unerring instinct, has cried down through the centuries: Holy Mary, intercede for us. As the following of Our Lord means union with the sacrifice of His

Atonement, so the following of the Blessed Mother means following her in the way of prayer. So closely are the two, Jesus and Mary, united that her prayer is always the echo of the Sacred Heart's desire. So ought it to be in a degree with us. We should desire what God desires to bestow. And we should have a greater faith in this principle of prayer: "Ask and you shall receive, knock and it shall be opened to you." The reason the great gift of prayer has been granted to man is because of love, for love ever desires to bestow gifts upon the object loved. Therefore, to ask belovingly in accordance with the divine will is certainly to receive. What a mighty instrument! So often we wear ourselves out thinking that all depends upon our hands and our heads, but prayer puts us in touch with tremendously efficient agencies, perhaps the minds and hearts of innumerable angels and human beings like ourselves. So even if our energies and efforts are sanctioned and dedicated ones, we can, by prayer, bring more pressure to bear upon the world hidden away from it, than going into it, with the prowess of an angel of light. Remember Moses on the mountain top. Let us realize the necessity of uniting our prayer, with Our Lady, for the furtherance of the great aims God has placed upon our hearts.

Consider the unselfishness of the Blessed Virgin's prayer. It was a request for someone else, so if we would please God, after praying for ourselves only that we may be conformed to the Divine Image and made perfect instruments in His hands, and these are not selfish prayers, then let us pray for others, bearing their needs before the throne of God. Oh may He show us more of that necessary part of perfection—the spirit of prayer. It is a very absolutely necessary part of our vocation. We started out at the beginning of our retreat, begging that we may, as a fruit of these days, grow in the way of prayer. Here the Child of God is differentiated from the child of the world for the latter cares not, believes not in prayer.

Said Our Lady: "Whatsoever He saith unto you, do it." She, who we hear inculcating obedience, is the obedient handmaid of the Lord. Let us consider the principle of authority. We become efficient servants in proportion as we reverence and yield obedience to those over us, and not just to the one remotely over us but to all who believe that one can transmit the claim to our obedience.

Our Lady was obedient first to God and by perfect obedience, we see her with a very real authority over the Christ Child's human nature. And now she is in Heaven, the Mother of that Sacred Humanity. The servants obeying Our Lady's word to hear her Son's command become efficient instruments in the working out of the great miracle.

Now we are servants and, in a very real way, Our Lady says to us: "Whatever He says unto you, do it." If we are self-willed and disobedient to authority we will wreck the work given us to do. Always must we work with deference to the will of those over us, if we are to assist in the turning of water into wine for the quenching of the world's thirst. Remember the self-will of Martin Luther and the wreck his disobedience wrought.

We have a very delicate and arduous task to perform, and only God knows how it is to be worked out. This, however, we do know, that God has given us gracious promises, and He has said that we shall *Repair the Breach*. Now, our Lady of the Atonement is the head of this movement. It is she who will assist us to know God's will and the manner of its performance. There is no confusion that we need fear her. Let us wait quietly the action of our superiors, knowing that we shall help best, by following those over us. We need not fear, as I said, a conflict between God's will and that of those over us.

Remember that authority is generally mediatory, coming down to us, that is, from God most certainly, but through those directly set over us. Protestantism, the spirit of contradiction and of making difficulties to every command must be purged out. Then God will bless our work and we shall see, in the beautiful working out of our tasks and labors, the continued miracle under our very hands of the turning of the water into wine. If we have not the spirit of submission to those over us, our work will be far worse than in vain, and we shall be most wretched and unhappy.

Let us renew in this votive Mass of Our Lady of the Atonement our resolutions, especially that one to "keep close behind" as Jesus goes to Jerusalem to perfect His Atonement. So shall we be able to convert the water into wine.

3. Devotion to Mary

Rose Leaves, May, 1908

I think you will agree with me that the individual members of the Rosary League are not all as enthusiastic and zealous for the propagation of devotion to the Mother of God, as we will say the Christian Scientists (falsely so-called) are for the spread of the anti-Christ cult of Mary Baker Eddy. A boy in Sunday school was asked by his teacher whether his father was a Christian. The lad replied rather dubiously: "Yes, I suppose so, but he is not working at it just now." The object of the Rosary League of Our Lady of the Atonement is according to the constitutions "to promote among Anglo-Catholics an increase of true devotion to the Holy Mother of God, thereby helping to win back for our glorious Lady her 'dowry' in the homes and hearts of American and English Christians, that Mary's Anglican children may once more become renowned throughout Christendom for the love and honor they show to the Blessed Virgin." Surely this is a splendid object for missionary endeavor. But, my fellow Rosarians, how hard are we working at it just now?

The origin of the use of the Rosary, as a popular Catholic devotion, was the campaign of St. Dominic against the Albigensians and other heretics of seven hundred years ago, and it was marvellously successful; and down through the centuries since many notable victories for the Catholic faith and the Catholic Church have been gained by means of the Rosary. And those in the Anglican Church, who have a true zeal for God and the Catholic Religion, can hardly do better in the present perilous times than to follow the example set us by that Sleuth-hound of Christ and of Mary, who pursued to their death the popular heresies of his day.

After the breach with Rome in the sixteenth century, the two truths which the Devil struck at most strongly in the English Church were the worship of Christ in the Mass and devotion to the Blessed Mother of God. In the present time, when the walls of the vineyard are being assaulted by those from within, who seek through "open pulpit" canons and other devices to let into the Church by wholesale heretical teachers who scorn a sacrificial priesthood and deny a supernatural religion, we ought to recognize, with clearest vision, that increased devotion to Jesus, present in the Mass and to the Holy Rosary of Our Lady, are the two principal weapons by which we resist the gates of hell and confound the wicked one. Therefore, awake, members of the Rosary League, to the vast importance of extending on all sides the use of the Rosary among Anglo-Catholics. Do not be discouraged at the difficulties of the enterprise, for even mountains can be moved by faith. In season and out of season preach the crusade of the Holy Rosary and presently we shall reap a generous harvest of converts to the League, "if we faint not". Let us hear from you individually in reply to this letter and may God and Our Lady strengthen you to battle for Catholic Truth.

4. Pray to Our Lady

Rose Leaves, October, 1908

The purpose of this series of letters is to stir you up to a livelier zeal in propagating devotion to God through the Mother of God by means of the most holy Rosary. If we would make our neighbor holier and more religious, we must persuade him to *pray more* and it was for this very purpose that Divine Providence placed in our hands the Rosary. In using the Rosary ourselves and persuading others to follow in this regard, our pious example, we are not venturing on a new experiment that may, in the end, prove an utter failure. On the contrary we have the experience of millions of Christians who, generation after generation have been using this instrument of prayer with all kinds of happy and blessed results for a period of no less than seven hundred years. The Catholic Church, which our Lord in the person of St. Peter and the Blessed Apostles promised to guide into all truth, has learned by rich and manifold experience to set such store by the Rosary as not only to dedicate the entire month of October to its honor, but during the forty days of Lent and the month of May and in fact all seasons of the year, the faithful are encouraged to its constant and ever increasing use.

The wisdom of the Church in this is manifest to none more than to those Rosarians who have grown by long practice most expert and spiritually skillful in the use of Mary's beads. It is only those, who are altogether ignorant themselves of its wonderful capacity for engaging the whole body, soul and spirit of man in devotion to God, that contemptuously speak of the Rosary as something that was invented in the dark ages as a prayer device for people who did not know how to read. As a matter of fact, the Rosary in the hand of an expert, in the art of mental prayer, is an instrument of wireless telegraphy by which the soul is put into communication with those sublime intelligences which encompass the throne of God. When Cardinal Gibbons, for his familiar walks through the streets of Baltimore, I am told, carries his Rosary in his hand; and we can well imagine how it helps him to keep his thoughts fixed upon heavenly things, while like the Blessed Virgin in the days of her earthly life, he ponders in his heart upon the mysteries of revealed truth.

I hope our Rosarians are something more than parrots when they recite their beads. While you tell the beads in your hand and with your lips repeat the Hail Mary and the Sacred Name of Jesus, try to cultivate more and more the spirit of interior recollection, always meditating upon some one of the joyful, sorrowful or glorious mysteries, until God the Holy Spirit has taken you down into their fathomless depths and flooded your soul with their wondrous light. I am sure as each one of you grows in the knowledge of how to use his Rosary, he will become more zealous in communicating its hidden treasure to his neighbor.

5. On Mount Calvary

Our Lady of the Atonement and St. John occupy the foremost place among the sacred personages who stood beneath the cross on Good Friday. "Seven times He spoke seven words of love" and the third occasion among the mystical seven can never be forgotten by His bride, the Church, "Woman, behold thy Son—Behold thy Mother." Henceforth the Mother of Jesus Crucified is to be our Lady of the Atonement, the Mother of all the elect of Christ, the Children of the New Covenant in His Blood. This third saying from the cross was too important for the commonwealth of redeemed humanity not to be recorded in the Gospels. Next to the unspeakable gift of Himself for our salvation, the most sublime legacy of the dying Redeemer was His own Mother to the Sons and Daughters of the Atonement. Of such vast concern was this gift of Mary to all believers that the

Incarnate Word of God Himself published it from the pulpit of the Cross.

But when Christ rose from the dead, the evangelists do not thrust the Mother of God forward into the limelight of publicity. The veil is drawn before the Holy of Holies, they tell us of the Lord's appearance to Mary Magdalene, St. Peter, and to the rest of the Apostles and the holy women, but not a word about the meeting after His Resurrection of Jesus and Mary. It was too sacred, even to be witnessed by Peter, James and John or Mary of Salome. Yet tradition confirms what has seemed most fitting to the pious instinct of all Catholics, whether of the Orient or of the Occident, the first appearance of the Risen Lord was to His Blessed Mother.

The sword of sorrow transfixed her Immaculate Heart on Mount Calvary; she shared the agony of His passion much more than the beloved disciple who leaned on His breast at the Last Supper, more than the other Mary's, or Nicodemus, or Joseph of Arimathea. It was fitting that in a sanctuary apart from the maddening crowd, like the cell where the Arch-angel found her praying and in whose privacy "the Holy Ghost came upon her and the power of the highest overshadowed her," she should quaff alone with her Divine Son, now risen and glorified, the cup of His unutterable joy and gladness, that those two sacred Hearts should beat with a single throb, their souls mingle into one.

How apt and beautiful, then, is it not to observe the novena of Our Lady of the Atonement at the very time we are approaching Easter. What a favorable occasion on which to approach the Mother of Christ with our petitions! Her heart is overflowing with radiant happiness and love. How can the Queen of Heaven better express her superabounding gratitude than by lavishing the gifts and graces of God upon her supplicant children. If "never was it known" that anyone sought her intercession in vain, at what particular time might we expect Our Lady to be more than ordinarily gracious, unless it be during Easter week? Then let us all unite in keeping the feast of Christ's Resurrection with a joy and gladness surpassing any we have even known before.

6. Our Lady of the Atonement, Standing by the Cross

The Lamp, March, 1915

The shadows of Lent are deepening. Passiontide and Holy Week will soon be here. Then on Good Friday we will follow our Prince of the Atonement outside the city walls to the place of the Crucifixion.

You know that the Sorrowful Mystery of Our Lady standing at the Cross is the one above all others that the members of our Rosary League should meditate upon so as to better understand and appreciate how pleasing it must be to the Mother of God to be addressed by the title of Our Lady of the Atonement. Hear Jesus say to her, "Woman, behold thy Son," and then to St. John, "Son, behold thy Mother." In these words, the Lord of Heaven and earth crowns Mary with the motherhood of all the sect, who should be redeemed by His *precious, atoning Blood,* and through St. John He addresses Himself to all the Children of the Atonement until the end of the world, saying, "Behold your Mother".

When Mary brought forth her first-born Son at Bethlehem, she experienced no suffering either in body or soul. It was only joy to give birth to the Word made Flesh. But when she became the Mother of God's elect on Mount Calvary, the pain and anguish of her travail was immense and indescribable. And in all the centuries since she has been travailing in union with the Holy Ghost to bring forth Sons and Daughters of the Atonement, and she will continue in her maternal labor until that blessed day when "without spot or wrinkle or any such thing" she shall present the whole innumerable multitude of them unto God the Father through His Son and hers.

Just so long as we continue in sin, we are a source of grief and sorrow to our Blessed Mother; when we keep ourselves unspotted from the world, abounding in the love of God and holy grace, we are her joy and delight. It was the look on Jesus' face when He turned and gazed on Peter that made the Prince of the Apostles go out and "weep bitterly"; and the thought of Mary's eyes full of tears, gazing down upon her sinful, wayward children ought to have a similar effect upon us and urge us on to amend our lives and to be good, just to win a smile from Our Lady of the Atonement.

We rejoice in the growth of the Rosary League and of the increasing devotion of its members to our Blessed Mother under her beautiful title of Mary of the Atonement. The ever growing list of testimonials of favors granted through the Novena of Last Resort is evidence that the Blessed Virgin is pleased with the love and confidence we repose in her and is exercising her intercessory power with God on our behalf, the Children of the Atonement.

We cannot too strongly impress upon the minds and hearts of all the members of the Rosary League the great importance, not only of reciting daily a decade of the Rosary with intention for all the members of the League, but, to say the "Common Prayers" of the Children of the Atonement also. We cannot conceive of anything that will more effectually bind all the Children of the Atonement together as constituting a united family, though widely scattered over all the earth, than to say the same Atonement prayers with the same intentions every day. And may our Blessed Lady of the Atonement embrace us all in her maternal heart, praying for us now and at the hour of our death.

7. Our Lady and the Unity Octave

The Lamp, January, 1917

Have you ever thought that the word "Atonement" means Unity, the state of being at one, At-one-ment? I am sure that it is because of this meaning that God has laid upon the Society of the Atonement, in a special manner, the burden of praying and working for Unity. We cannot have any doubt that our Blessed Lady of the Atonement herself is constantly repeating the prayer of her Divine Son that all believers in His Holy Name may be one, with something of that unity which exists among the saints in heaven. We can also have no doubt that it is very agreeable to the Sacred Heart of Jesus and the Immaculate Heart of Mary that we Children of the Atonement on the earth should pray unceasingly this same prayer for Unity. And since our Holy Father has seen fit to confirm the observance of the Church Unity Octave with an Apostolic Brief and to enrich it with indulgences, we ought to excel all others in the faithful observance of the Octave.

If the thirty thousand members of the Rosary League observe the Octave and receive Holy Communion either on the feast of St. Peter's Chair or the festival of the Conversion of St. Paul, it will not only be a blessing to themselves and to our fellow Christians for whom we pray on earth, but think what an exodus of souls from Purgatory into the Paradise of the Blessed will result from the securing of so many plenary indulgences.

Therefore, with all the power of persuasiveness that I possess in your regard, I entreat you beloved Children of the Atonement to keep faithfully this Octave.

Try to realize how blind our non-Catholic brethren are concerning the papacy. It seems to us as clear as the noon-day sun that Jesus commissioned St. Peter, and his successors, the Popes of Rome, to rule the Universal Church, and clothed them with His Supreme Authority. But our non-Catholic brethren cannot see that at all. It is their opinion that, instead of being the divinely-constituted center of Catholic Unity, the Pope is the chief obstacle in the way of Christians getting to-gether and being one again as they were in Pentecostal times.

Pray more earnestly, therefore, that God the Holy Ghost will open the eyes of our Protestant brethren to view the papacy just as we do; for otherwise it is in vain to talk of Unity. We can be friendly and act lovingly towards each other, but as to there being One Fold and One Shepherd, this can never be until our non-Catholic brethren see eye to eye with us in regard to the Chair of Peter and the infallible ruling and teaching authority of the Vicar of Christ. For this end pray without ceasing, not merely during the Octave but daily throughout the year. Who can tell? This prayer may be nearer an answer than we think.

8. Our Lady of the Atonement and Easter

The Lamp, April, 1919

"The times are very evil,
The days are waxing late,
Be sober and keep vigil,
The Judge is at the gate."

So wrote one of the Medieval saints, and his words are specially true at the present dark hour in the world's history. As a Franciscan, I love the joyous side of our holy religion, but I feel constrained now while we are in the shadows of the holy Passiontide to warn you, my dear children, to prepare for the dreadful things that are to come. As the multitude of the Jews rejected Christ and chose Barrabas to be released to them, so we see the leaders of the people assembled at the Peace Conference, ignoring the Vicar of Christ, going on, day after day, in their sessions without the slightest recognition of even one Our Father for guidance and in the meantime the world is growing more desperate in the economic, political and religious demoralization everywhere manifest. One does not know when he takes up the morning newspaper what new revolution, or new convulsion of society or new outbreak of madness of Bolshevism which has reduced Russia to a chaos of misery, famine, disease, brutal assassination, and is spreading over central Europe and moving swiftly westward, will be there. A little while ago it was a cloud on the Eastern horizon no larger than a man's hand. Today it is spreading half way across the firmament. No merely human cause is producing this insane infection of anarchy, ruin and bloodshed. There is a supernatural intelligence behind it. It is the work of the powers of Hell, and many of our Catholic theologians, profoundly versed in the prophecies of Daniel and the Apocalypse, believe we are about to witness a manifestation of the Beast, which will try the souls of God's elect as this generation has never been tried before, even during the war just past.

The program of Bolshevism is to destroy religion, property and all existing forms of government and to reduce society to a state of chaos, that on the ruins of the present order may rise the rule of the socialistic state.

Years ago the late Monsignor Benson wrote a book which created no small stir in literary circles and which was condemned by the critics as fantastic and absurd. "The Lord of the World" is now being read anew with wider eyes and a quicker pulse; and men are asking, was Benson a twentieth century prophet?

My dear children, it is a time for us to draw nearer together and shelter ourselves under the red mantle of Our Lady of the Atonement. Keep your rosary always with you, and use it often.

When, therefore, we invoke the Blessed Virgin as Our Lady of the Atonement, we should think of Our Lady of Reconciliation, of Unity. She is at the same time the Mother of Jesus and the Mother of the elect, that is, the regenerate. She cannot enjoy perfect unity with her Atonement children until they are entirely at-one in charity with God and with each other. The travail of Our Lady of the Atonement, Our Lady standing by the cross to whom Our Lord said, "Woman, behold thy Son," can never cease, until our Lord's prayer in the cenacle has been completely fulfilled and all Christ's elect are one in Him as He and the Father are one in each other. As far as Heaven is concerned, the attainment of Unity is already an accomplished fact. In Purgatory the suffering souls are being transformed and perfected in that Unity. It is only on earth that both Jesus Himself is "crucified afresh", and the sword of anguish still pierces the Mother's heart, because of the waywardness of Christian men and women, their lack of charity both towards God and towards each other, affording a spectacle both to angels and men, of positive enmity and hostility.

It is here on earth that the Holy Spirit still strives with the hearts of men to bring about those who profess to be the disciples of Christ "that peace and unity which are agreeable to the Divine Will."

It is for our Rosarians, as the Children of Reconciliation and Unity, to unite themselves in mind and heart with our Glorious Lady of At-one-ment, to further in our day and generation that Church Unity movement, which in the end will bring about the fulfillment of Our Lord's prophecy as the good Shepherd. "Other Sheep I have which are not of this fold (viz., the Catholic Church): them also I must bring and they will hear My voice, and there shall be one fold and one shepherd."

As we hold our beads in our hands and contemplate Our Lady of the Atonement on her throne in Heaven, let us unite with her in echoing constantly the prayer of Jesus, concerning His elect, that putting away divisions and all false doctrine, they may return to visible communion with the Apostolic See and that all God's elect on earth will obey Christ's "New Commandment" to His disciples that they love one another.

9. The Graymoor Prayer to Our Lady

The Lamp, August, 1919

I am writing this letter on the day which we are accustomed to observe at Graymoor in special honor of Our Lady of the Atonement, being the Saturday within our Atonement Week. This particular name of our blessed Mother is very dear to us, and we believe it is dear to Our Lady herself. We hold it as among the most treasured and sacred traditions of our Institute that it was the Blessed Virgin who first taught us to call her by that name and there are cogent reasons why she should give this title a favorite place among the many by which she is invoked.

First among these reasons must be her own devotion to the mystery of the Atonement, for it was by the death of her Son on the Cross, which cost Him the last drop of His blood and made her pre-eminently the Mother of Sorrows, that the wall of division between God and man was broken down and both were made one (Eph. 2:14) through Christ's Atoning Sacrifice.

As the Blessed Virgin is inseparably associated with our Divine Redeemer in the mystery of His Incarnation, so is she closely associated with Him in the great Act of the Atonement. Thus she is always represented in the gospel in the liturgy and thought of the Catholic Church as standing by the Cross, when Christ was crucified thereon.

> Stabat Mater dolorosa
> Juxta crucem lacrymosa
> Dum pendebat Filius.

There is a second reason hardly less weighty than the first, why the title, Our Lady of the Atonement, should powerfully appeal to the Mother of God. It was through the Incarnation that she became the new Eve and the Mother of all the regenerate, who being redeemed by the Precious Blood are predestined to eternal life as the adopted sons of God and heirs of the Kingdom of Heaven. The third time Our Lord spoke upon the Cross it was to emphasize this phase of the Atonement, when he said to His Mother: "Woman, behold thy son," and to St. John, "Son, behold thy mother." Thus by virtue of the Atonement, Mary is the Mother of all who live through Christ. Can anyone therefore rightfully, possibly conceive the depth of significance this title "Our Lady of the Atonement" must possess for Our Blessed Mother herself? But someone will ask, if so highly esteemed why should it be kept hidden for nineteen hundred years, to be made known to the faithful in the twentieth century? Is it not the custom of even earthly mothers to preserve the choicest fruits in the summer time and to hide them away under lock and key, to bring them forth to their children's delight in the depth of winter, and did not the Master of the Feast say to the Bridegroom at Cana: "Every man at first setteth forth good wine and when men have well drunk, then that which is worse. But thou hast kept the good wine until now." "My ways are not your ways," saith the Lord of Hosts.

The Name Text of our Institute runs as follows: "We joy in God through our Lord Jesus Christ by whom we have now received the Atonement." Although penned by St. Paul under the inspiration of the Holy Ghost, not even the great apostle himself can, even now, in heaven pronounce these words with such fullness of joy, of love and gratitude as the Blessed Virgin. Consider what the Atonement means to her. The end or purpose of Christ's sacrifice on Himself upon the Cross was the reconciliation of man to God and the establishment of a condition of at-one-ment or oneness between the divine nature and the human which has no equivalent in the relation of God to the angels or any other creature.

Thus, in anticipation of His death at the last supper, Our Lord, addressing His Father on behalf of His disciples, said:

> And not for them only do I pray, but for them also who through their word shall believe in Me; that they all may be one, as Thou Father in Me and I in Thee, that They also may be one in Us. (John 17:21)

It is recognized by all, that this at-one-ment or unity between God and the human creature reaches its highest perfection and glory in the person of Our Lady of the Atonement herself, for she thereby has become the Daughter of God the Father, the Mother of God the Son, and the Spouse of God the Holy Ghost. It is in recognition of this intimate relationship of Our Blessed Mother with the three Persons of the Holy Trinity that the Children of the Atonement are accustomed to address her by a Threefold Salutation as follows:

> I salute Thee, holy Mary, daughter of God the Father, and entreat thee to obtain for us a devotion like thine own to the Most Sweet Will of God.
>
> I salute Thee, Virgin Mother of God the Son, and entreat thee to obtain for us such union with the Sacred Heart of Jesus that our own hearts may burn with love of God and an ardent zeal for the salvation of souls.
>
> I salute Thee, Immaculate Spouse of God the Holy Ghost and entreat thee to obtain for us such yielding of ourselves to the Blessed Spirit that He may in all things direct our hearts and that we may never grieve Him in thought, or word, or deed.

We cannot recommend too strongly the daily use of this Threefold Salutation of Our Blessed Mother on the part of all members of our Rosary League. It sets Our Lady of the Atonement before us as the perfect pattern and model of union with God, whom we should strive to imitate as good children seek to follow the holy example of their Mother.

Is it union with God the Father we seek? Then Our Blessed Mother becomes our model and pattern of obedience and we know that the only way to please the Father is to follow His Will and avoid all sin.

Is it union with God the Son we strive to realize? Then it is union with the Sacred Heart of Jesus by means of Holy Communion, even as He promised: "Whosoever eateth My Flesh and drinketh My Blood dwelleth in Me and I in him," and we are reminded that He originally derived both that Flesh and Blood from His Immaculate Mother and so it comes to pass that union with Jesus is also union with Mary.

Is it union with the Holy Ghost that our soul craves for? Here again Mary is our example. How intimate was her relation with the Holy Ghost who caused her to be conceived without sin and chose her later to be His own Spouse. How perfect her love and devotion to the blessed Paraclete and how completely she surrendered herself to be illuminated and directed by Him in everything. What a model for us and, oh, how earnestly we should entreat her to obtain for us from her Divine Spouse the

grace of a perfect sanctification even as St. Paul prayed for
Thessalonians: "May the God of peace sanctify you in all things;
that your whole spirit and soul and body may be preserved
blameless in the coming of Our Lord Jesus Christ." Cultivate in
your own life an ever increasing devotion to Our Lady of the
Atonement, and preach that devotion among others.

10. The Triumph of the Rosary

The Lamp, November, 1920

There has just come into our hands the October issue of
"Notes for the Month" published by the Caldey Benedictines.
We quote from its pages the following description of how The
Rosary triumphed in the famous battle of the Christians at Le-
panto against the Turks.

"The great Turkish galleys met the little Christian fleet off
Lepanto, in the Gulf of Corinth, and contrary to all expectations, were scattered and destroyed after a furious battle. At
the time of the battle St. Pius was in Rome, doing business with
one of his Cardinals. Suddenly he broke off, walked to the
window and looked out. Then he turned to the Cardinal and
said: 'A truce to business; let us give thanks unto God who has
given us so great a victory.' He had received a divine intimation
that our Lady's weapon, the Rosary, that a child could hold in
the palm of his hand, had been stronger than all the massive
galleys of the Turks. This is not the only victory that has been
gained by this same means against apparently hopeless odds.
Over and over again our Lady has almost visibly intervened to
protect her clients."

No one knew this better than Pope Leo XIII. His great
series of Encyclicals on the Holy Rosary is a storehouse of
teaching on this subject, and it was he who raised the feast of
the Holy Rosary to its present rank, and added the invocation
"Queen of the Most Holy Rosary" to our Lady's Litany. Whether
we are great philosophers and statesmen as was the Holy Pope
himself, or whether we are simple children, there is no weapon
more powerful in the whole supernatural armoury than the
Holy Rosary."

The latest signal triumph of the Rosary over the Old

Dragon occurred last August when the vast hordes of the Red Army from Russia were sweeping like an irresistible torrent over Eastern Poland. Warsaw, the capital, was nearly surrounded and the Western World saw no hope of its escape. Poland seemed doomed to complete subjugation under Lenin and Trotsky, and the latter boasted that within a year the Soviet rule of Bolshevism would triumph in every part of Europe.

Then the Holy Father spoke to the Catholic world and asked that everywhere the Rosary should be recited for the salvation of Poland and the rest of Europe from the Red Menace out of Russia.

The hierarchy of Poland on the Sunday preceding the feast of Our Lady's Assumption summoned the Polish Nation to turn out in processions and supplicate God through His Blessed Mother to save not only Warsaw, the capital, but the entire country from the invasion of the Russian Armies. One hundred thousand of the people on that Sunday paraded publicly in processions throughout Poland reciting the Rosary. And wonderful to relate, a complete reversal of arms followed; before the end of August the power of the Red Armies was completely broken, and the Russian divisions were everywhere in retreat. It means, as far as we can foresee, the beginning of the end of Bolshevism, not only in Russia but throughout the world. It seems to us that this marvelous victory represents one of the most extraordinary triumphs of the Rosary in modern history, being hardly less signal than the celebrated victory of Lepanto, and in its consequences to Europe, and the Christian world, no less momentous. Pope Benedict has publicly ascribed the defeat of the Russians to Our Lady's intervention, and this death wound to militant Bolshevism in the hour of its greatest success should strengthen the faith of all our Rosarians in the wonderful power of God, placed in your hands by means of the beads as you daily whisper the Pater Noster, Ave Maria, and the Gloria.

We now ask our Rosarians to recite the Rosary for the confounding of the anti-Catholic Press which at the present time is poisoning the minds of the non-Catholic public in America against the Catholic Church. This is nothing else but the work of Satan to hinder the conquest of America, and through America the whole pagan world for Christ, and we should defeat him by the Rosary.

217

11. Rosary League—Letter to Rosarians

The Lamp, May, 1921

As the spiritual Director of the Rosary League, that is what the undersigned desires for you more than anything else. We are the Children of our glorious Lady of the Atonement, the heirs and inheritors of that salutation, which the Crucified Jesus, Son of Mary, addressed to Saint John, standing by the cross: "Son, behold thy Mother".

At Bethlehem, Mary became the Mother of the "Only begotten of the Father full of grace and truth," but while standing by the Cross, through the death of her Divine Son, she became the Mother of the children of the Atonement, and you and I belong to that category.

We are the children, over whom Our Lady has had to travail in sore pain and sorrow in order to bring us into the Kingdom of Heaven and present us "without spot or wrinkle or any such thing" before the Throne of Jesus Christ.

This earth is meant to be the theatre and training ground of our sanctification, the place where in the Providence of God we are to perfect ourselves in sanctity. What we fail to do in that regard, during the time of our earthly sojourn must be finished in the fiery furnace of purgatorial affliction. Far better, if, by our own cooperation with sanctifying grace, through the tutelage and prayers of our Atonement Mother in Heaven, that the work of sanctification is perfected here and now; therefore, to grow daily more like Mary of the Atonement, to have the image of her Child, Jesus, formed within us by the sanctifying hand of the Holy Ghost, this should be our supreme desire, the object of our ceaseless prayers, and the end of all our daily toils and sacrifices.

During Our Lady's own beautiful month of May, will you not take a firmer grip upon this supreme notice and purpose of your life, and strive henceforth, above all things, to become a saint, growing daily into the image and likeness of Jesus Crucified, and Mary, His Mother, standing by the Cross.

12. Our Lady and the Unity Octave

The Lamp, January, 1923

I appeal to all members of the Rosary League of Our Lady of the Atonement to spend devoutly the Church Unity Octave; hearing Mass, if that is possible, every day and not only hearing Mass but receiving Holy Communion, at the same time using the Rosary in fervent supplication, echoing the prayer of our great High Priest which he addressed to God the Father on the night of His betrayal, and which may be summed up in one brief petition: "That they all may be one". Here are the very words of Christ in that very wonderful prayer.

"Sanctify them in truth. Thy word is Truth, as thou hast sent Me into the world I also have sent them into the world and for them do I sanctify Myself that they also may be sanctified in truth. And not for them only do I pray, but for them also who through their word shall believe in Me; that they all may be one, as Thou, Father in Me and I in Thee; that they also may be one in Us; that the world may believe that Thou hast sent Me. And the glory Thou has given Me I have given to them; that they may be one; as we also are one, I in Thee and Thou in Me; that they may be made perfect in one; and the world may know that Thou hast sent Me and hast loved them as Thou hast also loved Me".

We behold Satan at this very hour setting up an anti-Christian kingdom of immense dimensions on the earth. It is known the world over as Communism. Its flag is red. What Mohammedanism meant for Christendom twelve hundred years ago, capturing Jerusalem, Antioch, Alexandria and Constantinople, out of five Christian patriarchates leaving only that of Rome un-subjected to its galling bloody and bitter yoke so Communism, rising in the East, threatens to subjugate to its ruthless tyranny, scourge and crucify the Christians of the world today. It possesses a hell-born, diabolic unity in itself which until now has broken down and crushed all resistance. It seems as though Satan had personified himself in one individual who rules over the Union of Soviet Republics with an absolutism transcending that of the Czars and their fore-bears, the Caesars of long ago. By no means satisfied with ruling over one hundred and fifty million in Russia, Siberia and central Asia, the Communists dream of conquering China, Japan, India, Africa, the rest of Europe and both North and South America. The red evangelists and propagandists are everywhere preaching the gospel of Sovietism with ceaseless fervor, agitating and plotting night and day to accomplish a world revolution. In the meantime Christendom is torn by internal divisions among those who confess themselves to be disciples of Christ, just as the Near East was rent by heresy and schism when Islamism lifted its banner against the Cross. Such was the hatred of the Egyptian Monotholites for the Catholics of Constantinople that they actually hailed the armies of the false prophet and Alexandria preferred the rule of the Mohammedan Caliph to the scepter of the Catholic Emperor. There is no doubt that many Southern Protestants would vote for a Communistic President of the United States in preference to the noblest and ablest Catholic who could possibly be nominated.

Never did Christendom need unity for its own preservation more desperately than at this very hour of supreme peril, when the whole religious, social, political and economic fabric is agonizing in the throes of an upheaval such as the world has not experienced in centuries.

Pray, therefore, during the Church Unity Octave with travail of mind and heart that Our Lord's own prophecy may be speedily fulfilled: "Other sheep I have which are not of this fold. Them also I must bring and they will hear My voice and there shall be One Fold and One Shepherd". Not only, dear Rosarians, pray for this consummation devoutly during the Church Unity Octave, but daily throughout the entire twelve months of year of grace, 1923.

When the Red Army of Russia invaded while Lenin was still alive and Trotsky was at the zenith of his career, they swept all things before them and Poland seemed doomed to be swallowed up by the Red Dragon of Sovietism.

It was in the month of August and the Pope sent forth a call to the faithful to recite the Rosary, particularly on the Feast of the Assumption, as Pius V bade Europe pray when Solyman II, Sultan of Constantinople, met the Christian fleet at Lepanto and was crushingly defeated on October 7, 1571.

All Poland responded as Europe answered the call of the Sovereign Pontiff against the banners of Mohammed, and with the same triumphant results. The Catholic victory of Lepanto was paralleled by the triumph of the Poles, supported by the

French, who drove back the Russian Reds and crushed completely their offensive. Who can know what glorious answers divine omnipotence may give to the prayers of our Rosarians, who uniting themselves to the Sacred Heart of Jesus and the Immaculate Heart of Mary, shall reiterate the prayer of Christ the King, that all who believe in Him may all be one, that the whole world may believe and accept His scepter and eternal salvation.

13. May Letter to Rosarians

The Lamp, May, 1923

It is the sincere desire of the Spiritual Director of the Rosary League that every Rosarian shall have this picture of Our Lady of the Atonement framed and placed where it can be venerated every day. For this purpose it should be in the place the Rosarians say their daily prayers, and an additional picture might be framed and placed in the parlor for the benefit of visitors.

It is the custom among the Russian and other Greek Christians, whether Catholic or Orthodox, to have hanging in their parlors an icon or sacred picture of the Blessed Virgin and usually a light burning before it. Where this custom can be followed, we recommend it to our Catholic readers in the West.

Outward and visible signs of our faith in Catholic homes are not as striking and pronounced as they should be. Before the Soviet Revolution in Russia, sacred icons or pictures of Our Lord and the Blessed Virgin hung in every railroad train, and passengers reverently saluted them on entering and departing from the trains.

Even Mohammedans of the Orient publicly acknowledge God, prostrating themselves wherever they are, as well on the street as in their private homes when the call for prayer is made, something which happens no less than five times every day.

Faith in God would be stronger among the peoples of the West did they more frequently give outward and visible expression to it, both within the home circle, and in their daily work and conversation abroad among their fellow men.

14. Promote Love of Our Lady of the Atonement

The Lamp, May, 1924

Thousands of your number will have had your thoughts directed towards the shrine of our Lady of the Atonement at Graymoor because it was announced in the April *Lamp* that for the first time in the history of Our Lady's Graymoor Novena it would be celebrated solemnly, beginning on the first Saturday in May; and that through the entire month that Thirty Days' Prayer to Our Lady would be recited by our Sisters and the Mass in the Convent Chapel every morning would be said for the intentions of those Rosarians who forwarded their petitions to the Sisters, in order that they might participate in this special month of prayer for our dear benefactors at the Graymoor Portiuncula.

It would be difficult to describe the beauty of Graymoor during the month of May when nature puts on her mantle of green, the fruit trees are in full blossom, the violets, the anemones, the wild columbine, and the jonquils, flower amidst the grass and beneath the trees on the wooded hillsides; while flocks of birds, returning after their winter exodus, make melody in the treetops.

I wonder if our Rosarians appreciate, as they should, the heritage of faith which the Catholic Church has preserved for us through devotion to Mary as the Virgin Mother of Christ, our God? At the time of the so-called "Reformation" the great enemy of our salvation aimed the envenomed arrows of heresy at three things that he particularly detested in the Catholic religion: the Real Presence of Jesus Christ in the Blessed Sacrament; devotion to His Virgin Mother, and to His Vicar, the Sovereign Pontiff. The Old Dragon succeeded in persuading the Protestants to abolish in their doctrinal system the Holy Sacrifice of the Mass; to affirm that the Pope of Rome was anti-Christ; and they did their best to tear Jesus out of the arms of His Mother, and relegate her to oblivion by destroying statues and sacred pictures of her, while the rosary was utterly tabooed. A widowed woman in the days of Queen Elizabeth had her house burned over her head because she insisted on saying the Rosary as she sat in the doorway of her cottage.

These deluded people thought they were honoring Christ,

by dishonoring His Mother, and are now, alas, denying His divinity, by denying at the same time His Virgin Birth of an Immaculate Mother.

Let us do all we can to make reparation; by increasing our own personal devotion to the Mother of Jesus, and by faithfully reciting our Rosary. There is much searching of heart going on, among our separated brethren, in the various Protestant denominations. Now is the time to pray with Mary, through Jesus, to God the Father, that Our Lord's Prayer on the night of His betrayal will begin to be fulfilled: "Holy Father, keep them in Thy Name whom Thou hast given Me; that they may be one, as We are also one." (St. John, 17:11)

15. Our Lady Prays for Unity

Annals of Our Lady of the Atonement.

Let the theme of our letter be Our Lady of the Atonement. Behold her standing in splendid self-control, though with heart transpierced with the sword of anguish; her eyes fixed upon the agonized form of her Divine Son, making Atonement, as the Lamb of God upon the Altar of the Cross, for the sins of the world. For a time the eyes of the Redeemer of mankind meet her glance and then amid tears of blood the Divine Victim turns His gaze upon the faithful John and then Jesus speaks, saying, "Woman, behold thy son"—"Son, behold thy Mother". In these words Jesus hails His Virgin Mother as the New Eve, and through John He addresses all the redeemed as Her children. The first Eve is the mother of all that live by natural regeneration from the first Adam; Mary is the Mother of all that live by regeneration as the sons and daughters of the New Adam. Mary is the Mother of the Elect, of all those whose names are written in the Lamb's Book of Life, of that "exceedingly great multitude, whom no man can number, out of all nations and tribes and peoples and tongues, standing before the throne and in sight of the Lamb clothed with white robes and palms in their hands" (Apocalypse). This is Our Lady of the Atonement; and if the Mother is so named, then it is fitting that her children should call themselves "Sons and Daughters of the Atonement".

But we must not think of the children of the Atonement Mother as confined to those Catholic Christians who are in

223

visible communion with the Apostolic See. All who have been validly baptized are also the children of Mary, even though they have gone astray from "Catholic Unity" and are identified with some Protestant sect or belong to some division of the Orthodox millions of Russia and the Near East. Mary loves them all and her heart is torn within her as she contemplates the unhappy divisions of Christendom and prays in union with the divine prayer of Christ Himself on the night of His betrayal: *"Ut Omnes Unum Sint"*, that all His disciples might be one in a unity similar to that which binds Himself and His Father together in the bonds of mutual charity.

It is to emphasize this unity aspect of Christ's Atoning Sacrifice that God called the Society of the Atonement into being.

The first purpose of Christ's death was to reconcile God to Man and Man to God. "The joy that was set before him" when "He endured the Cross" was the vision of the redeemed around the throne of God, constituting Himself an unity so complete as to be the very members of His Body: "bone of His bone and flesh of His flesh", enjoying thereby a fellowship of actual At-one-ment with God which transcends the intimacy which has ever existed between God, their Creator, and the holy angels since the first hour of their sinless existence. This was the unity in its perfect consummation which Christ besought for His elect at the last supper in the Cenacle at Jerusalem on the eve of His death: "I in them and Thou in Me that they may be made perfect in one. Father, I will that where I am they also whom Thou has given Me may be with Me ... that the love wherewith Thou hast loved Me, may be in them." The realization of this unity with God, when the elect shall attain to the beatific vision, demands, as its corollary, that the members of Christ's Mystical Body shall be one with each other perfectly fulfilling the New Commandment which Christ gave unto His disciples before He laid down His life for them that they should love one another.

16. Our Lady of the Atonement

Retreat Conference, August 7, 1925

The keynote of our Institute is union with God, which is, of course, the essence of the religious life. We have dealt with the different aspects of devotion to God the Father, God the Son, and God the Holy Ghost. Tonight we will direct our thoughts to Our Lady of the Atonement, for, next to God, our devotion is to her, for she is the Mother of us all. It is an inherent characteristic of the Catholic Religion to have devotion to the Blessed Virgin; it is one of the evidences of its being the true religion, because among heretics who have fallen away from the Catholic faith, many of them have repudiated devotion to the Mother of God for fear they might be guilty of Mariolatry. Monsignor Benson points out that the fatal results of taking Jesus out of the arms of His Mother and trying to separate those whom God has joined together—the Mother and the Son—and one of the fruits of heresy when they separate Our Lord from His Mother is that they, by and by, begin to deny the divinity of Christ. We see the Protestant world today honeycombed with all forms of so-called Modernism, and we see people occupying themselves—people that are supposed to boast of their knowledge—with absurdity, the ridiculous teaching of evolution, that a man emanated from a tadpole or a monkey.

Now the Catholic Church has always been devoted to our Blessed Lady, and in the Litany of Loretto we have assembled the various names and titles which have been incorporated in that Litany as some new title or new name has been added to those previous generations. When I was in Rome in the basilica of St. Mary Major, I saw there a beautiful representation of Our Lady in marble as "Our Lady of Peace", a special creation of Pope Benedict XV, who authorized that address to be inserted in the Litany. Now one of the special marks, it seems to me, of divine predilection towards our own holy Institute is that we are privileged to address the Mother of God by a title that is new and yet as ancient as Christianity. It is a title that has to do with her intimate relationship with the Redeemer of the world as He hung upon the Cross and offered Himself in sacrifice for the sins of the world. "There stood by the Cross, Mary," and the mother of James and the other Marys, and the faithful John, Nicodemus, and Joseph of Arimatiea. Now that God should have permitted us to address Our Lady by this title, I say, is one of the most extraordinary marks of divine predilection for the Institute. If we had no other reason for believing that this Society was dear to Our Lord than just that one thing, it would be ample ground for regarding our Society as something more than a religious foundation. Think of it, America is just now beginning to add a few saints to the calendar. There were some of our American Saints canonized at Rome this present year, Father Joques, for example, and the Jesuit Martyrs. But I do not think America has added a new title to Our Lady except the Society of the Atonement at Graymoor. It is a title that has already been recognized by the Holy Father, and a feast instituted in its honor and a plenary indulgence granted to those that join the Rosary League of Our Lady of the Atonement.

And, as I said in the address on the Feast of Our Lady of the Atonement, it is not one of the lesser marian titles, but it is a major one. Somebody pointed out to me while I was in Rome something that I did not know before. I use this simply as an illustration. He said that the *Congregatio pro Ecclesia Orientali* is one of the major Congregations, whereas the Congregation of Propagation of the Faith is not a major congregation, and the distinction is that a Cardinal is the prefect in a minor congregation, whereas in a major congregation the Pope is the prefect and a Cardinal is the secretary.

Now, Our Lady of the Atonement is not a minor title. A minor title of Our Lady would be Queen of Peace or queen of something else, Queen of Saints, but a major title would be Our Lady of Atonement because there is nothing more major than the Atonement. The two great pillars of Catholic theology are the Incarnation and the Atonement, and there is no place that Our Lady occupies in Gospel history of more prominence than the position which she occupies as mediatrix of the human family when she stood at the Cross when Our Lord was lifted up that He might draw all men to Himself. And, therefore, a Society to which the Atonement was given a name and then in connection with it this title was given to Our Lady, just must be of more ordinary importance, as the name itself was not given, by human wit or wisdom, but, by the answer to prayer in an extraordinary manner, showing by it the mind and intervention of God. So Our Lady's title we did not give to her originally ourselves, but it was bestowed upon her, so that we have the statue of Our Lady of the Atonement in the red mantle with the Christ Child in her arms and the cross in the hand of the child, indicating that this particular statue is not so much the Child of Bethlehem as the Child of the Atonement, as represented in that new birth as His Mystical Body of the elect.

Now if we are well grounded in our faith and confidence in

this new title as being given to us by Our Lady herself, it ought to inspire us with an extraordinary devotion to the Mother of God; we should have it in common with all religious, but as Children of the Atonement, we ought to excell in that devotion. We have our great devotion to the Holy Trinity, devotion to the will of God, devotion to Jesus present in the Blessed Sacrament in union with His Sacred Heart, devotion to the Holy Ghost as dwelling in us and making our bodies temples of the living God, and then this special devotion to the Blessed Lady. Now we should not only have this devotion ourselves, but it should be our duty as missionaries to propagate that devotion to our opportunities among those that are given to us to train in the things of God. There is a little five-point rule which I hope the Sisters will take down, the Mission Sisters and try to inculcate that rule in the children so that when they grow up, they will still observe it. The five-point rule consists of this:

1. That they should always say about their prayers, not only at night, but in the morning, and not only in the morning, but at night.

2. That they should always carry about and have with them a rosary, and that as a special act of love and devotion to the Mother of God, they should say that Rosary one decade every day. Impress upon them that this Mother will appreciate this act of love and that it will be more to their own advantage, because if she sees that they are devoted to her, she will watch over them and will also obtain favors for them. Of course, in that connection, if you can bring about and introduce into their homes a picture of the Lady of the Atonement, have them get it framed and hang it up on the wall where they say their prayers, you will do a very important thing. I went upstairs in a tenement the other day with one of our clerics, in one of the Italian quarters of New York. This house was very small, very much crowded. I noticed on the bureau in one of the rooms a statue, a couple of statues, one was of the Sacred Heart with the head off; nevertheless it was there; which shows, in that little thing, the piety of the people. And so you see a picture of Our Lady of the Atonement on the wall is an indication of devotion just the same at the crucifix on the wall. Those are practical things that you ought to try to promote among those with whom you are working.

3. That they should be very diligent to hear Mass every Sunday.

4. and 5. That they should go to Confession and Communion once a month. Now if you can get them to persevere in the practice of getting their religion to that degree, they are not going to get very far away from God. We, as priests, have an abundance of experience in the confessional. When we go to camp, we see the difference in the confession of the soldier who does not go to Mass and is very negligent in his prayers, if he says them at all, and does not say his Rosary, and the one who goes regularly and receives Holy Communion once a month and practices other devotions. It is a very, very different record they make in their confession, I can assure you.

Now, I am sure that by inculcating those practices and impressing on the minds of the children what we might call the five-point rule, you would do a great service, and particularly, try to get them in the habit of saying that one decade of the Rosary every day.

Then there is the importance of the literature. If you can get the people, all of them, to take the *Candle,* the little magazine of *Our Lady,* and practice devotion to Our Lady through the Rosary League, you get another influence in their homes which will link them with Graymoor and unite them through the Rosary League to this central shrine of Our Lady.

Then about the Three-fold Salutation, we say that, and we are apt to say it mechanically, just as we say the Lord's Prayer and the Hail Mary, but we have learned to put behind the Our Father and the Hail Mary a certain intention, and it is the intention that counts when we say them, as far as obtaining a result is concerned. It would be an excellent thing to meditate upon the significance perhaps more often than we do of the Three-fold Salutation. It sums up what we have been talking about—unity with God, each one of them emphasizing the Person of the Trinity that we desire for the time being to be devoted to.

The first salutation is taking Our Lady's devotion as a pattern to the most sweet Will of God, and there you have the beauty of obedience. If you want to hear God say in your soul what He said when St. John the Baptist was baptizing Our Lord and again when Our Lord was transfigured on Mount Thabor, "This is My beloved Son in whom I am well pleased," you must worship the sweet will of God. You must do everything from that supernatural motive because it is pleasing to God, because it makes you walk in the footsteps of Our Blessed Lady.

The second salutation is in regard to devotion to our Blessed Lord, devotion to His Sacred Heart so that our hearts may be united to His and, therefore, burning with love and charity and holy zeal for the conversion of sinners. Now all know that the center of the Sacred Heart, of course, is in the Blessed Sacrament; it is of the Sacred Heart an outward and visible reminder, but the Heart Itself is in the tabernacle, and in our devotion to the Blessed Sacrament we are expressing in the best possible way our devotion to the Sacred Heart, union with that Sacred Heart. And so there is our second salutation, for Our Lady to pray for us and cooperate with us in our devotion to our Blessed Lord.

The third salutation is the one in regard to yielding ourselves to the Blessed Spirit, who was the spouse of Our Lady, and she of course, is the pattern of that devotion. If you put behind that salutation your prayer and commit it to Our Lady with the intention which is vital to every day, that you may realize in your religious life more and more that union, that At-one-ment with God the Father, God the Son, God the Holy Ghost, it will be very wholesome and very effective. As far as your sanctification is concerned, I would recommend to you especially to address Our Lady with the prayer to intercede for you to the Holy Ghost, the Sanctifier, in regards to your faults and your weaknesses and your defects, whatever they may be, embody them more or less in your confession, in your self-examination during this retreat, and I trust, in the resolutions you form for the future. Now take these resolutions to Our Lady and ask her to address them particularly to the Holy Ghost that He may strengthen and sanctify you and confirm your will in running more diligently the race that is set for you in the way of holy perfection. The more difficulty you have in bringing your human nature to correspond to the divine nature of Our Lord, the greater will be your joy in the end.

I think that you will find that that particular kind of prayer is very efficacious. Place yourself before Our Lady and say, "Now, dear Mother, you know me better than I know myself, you know better my weaknesses and what needs correction. I pray you to direct yourself to the Holy Ghost that He may open my understanding, to see my faults, and then pour into my soul His sanctifying grace. He has made you without sin, and He will hear your prayer to keep me from sin and correct whatever is needful of correction, and to advance me year by year in the way of holiness, so that as I approach the day of my death, I will approach to the time of entering into that perfection 'without spot or wrinkle', which is that status of the saints before the throne of God."

I trust, therefore, that devotion to Our Lady, whether you are using your Rosary, or whether you are saying the Threefold Salutation, or whether you are kneeling before her picture, or statue, speaking to her in the way I have described to you, there will be in your life more and more love and confidence in that Mother who never fails any of her true children.

I pray God that this retreat may have permanent effects of sanctification in your souls, that you will go back to your posts of duty refreshed and strengthened, your ideals renewed and whatever darkness may have come over any of the ideals may be swept away and you will be as fresh and new in your enthusiasm and devotion to your holy vocation as it was on the day when you were first clothed as a novice or when you made your profession. May God give you all the grace of final perseverance. May this coming year be one of extraordinary unity among the Sisters, of extraordinary praising of God and fruitfulness in your labors and extraordinary sanctity among you all, together with that holy unity of charity both towards God and towards each other.

17. The Red Mantle of Our Lady

The Lamp, September, 1925

The connection of the Red Mantle with the Atonement is very obvious. It was during the shedding of the Most Precious Blood of her Divine Son, the very Blood which He had derived from her own Immaculate Heart, that the Redemption of the world was wrought, and an atonement made for the sins of the whole world by the Lamb of God.

Our Lady of the Atonement stood by the Cross when the Atoning Sacrifice of Calvary was enacted, and it is most fitting that she should wear a Red Mantle when accepting our homage and devotion under the title of the Atonement.

The Holy Father has not only sanctioned our use of this

title for the Blessed Virgin, but has granted a plenary indulgence to all who join the Rosary League of Our Lady of the Atonement. He has also sanctioned the observance of a special Feast Day in her honor, namely, the Saturday after the Seventh Sunday after Pentecost which comes in Atonement Week, the special time each year when the Society of the Atonement celebrates the founding of our Graymoor Institute.

18. Our Lady of the Atonement and Unity

The Lamp, February, 1926

I am writing this in the midst of the Church Unity Octave, and it suggests an explanation to you of Our Lady's Atonement title. As far as I am aware, there is no exact equivalent of the English word *Atonement,* etymologically speaking, in any other language.

The Latin word *expiatio* refers to the expiatory character of Christ's sacrifice of the Cross, but this aspect of Our Lord's Passion and death does not correspond to the significance of the word *Atonement.* Webster's dictionary derives *atonement* from the two words, *at-one,* which, as very primary, means "to be or cause to be *at-one,* to agree, to accord," whereas the secondary meaning is "to make reparation, expiation, or amends for an offense or crime." Hence *Atonement,* according to the same lexicographer, is literally a setting *at-one,* and in its theological sense, "a reconciliation between God and sinful man".

The word *Atonement* means *the end* of Christ's sacrifice on the Cross rather than *the means* of suffering and expiation through which that end was achieved. The purpose for which our Divine Redeemer offered Himself as a slain Lamb upon Calvary was to take away the sins of the world and restore that unity or *at-one-ment* which flourished between God and our first parents in the Garden of Paradise before the fall of Adam and Eve. Only the unity with God which regenerate man is destined to enjoy forever in heaven through the Incarnation and Atonement of Jesus Christ far transcends the intimacy which man enjoyed with his Creator in the state of primal innocence before the fall.

This is beautifully expressed by the text, found in the fifth chapter of Romans which contains the Name of our holy Society: "We joy in God through Our Lord Jesus Christ by whom we have now received the Atonement", or state of oneness, or reconciliation.

This unity of the elect with God and with each other in the final beatitude of Heaven was undoubtedly in the mind of Our Blessed Lord in the prayer, which He addressed, to His Heavenly Father on the eve of His Crucifixion: "Father, keep them in Thy Name whom Thou hast given Me, that they may be one as We also are. That they all may be one as Thou Father in Me and I in Thee that they also may be one in Us, and the glory which Thou hast given Me I have given to them, that they may be one as We also are one. I in them and Thou in Me. That they may be made perfect in one."

When we therefore give to our Blessed Mother the title of Our Lady of the Atonement we mean: Our Lady of Unity. As she sits enthroned, as the Great Wonder of Heaven, wearing a crown of twelve stars, clothed with the sun, the moon her footstool, she presents to the universe the highest possible approach of a creature to intimate and exalted union with God. She is at one and the same time the most perfect and the most beloved Daughter of God the Father; she is the Mother of God the Son; and she is the spouse of God the Holy Ghost.

But Our Lady of the Atonement is not alone the Mother of God, she is also the New Eve, the Mother of Redeemed Mankind; she is the center of that family unity which Christ prayed and willed might flourish among the Sons and Daughters of the Atonement. As the Mother is the center of the home binding together the love of her husband and her children, so Our Lady of Unity cooperates with the Holy Ghost and the Sacred Heart of Jesus to bring about that blissful state of Unity which will constitute the joy of Heaven, and towards which the souls of men approximate upon earth in the measure and degree that they correspond to the vocation God had imposed upon His elect children and which St. Paul expressed in his letter to the Romans when he tells them: "Ye are all called to be saints."

When, therefore, we address the Blessed Virgin as Our Lady of the Atonement, we think of her as the connecting link between ourselves and God; and while we gaze fondly upon her as our Mother, we should try to correspond with the work of the Holy Ghost, the Sanctifier in our mind, heart, and soul to make us like unto her as children resemble their parents.

It is St. John, the devoted Son of Mary, who writes: "Dearly beloved, we are now the sons of God; and it hath not appeared to what shall be; but we know that when He shall appear, we shall be like unto Him." And this resemblance will not alone be to Jesus who has become the New Adam or Father of the redeemed humanity, but also to Mary, the Mother of the Children of the Atonement. As man, Jesus must have been the living image of His Mother; for having no earthly Father, he derived His humanity entirely from Her; so if in heavenly glory we are to be like unto Jesus, Mary's Son, we will of necessity be like unto Mary, since He, the Perfect Son, resembles the most perfect of all Mothers.

We read in Genesis that God the Divine Creator decreed that every tree should produce seed after its kind, and these seeds in return should reproduce the image and likeness of the original tree and plant. So will it be in the unity of the perfected Atonement Family in Heaven. All the Children of the Atonement will reflect the image of Jesus and Mary. Nor will this likeness be simply external, it will also be interior, a likeness of soul and heart, a oneness, such as that which flourishes between the three Persons of the Adorable Trinity, even as Our Lord prayed, "As thou Father in Me, and I in Thee, so also that they may be One in Us."

Now it has been divinely revealed that God is Love, and what blood is to the body coursing through every vein and artery and uniting every member with every other member, so love is the very essence of the Divine Trinity. Moreover the unity of the Sons and Daughters of the Atonement not only with each other but with Jesus and Mary, and through them with God the Father and Holy Ghost, will be a unity of love—the perfect fulfillment in fact and through eternity of the Divine Law, "Thou shalt love the Lord thy God with all thy heart and with all thy soul and with all thy strength," and that new commandment which Christ gave to His Disciples at the last supper, saying: "A New Commandment I give unto you that you love one another." Lest we make this letter too long, I must stop here, but next month we will consider Our Lady of the Atonement in special relation to the all important questio nof Church Unity or the return of all outside the Fold of Peter to the Unity of the One, Holy, Catholic, Apostolic and Roman Church.

Our Blessed Lord, while making an Atonement for the sins of the world upon the Altar of the Cross (He Himself being both Priest and Victim) did not forget His Mother nor the beloved disciple, John. Fixing His eyes upon Our Lady of the Atonement, standing near the Cross, He said to her: "Woman, behold thy Son," and to John He said, "Behold thy Mother."

By this, His last will and testament, He constituted the Blessed Virgin the New Eve, the Mother of all the Redeemed; that is to say, of the Children of the Atonement, they that have been baptized or shall hereafter receive the new birth of the Spirit, and enrolled in the Lamb's Book of Life as the elect sons and daughters of God by the adoption of Grace, destined, if found faithful, to occupy those seats in Heaven from which Satan and his apostate angels fell.

When, therefore, we address the Blessed Virgin as "Our Lady of the Atonement," we conceive her to be our Mother, and we her Atonement Children. Nor, because we are Catholics, do we assert that she is the Mother of Catholics only; she is the Mother of all the baptized whether they be in the Fold of Peter, or belong to "the other Sheep" mentioned by the Good Shepherd, scattered abroad in the desert places of heresy and schism, yet dear to Jesus and the Mother heart of Mary.

In the parable of the Prodigal Son, Jesus revealed to us how the father's heart went out to the younger son who left the paternal roof and going into a far country, wasted his sustenance with riotous living. So we can very readily conceive the Heart of Mary going out in yearning over her children who have wandered far from the Holy Father's House, and from the Fold of Peter, the Universal Shepherd.

How very strange that God should have hidden from the eyes of so many religious founders within the Catholic Church that most glorious name of the Atonement and revealed it to someone outside the Fold and that Our Lady herself should have taught these "other Sheep" while still in "the far country" to invoke her as Our Lady of the Atonement, i.e., of Reconciliation and Unity. Surely it ought to be obvious to all of us, that whatever other good work the Society of the Atonement has been called into being to do, its first and primary, mission is that of Church Unity, to prepare the way like John the Baptist so that when the Good Shepherd sounds the Call to the "other Sheep" to return to the Unity of the One Catholic Fold under the benign rule of Peter, all the obstacles that block the path shall be removed.

Our Lady has long been known as the destroyer of all heresies; let her now be looked up to and invoked as the Mother who will not rest until her children, long estranged from each other by schism, shall sit down together at the same table, knowing and loving each other as true brethren, and realizing in the glorious fellowship of the one household of faith, the answer of Our Divine Lord's Prayer; "That they all may be one as Thou Father in Me and I in Thee, that they may be one in Us; that the world may believe that Thou hast sent Me." It was Our Lady of the Atonement whom Isaias prophesied long ago under the inspiration of the Holy Ghost: "And they that shall be of Thee shall build the old waste places; Thou shalt raise up the foundations of many generations; and thou shalt be called the *Repairer of the Breach,* the restorer of paths to dwell in."

When, therefore, we as the Children of the Atonement address Our Blessed Mother under that beautiful title, let us think of her as "Our Lady of Unity", and let us consecrate ourselves afresh at her altar to contribute what lies within our power of prayer, of sacrifice, and charitable endeavor, to bring the separated brethren of the East and West into the unity of the One Fold under the One Shepherd.

Let us not make the mistake of imagining that Unity of faith is the only thing required to bring all Christians into the Communion and fellowship of the Apostolic See. "Now abideth faith, hope and charity," says St. Paul, "but the greatest of these is charity." And again: "Though I have all faith so that I could remove mountains, and have not charity, it profiteth me nothing." There were other Catholics as orthodox as St. Francis of Assisi in the thirteenth century, but he excelled them all as the Apostle of Unity because he surpassed all men in the burning charity with which he was daily consumed towards God and towards man.

St. Francis de Sales converted seventy-five thousand Calvinists by love and neither the Orthodox of the East, nor the Anglicans, and other Protestants of the West will return to unity of Peter's Chair unless we can convert them through love. Cardinal Mercier did more to bring the Anglicans back to Unity

by his loving sympathetic heart than tons of controversial literature could do though written with the wisdom and logical force
of the highest archangel.

Our Lady of the Atonement, is herself "the Seat of Wisdom,"
as the Spouse of the Holy Ghost, and is supported by countless legions of angels. We may rely upon her maternal heart
never to rest until the words of her Divine Son has been fulfilled:
"Other Sheep I have which are not of this Fold, them also I
must bring and they will hear My voice and there shall be One
Fold and One Shepherd." Satan by fomenting strife and fostering heresies and schisms has separated many millions from the
unity of the Church and greatly hindered thereby the conquest
of the world by the missionary hosts of Our Lord Jesus Christ,
but Our Lady of the Atonement will yet crush the serpent's
head even where he has until now achieved his greatest victories.

Through her all prevailing intercession the Holy Spirit will
bring about such a world-wide movement of dissident Christians
to the center of Catholic Unity that the return of the Wandering
Sheep to communion with the Apostolic See will far transcend
in magnitude and importance the lapse of the Greeks from Unity
in the tenth century and the Protestant defection of the sixteenth
century combined. We dare to make this prophesy not because
we have the vision of the seer but because we believe that God,
the Father Almighty, will answer the prayer of His Son, Jesus
Christ, and Our Lady of the Atonement will have a leading part
to play in this glorious accomplishment.

19. Our Lady of the Atonement—Mother of Unity

Feast of Our Lady of the Atonement
Sermon, July 9, 1930

There are many aspects from any one of which we might
treat the theme of Our Lady of the Atonement's title, but we
shall confine ourselves to the meaning of this new name for
the Blessed Virgin which sets forth her mission as Our Lady of
Unity.

The word "Atonement" in its original significance means
the state of being *at one*. Etymologically speaking, the exact
Latin equivalent of the English word, at-one-ment, is *adunatio*

(ad-at, una-one) and thus we translate Society of the Atonement as *Societas Adunationis* and Our Lady of the Atonement as *Domina nostra Adunationis*.

We know that one of the special purposes for which our Institute was called into being is to assist in bringing to its fulfillment the prayer made by Our Lord on the night of His betrayal when He besought His Father: *"That they all may be one, as Thou, Father, in Me, and I in Thee, that they also may be one in Us; that the world may believe that Thou hast sent Me."* (John 17:21)

First of all in the Person of Our Lord Jesus Christ, through His Incarnation, God and Man were made one. Our Lord has two natures, the divine and the human, united in the one divine Person, Himself, in which Person, man and God are perfectly at one. Our Lady of the Atonement was God's instrument by which this hypostatic union, as it is called, was accomplished when the Word was made flesh. Moreover, in the oblation of Himself on Calvary the Incarnate Word shed the Blood which He had derived from His Mother, Our Lady of the Atonement; and when the sacrifice was completed, He addressed her from the cross, "Woman, behold thy Son," and to John He said, "Behold thy Mother."

Not only did Our Lady of the Atonement cooperate with Our Lord by giving Him her blood for His Incarnation, but when He poured out that same Blood for our salvation, she again cooperated in her acceptance of the second Motherhood which He bestowed upon her as she stood by the cross.

Our Lady by virtue of the Incarnation and the Atonement is herself brought into a most intimate relationship with the Blessed Trinity, for she becomes the Daughter of God the Father, the Mother of God the Son, and the Spouse of God the Holy Ghost.

Now the purpose for which God took unto Himself man's nature was, by that means to reconcile mankind unto Himself through the Atonement and further to collect souls out of the human race and draw them into His divine nature, as the tree drives its roots down into the soil and draws up into itself the earth's substance, which substance becomes ultimately part of the tree's organism.

This intimacy of union with God which Our Lord's Atonement achieved is marvelous beyond our power to comprehend.

In order the better to grasp it, let us consider at the fall "by the disobedience of one man," as St. Paul writes to the Roman Christians, "many were made sinners": the fall of our first parents in Eden polluted the fountain of humanity at its source. And as the sons and daughters of men increased, they became more and more "the children of disobedience"; for the gulf of separation between God and man widened with the lapse of centuries. This universality of sin made men everywhere rebel against the Divine Majesty, and the gravity of the offence could be measured only by the supreme dignity of Him who was sinned against. Great barriers, therefore, existed between man and God, not only the barrier of sin itself, but the impossibility of any unity between God and the concupiscence with which our race was infected. Our Lord, by His Incarnation, became the link between God and Man, nay, much more, He at the same time remaining God became Man, and as such, by His Atonement of the Cross, He was able to render infinite satisfaction ultimately more than its primal rectitude.

In the Catholic Church all this becomes operative for us by means of sacramental union and sanctifying grace, so that we are now, indeed Children of God the Father and reinstated heirs of the Kingdom of Heaven. Of this regenerate humanity of ours let us ever remember that Our Lady of the Atonement is the Mother and the New Eve, and shall be through all eternity.

Because of this accomplished unity between God and Man, God wills that there should follow as a consequence a union of the Children of *God one with another* in the House of Peter, their common Father, the Shepherd of Christendom and Vicar of Jesus Christ. This Unity which shall be most perfectly realized in Heaven, where the Saints dwell together in a oneness reflecting that which exists between the three persons of the Adorable Trinity.

The Disunity of Christendom

Because of Satan's war on the Church and through the perversion of the human heart in which dwells the natural pride of man and his spirit of rebellion, it has come to pass down through the ages that since the night of Our Lord's betrayal and His prayer for Unity, the many heresies have corrupted and schisms have divided His followers, but the unity of the Catholic

Church has been visibly preserved, and this was necessary for the *esse*, or being, of the Church, for one of her essential marks is that she is one. But still, as said above, there have been, and there are still, vast lapses from her Fold, children who while still hers by lawful right and are yet grievously alienated. It is this vast multitude outside the Unity of the Apostolic See (which Unity is the test of Catholicity) for whose return we must unceasingly invoke our Lady of the Atonement, whom we call in her Litany: *"Pillar of Unity and Shepherdess of the Wandering Sheep."*

The Word Adunatio in the Liturgy

It is most interesting to find our word "Adunare" used to express oneness, appearing no less than four times in the Liturgy of the Mass.

First, in the Canon of the Mass, where "the priest with outstretched hands, prays for the Church Militant"..."*in primis quae tibi offerimus pro Ecclesia Tua sancta Catholica; quam pacificare, custodire, ADUNARE, et regere digneris toto orbe terrarum."* ("Thee in the first place we offer up to Thee for Thy Holy Catholic, that it may please Thee to grant her peace, to protect, Unite, and govern her throughout the world.")

Second, in the Church's great prayer for the Unity of the Church said by every priest every day at Mass just before his communion: "O Lord Jesus Christ, who saidst unto Thine Apostles: Peace I leave with you, My peace I give unto you; regard not our sins, but the faith of Thy Church, and grant unto her that Peace and *Unity* which are agreeable to thy Will."—*"Secundum voluntatem tuam pacificare et COADUNARE digneris."*

Third, in the Mass of Holy Saturday, after the tenth Prophecy we find the beautiful prayer: *"Deus, qui diversitatem gentium in confessione tuae nominis ADUNASTI; da nobis et velle et posse quae praecipis ut populo ad aeternitatem vocato, una sit fides mentium, et pietas actionum."* ("O God, Who hast united in the confession of Thy Name, the several nations of the Gentiles; bestow upon us, we beseech Thee, both the power and the will to keep Thy commandments; that all whom Thou callest to eternal life may be one in faith, and likewise one in fervor of life.")

The *Fourth* example is in the oration for the Thursday in Easter week: *"Deus qui diversitatem gentium in confessione tuiae nominis* ADUNASTI: *da, ut renatis fonte baptismatis, una sit fides mentium, et pietas actionum."* ("O God Who hast united —*adunare*—many nations in confessing Thy Holy Name: upon those who have been born again in the waters of baptism, bestow unity in faith and like zeal in the doing of good works.")

We understand, therefore, that the particular aspect of the Atonement which we are to emphasize is Oneness with God and with one another, this being the end for which our Lord was raised up upon the Cross even as Moses lifted up the serpent in the wilderness, that great figure of Christ's Atonement for sin. Our Lord on the night of His betrayal prayed for the perfecting of this Double Unity in those unforgettable words, voicing His dying desire and testament, *"That they all may be one, at Thou, Father in Me, and I in Thee; that they also may be one in Us—I in them and Thou in Me; that they may be made perfect in one."* (St. John 17:21,23)

Let us then—and we cannot stress this too often—invoke and make known Our Lady of the Atonement as *Shepherdess of the Wandering Sheep and the Pillar of Unity.* Let us never doubt that by her powerful assistance, and with our cooperation, she will draw them back into Unity with God and with each other in the communion of the one, Holy, Catholic, Apostolic and Roman Church.

On the first Christmas night, most joyfully, she brought forth Jesus in Bethlehem, but on Calvary she travailed in agony to mother the new children He left to her in the person of St. John. Among these are the poor wandering ones whom she is calling to return to God and God's Church and to the fraternal love of their brethren. She knows so well that only by such a return shall they be wholly delivered from their bondage and enter into the glorious liberty of the sons of God, the liberty of the Faith, "once delivered to the Saints".

Let us look up to her all radiant on her throne, our beautiful Mother of the Atonement, apparelled in the crimson robe of the Precious Blood, interceding at this moment for the great AT-ONE-MENT; and may we never cease to unite our prayers with hers that the scales may fall away from the Great Shepherd whom Our Lord has appointed as His Vicegerent on earth is *Their* Father and *Their* Shepherd.

Make known then Our Lady of the Atonement as the "Mother of Conversions", spread the knowledge of her as the

Shepherdess of those of whom Our Lord spoke, "Other sheep I have that are not of this fold; them also I must bring, and they shall hear My voice and there shall be one Fold and one Shepherd". (St. John 10:16)

Pillar of Unity,
Shepherdess of the Wandering Sheep
Mother of Conversions, *Pray for us.*

20. Our Lady of the Atonement and Graymoor

Radio Broadcast, March 9, 1936

We call this Carmel of America the "Holy Mount" and we certainly believe that God had the Society of the Atonement in mind when He created it. But a holy thing is something that belongs to God, and as we have said only 25% of the Mount of the Atonement has been purchased as a patrimony of the Lord of Hosts up to the present time. It is unthinkable that three-fourths of this beautiful mount should be permanently estranged from the Friars and other Children of the Atonement. None of us should rest secure in our thoughts about the Holy Mountain until every inch of its extent is held in sacred trust for the religious uses of the Atonement.

A few lines above we called it an American Carmel, and we did so advisedly. Carmel was the home of the prophets of the New Law. After her assumption into heaven, Carmel became a center of devotion to the Blessed Virgin, which gave rise to the invocation of Our Lady of Mount Carmel; here upon this holy mountain is promoted a corresponding devotion to the same mother of God under the title of Our Lady of the Atonement. We do not doubt that as the Blessed Virgin showed a predilection for Mount Carmel, so she chose this mountain long before the coming of the Friars and set her affection upon it as a sacred eminence, where the Atonement of her Divine Son in which she so intimately participated would be illustrated and magnified in the last days of the world.

Many of our Protestant friends have the idea that Catholics do not read the Bible and that the Catholic Church has no use for the Holy Scripture. That is a big mistake, the Catholic

241

Church has always been the guardian and the defender of the Holy Scriptures, and today is conducting a campaign in defending the Bible against so many Protestant rationalists who have been denying miracles and tearing Scriptures to pieces generally. The Catholic Church is the only religious organization that fully lives up to the teachings of the Bible. For example, the Bible tells us that Our Lord said to St. Peter: "Thou art Peter and on this *Rock* I will build my Church and the gates of hell will not prevail against it—and I will give unto Thee the keys of the Kingdom of Heaven (that is to say My Church) and whatsoever thou shalt loose on earth, shall be loosed also in Heaven." All Protestants reject the Pope in succession to St. Peter, and refuse to recognize him as not only the foundation on which Christ built His Church, but as having the power of jurisdiction and government over His sheep, as Christ said to St. Peter, "Feed My sheep, Feed My lambs." Catholics are the only ones who are loyal to the Vicar of Christ and obey him who according to Christ's own word was given the keys of power and jurisdiction over His Church. Once again our Lord said to the Apostles that He would send the Holy Ghost and then He, the Holy Ghost, would guide them unto all truth so that all truth is preserved and taught under the guidance of the Holy Ghost by the Apostles who are in communion with St. Peter's successor and outside and apart from that body, who are the successors of the Apostles, the whole truth is not accepted, nor is it taught to the faithful.

We Catholics believe and accept the declaration of St. John and St. Paul that there is only one Mediator between God and man, Christ Jesus, the Incarnate Word of the Most High. Jesus alone, by taking our flesh and human nature, in union with the Godhead and becoming a man, offered Himself as a victim on the cross, and thereby opened the gates of heaven to all believers, obtaining pardon and redemption for mankind, and as St. Paul says: "He ever liveth to make intercession as our great High High Priest before His Father in Heaven." But that would not prevent the great High Priest from ordaining priests that should exercise His mediatorial office on the earth. In fact He said to the Apostles: "As the living Father has sent Me, so send I you—Go, ye into all the world, make disciples of all men, baptizing them in the name of the Father and of the Son and of the Holy Ghost." And immediately after His resurrection from the dead, He breathed on them and said, "Receive ye the Holy Ghost, whose sins ye shall forgive, they are forgiven and whose sins ye shall retain, they are retained." He also ordained them and commanded them to offer the Holy Sacrifice of the Mass as priests of the New Testament and as the great High Priest pleads His Atonement in Heaven so the priest on earth, in union with Him, presents that great Sacrifice before God the Father at the Catholic altar, throughout the world every day and every moment of every day. He that has the mediatorial office has commissioned His ministers to exercise that office among men and that it is not only the teaching of the Holy Scriptures but it has been the practice of the Church, which is the Mystical Body of Christ, down through the centuries, and will continue to be until the end and this is not contrary to the Word of God. Neither does it make God a liar, but it is so by the direct command of God, by His spoken word.

Now about the Blessed Virgin, the Mother of Christ. It was to St. John, who stood by the cross and who is quoted by our correspondent as saying: "If a man sin, we have as advocate with the Father, Jesus Christ, the righteous."—I say that it was to this same John that Our Lord on the cross said: "Behold thy Mother," after He had addressed Himself to that same mother saying: "Woman, behold thy Son." And we read in the Scripture: "From that hour St. John took her into his own home," and he acted in Our Lord's place by delegation, in caring for and proving a dutiful son to the Blessed Virgin, Christ's own mother.

Our Lord said to the multitude while He was on the earth. "Call no man your father upon earth for one is your Father who is in heaven." Some have interpreted this to mean that we were not to call anybody by the name of father, but that Our Lord could not have intended because the first commandment of promise in the decalogue is "Honor thy father and thy mother, that their days may be long in the land which the Lord thy God giveth thee." He meant for us to realize that in a supreme, eminent sense we have but one Father, and the earthly parents are only the delegated ones which the providence of God has commissioned to take care of us, not only to bring us into the world but to nourish, feed, clothe, care for us until we have arrived at the age when we can take care of ourselves. Our Lord is the one Mediator, but He has assigned His mediatorial office

243

in its exercise, particularly to His ministers. In the same way when Our Lord said to St. John, "Behold thy Mother", He gave His Mother not only to St. John but to all the faithful down through the Christian centuries, but in giving her that office He also endowed her with the qualities and the power to prove herself a real Mother.

I remember once calling upon a Baptist lady who was married to a Catholic gentleman, and she said that she prayed only to God, and she would not ask anything through the Blessed Virgin. She had only one child, a little girl. I said to her: "When your little girl comes to you and says, 'Mama, please do so and so for me,' do you say to her, 'Oh, my child, you mustn't pray to me, you must pray only to God; don't ask me for anything, go straight to God?'" The principle is the same in the divine economy. Catholics not only say the "Our Father", which is a direct address to God the Father in Heaven, but they also say the "Hail Mary", asking the Blessed Virgin their Mother, to take up their prayer and address God the Father on their behalf. This does not make God a liar. It is only putting into practice the very words of Christ when He said, "Son, behold thy Mother." If I behold the Blessed Virgin as my mother, I should expect her to be a mother. Mothers on the earth are the representatives of God in taking care of, nourishing and obtaining things for their children.

The correspondent says, "Brother, you are bound. Satan has blinded your eyes . . . he will do anything, even to deceiving the very elect by miracles and lying wonders." Now the devil is not going to work any miracles so as to get us to have a devotion to the Mother of Christ and to invoke her. He hasn't forgotten the judgment that was passed upon him by God after he seduced our first mother Eve, for the Lord said: "I will put enmity between thee and the woman and between thy seed and her seed, and she shall crush thy head." The woman referred to is the Blessed Virgin, the New Eve. In the Book of Revelation (of Apocalypse) St. John saw in Heaven a woman clothed with the sun, the moon under her feet and a crown of twelve stars on her head; that woman, the woman of the vision, is believed by Catholic theologians to be the Blessed Virgin. But then the scene shifts and the woman with the Child is pursued by the old red dragon who throws water out of his mouth to seek to destroy both her and her Child. This is Our Lady of

244

the Atonement and the Child represents her children of the cross, those that Christ gave to her redeemed by His Precious Blood and born again into the Kingdom of Glory. The devil is not going to work miracles to get any of her children on the earth to invoke and call upon their mother in Heaven to help them save their souls and escape the devil's clutches—far from it.

Now the Blessed Virgin has appeared on the earth many times in the past 1900 years, and she has repeatedly told those to whom she appeared to regard her as their Mother and to call upon her and that she will help and assist them and prove herself a real mother and a real intercessory before the throne of her Divine Son and also that of God the Father. Now the Blessed Virgin wouldn't do anything that was contrary to the divine will or in contradiction to the word of God, that is absolutely sure. The only way out of it would be to say, "Well, it wasn't the Blessed Virgin who appeared at all, it was only the devil who disguised himself into the form of the Blessed Virgin so as to deceive and to bind the elect and get them under his control", but that is really absurd and can be demonstrated as a false hypothesis. For example, the Blessed Virgin appeared to Bernadette at Lourdes and she told the child that a fountain would spring up out of the rock on which she stood and that the people who came there and bathed in that fountain and called upon her would be healed of all manner of incurable diseases. Now it not only is by bathing in the fountain that people are healed nowadays, but a large number of the people are healed when the Blessed Sacrament is carried in procession through the streets, just as Our Lord, when He was on earth, gave sight to the blind, healing the sick. Well, the devil doesn't do all that. It would give too much glory to God and strengthen the faith of too many people in Jesus as their Savior.

Let me tell you one of my own experiences. When I was head of the Associate Mission of the Episcopal Church in Omaha, I twice anointed a young woman, who the first time through the prayer of faith was healed of valvular heart trouble and the second time was brought back to consciousness after she had been in a coma for two days through concussion of the brain, and there seemed little hope of her recovery. Shortly after that I came to Graymoor and one day in February, 1900, I received a telegram from this young lady, stating that her father was ill with double pneumonia and her sister, Emily, was dying, pray for them. This young lady developed a religious vocation and wished to become a Sister, and the only reason she wouldn't come to Graymoor was because she knew we said the Hail Mary, and like our good friend who wrote this letter, she had conscientous objection to saying the Hail Mary. I sat down and wrote to her, "You have faith enough in my prayers to send me a telegram 1500 miles. I have sent that telegram to the Queen of Heaven and if your father and your sister get well, you will know it is because the Blessed Virgin can hear prayers and answer them." Before my letter reached her, she wrote a letter to me, stating that on the next day her father made a sudden recovery and her sister, who had become blind, her feet were swollen with every indication of the immediate approach of death, was making a rapid recovery to the astonishment of the doctors. Convinced by this miracle that it was right to invoke the Blessed Virgin and say the Hail Mary, this young lady came at the end of the same year to Graymoor.

Believe me, my dear non-Cathloic friends, we have had quantities and quantities of experiences and demonstrations, not only that the Blessed Virgin can hear prayers, but that it is the will of God and of her Divine Son that we go to her as our Mother and expect her to give to her children that assistance and help which they need.

21. The Feast of Our Lady of the Atonement

The Lamp, June, 1938

In the Royal Month of June we can wish you no better grace and greater joy than a close, personal and intimate union with the Sacred Heart of Our Divine Redeemer, whose delight it is to dwell with the sons of men, and in order that He might do so more perfectly, united our humanity with His Godhead. Taking a body like ours, the corruption due to sin excepted, He, by His death on the Cross, made it possible to unite His Flesh with ours in the Sacraments of the Catholic Church; and by taking up His abode in our hearts as in a Tabernacle, He will establish a vital and supernatural union between His own Heart and those who like St. John love Him supremely, giving love for love.

246

I beg to remind our Rosarians that Saturday, July 9th, will be the Feast of Our Lady of the Atonement, and we recommend, as far as possible, that all Rosarians observe the novena, which leads up to it, beginning on July 1st, the *Feast of the Most Precious Blood*, which is also the First Friday. It will be the 45th Anniversary of that momentous day, the 7th Sunday after Pentecost, July 9th, 1893, when the Father Founder received the Name of the Institute.

In observing the novena, do your best to receive Holy Communion as often as possible and wear the medal of Our Lady of the Atonement attached to a piece of red ribbon in special honor of the *Most Precious Blood*, through the shedding of which Christ made Atonement for the sins of the world and opened the gate of heaven to all believers.

22. Our Lady of the Atonement and Mother's Day

May 14, 1939

Today is Mother's Day—and those of you who are so fortunate as to have your mother still in the land of the living, will be sending to her some message or token of your love, which is quite as it should be. But we, Children of the Atonement, should never forget that Lady of glorious beauty, "the Great Wonder of Heaven", who is described by St. John in the Apocalypse as seated on a throne of surpassing magnificence, her vesture the glory of the sun, her crown consisting of twelve brilliant stars and the moon constituting her footstool, for she is the Mother of us all, whom we invoke at Graymoor under the title of Our Lady of the Atonement.

Let us this afternoon try to convey to you a finer conception of what the Motherhood of Mary is in relationship to yourself and of your own glorious dignity and destiny as a Child of Mary. You will remember that when the Blessed Virgin gave birth to our Savior at Bethlehem, the Evangelist states that she "brought forth her first born Son and laid Him in a manger". Some students of the Bible, not belonging to the Catholic Church, have concluded from this statement that the Blessed Virgin, after she brought forth her Divine Babe, produced other children as a result of her marriage with St. Joseph. This idea,

247

as you all know, is quite abhorrent to the Catholic who believes that the Blessed Virgin was not only immaculately conceived but that she continued to be a stainless virgin, during her entire lifetime. In fact, we confess her to be "Ever-Virgin", and yet that expression "first born son" is true, because by the travail of her soul united with the death agony of her Son, Jesus, on the Cross, the Holy Ghost still being her spouse, she became the New Eve, the Mother of the Children of the Atonement, the race of the redeemed, who in union with Christ, her first-born Son, should be the heirs of the kingdom of heaven and of Christ's eternal glory.

This is very important for us to understand. We are not the children of the Blessed Virgin just because she has adopted us, but, intrinsically because through the Sacrament of Baptism we were regenerated by the Holy Ghost, given a new birth, and incorporated into the Mystical Body of Christ, becoming as St. Paul says, "Bone of His bone and flesh of His flesh." Now the bone and the flesh of Jesus was derived from His Mother while He slept within her womb. Therefore, it is a blood relationship. You know, once in a while, when two people are married, they are not blessed with any children, and they go to the foundling hospital and get a baby and adopt the little one, but though they lavish much love upon the child, they will never forget that the child is not theirs by blood relationship. We must understand by virtue of our new birth into the Kingdom of God that the Blessed Virgin is our real Mother and not merely a Mother that has just adopted us. By Baptism, as I said, a moment ago, we are incorporated into the Mystical Body of Christ and by that process of incorporation we are also brought into relationship with the Blessed Virgin, which is intrinsically similar to the relationship which Christ has to the Blessed Virgin as His Mother. Don't you see how tremendously important that is and how, when we realize it, the greater love and affection we should have for our Mother in Heaven?

Sometimes on the earth the wife dies, and the husband marries again and brings another Mother into the family, but the children of the first Mother cannot forget that this new Mother is only a stepmother, no matter how kind she may be. She may be very lovely, but she is a stepmother at the best. The Blessed Virgin is not our stepmother. She is our real Mother in so far as we are the Sons and Daughters of the Atonement and members of the Mystical Body of Christ.

What a wonderful Mother she is! This is illustrated by the novena to Our Lady of the Atonement, which is conducted at Graymoor by the Sisters and Friars, beginning always on the first Saturday of the Month. So many are the favors granted by our Atonement Mother to her children, who invoke her and through this Novena that it has become popularly known as the Novena of Last Resort. When Jesus constituted Our Lady of the Atonement the Mother of all that should be redeemed by His Precious Blood on Calvary's Cross, He endowed her with abundant capacity to discharge her functions as a Mother; and although her family is so huge and immense and scattered all over the world, God has given her capacity of mind and of heart to think about and watch over all her children no matter where they are on the earth.

It is part of the revelation that Our Lord made to His people on the earth that everyone has a Guardian Angel, a ministering spirit that goes forth from God to watch over and assist us. Now these Guardian Angels, I have no doubt, are under the particular direction of our Atonement Mother in Heaven; and if need be, she sends forth other angels to assist her children. For example, our Sisters often receive thanksgivings from somebody getting a job after he had been out of work a long time because he sent in his petition to the novena of Our Lady of the Atonement. What, probably, was the way Our Lady brought it about? Perhaps she sent an Angel all the way from Heaven, to find that job for her son who called upon her. Very often somebody's influence secures a job for a friend or a politician gets a job for somebody through his influence. Now the Angel sent by Mary may go to the boss of the factory and although the boss does not see the Angel or hear his voice, this Angel brings the pressure of his mind upon that of the boss and suggests to him that he employ such and such a man or such a girl. But the real agent who secured that job was the messenger of Our Lady.

She is such a wonderful Mother! How you ought to love her and how you ought to trust her and invoke her, remembering that this beautiful stainless Mother in Heaven wishes her children to be pure and holy on earth and to obey God as she obeyed Him. So—let us not only cultivate a beautiful devotion to the Blessed Virgin, but strive ourselves to be saints, reflecting not only the image of Christ in our soul and His conduct in our life, but that of our altogether lovely Mother, the stainless one, the Queen of Heaven, and the consort of Jesus Christ upon His throne.

23. Feast of Our Lady of the Atonement

Convent Grounds, Graymoor
July 9, 1939

Now there stood by the cross of Jesus, Mary, His
Mother, and Mary Cleophas and Mary Magdalene.

As it has already been announced to you, we observe to-day the feast of Our Lady of the Atonement, a feast peculiar in its origin to Graymoor and the Society of the Atonement, a great favor that we were able to obtain by the *Motu proprio* of the Holy Father—or the permission to observe this feast. In time, we have no doubt, the devotion to Our Lady under that title will extend throughout the Universal Church. We consider it the mark of the divine favor that we have been permitted to introduce the Blessed Virgin under that title to the Church at large. Because of the high significance of the title and its primary importance and what it must be to Our Lady herself, we have no doubt that in time to come it will be celebrated by the whole Church throughout the world. We started in 1908 at Graymoor when we were very small, the Church Unity Octave. It has already spread throughout the universal Church, but it is also observed by many thousands among our separted brethren—and we feel that this devotion will spread far and wide. Let us think this morning of the title and how precious it must be to the Blessed Virgin herself.

St. John in the Apocalypse speaks of the Lamb of God and His exaltation in heaven, of the honor and worship that is paid to Him and he refers to Him as slain before the foundation of the world, foregoing in the mind of the Almighty before the world was created, the Atonement of Christ upon the Cross in the mind of God all these centuries, aeons and ages a preparation in the mind of God for that great sacrifice Christ made of Himself upon the Cross. As the Lamb of God, He shed His blood to take away the sins of the world and organize a new race with its Creator and Redeemer. Now the Church in proclaiming the Immaculate Conception of the Blessed Virgin and her great privilege of never having been touched by original sin, or by any other actual sin, during the full career of her being, is careful to declare this came to her by anticipation of Christ as the Lamb of God who offered Himself on the Cross to take away the sins of the world as St. John said: "Behold the Lamb of God who taketh away the sins of the world."

And just as the sacrifice of the Old Law took away sin by anticipation of the sacrifice of the Lamb of God on Calvary, so the Blessed Virgin had the wonderful privilege of being conceived without sin which came to be hers through the Atoning Sacrifice on the Cross. Consequently, she who must have a keen appreciation of her dignity and glory as "blessed among women" and she must have a tremendous respect and affection for that Atonement of Calvary because it means so much to her. Consequently, that title must be especially pleasing to her. It was not only her creation without fault or stain of sin, but that Atonement Sacrifice, which brought her into a wonderful relation with the three Persons of the Adorable Trinity. God the Father became her Father. God the Son became her Son and the Holy Ghost became her Spouse for before there could be any Atonement, there must be an Incarnation which was a preparation for the Atoning Sacrifice of Calvary. That is a reason Christ became incarnate that He might offer His life to take away the sins of the world; in order to make this sacrifice He had first to become incarnate and it was all because of the Atonement which brought the Blessed Virgin into a marvelous relationship with God and she has to thank the Atonement for that. So that name to her must be exceedingly great and immensely precious.

Then as a result of the Atonement, the Blessed Virgin became the New Eve. When the Evangelist describes the birth of Jesus at Bethlehem, he says of the Blessed Virgin that she brought forth her first born Son, clothed Him in swaddling clothes and laid Him in a manger. That would indicate some other children and the children that would be indicated were the children of Calvary, where she became the New Eve, of the baptized of all that live in Christ, so Our Lord addressed her on the Cross, "Woman, behold thy Son; Son, behold thy Mother".

251

Consequently the motherhood as far as the redeemed humanity are concerned is bound up with the Atonement, and the Blessed Virgin must value it accordingly; and therefore the title when applied to herself must be exceedingly precious.

I dare say Our Lady values with different degrees the titles that are given to her in the Litany of Loretto, and I am satisfied that there are none that appeals to her more than that of the Atonement. One of the popular devotions to the Blessed Virgin is that of Our Lady of Sorrows conducted and sponsored by the Servites of Mary,—but the sorrows of many are only incidental to the Atonement. One of the incidents connected with the Atonement was sorrow, for although Mary brought forth her first born son in Bethlehem with joy, she had to travail with sorrow in bringing forth the Children of the Atonement, because they were conceived in sin and this new birth in God involved the very death of the Redeemer of the world. All the sorrows of Our Lady by perfect sympathy were expressed in the heart of Mary. Our Lord in death was pierced by a spear, and her heart was pierced by a sword of anguish. But sorrow was incidental. It was not the great thing of the Atonement and would result from the Atonement even as Our Lord said in one of the addresses to the Apostles before He took His departure from them. "In a little while and you shall see me not because I go to the Father." Your sorrows are for a little while. Your joys are eternal. "A woman when she is in travail has sorrow but when the child is born, she remembereth no more the sorrows because of the joy that a son is born into the world." So the sorrows of the Blessed Virgin are transitory. They are not permanent, but the joy that comes to her through the Atonement, that is eternal. In sorrow she brings forth the children of the Atonement, but when that is passed she forgets the sorrow when the Children of the Atonement are brought into the Kingdom of God in eternal glory.

As the title must be dear to the Blessed Virgin, so must it be dear to us. So let us spread this devotion, knowing that those who preach her under that invocation will find her expecially gracious.

24. The Rosary League of Our Lady of the Atonement

The Graymoor Friars and Sisters never cease to pray for the "Sanctification and Increase of the Children of the Atonement". Attached to the white cord of every Atonement Religious is a seven decade Franciscan Rosary, and no day passes without the recitation of either the seven joys or the seven sorrows of our Atonement Mother. Whether it is the joys or the sorrows of Mary, we are commemorating, when we come to the third decade; i.e., the Holy Nativity of Mary's Child, or the Losing of Him in Jerusalem, the intention wherewith that third decade is recited every day is the Sanctification and the Increase of the Children of the Atonement.

That prayer will undoubtedly be answered because it finds its response in the fervent desire of the Sacred Heart of Jesus and the Immaculate Heart of Mary; moreover, the Most Holy Trinity so wills it. "This is the will of God," says St. Paul, "even your sanctification." To the Roman Christians he wrote: "Beloved of God, ye are called to be saints." (Rom. 1:7) To the Thessalonians: "May the God of peace Himself sanctify you in all things; that your whole spirit, and soul, and body may be preserved blameless in the coming of our Lord Jesus Christ, He is faithful who hath called you, who also will do it."(1 Thess. 5:23,24)

But the paternity of God and the maternity of Mary will never be satisfied with just a few very choice and very select children. The Sons and Daughters of the Atonement must not only be saints, holy and most beautiful in the eyes of Christ the New Adam and Mary the New Eve, but they must increase exceedingly and be multiplied until they not only fill the world but also the high courts of Heaven. When Jehovah made covenant with Abraham, He declared: "By My own self have I sworn. I will bless thee, and I will multiply thy seed as the stars of heaven, and as the sand that is by the seashore." (Gen 22:16). To Isaac God renewed the covenant, saying: "Go not down into Egypt but stay in the land I shall tell thee of. Sojourn in it, for thee and to thy seed I will give all these countries to fulfill the oath which I swore to Abraham thy Father. And I will multiply thy seed like the Stars of Heaven." (Gen. 26:2-4). And finally to Jacob, appeared the Lord in a dream leaning upon the ladder and saying to him: "I am the Lord God of Abraham, thy Father, and the God of Isaac . . . thy seed shall be as the dust of the earth . . . and in thee and thy seed all the tribes of the earth shall be blessed". (Gen. 28:13).

If God, in fulfillment of His covenant oath to Abraham, Isaac and Jacob, has so multiplied and increased their posterity that the Israelites, the Ishmelites and the other descendants of Abraham are to be encountered, north, south, east and west, wherever the traveller goes in any and every portion of the earth, how much more will the seed of that new and everlasting covenant which Jesus Christ, the New Adam, made with God the Father in His own Blood, multiply and increase until the Children of the Atonement replenish the whole earth and the words of St. John in the Apocalypse are fulfilled: "The seventh angel sounded the trumpet: and there were great voices in Heaven, saying: The Kingdom of this world is become Our Lord's and the possession of His Christ, and He shall reign forever and forever."

We ask all members of the League to adopt the practice of the Graymoor Friars and Sisters and to say one decade of the Rosary every day for the Sanctification and Increase of the Children of the Atonement and let this be over and above whatever other decades you may say. If you are reciting the joyful mysteries associate this special intention always with the mystery of the Holy Nativity; if it be the sorrowful mysteries, link up the same intention with the Loss of Jesus in Jerusalem.

All the regenerate, who have been redeemed by the Blood of Christ, may rightly call themselves the Children of the Atonement, as well as the members of our Atonement Society, the Union-That-Nothing-Be-Lost and the Rosary League. We have no desire to restrict the name to ourselves but as a title for the elect seed of Jesus crucified and Mary, the New Eve, it originated at Graymoor, just as did that glorious name of the Virgin Mother herself, Our Lady of the Atonement.

25. Mother of the Mystical Body

The Lamp, October, 1939

Not only was the Name of our Holy Society specially revealed to the Father Founder seven years before it developed into a Religious Institute with its three congregations organi-

254

cally formed, but simultaneously with that formation for the first time in the history of the Catholic Church was the Blessed Virgin, the Immaculate Mother of God, addressed by the title, Our Lady of the Atonement. It was in October, 1901, that the Rosary League of Our Lady of the Atonement was formed and eighteen years later (1919) the Holy Father, by a *Motu proprio*, instituted a feast in her honor under that title and granted indulgences to the members of the League.

Have you ever taken special note of the way I address you as Rosarians? Did any one else ever call you a Child of the Atonement except the writer of these letters? Others have called you repeatedly, and you have called yourself—a Child of Mary—but a Child of the Atonement, never perhaps. Yet it was by reason of the Atonement that the Blessed Virgin became your Mother and you became her child. No words of mine can adequately describe the grandeur of Mary's Atonement Motherhood and the sublime dignity which has befallen us by virtue of our Atonement Birthright.

Do let me give you a larger and more vivid conception of both the one and the other—that is, on the dignity and transcending glory of Mary as Our Lady of the Atonement and your filial relation to her. As Catholics, we have been well instructed concerning the relationship of the Blessed Virgin to the Three Persons of the Adorable Trinity. On account of the Incarnation of Our Lord she has become the Daughter of God the Father, the Mother of God the Son, and the Spouse of God the Holy Ghost, she reigns in heaven Queen of Angels and Saints. St. John, while a prisoner on the Isle of Patmos, was caught up into heaven, and saw many wonderful things which he describes in the Book of the Apocalypse, by the "Great Wonder of Heaven" as he calls it, was the Woman, crowned with twelve stars, encompassed about with the glory of the sun as her vesture and the moon humbly serving as her footstool. All this glory comes to her by virtue of Christ's Incarnation.

But what did His Atonement on Calvary's Cross do for Mary? Let us see. The theologians speak of Jesus Christ as the "New Adam", and the Blessed Virgin as the "New Eve". But when did Christ become the "New Adam" and when did Mary become the "New Eve"? Was it not on Mt. Calvary and was it not by virtue of the Atonement, the Sacrifice of Himself, which He made into death on Calvary's tree, not alone by the shedding of His Blood, as the Lamb of God, to take away the sins of the world, but to create a New Race of Men, the Atonement Race, of which He Himself is Head, the Father, and the Blessed Virgin is Mother, who stood by the Cross, one heart and one soul with Him in making that Sacrifice to become the New Eve, the Mother of all that live in and through Christ?

Every child of the Church has been taught from infancy to call Mary his or her Mother. But what kind of Mother, is the Blessed Virgin to the children that Christ gave to her when he said from the Cross, "Woman, behold thy son," and to St. John, "Behold thy Mother"? Is she our Mother only in the sense which often happens on earth when a man and his wife fail to have any children of their own and then go to a foundling hospital and select a baby, adopt it, bring it up and teach the little one to call them "Papa" and "Mama"? Did Jesus Christ on the Cross just ask His Mother to adopt all children, the Christians of future generations and watch over them as a Mother Superior might watch over the orphan children committed to her care in an asylum? No—a thousand times, no! To appreciate this we must understand that Jesus, as the New Adam, begot us when He travailed with the Blessed Virgin to bring us forth on Calvary, He in His Sacred Humanity as the Father and the Blessed Virgin as the Mother of the Children of the Atonement, among whom are you and I happy to be numbered. Let me remind you of a prophecy made by Isaias, concerning the Messias. He prophesied saying: "Unto us a child is born and He shall be called Wonderful, Counseller, the Almighty, the Father of the World to come." Jesus on the Cross became this "Father" and "world to come" is heaven, peopled by the Children of His Atonement.

Speaking of Himself before He was crucified, Jesus said: "A corn of wheat, except it die, abideth alone, but, if it die, it bringeth forth much fruit." Take a grain of wheat, plant it in the ground and in due time, it will spring up "first as a blade, then the ear, then the full corn in the ear," to use the very words of Christ Himself, and, when it is ripe and golden for the harvest, if you take the head off the stock and rub it in your hands, you will discover that it contains perhaps twelve grains of wheat exactly like the one that died. Now the "grain of wheat" is the father and the twelve grains that were produced by its death are its children, and in the same way Jesus is the Father of the baptized.

You will remember how Nicodemus, the ruler of the Jews, came to Christ by night and how Our Lord startled him by saying: "Except a man be born again, he cannot enter into the Kingdom of God." And, when Nicodemus wondering, asked the Divine Master, "How can a man, when he is old, be born again? Can he enter a second time into his mother's womb and be born?" The only answer that Jesus gave him was, "Except a man be born of water and of the Spirit, he cannot enter into the Kingdom of God." The "Kingdom of God" is that kingdom which Christ came into the world to establish, and which shall have no end. And the citizens of that kingdom are His sons and daughters, redeemed by His Precious Blood and begotten by Him as Princes of the Royal Family over which He reigns as King of Kings in Heaven.

As Savior of the world, He might have been content with shedding His Blood, washing away the guilt of the sinner, reconciling him to God the Father and giving him grace enough to keep the holy Commandments of God and preparing him a planet somewhere in the universe, perhaps a hundred times as big as this world in which those redeemed by *His Blood,* pardoned of their sins, might have continued the race of Adam, multiplying and replenishing the new world that God had given them. But He did much more than that. He incorporated us into His Mystical Body and through the extension of His Incarnation made us along with Himself "partakers of the Divine Nature" (2 St. Peter 1:4).

As Abraham was the father of many nations by reason of his numerous posterity and they all have the mark of Abraham upon them, whether they are the tribe of Judah, or Dan, or Reuben, or any other of the twelve tribes of Israel, so those that are begotten of Christ and through baptism made members of His Mystical Body are His sons and daughters of the Atonement through eternity. And if by correspondence to grace they prove themselves worthy of the heavenly mansions in the Father's House, they will be received into heaven, not as ordinary citizens but they will be received into the palace as the King's sons and the King's daughters, Kings and Queens through eternity. When we arrive in Heaven, we will be welcomed there by Jesus Christ and His Mother, as the two little princesses were gathered into their arms by King George and Queen Elizabeth, his consort, when they arrived back into England after their visit to

Canada and the United States last summer. As the royal motor carriage drove through the streets of London, on the way to Buckingham Palace, the common people stood upon the curb and crowded the streets to do their sovereign honor and extend to the royal personages a hearty welcome to their own country, but it was only the little Elizabeth and her sister, Margaret Rose, with some of the maids of honor and the servants that were in immediate attendance upon the King and Queen that were received into Buckingham Palace.

When we get to Heaven, we won't be assigned to a tenement house or be permitted to stand on the curb and applaud when the King passes by, but the Royal Lady, Queen of Angels and of Saints, as the consort of Christ, the King, will welcome us into the very palace of God Almighty; and there will be fulfilled the promise Jesus made to His Apostles before He left them saying, "Let not your heart be troubled. You believe in God. Believe also in Me. In My Father's house are many mansions; and I go to prepare a place for you that where I am there ye may also be."

Understand that the Royal Blood of Jesus Christ flows through the veins of the baptized, particularly after they have received Him in Holy Communion, according to His own word and promise, "Who so eateth My Flesh and drinketh My Blood abideth in Me and I in him. He shall have eternal life, and I will raise him up at the last day." We must not forget that the Royal Blood that flows in the veins of Jesus Christ was derived from Mary, His Mother, when His humanity was formed in her womb by the Holy Ghost; and it is the same Holy Ghost who in the Sacrament of Regeneration causes Christ, the son of Mary, to be born again in us; and we are made "members of His Body, of His flesh and of His bones" (Ephesians 5:30). It was in our Baptism we became sons and daughters of the New Adam, even Jesus Christ, and His Mother as the New Eve, became our Atonement Mother.

VI

Father Paul of the At-one-ment

IN THIS SECTION *of our work we have chosen Fr. Paul's words that refer to him in a personal way, such as the accounts of his life and conversion, his entrance into the Church, and some thoughts on Mother Lurana, who was so closely associated with him in the Society which they founded and in the apostolate of Christian Unity. We have included an account of the Union-That-Nothing-Be-Lost, a missionary agency which Fr. Paul began in 1904 and developed in the Church in 1911. It was inspired by the words of Our Lord: "Gather up the fragments that remain that nothing be lost" (Jn. 6:12). We have chosen, too, a few selections on the favorite theme of the Graymoor founder, on Christian Unity, under the name that he originated, At-one-ment or At-one-mentism.*

Paul of the Atonement became Paul of the At-one-ment. He was fond of quoting the words of St. Paul from the epistle to the Romans in this form: "We joy in God through Our Lord Jesus Christ, by whom we have now received the At-one-ment."

We are told that after St. Francis received the wounds of the stigmata on Mt. Alverna in 1224 he did not speak of Jesus Crucified, or of the Mystery of the Cross, but of the Divine Trinity and of the soul's union with God. So too with Fr. Paul. As he advanced in age he spoke and wrote more than ever on Unity, of man's union with God, achieved through grace.

Unity was the great ideal and the consuming passion in the life of Fr. Paul and as he grew in years, this theme became more urgent and compelling. To it he devoted all his energies and talents and spent himself without reservation. He was an Apostle of Unity in the finest sense of the word.

Unity was his special vocation and the destiny of his two religious communities. He wished everyone would be an apostle of unity according to the opportunities in which Providence had placed him. Fr. Paul longed to bring all the world to unity with the Sacred Heart of Christ and in this sacred endeavor he was surely an Apostle of Reunion. His legacy is a precious gift to his spiritual children which reaches out to all the world.

1. The Story of the Conversion of Father Paul

(*From Beyond the Road to Rome,*
Compiled and edited by Georgina Pell Curtis,
St. Louis Herder, 1914, pp. 202-219)

My thesis is this: The so-called Oxford Movement in the Anglican Church is a Romeward Movement and its *terminus ad quem*, a return of the Catholic Remnant in the Anglican Body to communion with the Apostolic See. So far as this has been, now is, and shall hereafter prove to be the outcome of the Oxford Movement, it is inspired and directed by God and is the work of the Holy Ghost. To this movement I owe conversion to Catholicism, and being correspondingly grateful, I wish to win for it among my fellow Catholics as much sympathy as possible; and it is to this end—and not for self-laudation—I contribute this story.

I have sometimes said that it took Divine Providence seventy-five years to make me a Catholic. Not that I wish to add twenty-five years to my actual age, but in reality my conversion began with my father; yet in his case it never got beyond the High Church Anglican stage. To tell my story, therefore, I must start with my father. He belonged to an honorable Welsh family proud of their sterling integrity, who migrated from the old country to Philadelphia in the early part of the nineteenth century. I have often heard my father tell of his uncle, Tom Wattson, a wholesale baker of the Quaker City, who contracted with the United States government to supply breadstuffs to the army during the war with Mexico, but owing to the uncalculated rise in the price of flour, he was ruined financially. He might have compromised with his creditors at twenty-five cents on the dollar, but he was too honest for that, and before he died he discharged every obligation he had contracted, dollar for dollar.

Joseph Newton Wattson, for that was my father's name, was born in Lewistown, Pennsylvania, and as a young man began his professional career as a law practitioner. His elder brother, Lewis T. Wattson, after whom I was named, became a wealthy iron manufacturer whose mills were located in Lewistown and he became president also of the Huntington and

Broad Top Railroad, one of the earliest and still existing railroads of Pennsylvania. The family was Calvinistic and its members were adherents of the Presbyterian Church, in which my father was strictly reared.

He had not long been practicing law when he providentially became interested in a controversy which occurred at the time between Dr. Potter, the Anglican Bishop of Pennsylvania, and a prominent Presbyterian Doctor of Divinity. My father's legally trained mind soon convinced him that Bishop Potter had the better of the argument, and being an extremely conscientious man, he was true to his convictions and not only submitted to the Apostolicity which the Episcopal Church claimed, but more than that, he actually abandoned the practice of law and entered the General Theological Seminary, Chelsea Square, New York City to become a clergyman of the Episcopal Church.

This was in the early forties and shortly after the submission of John Henry Newman to the jurisdiction of the Apostolic See. The ritualistic, or "Puseyite" movement, as it was then commonly called (for Dr. Pusey succeeded Cardinal Newman as its moving spirit) had taken root in America and the General Theological Seminary had become a "storm center" of agitation between the ritualistic and the Evangelical parties. My father entered the controversy with the enthusiasm of a young convert and became a pronounced "Puseyite". So many of the young men of the seminary followed Newman's example and entered the Catholic Church—notably Wadhams, afterwards first Bishop of Ogdensburg, Monsignor Preston, Rector of St. Ann's, New York, Father Walworth, one of the first associates of Father Hecker in founding the Paulist Congregation, and McMasters, the founder and editor of the *Freeman's Journal*, that the suspicion took fast hold of the minds of the dean and faculty of the seminary, that certain "Jesuits in disguise" had entered the institution and were responsible for these transmigrations. My father and a young man named Donnelly, who formerly had been a Congregationalist, became the scapegoats of this false suspicion and actually were expelled from the institution as the ringleaders of this imaginary "band of Jesuits".

It seemed an irony of Providence that, about forty years later, the son of Joseph Newton Wattson studied for Anglican Orders in the same General Seminary and my father was at the time a trustee of the institution, yet the son was much further

262

advanced in ritualism and Catholic practice than his father had been in his day as a student.

Another striking coincidence was the following: When my father's dismissal from the seminary took place he went to Wilmington, Delaware, to call upon Dr. Lee, his bishop, who was an Evangelical of the Evangelicals; and the counsel he received was, "Young man, go to Rome, that's where you belong!" It was not, however, given to my father to see his duty with the bishop's eyes, and finally he was adopted and ordained to the Anglican ministry by Bishop Whittingham of Baltimore. Yet such was the cloud of suspicion that still hung around him by reason of his expulsion from the New York Seminary, that the best his bishop could do for him was to assign him a country curé of souls on what is known as the "Eastern Shore" of Maryland.

Once he was called by the vestry of St. Luke's Church, Baltimore, to be their rector; but a church bookseller of the Monumental City quickly secured a recall, by informing the vestry that this "Eastern Shore" clergyman was a "Jesuit Emissary", and thus it came to pass that my father, notwithstanding mental abilities of a high order and an attractive personality spent thirty years of his ministry in two obscure country parishes, the victim of Popish bogey, pure and unadulterated.

It was in 1885 that I was graduated from the General Theological Seminary and returned to the eastern shore of Maryland to be ordained a deacon. My diocesan, Bishop Henry C. Lee, was at the time to officiate and he called upon his venerable brother, the aged Bishop Lee of Delaware, to act in his place. And so it came to pass that my father presented his son for ordination to the Bishop, who, forty years before, had turned him from the door as a Roman suspect. When we sat at dinner that day, after the ordination was over, it was noticed that tears of emotion were in the eyes of Bishop Lee.

My vocation to the *ministry* must have been infused at the same time with the grace of Holy Baptism, for it was recognized by my parents and others, while I was still an infant, and it was in my mind when I first began to think. As far as vocation to the *Religious Life* is concerned, I am sure that it first came to me at the age of about ten years, when my father was recounting to me the story of his expulsion from the seminary and incidentally mentioned the Paulist Fathers. It was summer time.

We sat in the rectory hallway and I remember distinctly how an interior voice—inaudible yet quite clear—said: "That is what you will do some day, found a Preaching Order like the Paulists."

Through all the vicissitudes and changes of my subsequent career as a college student, a seminarian and an Episcopal clergyman, I never lost the remembrance of that voice. I had been rector of St. John's Church for some eight years, when, at the age of thirty, it seemed to me that the time had arrived for my resignation from parochial work and I contemplated retiring to the Mission Church of the Holy Cross which I had been instrumental in establishing, two years previously, as a chapel-of-ease of St. John's, there to begin the formation of the Society. But *what to call it* perplexed me more than anything else. I felt the attraction to the cross and Passion of our Divine Redeemer; but every name I could think of in that connection already had been appropriated by some religious community, either in the Catholic or Episcopal Church.

It was at this time that St. Francis of Assisi began to exercise a dominating influence over my life, and having read how he had based the Rule of the Friars Minor upon three Scripture texts which he had obtained by having a priest open before him the missal three times in the name of the Holy Trinity, I was strongly moved to seek of God in the same way the name of the new Institute.

Accordingly, after early celebration of the Holy Communion on the Seventh Sunday after Pentecost, July 9, 1893, I knelt before the altar in St. John's Church, and having invoked the Holy Trinity opened the volume of the Scriptures three times and thereby obtained not the name alone, but like St. Francis, the three texts which till this day remain the foundation of the Constitutions of the Society of the Atonement. Going from the Church to the rectory, I first wrote down the name, *Society of the Atonement,* at the top of a sheet of notepaper and underneath were carefully recorded the three texts, of which the central one contained the name: "We joy in God through Our Lord Jesus Christ by whom we have now received the Atonement." (Romans 5:11, King James Version)

Undoubtedly I would have carried out my intention of resigning St. John's and retiring to the Mission Church of the Holy Cross had I not been interrupted then and there by the same interior voice that twenty years before had given me the first

264

intimation of religious vocation. This time the "still, small voice" said: "You will have to wait seven years for this to be realized." I was distinctly disappointed; nevertheless in obedience I laid the paper aside as if nothing had happened and went quietly on with my work as a pastor of souls.

Two years later I went West and assumed the headship of the Associate Mission of Omaha—exchanging a salary of $100 for one of $15 a month—because I hoped that there I would be able to convert an association of unmarried clergy into the religious congregation of the Society of the Atonement. The term of pledged service in the Associate Mission was three years, subject to renewal at the will of each member. My companions were zealous, godly men whose theology and ritual practice were modeled after the Roman pattern. To illustrate their self-denial and serious piety, it will suffice to say that for a considerable time we observed a retreat of one day in every month when no one ate or drank anything until 6 o'clock in the evening. We had four mission congregations in Omaha and as many more in outlying towns. So successful was the work of the clergy of the Associate Mission that it presented twenty-five per cent of all the candidates confirmed by Bishop Worthington in his entire diocese. Yet the Associate Mission was not destined to eventuate in the Society of the Atonement, and now it lies buried in the same grave with so many like ventures in the Episcopal Church.

It was on the feast of the Dedication of all Franciscan Churches, July 4, 1898, that for the first time in my life I truthfully could say: *"I believe in the universal jurisdiction of the Roman Pontiff as the Successor of St. Peter and the Vicar of Jesus Christ."* From my youth I had studied the question of Papal Supremacy far more than any other single historical and theological proposition connected with Christianity. Moreover, I had prayed constantly for supernatural light; but until that day I had still remained in the dark, and quite at sea as to the truth or falsity of the Petrine Claims. Truly, faith is a supernatural gift of God and the study of books, without divine illumination, is not sufficient to convince these born outside her pale of truth of the Catholic Religion, even though to those who enjoy that supernatural gift it all seems as clear as the sunlight.

I immediately wrote to Bishop Worthington, told him what had happened, and tendered my resignation to take effect on the feast of St. Michael the Archangel, when my term of pledge service in the Associate Mission expired. After that I would go into retirement until I was quite sure whether it was the will of God for me to enter the Catholic Church.

It would take far too long were I to recount in detail the succession of Providential links which drew together at Graymoor not only the Friars but also the Sisters of the Atonement. Suffice it to say that exactly seven years after receiving the Name and Texts of the Society in St. John's Church, Kingston, I found myself wearing the habit of St. Francis and making my vows on the Mount of the Atonement, in the presence of Dr. Leighton Coleman, Anglican Bishop of Delaware and successor to Bishop Lee. The first service was held in a tent pitched upon the mountain summit, on the seventh Sunday after Pentecost, July 22, 1900, and my profession under the Franciscan Rule was made in the same tent on the following Friday. There were present thirteen members of the Society representing its three congregations, viz., the Friars, the Sisters and the Tertiaries. Thus was literally fulfilled the words I had heard in Kingston in 1893: "You will have to wait seven years for this to be realized."

The convent of the Sisters of the Atonement was erected alongside the Mission Church of St. John Baptist, Graymoor, in the summer of 1899; and St. Paul's Friary, on the Mount of the Atonement, was dedicated by Bishop Coleman, December 8, 1900, in honor of the Immaculate Conception of the Blessed Virgin Mary.

Then there followed the years of waiting for that glad day when the doors of Peter's Sheepfold were opened and the Society was admitted into communion with the Vicar of Christ. Those nine years were not ideal years; far from it. We, of the Society of the Atonement, very keenly realized we had a message to deliver to our fellow Anglicans and in many ways we suffered in delivering it. Its announcement meant isolation, contempt and to some extent, ostracism more than actual persecution.

When we first began to lay the foundation of our Institute at Graymoor, we met with considerable success from a popular viewpoint. Franciscanism (apart from the papacy) has enthusiastic admirers not a few in the Anglican Church; and these were naturally pleased at the prospect of two Congregations of Franciscans, the Friars of the Atonement and the Sisters of the

Atonement, taking their rise at Graymoor. But in 1901 we began openly proclaiming our faith in the jurisdiction of the Apostolic See and that we believed all that Rome believed. We did not hesitate to say to our Anglican hearers that Henry VIII and Elizabeth were entirely wrong in having repudiated the Papacy and in separating England from the Holy See. Furthermore, we stated that the sole salvation for Anglicanism was wholesome repentance, retraction of error, and corporate submission to the successor of St. Peter.

Never shall I forget my experience one evening at an archdeaconry meeting on Long Island when, in the presence of a large body of clergy and a congregation that filled the church, I enunciated the foregoing truth. In the middle of the sermon the archdeacon ascended the steps of the altar and shouted in stentorian tones, "Let your light so shine before men that they may see your good works and glorify your Father which is in Heaven." This was not intended as an exhortation to the preacher, to go onward bearing his witness; but in the Episcopal Church it is the offertory sentence, usually pronounced as the signal for the collection to be taken up. The preacher, of course, took the hint and sat down.

But, in a way the archdeacon never intended, I took his advice and continued to "let my light shine" by publishing *The Lamp*, which proved a much more effective method of illuminating the minds of Anglican readers on the burning question of papal jurisdiction than if I had preached on the subject to hundreds of congregations in every part of the country. There was no portion of the Anglican Communion, whether in Europe, America, Africa or Asia, where the rays of *The Lamp* did not penetrate, or where its gospel of papal submission did not find hearing. The message of *The Lamp* continues to this day bearing fruit in the Anglican vineyard. Not only through its influence have many Anglicans, both clerical and lay, found their way into Peter's Fold, but it has contributed its share to the formation of a new party in the Anglican body, that of the advocate of corporate submission to the Apostolic See, which in the popular parlance is called the Pro-Roman Party.

After the preaching experience recorded above, invitations to fill Anglican pulpits rarely came my way and I became to some extent a street preacher in consequence. One summer, by permission of the President of Manhattan Borough, I preached once a week on the steps of City Hall in New York; and another time, on a street corner in Newburgh.

As the Society of the Atonement persisted in propagating its Church Unity principles, efforts were made to silence us altogether; and Bishop Coleman, under pressure from certain of our antagonists, actually took the preliminary steps towards my deposition from the Episcopal ministry; but as I showed a disposition to fight the matter to the finish by demanding an ecclesiastical trial, the threatened disposition was allowed to fall into "innocuous desuetude", and ended in the good bishop letting us severely alone until his death, which occurred in December, 1907.

The Rt. Rev. Frederick J. Kinsman, D.D., succeeded him and at the hands of Bishop Kinsman I received the kindest and most considerate treatment. He invited me to Bishopstead, his residence in Wilmington, and afforded me the opportunity of explaining to him in full what I considered to be the providential mission of the Society of the Atonement; and at the same time, with the greatest freedom and clearness, I explained to the bishop just what I and my associates in the Society of the Atonement believed.

He informed me that he would take the whole subject under careful consideration and that, in about a month's time, he would write me his mature judgment. And once more, in connection with the Episcopal Diocese of Delaware, there occurred a singular coincidence; when his letter came it contained in substance—though more elaborately expressed—the identical advice which Bishop Lee 65 years before, had given my father, namely: "Make your submission to Rome; that is the only thing in consistency with your principles that is left open for you to do." Contrary, however, to my father's action, I accepted the counsel of the bishop as a providential manifestation of the will of God, and in August of that year, 1909, I went to Washington and called the Apostolic delegate, then the Most Reverend Archbishop—now His Eminence—Cardinal Falconio.

Immediately upon my return to Graymoor I drew up a petition addressed to His Holiness Pope Pius X, professing our faith in the Holy Roman Church and all her teachings, and asking the Holy Father to take our Institute under his protection and to observe its name and identity. This petition was forwarded by the Apostolic Delegate to the Vatican; and on October the seventh we received through His Excellency, Monsignor Falconio, the reply of the Soverign Pontiff graciously granting our petition. It was on Saturday, October 30, that our corporate reception took place, His Eminence Cardinal Farley having deputed Monsignor Joseph H. Conray, now auxiliary Bishop of Ogdensburg, to reconcile us to the Holy See and to receive the Graymoor Community into the Catholic Church.

At that time the Society consisted of about twenty-five members—two Friars of the Atonement, five Sisters, and the rest Tertiaries—all of whom, with one or two exceptions among the Tertiaries, at that time or since, have entered the Fold of Peter. Had we persisted in remaining outside once the door of entrance into the Fold had been providentially opened, I have not a doubt that the Society of the Atonement would sooner or later have become extinct; but now, under the blessing and fostering care of Christ's Vicar, it is pulsating with divine life and making most encouraging progress. Already we have had the satisfaction of seeing its example followed, in the submission of two religious communities much more numerous than our own, namely, that of the Benedictine Monks of Caldey Isle, off the coast of South Wales, and the Benedictine Nuns of St. Bride's Abbey, Milford Haven. Nor do we believe that this is the end of the list of corporate receptions from Anglicanism into the bosom of the Catholic Church. We believe there has always been a Catholic-minded Remnant of the Church of England since the days of Elizabeth; and, in point of fact, nothing has been more remarkable in the religious phenomena of our time than the steady, persistent and advancing Catholicizing of the Anglican Body, since the Oxford Movement, not in one part, but in every part of Great Britain and America.

We do not expect a corporate submission of *all* Anglicans to the Apostolic See, in either this or any subsequent generation, but we *do* anticipate the home-coming of the Catholic Remnant. How extensive the numbers will prove to be God alone knows.

What has been thus far most unique and significant in the Society of the Atonement is that it had its origin outside the Fold of Peter and yet from its beginning all its members have held the Catholic faith and have breathed the spirit of loyalty to the Apostolic See. It is but another illustration of the fundamental principles of redemption recorded by St. Paul in the fifth chapter of Romans: "As by the disobedience of one man many were made sinners, so also by the obedience of one many shall be made just" (5:19). By the disobedience of one man, Henry VIII, a whole nation and people became rebels to the Apostolic See. So also "by the obedience of one, many shall be made just," found illustration in the submission of John Henry Newman—to be followed in each successive generation by increasing numbers of Anglicans returning to the jurisdiction of Christ's Supreme Vicar; and in our isolation upon the Mount of the Atonement—when for so long a time there was only cleric and one lay brother—it was borne in mind upon us as a covenant promise from God, that the Children of the Atonement, with whom are included all the Children of Reconciliation to the Apostolic See, will be increased and multiplied until they become "as the stars for multitude".

When God sought to save a rebellious race He gave His only-begotten Son not to thunder down from Mount Sinai the law of God and His judgment upon the wicked, but "the Word was made flesh and dwelt among us." Christ identified Himself with the race He sought to redeem, and glorified the title, "Son of Man". There was, however, this difference between Himself and them. They were the children of disobedience while He "came down from Heaven not to do His own will but the will of Him that sent Him" (John 26:38).

Indeed it was by being obedient unto death, even to the death of the Cross, that He made possible the reconciliation of sinners with God, or in other words, the At-*One*-Ment between God and man. He said: "Except a corn of wheat fall into the ground and die, it abideth alone, but if it die it bringeth forth much fruit." By His own death He propagated among the disobedient the seed of the Atonement, that is, the Children of Obedience. And this seed will go on increasing and multiplying "until the kingdom of this world is become the kingdom of our Lord's and His Christ's, and He shall reign for ever and ever. Amen" (Apoc. 11:15).

This, I think, explains the providential meaning of the Society of the Atonement's Anglican origin, and although it has now happily emerged from Anglicanism, its message to Anglicans has not ceased to be, but aided by its witness and example, the seed of obedience to papal authority will go on being propagated in the Anglican Communion until the conversions and submissions hitherto experienced will be as nothing to those that shall hereafter be recorded. Hence we close our thesis where we began it, namely, that the so-called Oxford Movement in the Anglican Church is a Romeward Movement and its *"terminus ad quem"*, the return of the Catholic Remnant in the Anglican Body to communion with the Apostolic See; and this, I think, answers the question as to whether I am satisfied, beyond all shadow of doubt, that my share in that movement was according to God's Will.

2. The Name and Texts of the Society of the Atonement

Holy Cross Day, September 14, 1897

Dear Sister Lurana:

I found your letter awaiting me yesterday on my return from a few days spent among our outlying missions.

Will you pardon me if I reply by means of typewriter? I have so much to say and I can write so much more rapidly in this way and my time is so fully occupied that I am compelled to use every timesaving expedient that offers itself.

Whether at the expiration of the year the way opens in the Good Providence of God for you to come to Omaha, or you are called with your co-workers to labor in some other portion of the Lord's Vineyard, I am in any case deeply and intensely interested in watching the unfolding of the purpose of the Holy Spirit in your life.

In what you write I can see nothing fanatical, or strange. It all harmonizes too well with my own conceptions of spiritual things.

As to the rule of absolute poverty, undoubtedly right in principle, the difficulty is to carry it out, not because the thing is impossible, but because human nature is so earthly and weak. St. Francis realized the ideal himself, but his followers soon fell from the standard their founder had set them. How to perpetuate the real spirit of poverty in your community will be a very difficult problem. But then as you quite truly say we ought to aim at heavenly ideals, although we do not fully attain unto them.

A Third Order of lay people, living under a rule adapted to

271

their several stations of life is something we were discussing among ourselves at the Clergy House a few weeks ago, and such an Order I believe to be entirely feasible.

Now in regard to the Name of the Community I trust you will not set your heart too much on the name of Saint Francis.

If in the will and purpose of God the Associate Mission of Omaha should eventuate in the formation of a Religious Order both of Priests and Mission Sisters, each the complement of the other and working in concert for the up-building of the Kingdom of our Lord that unity of purpose in life ought to find some expression in the Name by which the two Orders are to be known to the world. Now whereas you might take the name of Francis of Assisi, as far as we of the Clergy are concerned that name is pre-possessed by the Franciscans.

Better let us stand for some great central truth of the Gospel of Jesus Christ and let that truth stand forth in the Name we bear. It is true that many and most of these names are already appropriated, e.g., Society of Jesus, Order of the Holy Cross, Community of the Resurrection, Sisterhood of the Holy Nativity, the Passionists, the Redemptorists, Sisters of the Annunciation.

But strange to say one of the grandest names of all has yet to be borne before the world by a Religious Order, viz., The Society of the Atonement.

If I be not deceived, God Himself has already given this Name to us. I do not hesitate to tell you why I think so, for we breathe the same atmosphere of faith.

I told you how almost from childhood the thought of a religious order for the American Church has been present with me.

While at Kingston I studied the life of St. Francis with intense interest and he became my ideal of a monk and mission preacher. I was especially impressed with the way he sought of God a constitution for his Friars Minor. After weeks and even months of prayer, on the Sixth Sunday after Trinity, four years ago I celebrated Mass, knelt before the altar with the Holy Scriptures in my hands and opened them three times in the Name of the Three Persons of the Blessed Trinity.

The first passage related to the Holy Ghost as the well of living water which should spring up within those who believed in the Son of God. (St. John 7:37-39)

The second contained these words: "We joy in God through

Our Lord Jesus Christ by Whom we have now received the ATONEMENT." (Rom. 5:11) And the moment my eyes rested upon that word it seemed to stand out from the sacred page with a distinctness all its own and it flashed upon me as I believe from heaven, that the community God was preparing should be called the Society of the Atonement.

The third passage was St. Paul's address to the Corinthians on the Holy Eucharist. (1 Cor. 11:23-92)

Thus has God Himself outlined for us the Constitution of our Order. (1) The Holy Spirit our Inspirer and Guide and Comforter. All preaching and mission work to be successful must be done "in the power and demonstration of the Spirit." (2) The doctrine we are to preach and ever hold before the eyes of men is the At-ONE-ment of man with God and the sole instrument of its accomplishment is the Holy Cross. (3) The Central Means of Grace by which all that Christ wrought for us on the Cross and by which the Atonement is made real between God and man is the Real Presence of Jesus Christ in the Blessed Sacrament of His Body and Blood.

By a coincidence, which I love to regard as of Divine intention, on the Sixth Sunday after Trinity two years later, the Chapter of the Associate Mission elected me its head and the letter was written notifying me of the fact.

I also notice that your letter with reference to your coming to Omaha, should God so will it, bears the date of July 30th, being the Friday within the octave of the Sixth Sunday after Trinity, two years later still.

All this may be pure accident, but I rather believe that nothing happens by pure accident; for are we not told that "not so much as a sparrow falleth to the ground without His knowledge and the very hairs of our head are all numbered."?

Bishop Worthington, I understand, expects to sail for home about October 1st. I hope he manages to see you before his return.

With oft repeated intercessions for you and your companions at the Altar and in offering up the Holy Gifts, I remain,

Faithfully yours,

Lewis T. Wattson

3. Reception into the Church

Lamp, November, 1909

The present issue of *The Lamp* has been held back in order to make the following announcement to our readers: On Saturday, October 30th, in the Chapel of Our Lady of the Angels, Graymoor, the Right Reverend Joseph Conroy, Vicar General of the Diocese of Ogdensburg, acting under faculties from the Most Rev. John M. Farley, Archbishop of New York, received into the Holy Catholic and Roman Church, all members of the Society of the Atonement resident at Graymoor or who could conveniently be present from a distance.

Msgr. Conroy was assisted in the ceremonies incident to the reception by the Rev. Paschal Robinson, O.F.M., distinguished among the Friars Minor as one of the greatest living authorities in the field of Franciscan literature, and by the Rev. Patrick Drain, Pastor of the Church of Our Lady of Loretto, Cold Spring in whose parish Graymoor is situated.

Not to go into details suffice it to say that previously application was made to Pope Pius X through the Apostolic Delegate at Washington, Monsignor Falconio, to take the Society under his "protection and governance" and to preserve its "Name and Institute." On October 7th the answer was returned by His Excellency, the Apostolic Delegate, in the affirmative.

During the ten days previous to the reception of the Society the Right Rev. C. G. O'Keefe, Pastor of the Church of the Sacred Heart, Highland Falls, N.Y., several times visited Graymoor to examine the members of the Community preparatory to their admission.

It is the wish of the ecclesiastical authorities that the publication of *The Lamp* should continue.

4. The Sacerdotium

Lamp, July, 1910

On Thursday, June 16, the Feast of Our Lady of Perpetual Help (according to the Franciscan Calendar) the Most Rev'd. John M. Farley, D.D., Archbishop of New York, in the Chapel of St. Joseph's Seminary, Yonkers, ordained to the priesthood the Rev. Paul James Francis, Superior of the Society of the Atonement.

It is to be remembered that for ten years the Graymoor Community has held *in toto* the Catholic Faith and borne witness thereto openly and before the world, as the files of *The Lamp* abundantly testify.

One practical demonstration of the Society's loyalty to the Holy See is the fact that twice each year St. Peter's Pence was sent to Rome.

During this period the ceremonial and liturgical usage of the Roman Catholic Church was followed with painstaking exactness; an English translation of the Breviary being used for the daily recitation of the Divine office and the text of the Anglican communion service adapted to the rubrical directions of the Latin Missal. During Holy Week the ceremonies of the Catholic Church were carried out in full. The rule of weekly confession and of fasting before communion was faithfully adhered to.

It is also to be taken into consideration that practically the whole life of the head of the Society of the Atonement has been prepared for the Catholic Priesthood. Trained from childhood to reverence John Henry Newman and the other great leaders of the Oxford Movement and consecrated to God from infancy there never has been a time in his life when he did not love and venerate the Catholic Church and always mourned for the causes which separated England from the Holy See.

Carefully and thoroughly educated for the Anglican ministry in school and college and seminary the educational process has proved a providential preparation for that specialized study of Roman theology and the claims of the Roman Papacy, which during a score of years has gradually dissipated every non-Catholic postulate of the Anglican system.

Immediately after the admission of the Society to Catholic communion and jurisdiction its Superior was sent by the Archbishop to the splendid Seminary of the Archdiocese and no pains have been spared to fit him in every way for the Catholic Priesthood.

The Catholic Church is endowed with that supernatural illumination, which not only watches constantly for the manifestation of the Finger of God, but promptly and with confidence takes the line of initiative where it points the way. That the Society of the Atonement is a providential instrument, designed to accomplish a notable work in the return of the "other sheep" to the "one fold" of the Universal Shepherd must be the explanation of the favor it has received from the Holy See and if it is to do that work without delay it was a necessity that the sublime gift and power of the Priesthood should be imposed upon the Society's founder and leader; and that is the simple explanation of the solemn and beautiful ordination which took place at St. Joseph's Seminary on June 16th.

Will not all who have any interest in or love for the Society of the Atonement, from this time forward, pray to Our Lord to call whom He will, both men and women, to attach themselves in larger numbers to the Institute, but more particularly to the First and Second Congregations of the Society, that is to say, to the Friars of the Atonement and to the Sisterhood, in order that when the call comes we may have laborers to send forth into the harvest.

5. A Year in the Catholic Church

The Lamp, November, 1910

A year has gone by since the reception of the Society of the Atonement into the Catholic Church on October 30th, 1909. Seventeen were received in a body on that day and other members of the Society in various places made their submission subsequently. In all about twenty-five. Of these, two were friars of the first congregation, five were sisters of the second congregation and the rest were tertiaries, some attached to the Graymoor community but the majority living in the world. Certainly all told a tiny company. It is, however, noteworthy, that only two members of the Society have held back from entering Peter's Fold and both of these are likely to become Catholics in the near future. Also in addition members of the Rosary League of Our Lady of the Atonement, of the Anglo-Roman Union, Anglican clergy and Religious, more or less associated with the Society, have either already made their submission or are preparing to do so in the near future.

The arch-enemy of souls has not been inactive and during the years has directed more than one assault against the Graymoor foundation. Notable among these attacks was the effort to wrest from the Society the half acre of ground on which stands the Convent of St. Francis and the Mission Church of St. John the Baptist which we have been wont to call the Graymoor Portiuncula, but the attempt seems to have failed and the end of the year has been crowned by the dedication of St. John's Church after having been thoroughly renovated and repaired by his Grace, the Archbishop of New York and furnished with many beautiful gifts.

Room also has been provided for the future growth of the Second Congregation (the Sisters of the Atonement) by their acquiring possession of nearly an acre of ground to the south of their convent and two benefactors have purchased nine acres to the north with the intention of holding it for the Sisters until they are able to purchase the same.

The prospect of the increase of the Sisters of the Atonement is encouraging, and before long an enlargment of their present rather cramped quarters may be a necessity.

As for the First Congregation, no growth could be expected until Friar Paul, the Father Minister of the Society, has received priest's orders in the Catholic Church. This sublime gift was conferred by Archbishop Farley in the seminary chapel of the Archdiocese on June 16th. It was not, however, until the middle of September that St. Paul's Friary was opened to religious aspirants. The end of the first year in the Catholic Church finds the little building nearly full, which means that if our aspirants preserve that ere long the First Congregation as well as the Second will be required to "enlarge the place of their tent, lengthen their cords and strengthen their stakes".

It is hardly worth while adding that members of the Society have only feelings of profound gratitude when they consider the step of a year ago; eternity itself will not be too long in which to magnify God and praise Him for the benefits which have come to us by virtue of our citizenship in the Catholic Church. The words of St. Paul to the Ephesians have acquired a new and personal meaning for us: "Now, therefore, you are no more strangers and foreigners; but you are fellow citizens with the saints, and the domestics of God, built upon the foundation of the Apostles and prophets, Jesus Christ Himself being the chief corner stone."

As for those we left behind in the Anglican Communion our heart's desire is that they too may have the gift of Peter's faith and follow us into the Catholic fellowship, which is theirs quite as much as ours, if they will but free themselves from that intellectual and spiritual bondage wherewith the Tudor Pharoah bound our forefathers and their posterity in the House of Anglicanism.

6. Anniversary of Reception into the Church

Our Lady of the Angels Chapel
Graymoor, October 30, 1929

"As by the obedience of one many shall be made just." Fifth chapter of St. Paul's Epistle to the Romans, following immediately after the central Basic Text of our Institute: "We joy in God through Our Lord Jesus Christ by Whom we have now received the Atonement."

Twenty years ago today a transaction unique in the history of the Catholic Church took place in this sanctuary. The present bishop of Ogdensburg, acting for the Archbishop of New York, and later on, Cardinal Farley, by the authority and mandate of the Apostolic See received corporately into the Catholic Church the Society of the Atonement. It was not only an important event in the history of our Institute, but all its future consequences important in the history of the Catholic Church itself.

It is no discredit to the Society of the Atonement that it is a convert society, that it originated outside the Fold of Peter. There was in the purpose of Almighty God a special design that it should be so. Take the Atonement itself—how was it accomplished? "As by the disobedience of one many were made sinners, so by the obedience of one shall many be made just." The human family in its origin through our first parents, became rebellious against the Almighty and as a consequence were punished by the eternal banishment from God in the torments of Hell. God, to save and redeem humanity, permitted that His only-begotten Son should become a member of this human race, identifying Himself with them, call Himself the Son of Man, in order that He Himself in becoming one of them, might lead out of the midst of the disobedient, the children of atonement, obedience, reconciliation, and all the heirs of heaven. By the disobedience of one man, Henry VIII, a whole nation became rebellious, or protestant against the authority of the Vicar of Christ and broke off communion with Him. God desiring to bring back these rebellious and disobedient children to the obedience of the Holy See, saw fit to choose out of their midst one or two that through their obedience many might return to the obedience of the Catholic Rock of Ages. The process, therefore, was a divine one and because this was the Society of the Atonement, it was modeled after that original atonement that was wrought through God's Only-begotten Son identifying Himself with a fallen race that He might redeem that race and exalt it to heavenly glory; that is the reason why this unique thing happened.

God, desiring to lead back to communion with the Apostolic See those that had gone astray, took out of their midst members of the Anglican communion, inspired them with the full faith of the Catholic Church and a loyalty and loving obedience to the Vicar of Christ. From the very beginning of this Institute its Founders were not Protestant; they believed in the Catholic Religion, loved the Catholic Church, understood what the Catholic Church was, and they had a special loyalty and devotion to the Vicar of Christ, and sought not alone for themselves but for their companions in schism a return to the Apostolic See that had been broken off not by the fault of the English people themselves, but by the force and power of their king and queen.

Thus the reception of the Society of the Atonement into the Catholic Church which took place twenty years ago, was only a development and logical consequence of its origin and purpose and now that we have had twenty years of life and growth in the Catholic Church, we rejoice at the consequences. God has fulfilled the Covenant Promise in a wonderful way already. "Blessing I will bless you." I will multiply and increase your numbers. Twenty years ago the First congregation of our Institute was represented by one cleric and one lay brother; after twenty years, including the students in our preparatory college, we number ninety. There were five Sisters received corporately; today, including postulants and oblates, our numbers are over a hundred. There were ten members of the Third congregation received twenty years ago; today, they number over a thousand. The members of the Rosary League and the Union-that-Nothing-be-Lost at that time were a handful. and today they number a hundred thousand.

Consider how much this growth will increase when these that are now in the course of their studies for the priesthood in a few years have been ordained and larger numbers have taken their place in the preparatory college and in the Seminary in Washington. The Sisters are already multiplying their activities in the various centers from coast to coast and from the Gulf of Mexico to the Northern border of Canada and what will happen in the next twenty years, God only knows, but we look forward with anticipation to the marvelous increase and development until the prayer which we say every day is fulfilled, that the sons and daughters of the Atonement will be missionaries in all lands.

Really that is a glorious and magnificent program. God does not do things without being behind them, that His purposes may be accomplished. Consider that first purpose of our Institute in regard to those outside of the Fold of Peter. We know that more than at any time perhaps in our history of the Church the minds of men have been agitated over the question of reunion, the return to Catholic unity of those that have gone astray. At this very time there is pending in the Sacred Congregation of Rites in Rome a petition signed by thirteen hundred Cardinals, Archbishops, Patriarchs, Bishops, Vicars and Prefects Apostolic, Heads of Religious Congregations and rectors of colleges in Rome, asking the Holy Father by His Apostolic Authority to call all Catholics of the world from the least to the greatest, for eight days to pray that those words of His on the night of His betrayal, *Ut omnes unum sint*, for the return of separated Christians to unity with the Apostolic See. If the Holy Father grants that petition, and we hope he will, and if the Society of the Atonement had never done anything else in fulfillment of its vocation in bringing back the wandering sheep to the Fold of Unity, it would have done an enormous work because after all prayers are the way by which God accomplishes things; first, He makes His servants ask and then by His power He accomplishes their requests. So that this Unity Octave originating here at Graymoor will be a potential power to bring the very thing to accomplishment which our feeble intellects are not able to measure outwardly and to comprehend.

Let us consecrate ourselves afresh at the altar and in Holy Communion today that each of us may be a vessel of sanctification fit for the Master's use in accomplishing His purpose in our glorious Institute, and at the same time let us not forget to thank God with the profoundest gratitude for the Society and for our vocation in the Society.

7. The Homecoming of the Other Sheep

Holy Cross Cathedral,
Boston, November, 1910

"Other sheep I have which are not of this fold; them also I must bring, and they shall hear My voice, and there shall be one fold and one shepherd." (John, 10:16)

The burden of my message to you this morning, dear brethren, is about the homecoming of the "other sheep" and in consequence of that homecoming the conversion of the heathen world to Christ and the Catholic Church.

Who among us can ever forget our Blessed Lord's prayer to His Heavenly Father on the night of His betrayal that His disciples might all be one and what was the reason that He gave for asking this? It was "that the world may believe that Thou has sent Me."

One of the most vivid memories of my life was the first time I went to His Eminence, Cardinal Gibbons, with the homecoming of the other sheep in my heart and on my lips, and how he responded with the swift exclamation: "If we had the Anglicans with us we would conquer the world." By which I understood His Eminence to mean not merely the Episcopalians, but that of all the Christian forces of the great Anglo-Saxon and English speaking world were united in the one fold of the Catholic Church and under the banner of His Holiness, the Vicar of Christ, such an impulse would be given to foreign missions that the powers of hell could not withstand the march of the Church's conquering hosts; Asia and Africa would be converted and the whole world would soon believe in Christ.

And indeed, does it not seem that upon the conversion of America and England to Catholicism depends in a very large degree the future of Christianity throughout the world?

We all know something of the distressing state of religious affairs on the continent of Europe. A more tenable apostasy of the nations even than that which characterized the Sixteenth century seems imminent.

France is in the grip of a government not merely hostile to the Holy See but frankly atheistic; the religious who thirty years ago taught in their schools two million of the French children have long since been expelled by the civil arm and their convents and monasteries confiscated. Even the churches have been taken over by the government and are falling into ruins, because its representatives will neither repair the buildings themselves nor permit the clergy to repair them. Whether they will go a step further, close the churches altogether and drive out the bishops and the priests no one can with certainty say. Italy likewise has become, in politics at least, rabidly anti-clerical and the mayor of the city of Rome is an atheistic Jew, who on the occasion of a political demonstration recently offered the grossest insults to the Holy Father. Catholic Portugal too has suddenly become the prey of anti-clerical revolutionists and a few weeks ago celebrated its debut as a republic by banishing all religious of both sexes from the country, accompanying the process with the brutal treatment of priests and nuns, the pillaging of convents and the looting of churches. The same satanic forces are at work in Spain and where it will end, who can tell?

When the tide of Lutheranism swept Germany, Norway and Sweden out of the column of Catholic nations and Calvinism did the same for Switzerland, Holland and Scotland, and Henry and Elizabeth Tudor snatched England from the Sovereign Pontiff, these tremendous losses were in a measure compensated for by fresh conquest in the New World and in Asia. To the Emperor, Charles V, was reported the conversion of twenty millions in North and South America, while St. Francis Xavier cheered the heart of the Vicar of Christ by his brilliant missionary conquests in India. So now, the Catholic Church of the twentieth century must not suffer loss. If hundreds of thousands apostatize from the faith and swell the ranks of anti-clerical Socialism in Europe, *millions* here in America and in Asia and Africa must be rallied to the papal standard to offset the European apostasy.

The brightest day in the history of American Catholicism has already dawned and we must rise up to the tremendous opportunities which are ours to dispel the clouds which now hang black and threatening over the Vatican and to make the present century the very greatest in missionary conquest which the Church of God has experienced since the day of Pentecost. But that this may be so, we must somehow win the non-Catholic millions of our fellow American citizens to the allegiance of the Apostolic See, we must echo the Good Shepherd's call and lift our voices loud and clear in ceaseless invitation to "the other sheep" to become one with us in Catholic faith and worship within the One Fold and under the One Shepherd.

The outlook and the time is ripe here in America. It is evident that old-fashioned Protestanism is falling to pieces but out of its decaying systems there is emerging, thank God, an extraordinary Catholic reaction. Under what we may confidently believe to be the directive hand of the Holy Ghost this Romeward trend has taken the form of a universal cry among all the sects for Christian Unity. As yet only here and there may be found a Protestant leader who has even now caught the vision of what will be the end of this unitative movement; but we Catholics know perfectly well where it is bound to end, if, as we hope, this unity movement among the Protestants is truly of God. There is no other foundation divinely laid of Catholic unity than that which Jesus Christ Himself laid when He said to His personal representative among the blessed Apostles: "Thou art Peter and upon this rock I will build My Church."

A generation ago the Protestant portion of Christendom was entirely blind to this but now by a miracle of divine grace the scales are falling from their eyes. Dimly as yet, like men who grope in a fog, the Protestants themselves are beginning to see that reunion with Rome, and not mere denominational federation, is the God-intended *terminus ad quem* of the Church Unity movement. For evidence of this we need not look across the sea to the Church of England and to such well known advocates of Reunion with the Holy See as Lord Halifax and the Rev. Spencer Jones, but we may begin right here at home among the Puritans of New England. The Congregational Church has its apostle of Church Unity in the person of the Rev. Dr. Newman Smyth of New Haven, and when he named his book on Unity, "The Passing of Protestantism and the Coming Catholicism," he stereotyped on its title page his vision of the future. It is true that the contents are very unsatisfactory to a Catholic, Dr. Smyth built his hopes too much on the sands of Modernism. But then it is not to be expected that through the mists of

Puritan tradition he has caught a far-off glimpse of the Eternal City and prophesies of a time when the scattered sheep will all be folded by the Successor of St. Peter.

Then in New York we have that remarkable scholar, Dr. Charles Augustus Briggs, whose passionate study for thirty years has been the problem of Church Unity. Wishing to unite the Presbyterians and the Episcopalians, as one forward step in the right direction, Dr. Briggs, while still retaining his chair in a Presbyterian Seminary, received ordination to the Anglican ministry. But looking upon this as merely a means to an end, he has not hesitated to declare that Rome is the goal of unity and that no one but the Pope can unite the divided followers of Christ. Or to use language most readily understood by Bostonians, that Rome is by divine selection the Hub of the Christian Universe.

We all know that nearest to the Catholic Church of all the denominations around us is the Episcopal Church, or as they best love to style themselves, the Anglicans. So near the borderline in fact are many of the High Church Episcopalians that should a Catholic stranger find himself in an ultra-ritualistic Church on a Sunday morning he would certainly think himself in a Catholic Church, unless he discovered his mistake by hearing the Introit, the Credo and the Gloria in Excelsis sung in English. As for the images of Our Lady and St. Joseph, the sanctuary lamp with its red light, the confessional boxes and the holy water stoups these would all be in evidence. So close a neighbor has the Episcopal Church become that the Anglican shepherds and many of their sheep are learning to pass from Anglicanism to the Fold of Peter as graduates from the high school pass into the University. Barely a month ago in a certain English City, after which your own Brighton takes its name, five clergy of the English Church made their submission to the Catholic Church and fifty of the laity immediately followed their example, while others are preparing to follow later. Here in this country within the last three years over a score of Anglican clergymen have become Catholics. The Catholic seminary of Philadelphia and the Catholic University of Washington contain at the present time the ten men who were formerly part of the very cream of the Anglican ministry, and at St. John's Seminary of this city there is a native of Boston, who once wore the habit of the Anglican Order of the Holy Cross, served as novice master and superior for a term of years and next to the founder did more than any man to make the order the great spiritual force it unquestionably is in the Episcopal Church.

And now what shall be the attitude of the Catholics themselves towards this Romeward movement among those still outside the Church? I am sure you will answer with me that it should be one of the intensest sympathy, yes, dear brethren, and more than that, it should be an *intelligent* sympathy that puts itself, as far as it can, in the place of those outside the fold and tries to realize how very dear those "other sheep" are to Jesus and His Blessed Mother Mary, and how we must co-operate with the designs of the Sacred Heart "to bring home again His own exiles." (Kings 2, 14:13)

What we need most of all fellow Catholics, is the heart and the spirit of St. Francis of Assisi. You know that the Seraphic Saint saw God in everything and loved all creation for the Creator's sake, calling even the birds and the rabbits his sisters and brothers. How eager he would have been to encourage every one of our separated brethren, whose face was in the least degree turned towards the Vicar of Christ. How he would have bent, like His Master, over "the smoking flax" of Catholicism smouldering in the breast of our Protestant fellow citizens, whose ancestors over four hundred years ago were as Catholic as our own. I once asked a street-car fare, in Washington, of a Protestant minister in the name of St. Francis of Assisi and he gave it to me with alacrity, exclaiming as he did so, "Francis of Assisi is the saint of us Protestants." Then by the constraining power of that same charity which burned so warmly in the breast of the Seraphic Francis let us mightily persuade those "other sheep" to have forever done with their Protestant shibboleths and to herd with us in the one fold under the one shepherd.

As a practical illustration of what I mean by a sympathetic attitude towards those outside the fold I am glad to say that among the letters I shall always keep in my file of select correspondence is one that I received from your Most Reverend Archbishop some two years ago in reply to a letter I had addressed to him telling him of an Octave of prayer the Society of the Atonement had inaugurated and asking his Grace's prayers during the Octave in union with our Anglican ones for the return of all the stray sheep to Peter's Fold, and this was his reply: "You may rest assured that I, myself, my clergy and people will join their prayers with yours for the holy purpose you outline in your note."

I wonder now at my temerity in writing the note but I wonder yet the more at the Archbishop's gracious condenscension in making such a generous answer. At that time I was one of the sheep outside the fold and the thought of the chief shepherd of the great Archdiocese of Boston, his clergy and his people uniting their prayers with those of the "other sheep" was a tremendous inspiration. It helped to hasten the day of our homecoming.

Another essential element in attracting to the Fold of Peter our separated brethren is the eloquent persuasiveness of holy living. If we Catholics can only prove by our daily conduct that we keep the commandments of Jesus Christ better than they do themselves, in other words if we practice faithfully our holy religion we cannot fail to draw all good men to our fellow-ship.

Our Holy Father in his inaugural encyclical on how all things should be restored in Christ declared that it was not the spirit of controversy that was needed but the faithful and consistent practice of the Catholic Religion. "When," exclaims Pope Pius, "in every city and village the law of the Lord is faithfully observed, when respect is shown to sacred things, when the Sacraments are frequented, and the ordinances of Christian life fulfilled, there will be no need to labor further to see all things restored in Christ."

The third essential to unity on our part is that we keep the faith. When Protestants say that the Church of Rome must change her doctrines before there can be any hope of a reunited Christendom, they really do not mean it. One of the principal attractions of the Catholic Church to those outside her communion is that she continues to hold uncompromisingly to the faith of the ages, amplifying her dogmas and giving fuller explanations of the original deposit from time to time, but never discarding "one jot or tittle" her holy doctrine to please any man. As they see the theological systems of Calvin, Zwingli and Luther crumbling to dust they look with the greater admiration and longing to that Rock of Roman orthodoxy which has withstood the storms of nineteen centuries and, if the world lasts so long, will stand unshaken the mad waves of nineteen centuries more.

Charity towards our separated brethren, the faithful practice of our holy religion, unswerving orthodoxy, these three things which must signally characterize the Catholics of America, if we are to make our land altogether Catholic, but there is a fourth characteristic which American Catholics must emphasize more even than they have done in the past, and that is personal loyalty, fealty and devotion to the successor of St. Peter, because he is the Sovereign Shepherd and the Vicar of Jesus Christ. When the multitude of Protestants who love our Blessed Lord in sincerity and are trying so hard to serve and obey Him, come to realize that the voice of Peter is the voice of Christ, then they will harken to his call and thus hearing the Divine Master speaking through His Vicar, the problem of a reunited Christendom will be solved and there will be one fold and one shepherd. And how shall they have this tremendous and essential fact brought home to them except by the magnificent spectacle of 250,000,000 Catholics throughout the world obeying as one man the voice of Christ's Vicar following his leadership as a flock of sheep follow their shepherd.

The most terrifying of all the perils which menace America at the present hour is the progress which anti-christian Socialism is making in our land, and this Socialism is one with that which boasts of its determination to throttle and exterminate Christianity in all the countries of Europe. Its universality and its deadly malice toward the Catholic Church betray its satanic origin and generalship. We wrestle not against flesh and blood but against principalities and powers of hell, against the rulers of the world of darkness. Father Hugh Benson in his remarkable book, *The Lord of the World*, with a vividness of imagination and a wealth of description which few writers can equal pictures the universal kingdom of Satan in the last days, governed by Lucifer himself visible and incarnate as "Feesenburgh hailing from America and ascending the throne of the world." The prophecy is a gloomy and pessimistic one, but perhaps the author only intended to warn us of what we may expect from socialistic democracy unless all the Christians of the western world can get together and sink their differences of creed and ecclesiastical government under the one faith and the one rule of the one man, who represents pre-eminently the sovereign authority of Jesus Christ. Combination, consolidation and universality are the hall-marks of the gigantic age in which we are now living and it does certainly appear that a titanic struggle

287

is being enacted before our eyes between the *Psuedo*-Prince of this world and the Lord Jesus Christ to establish a world-wide government, which shall be either eminently Christian or supremely satanic.

That Protestantism can ever produce a single ruler or a council of rulers whom Christians of every nationality, tribe and kindred will by common consent follow and obey no one would be so ridiculous as to assert. The profoundest of Protestant thinkers are one with us in recognizing that the successor of St. Peter alone is the hope of a re-united Christendom. Therefore it behooves us Catholics in season and out of season to uphold and magnify the teaching and ruling authority of the Vicar of Christ as the supreme test of loyalty and obedience to Christ Himself.

And now in conclusion one word to those non-Catholics who are present in the Cathedral this morning. Will you permit me to quote the words of the Rev. Charles Edward Stowe, a New Englander, a Congregationalist minister and the nephew of Henry Ward Beecher. Surely you will take these eloquent sentences more kindly as coming from one to the Puritan-manor born, than if I should pronounce them as my own:

"Our puritan Fathers never would have made the break they did with Catholic Christianity could they have foreseen as the result thereof the Christless, moribund, frigid, fruitless Protestantism that can contribute neither warmth, life, inspiration nor power to lift us above the weight and weariness of sin. It is only too true that the heavenly city which our Puritan Fathers yearned for and sought with prayers and tears has become to many of their Christless descendents a frigid city of icy palaces built of pale negations, cold, cheerless, and shining in a pale winter sun, with an evanescent glitter of a doubtful and unsubstantial intellectual worth. The full, rich glorious Christ of a Catholic Christianity had been dragged from His throne by the advanced thinkers and reduced to beggary. A pale, bloodless, emaciated, Syrian Ghost, He still dimly haunts the corridors of this twentieth century Protestantism, from which the doom of His final exclusion has been already spoken.

"Then in their bluntless arrogance and self assertion they turn upon us who still cry with Thomas before the Risen One, 'My Lord and my God,' and tell us there is no middle ground between their own vague and sterile rationalism and the Roman

Catholic Church. If this be so, then for me, most gratefully and livingly, I turn to the Church of Rome as a homeless, houseless wanderer, to a home in a continuing city.

"We are hungry for God: Yea, for the Living God, and hence, are so restless and dissatisfied."

These last words of the Congregationalist preacher remind one of the saying of the prodigal son: "In my father's house there is bread enough and to spare and I perish with hunger."

My dear non-Catholic friends, if you can only come to realize two things you will not long tarry outside the Catholic Church, first, your own spiritual hunger for the Bread of life and, secondly, that the Living God offers Himself as that bread on the altars of the Catholic Church. After all, the most potent magnet to draw you to the Catholic Church is not that we have Christ's own Vicar to rule over us in the Chair of Peter, but it is that Jesus Christ, Himself, is always present with us, according to his own promise, "Lo, I am with you all days, even to the consummation of the world." It is the Mass that matters most to the Catholic. It is the belief in the Real Presence of Jesus Christ upon the Altar and in the tabernacle because the Holy Eucharist is His Body and Blood. This, dear brethren, is the irresistible attraction of the Catholic Church; there is no room for doubt as to the real presence any more than there is room to doubt the truth of Christianity itself. Here is the Living God and here is the fulfillment of His own words: "I am the living bread which came down from Heaven. If any man eat of this bread he shall live forever and the bread that I will give is My flesh, which I will give for the life of the world. My flesh is meat indeed and My blood is drink indeed."

So my friends, do not wait until the landslide of your fellow non-Catholics hurries you pell-mell into the Catholic Church, but forestall the march of the returning hosts by coming home here and now. I am so glad I did not wait any longer for the slower movement of my fellow Anglicans. Come home at once, dear brethren, and share with us the delectable things provided for all her children by our good Mother, the Catholic Church.

8. The Society of the Atonement

America, February 25, 1914

As a straw upon the surface of the waters, though so small a thing, will, nevertheless, indicate the way the tide is running, so the corporate action of the Society of the Atonement four years ago last October, in passing from Anglicanism into the Catholic Church, marked a new stage in that remarkable Romeward movement which has asserted itself so persistently in the Church of England, and her branch communions during the last two generations.

The movement began, as all the world knows, at Oxford in 1833, exactly three hundred years after the setting up of the royal supremacy in England and the rejection of king and Parliament of the Papal authority. Newman, who was the corypheus of the movement, revealed its providential, as well as logical *terminus ad quem,* by becoming Catholic. Many followed his example and the stream of individual conversions gradually has swollen from Newman's day to this; yet the movement within the Anglican body has suffered no reaction on that account and it has steadily progressed, both doctrinally and numerically. The Catholic leaven is ever, more and more, permeating the Anglican lump.

That a Religious Institute, comprising a community of Friars, another of Sisters, and a small band of secular tertiaries could have existed for ten years in the Episcopal Church, and all this time holding the Catholic Faith in its entirety, inclusive of the Immaculate Conception of the Blessed Virgin Mary, and of Papal infallibility, was astonishing to many. Yet this was done by the Society of the Atonement, not in secret, but openly and with a monthly magazine boldly proclaiming the fact to the world. This was simply one of the psychological phenomena in connection with the Romeward trend in the Anglican Church. That it was not a bit of mere individual eccentricity has been demonstrated since by the reception into the Catholic Church, a year ago, of two much larger communities in England, viz., the Benedictine Monks of Caldey and the Benedictine Nuns of of Milford Haven, South Wales. A new pro-Roman party now exists in the Church of England; and the present agitation over the kikuyu affair is likely to bring the fact into ever-increasing prominence.

The home of the Society of the Atonement is Graymoor, in the Highlands of the Hudson, three miles back from Garrison, a town on the east bank of the river and connected by ferry with West Point. At the summit of the Mount of the Atonement, having an elevation of 700 feet, and commanding a stretch of magnificent river and highland scenery, stand clustered together the community buildings of the Friars of the Atonement—St. Paul's Friary, erected in 1900; St. Francis Church, which was dedicated on the feast of St. Peter's Chair, January 18, 1912; and St. John's House of Studies, completed in the summer of 1913, and now rapidly filling with young students who are eager to qualify as members of the congregation.

On the southern slope of the mountain, hardly more than a stone's throw from the Friary, there lies almost hidden among the trees a poor log cabin, which has afforded shelter to many thousands of homeless men in the five years of its existence. It bears the name of St. Christopher's Inn, not alone because of its dedication to the patron saint of travelers, but because the wayfaring men, commonly styled tramps, are at Graymoor, Brothers Christopher (Christ Bearers). To make a frank confession, I would blush to have any of our fine friends visit this hostelry of our penniless guests—it is so desperately poor and rough. In fact, it was originally intended for a chicken house; and it was a photograph of the log cabin in which Lincoln was born that inspired the idea of converting it into a St. Christopher's Inn.

Down in the beautiful Graymoor Valley, just at the foot of the Mount of the Atonement, and half-mile distant from St. Paul's Friary, are the grounds—ten acres in extent—of the Sisters of the Atonement, and all has been acquired since the Society became Catholic, except the original three-quarters of an acre on which stands St. John's mission Church, erected about 1875, by Dr. Gray, the Episcopal rector at Garrison, and St. Francis's House, the Sister's Convent, which was built in 1899. Soon after the coming of the Sisters this tiny bit of ground acquired the name of the Graymoor Portiuncula, after the famous Portiuncula of St. Francis at Assisi, and no doubt the name will cling to it always.

Submission to Rome has meant growth and expansion to the second, as well as to the first, congregation of the Society;

and this is evidenced by the enlargement of St. Francis's House to twice its former size, a work that began last September and which will not be completed until May or June. In its Anglican days the Sisters' convent chapel was ample to accommodate the few people from the neighborhood who occasionally came to worship or to hear a sermon, and the large building, St. John's mission church, was seldom used. Now the Church is filled at Mass on Sundays, even in the winter, and in summer it is so crowded that its enlargement, too, will doubtless soon become a pressing necessity.

The motto of the Society is *Omnia pro Christo et Salute Hominum* (All things for Christ and the Salvation of Men) and it voices the missionary purpose of its existence. When His Holiness Pope Pius X was humbly besought to take the Institute under his sovereign care as Shepherd of Christ's Sheep, the three-fold mission of the Society of the Atonement was defined to be: First, to labor for the reconciliation of sinners unto God through the Precious Blood of the Atonement; second, to pray and work for the return of Anglicans and other non-Catholics, to the unity of the Catholic Church; third, the conversion of the heathen.

It is too early in the life of this young Society to show much work actually accomplished on these lines. It has taken the past four years to lay foundations, which is always slow and tedious work and one that requires great patience and even greater wisdom. But anyone who takes the trouble to scan from month to month the "Graymoor Annals" as these are published in *The Lamp,* the organ of the Society, cannot fail to see the hall-mark of progress clearly inscribed upon every department of its work. As for the writer, I have always believed that the Society of the Atonement from its infancy has been of God; and certainly this faith has not been lessened upon the Institute during the last five years of its flourishing existence.

9. Oneness with Christ

The Lamp, December, 1914

Peace be unto you from the Babe of Bethlehem and His Blessed Mother and ours. After we have listened to the song of the angels until our hearts are brimful of Christmas melody, let us go in company with the Shepherds even unto Bethlehem and entering the stable on bended knee before Mary's new-born Child, recall to mind His words in after life: "Except you (too) become as little children and be born again, ye cannot enter the Kingdom of Heaven." The Infant Jesus was that "Stone" of prophecy seen by Daniel in the vision, "hewn out of a mountain without hands," which was to grow until it should itself "become a great mountain and fill the whole earth." What Christmas began, Calvary has fulfilled.

Mary's Babe was the "corn of wheat" which, by falling into the ground and dying, has multiplied His own infancy in the regeneration of the Children of the Atonement until the multitude of them who constitute His Mystical Body more and more fill the whole earth. Two great mysteries of the Catholic religion perpetually continue the divine process by which originally the Word was made flesh in the womb of Mary and was born at Bethlehem; the first is the Mystery of Regeneration, for in this Mystery the baptistry becomes a new Bethlehem and within the bosom of the infant, or adult, who is baptized, Mary's Son is born again by the operation of the Holy Ghost. The second mystery is the Holy Eucharist, whereby the Catholic Church or chapel also becomes a new Bethlehem (*House of Bread*), and the altar, the manger on which the Infant Christ lives afresh in the Host as the priest, bending over the tiny particle of snowy bread whispers the mystic sentence of the new creation: *Hoc est enim Corpus Meum.*

Rejoice then, in thy oneness with Mary, O thou Child of the Atonement, for by virtue of the two greatest sacraments of the Catholic Church the Babe of Mary has not only been born in thee, but as often as thou dost partake of the Holy Eucharist, it is the Jesus Christ, under the appearance of a small host, who passes through the door of thy lips into the tabernacle you have lovingly prepared for Him in thy heart. Pray not only for spiritual understanding great enough to worthily appreciate this marvelous truth, but for grace also to love and serve the Divine Infant as faithfully and unselfishly as Mary, His Immaculate Mother. Hide thyself so completely in Him that, with His great servant, St. Paul, you may be blest truthfully to say: "It is no longer I that live, but Christ that liveth in me."

But this possession of the Babe of Bethlehem as our very own involves a duty of charity to our fellow Christians, which every true Child of the Atonement must be keen to fulfill. Because of our spiritual oneness in Christ Jesus, on us rests the burden of that New Commandment that Christ gave to His disciples, "that ye love one another, as I have loved you that ye love one another."

God hasten the day when Pentecostal love and unity shall flourish again among all Christians, beholding which the pagan world shall exclaim again as it did of old: "Behold how the Christians love one another." With a heart full of affection towards you in the Lord, I wish you all a Merry Christmas, and from His throne in Mary's arms, may the Divine Infant Bless you every one.

N.B. As far it is practicable, I ask that all members of the Rosary League, on Christmas Day, wear a piece of red ribbon in connection with their medal, when they receive Holy Communion (if they be men) and that the medal be suspended around the neck by a scarlet cord or ribbon (if they be women). It will be remembered that Rahab, in the fall of Jerico was commanded to suspend a scarlet cord out of the window of her house and by obedience, she and all her household were saved from death in the destruction of the city. Through the scarlet Blood of the Atonement, we children of Mary know that we have passed from death unto life, and by wearing the red ribbon in connection with your medal of Our Lady of the Atonement, you will give visible expression of your faith in the Precious Blood and gratitude to God for the unspeakable gift of His dear Son.

10. Comment on the Apostolic Brief of Pope Benedict XV

The Lamp, April, 1916

It is with great joy we publish for our readers and indeed, for the whole Catholic world, the brief of His Holiness, Pope Benedict XV, granting under the usual conditions, a plenary indulgence, which may be obtained every year, whether on the Feast of the Chair of Peter at Rome, January 18, or of the Conversion of St. Paul, January 25, and also on each day during the Octave a partial indulgence of two hundred days by the devout recital of the form of prayer, set forth by the Holy See for use during this annual period, henceforth dedicated to the repetition on the part of the faithful on Our Lord's own prayer, that all who believe in Him might be one.

In spirit, we kneel with profound veneration at the feet of the Vicar of Christ to thank His Holiness for the immense favor he has granted and we promise in return to labor more zealously and with all our strength, to propagate this same Octave of Prayer, not only in the United States of America and Great Britain and Canada, but among all nations and in all parts of the world. Nor must we forget to give full credit and profound thanks to the Cardinals, Archbishops, and Bishops of the United States, England, Ireland, and Canada, together with His Eminence, Cardinal Falconio of Rome, who from year to year increasingly have endorsed and fostered the observance of the Octave. Worthy of particular mention in this regard are the Cardinal Archbishop of Boston who, while the Society of the Atonement was still without Peter's fold, took the lead among Catholic prelates in approving of the Octave; the Rt. Reverend J. H. Regis Canevin, D.D., of Pittsburgh, who was among the earliest to officially recommend its observance in his diocese; His Grace, Archbishop Blenck, of New Orleans, who several years ago published a pastoral directing it to be observed by the clergy and people throughout his archdiocese and the Right Rev. Joseph Schembs, D.D., Bishop of Toledo, who for two years past has commanded his pastoral letter to be read in every church of the diocese, explicitly setting forth the way and manner in which "this Octave of Prayer shall be, as far as possible, observed," and appointing a collection to be made for missions on the Sunday within the Octave. The late Bishop Conaty of Los Angeles, and the present Bishop of Sacramento, California, are also to be lovingly remembered as devoted friends of the Octave from its very commencement.

It remains for us to say with the greatest gratitude, that the obtaining of the Papal Brief, is directly due to His Eminence, Cardinal Farley, Archbishop of New York, who made application to Rome for it, and to His Eminence, Cardinal Merry del Val, Secretary of State in the Pontificate of Pope Pius X, and at present Prefect of the Congregation of the Holy Office.

Now that the blessing originally bestowed upon the Octave by the late Holy Father has been supplemented by the brief of His successor, Pope Benedict, happily reigning, we may confidently anticipate for the Church Unity Octave an immense increase of popularity and its propagation by the hierarchy, the clergy and the faithful on every continent and in all lands. May the innumerable multitude which it will cause to rise heavenward for the reunion of Christendom, hasten that blessed day, when there shall be but one fold under one shepherd and the kingdoms of the whole world shall be united in loyal submission to the scepter of Jesus Christ.

11. Our Cardinal Ugolino

The Lamp

When God inspired the Seraphic Patriarch of Assisi to found his three great Orders, He raised up for him a special friend at the Papal Court and defender of the Franciscan Institute in the person of Cardinal Ugolino, afterward Pope Gregory IX. When the Society of the Atonement, as a tender shoot, was grafted into the Franciscan vine, the same Divine Providence gave it a nursing father and protector in the person of Cardinal Diomede Falconio, whose summons to take passage from the City of Peter to the Jerusalem which is above, came from Almighty God on February 7th.

During his long and illustrious career as a Friar Minor and trusted ambassador of the Holy See, he placed an innumerable multitude of people, clerical and lay, religious and secular, under obligation to remember him after his decease, with gratitude and to breathe a prayer for the speedy entrance of his soul into the Paradise of God. But we can hardly imagine any individual or collection of individuals who have greater cause to hold in grateful memory the name of Cardinal Falconio than the members of the Society of the Atonement. To substantiate this statement we have but to remind our readers that it was His Eminence in his official capacity as Apostolic Delegate to the United States of America who obtained from Pope Pius X, the Society's corporate reception into the Fold of Peter.

It has already been recorded in the annals of the Society how the Father Minister, clothed in the garb of a Franciscan Friar, and traveling without money, on Friday morning, August 13, 1909, knocked at the door of the Apostolic Delegation in

Washington, and being admitted into an ante-room, suddenly found himself in the presence of His Excellency, the Apostolic Delegate, wearing a dove-colored cassock, much the worse for wear, and on his feet a pair of carpet-slippers. This venerable representative of the Soverign Pontiff, and son of St. Francis, with the utmost simplicity and friendliness of manner patiently heard the story of the Graymoor Institute and the evidences advanced in its support. The wise and holy man of God, trained as he was in the school of ecclesiastical diplomacy to judge the merits of a case swiftly and almost unerringly, seemed to recognize at once that the Society of the Atonement, in spite of its smallness and the contempt in which it was held, was nevertheless, a vine of the Lord's own planting; and, when on his return to Graymoor, the Father minister addressed a letter to the Apostolic Delegate asking him to entreat His Holiness, Pope Pius X, to receive the Society of the Atonement under his protection, and to preserve both the Institute and its Name, His Excellency became such an effective advocate with the Holy See, that in due time a favorable response was received from Pope Pius X, and on October 30, 1909, the corporate reception of the Society of the Atonement took place at Graymoor.

Nor was this the solitary service rendered by the great Franciscan Churchman to the Graymoor Institute.

And when Cardinal Falconio bade farewell to the beloved country of his adoption, and sailed for Rome to receive the red hat, he did not forget the youngest Child in the Franciscan Family, and still followed us with his prayers, benediction, and loving assistance, and always to the last he held Graymoor in loving affection.

He ever had a predilection for *The Lamp*. It was *The Lamp* that first introduced Graymoor to his attention and directed our steps to Washington. On the occasion when we had encountered a former secretary of Monsignor Falconio, he said to us: "Why do you not go and present your case to the Apostolic Delegate? I know that you will receive from him a favorable hearing; not only because he is himself a Franciscan, but he is a most interested reader of *The Lamp*, and I have heard him express himself as deeply sympathetic with your aspiration to bring about the corporate return of Anglicans to communion with the Apostolic See."

Since 1914 we have carried most of the time upon the second page of our cover a letter from Cardinal Falconio cordially endorsing our magazine.

Not long after he became Cardinal he was appointed by Pope Pius X, protector of St. Clare's Church in Assisi, and after his first official visit to the tomb of the Mother Foundress of the Poor Clares in this capacity he congratulated and thanked *The Lamp* for having raised the sum of five thousand dollars for the restoration of the venerable edifice in honor of the Seventh Centenary of the founding of the Poor Clares.

We ask on behalf of this our Cardinal Benefactor the prayers of all our readers, and let us entertain the confident hope that when this illustrious Son of St. Francis and Cardinal Bishop of the Holy Roman Church appears before the Throne of God and Our Lady of the Atonement, he will prove our most faithful advocate with God against the subtleties of Satan and his undying malice. "Eternal rest grant unto him, O Lord, and light perpetual shine upon him."

12. Cardinal Gibbons

The Lamp, November, 1918

We once begged a car-fare on board a trolley in Washington and explained to the Protestant Minister, who right cheerfully gave it, that it was in obedience to the rule of St. Francis of Assisi we were traveling without money whereupon the worthy man exclaimed: "St. Francis is the saint of us Protestants."

One of the finest tributes we can pay to His Eminence, Cardinal Gibbons whose jubilee is commanding such universal attention at the present time is that he is the Cardinal in a unique sense of the whole American people, Protestant and Jew as well as Catholic. The Catholic Church in this country has produced a long list of illustrious prelates, who have won their way into the affection and esteem of the entire nation, regardless of the creedal differences, but as Saul towered head and shoulders above all the men of Benjamin, we think by general consent, the place of greatest prominence among this illustrious company will be awarded to James Cardinal Gibbons.

A Prince of the Church and "the noblest Roman of them all," the red hat and the ecclesiastical purple has never weaned him from the simplicity of the plain American citizen. We have had the high privilege of eating at His Eminence's table, of talking with him in his private study and sleeping in a room adjoining his own, and our eyes have witnessed the severe plainness of his surroundings. His bed and sleeping apartment is as poor and simple as that of a Franciscan Friar.

It is his simon-pure Americanism coupled with his perfect Christian courtesy and his sublime greatness as a Catholic Churchman that has made him everybody's Cardinal and won for His Eminence the good will of the whole American people.

The editor of *The Lamp* embraces the present occasion to put on record something of the personal debt he owes the Cardinal Archbishop of Baltimore. Once in the early days of our ministry as an Episcopal clergyman we were conducting a mission in Queenstown, Md., when we picked up on the table of our host a copy of Cardinal Gibbon's "Faith of Our Fathers" and spent considerable time reading it. Our ultimate submission to the Catholic Church did not occur until more than twenty years later, but the reading of that most popular and famous of all apologies for the Catholic Faith in the English tongue was one of the links in the long chain which finally produced *The Lamp* and brought the Society of the Atonement to the feet of Peter nine years ago.

Shortly after *The Lamp* shed its first beams on a divided Christendom the Editor made a pilgrimage to Baltimore for the sole purpose of paying an humble act of respect and veneration to the only Cardinal of the Holy Roman Church at that time in all America. His Eminence received us with that inimitable cordiality which characterized him and when we spoke of *The Lamp* and our desire to lead souls to the Apostolic See, His Eminence exclaimed with an emphasis we shall never forget: "If we had the Anglicans with us we would conquer the world for Christ." Before departing from that august presence we knelt to receive the saintly Cardinal's blessing and again acting, as it still seems to us under a strong impulse of the Holy Spirit, he laid his hands tremblingly upon our head and spoke these words, which have been so wonderfully fulfilled: "And may you and your Society be corporately united with the Holy See before you die."

Five years later we came again to his residence and in the same room sought his counsel and assistance in securing for the

Society of the Atonement, a way of entrance into the Fold of Peter. His answer was: "Follow implicitly and in good faith the guidance of the Holy Ghost and go no faster Romeward than He, the Parclete, reveals the pathway for your feet to tread." To this counsel we were obedient and through his Eminence had no further hand in directing our steps yet within twelve months the reception of both the Society of the Atonement and *The Lamp* into the one Fold under the One Shepherd was an accomplished fact.

13. Oxford and Graymoor (1)

The Lamp, July, 1923

Two important anniversaries are being celebrated simultaneously during the present month of the Precious Blood.

Thirty years ago, the Seventh Sunday after Pentecost, (July 9th, 1893), in St. John's Church (Anglican), Kingston, New York, the future Father Founder of the Society of the Atonement sought of God after the manner of St. Francis of Assisi the Name of the Institute which already occupied his mind and heart day and night. In answer to that fervent prayer he not only received the Name—Atonement—but the Three Basic Texts which have served the same purpose in the after development of the Society of the Atonement as the Three Texts which Saint Francis received in Assisi guided the Seraphic Patriarch in forming the Rule of the Friars Minor.

The other Anniversary, which coincides in its observance with this one of the Society of the Atonement is the celebration (July 8-13) by the *Anglo-Catholic Congress in London of the Ninetieth Anniversary of the Oxford Movement,* so-called. The connection between the two is too important for *The Lamp,* as an organ of Church Unity, to ignore.

By unanimous consent of its historians, the Oxford Movement had its beginning with the Sermon preached by John Keble in St. Mary's Church, Oxford, on "The National Apostasy" in July 1833, the particular Sunday being the Seventh Sunday after Pentecost, (or Sixth Sunday after Trinity, according to the Anglican Calendar.)

It is to be noted, therefore, that the Sermon which inaugurated the Oxford Movement, and the receiving of the Name and the Basic Texts of the Society of the Atonement both occurred on the Seventh Sunday after Pentecost, and consequently, the ninetieth anniversary of the Oxford Movement is celebrated in London this year during our Atonement Week, which always begins on the Sunday just mentioned.

Now for the providential connection! To discover this we must travel back in time to the reign of Edward the Confessor, that saintly King of England who was the principal builder of the great historic Church of London, Westminster Abbey. Edward the Confessor was richly endowed with the gift of prophecy, and among the prophetic visions vouchsafed him that have been preserved among the historic records of his reign was a notable one conceiving the Church of England.

In this vision he saw the Church of England as a great tree severed from its stock and carried a distance of three furlongs, and then in the same vision he saw the tree brought back by no human power and reunited with its orignal stock.

Nothing in the history of English Christianity seems to fulfill the first part of the vision except those drastic acts of Parliment in the days of Henry VIII and Elizabeth, by means of which the Church of England was cut off by schism from its root foundation in the Apostolic See of Rome. If we may interpret the Three Furlongs by a measurement in time, and give to each furlong the space of a century, then indeed it is most noteworthy that exactly three centuries intervened between the breach with Rome and took place in the reign of Henry VIII, and the beginning of the Oxford Movement. It was in 1533 that the first Acts of Parliament were passed by which the cleavage between England and Rome began, and it was in 1833, as mentioned above, that the Oxford Movement began.

Up to 1833 the Reformed Church of England was undeniably Protestant. The revival of religion which took place in that moribund organization as a result of the Movement inaugurated at Oxford by Keble's Sermon, and the publishing subsequently of the "Tracts for the Times," has been characteristically Catholic in its trend and has changed the whole face of Anglicanism which has continued to develop during the ninety years since its beginning in a persistently Romeward direction.

It was in 1903, just seventy years after the Oxford Movement, and ten from the time we received the Name and Texts of our Institute, that *The Lamp* made its appearance, affirming from its very first issue that the *terminus ad quem* of the Oxford Movement was designed by God to be the *Corporate Return of the Anglican Body to Communion with the Apostolic See.*

At the time the Editor of *The Lamp* made this assertion the pro-Roman Party in the Anglican Church was still non-existent, and as far as he knew he was practically alone among thirty thousand Anglican Clergymen in holding to such a conviction. But, in the last two decades the Oxford Movement has inaugurated, particularly in England, what has been called by one of its advocates, "a Counter Reformation," having no final end in view short of corporate submission of the entire Anglican Communion to the spiritual jurisdiction of the Successor of St. Peter, and the return of the Church of England to the same relationship with Rome in Faith and Discipline as existed prior to Henry VIII and Thomas Cranmer.

There lies before us on our desk one of the straws which shows the way in which the tide of the so-called Oxford Movement is running at the present time in England. This straw is a four-page leaflet entitled, "The Messenger of the Catholic League," an organization of clergy and laymen flourishing in England. The entire leaflet is an exposition of the Primacy of Peter, as able and conclusive in its argument as anything we have found among the apostolic literature of the Catholic Church herself.

We ask our readers of *The Lamp* to support this wonderful movement of the Holy Ghost within the Anglican Body, which, in spite of all contrary winds and oppositions of devils and of men, has continued to guide the Anglican Ship in the direction of the Rock of Peter and the Harbor of Catholic Unity.

The difficulties to be overcome from the human standpoint we confess to appear insurmountable. Yet with God all things are possible! Our faith and confidence should be strong that God, having begun the marvelous work at Oxford in July, 1833, will carry it on to a complete and triumphant conclusion, the gates of hell and the infirmities of human nature to the contrary notwithstanding.

The first-fruits of the Oxford Movement indicative of the larger fruitage of the future was the submission of the coryphaeus of the Movement, John Henry Newman, to the Apostolic See, and his subsequent elevation to the office of a Cardinal

Prince of the Holy Roman Church. His example has been followed by a long list of individual converts drawn from Anglican ranks, both clerical and lay.

But that God's purpose in the Oxford Movement might be made manifest as something more than a series of individual conversions, there took place in 1909 the corporate reception into the Roman Fold of the Society of the Atonement. This was followed a few years later by a similar corporate reception of the Anglican Benedictine Monks of Caldey, and simultaneously with them of the Benedictine Nuns of Milford Haven, South Wales.

May we not accept these three models as illustrative of what on a far vaster scale God will yet bring to pass in the future development of the Oxford Movement so that in the not far distant future another chapter in the history of the Anglican Church will record the complete fulfillment of the vision of Edward the Confessor; when the tree severed from its parent stock by the violent hands of Henry VIII and his daughter, Elizabeth, will by the omnipotent power of God, miraculously return and take root once again in its parent stock, the Holy Roman Church which, as "The Messenger of the Catholic League," affirms, "is the Mother and Mistress of all the Churches."

14. Oxford and Graymoor (2)

The Lamp, July 1923

Last month I asked you to read with special attention the Editorial on "Graymoor and Washington". This month I am asking you to read the one that bears the title "Oxford and Graymoor". It will help you to realize more vividly a very important part of the Church Unity vocation of the Society of the Atonement.

While the original members of our Holy Institute were still members of the Anglican Communion it was clearly recognized by them that God willed the Society to bear witness to the Chair of Peter at Rome as the divinely constituted center of Catholic Unity and to labor more particularly for the return of England to its ancient allegiance to the Holy See. The corporate reception of the Society itself into the Catholic Church fourteen years ago and its subsequent development has only served to strengthen and confirm our belief that what John Henry Newman began to do at Oxford ninety years ago the Society of the Atonement is destined to take a leading part in completing.

That the sixteenth century breach between England and Rome is being repaired from both the Catholic and the Anglican side at the present time, much circumstantial evidence might be adduced. Lord Halifax, the venerable president of the English Church Union, has been working persistently for twenty years to bring the Church of England into communion with Rome and the last decade has seen a powerful pro-Roman party take the pilot wheel of the Oxford Movement into their hands and they are steering the Anglican ship straight for the Roman harbor.

His Eminence, Cardinal Gibbons, the first time we met, said to me: "If we had the Anglicans with us, we would conquer the world." Undoubtedly the return of England to communion with the Apostolic See would not only immensley facilitate the return of the other Protestant sheep to the Fold of Peter but also the return of the Oriental Orthodox Churches over whom Great Britain at the present time exercises a powerful influence, for political reasons that have always played so dominant a part in Eastern ecclesiastical history. Great Britain and America combined have a preponderating influence among the nations of the whole world and were all English-speaking peoples, now predominantly Protestant, to return to Catholicism the conversion of Asia and Africa would be accomplished in a very short time and so Cardinal Gibbons' prophecy would be fulfilled: "If we had the Anglicans with us, we would conquer the world."

From our Lord's own prayer that His disciples might all be one, and His foretelling the day when that prayer would be answered ("other sheep have I which are not of this fold; they also will hear My voice, and there shall be One Fold and One Shepherd") we know how very dear to the Sacred Heart the cause of Unity among Christians is; and as the Immaculate Heart of Mary, His Mother, beats in perfect union with the Sacred Heart of her Divine Son, we can readily perceive how dear the cause of Catholic Unity is to her also. It should be the desire of our Rosarians, as loving Children of the Atonement, to be united in all things with the Sacred Heart of Jesus and the Immaculate Heart of Mary, and therefore we too should ardently desire the return of the "other sheep", particularly those of the Anglican household of Faith, to the unity of the One Fold under the One Shepherd, the Pope of Rome. Therefore, I ask you to cooperate with the Friars and Sisters of the Atonement in our Church Unity vocation by praying daily for its fulfillment.

Let me point out to you how this is provided for in the rule of the Rosary League. The second degree calls for the recitation daily of the Threefold Salutation of the Blessed Virgin and the Morning Offering. Now the Morning Offering concludes with this petition, "the Unity of Christians and the Conversion of the world through Christ Our Lord." The third degree of Membership provides for the receiving of Holy Communion once a month "with the intention that all sinners may be reconciled to God through the Precious Blood of the Atonement and *all Christians be made one,* that the whole world may believe and be saved." We have one hundred thousand Members of our Rosary League and if every one of these practices this rule of daily prayer for Church Unity and received Holy Communion once a month for the same intention the result would be immense beyond computation.

Through the intercession of Our Lady of the Atonement may God inspire you all with a wonderful faith in our Church Unity vocation and a faithful performance of your own duty of prayer and work for the reunion of Christendom as loyal members of the same Holy Society.

15. The "Terminus Ad Quem" of the Oxford Movement

An Address to the Anglican Clergy

Antidote, July, 1923

It was stated in the *Antidote* last month that the ninetieth anniversary of the Oxford Movement would be celebrated in London from July 8th to July 13th by an "Anglo-Catholic Congress," which notable event will be taking place on or about the time this issue of The Antidote reaches its readers.

A wonderful transformation has taken place in the Church of England and those other national or colonial Episcopal Churches in communion with Canterbury since the so-called Oxford Movement began just ninety years ago. The three-decker pulpit which, until then, was an outward and visible sign of the

Protestant teaching and practice which had prevailed for three hundred years in the Church of England has long since given place to the altar against the east wall of the sanctuary and an increasing number of those other outward and visible expressions of a sacerdotal and sacrificial religion are now common in Anglican Churches which have always characterized the faith and worship of the Catholic Church. Both sacramentally and ceremonially the Church of England has steadily gravitated in a Romeward direction since 1833. Those who call themselves Catholic priests and hold the Catholic doctrine of the Sacrifice of the Mass, who hear confessions and grant priestly absolution among the Clergy of the Anglican Communion have constantly grown in numbers until they now comprise if not a majority, at any rate a very large percentage of the clerical body and even among Anglican Bishops who were and always have been the slowest to accept and promote the movement originating at Oxford, the percentage who wear capes and mitres and glory in the names Catholic are greater now than ever before. In fact, from His Grace of Canterbury to My Lord of Liverpool none of the Anglican prelates have entirely escaped the influence of the Oxford revival, being to a greater or lesser degree affected by it in getting away from the old fashioned Protestant traditions which prevailed in the Church of England by law established before the days of Keble, Newman, Pusey, Neal and Little.

And where is it all tending? From the very beginning the leaders in the Oxford Movement have been called "Romanizers," and, although for the most part they have quite sincerely denied the imputation, yet in the determinate fore-knowledge of Almighty God, Romanizers, in a real and good sense they most certainly have been. For, after all, is not the providential *terminus ad quem* of the Oxford Movement a return of the Church of England to Communion with Rome and the re-establishment of the same relationships between the See of Peter and the Sees of Canterbury and York, which existed prior to the days of Henry VIII, Edward VI, and Queen Elizabeth, the three Tudors, who, by their royal wills, created in the XVI Century a breach between England and Rome, ecclesiastically speaking?

By a certain coincidence, which can hardly be accidental, the Society of the Atonement is this month celebrating the 30th anniversary of a very important event in its history which corresponds exactly in date with the celebration in London on the

Sixth Sunday after Trinity (7th Sunday after Pentecost, Catholic Calendar) of the 90th Anniversary of the Oxford Movement. It was on this particular Sunday (July 9th) in 1893 that the future Father Founder of the said Society in imitation of St. Francis of Assisi, kneeling before the altar in St. John's Episcopal Church, Kingston, of which he was then Rector, sought by opening the volume of Holy Scripture the name which the Society he believed God was calling him to found should bear. He received not only the name but also the three basic texts for the future Society corresponding to the three texts which St. Francis received in the same manner, and which became the rule of life for the greatest missionary order in the Catholic Church.

A photograph of these three texts as they were actually written down on that eventful day appears on the next page. It was not till years afterwards that we made the discovery that this memorable Sunday in the history of the Society of the Atonement was the sixtieth anniversary of the Sunday in 1833 on which John Keble preached his famous Assize Sermon on "the National Apostasy" which ever since has been recognized as the Pentecostal Day of the Oxford Movement.

Please note on the photograph that the Central Text, containing the Society's Name, is recorded as Romans v.2 (King James Version). By taking your bible, or new testament you will note that the 19th verse of that Chapter reads as follows: "For as by one man's disobedience many were made sinners, so by the obedience of one shall many be made righteous." In the famous book written by Henry VIII against Martin Luther which earned for him from the Pope the title of "Defender of the Faith", these very words are quoted in condemnation of the German Reformer. See how this one man's disobedience, Henry says, has caused so many in Europe to become sinners against the Divinely constituted authority of St. Peter's successor. Ten years later Henry himself comes under the same condemnation through his headstrong determination to have his secret alliance with Anne Boleyn dignified by the name of marriage. But who is Henry Tudor's counterpart to fulfil entirely the parallelism of the text? If Henry is the one man whose disobedience will serve to make many in England Catholic and to thereby reconcile that rebellious nation to the Vicar of Christ? To what one man, more than to another can that high dignity be attributed so well as to John Henry Newman, the coryphaeus of the Oxford

307

Movement? Note the very significance of his name John, the faithful, Henry, filled with the Spirit of Christ, the New Man; whereas the rebellious spirit of the Old Man of Sin actuated the disobedient Henry Tudor. In this connection observe how in John Henry Newman was epitomized the entire course of the Oxford Movement. Tract Number One began at the very foundation of the Catholic religion in reaffirming the fundamental, primary doctrine of Baptismal Regeneration and tract 90 romanized the 39 articles of Religion. Newman, himself did not stop developing until he was prostrate at the feet of the Successor of St. Peter and died a Cardinal of the Holy Roman Church. In that one many see fulfilled the God-intended line of development of the Oxford Movement.

Another straw upon the Anglican waters to show the direction the tide is running, was the corporate reception of the Society of the Atonement into the Catholic Church in 1909; the remarkable history of the Society until now is, in itself, an illustration of the providential destination of the Oxford Movement. Having its origin in the Anglican Communion as a direct product of the Oxford Movement it effected a perfect corporate re-union with the Apostolic See fourteen years ago and its Church Unity Mission, particularly in helping to repair the breach between Rome and Canterbury is clearly recognized by many in Israel today.

In view of all we have said it could hardly have been accidental that the Name and Basic Texts of our Graymoor Institute were revealed on the 7th Sunday after Pentecost just 60 years after the Birthday of the Oxford Movement. Ten years later, or 70 years after the commencement of the Oxford Movement, *The Lamp,* our Graymoor magazine, proclaimed the *terminus ad quem* of the Oxford Movement to be the corporate re-union of the Church of England with the Apostolic See. Almost at the same time the Reverend Spencer Jones, M.A., with an introduction by Lord Halifax, President of the English Church Union, published his famous book "England and the Holy See", asserting practically the same thing. *The Lamp* was greeted with a storm of protest throughout the length and breadth of the Anglican Church. *The Living Church,* the leading High Church organ of the Episcopal Church in the United States, hastened to explain to its readers that the Editor of *The Lamp* was an erratic monk living in solitude on a mountain at Graymoor and described him as a chaser of irridescent dreams. Later when the Reverend Arthur Lloyd, M.A., of Japan now dead, and the Reverend Spencer Jones came to the support of the Editor of *The Lamp* in bearing witness to the Chair of Peter as the *de jure divino* center of Catholic Christendom, *The Living Church* was constrained to confess that there were three pro-Romans in the Anglican body, but insisted that there were only three. A few years later *The Living Church* began to talk about the Pro-Roman Party. Now we find in England the Catholic League, openly acknowledging the Primacy of the Roman See and a formidable number of clergy advocating a Counter Reformation which shall have the beneficent result of bringing *Ecclesia Anglicana* into the same spiritual relationship with Rome which prevailed in England prior to 1533.

The editor of the *Antidote* thanks God for the Oxford Movement and prays that through its instrumentality the entire Anglican Communion during the 20th century may be corporately united with the Petrine root from which the Church of England was ruthlessly torn four hundred years ago.

16. Audience with the Holy Father, Pope Pius XI

Journal of Trip, May, 1925

Rome, Thursday, May 14, 1925: Four busy days have passed in which I have had no time to jot down anything in my "Diary Abroad".

Two questions are uppermost in the minds of Father Gabriel and myself. Will we secure, after our long waiting and such persistent effort, the private interview with the Holy Father and, in spite of the good offices of the Cardinal Protector of the Franciscans will we fail to secure a place in the procession at the canonization of the Little Flower? Almost, if not quite, the eleventh hour has arrived and still we are left wholly in the dark. Day by day we have been waiting for the customary notification, sent by a special messenger from the Vatican, stating the day and the hour of the appointment with His Holiness, but the cries of the priests of Baal, on Mount Carmel, to their God and to send down fire from Heaven to kindle the dry wood laid upon the altar of their desire was no more futile than until now appear all our efforts to secure the coveted audience with the Vicar of Christ. In using such a simile I, by no means, wish to give expression to despair or to imply that I have lost faith in ultimate success. I know how sorely beset the Holy Father at the present time is with application, not only from ordinary mortals, but from scores upon scores of Bishops assembled in Rome from all parts of the World, having purposely directed their steps towards "the Threshold of the Apostles" so that they might reach the Eternal City in time to be present at the canonization of St. Theresa of the Child Jesus. I was told, the other day, that as many as five Bishops were received by the Holy Father in audience at *one time,* something almost unprecedented in the annals of the Vatican.

In case Monsignor Cassia is able to secure for us an audience even for five minutes with His Holiness, I have the pledge of Father Michel d'Herbigny, S.J., head of the Oriental Institute, to accompany us. Not only does this learned ecclesiastic stand high in the favor of His Holiness, speaking Italian fluently and having experience with papal audiences, but he is deeply sympathetic with the petition concerning the observance of the Church Unity Octave which is the main purpose of the so much coveted audience.

Friday Evening, May 15th: The longed for audience with the Holy Father, is no longer a mere possibility of the future, it is now an event of the past.

Late last evening the bell of the monastery door rang and the messenger from the Vatican delivered the notification from Monsignor Cassia that the Holy Father would see us at eleven o'clock on the following morning. Promptly at the hour named, Fathers d'Herbigny, S.J., and Gabriel, S.A., stood with me at the entrance to the Vatican and bearing the papal invitation in our hands the Vatican soldiers on guard bowed their heads and motioned us to pass on. At first we were accompanied by many others as we walked across the courtway and up the broad flight of marble stairs that led to the audience chambers of the Vatican Palace. Our companions were pilgrims that hoped to see the Holy Father also at the hour of noon, but only in *public* audience. These were stopped by the guards after we had entered the outer rooms where the Holy Father sees hundreds at a time, being generally pilgrim groups, this one from Germany, that one from England, the other from South or North America.

The letter we bore was the "sesame" which opened the doors that left our pilgrim companions behind, nor was it a single anteroom we had to pass through. There were at least three of these and, in each, a time pause and waiting. Here we met and held conversation with elegant gentlemen wearing gorgeous uniforms and called Papal Chamberlains. Men of aristocratic rank and wealth who, nevertheless, as devoted sons of the Church, esteemed it an honor of the highest order to act as gentlemen in waiting upon His Holiness, the highest earthly Representative of the Lord of lords and King of kings.

At last we found ourselves standing at the portal of the last anteroom to pass through before entering the audience chamber where the Pope receives Cardinals and Bishops in private audience and confers with the Chief Shepherds of Christendom concerning the state of the Church in their several dioceses of missionary jurisdictions. Just as we were about to enter a Bishop appeared upon the scene with his tale of woe. When the Papal messenger arrived at his temporary abode to notify him that the Pope would receive his lordship at a certain hour, he was absent and accordingly had missed his appointment. He was in great distress, because he had come very far and wished to discuss with His Holiness matters of great importance in his own portion of the Lord's Vineyard. Being a Bishop, he had the right of way, therefore our little trio stood aside while his lordship passed within. His interview with the Soverign Pontiff was extremely brief. Less than ten minutes elapsed when he again passed us by on his way out from the august presence of the Vicar of Chirst. Then the Master of Ceremonies beckoned us to follow and we passed within, but we were only half way through the last anteroom when our guide whispered to us: "Kneel" and there standing before us—was Pope Pius XI.

The time had arrived for His Holiness to greet the throngs that were waiting for Him in the outer chambers, he could delay no longer. Nevertheless, the Holy Father looked down benignly upon us, as we still retained our kneeling position and patiently listened to what we had to ask the Vicar of Christ. We held out towards him the petitions, typewritten in both Latin and Italian, and as briefly as possible tried to tell him what they were, namely: First: A petition signed by over two hundred Bishops of the world asking His Holiness to further confirm the Papal Brief of His Predecessor, Benedict XV., extending the observ-

311

ance of the Church Unity Octave to the Universal Church and to make the observance of holy obligation by a Papal Rescript similar to the decree of Pope Leo XIII concerning the October devotion to the Blessed Virgin which, in consequence, are faithfully observed in Catholic Churches and religious houses in every part of the world. Second: permission to change the feast-day of Our Lady of the Atonement from the seventh Saturday after Pentecost to a fixed date, namely July 9th, the octave of the feast of the Visitation of the B.V.M. Also to sanction a special Mass and Divine Office in her honor. Third: To bless the *Rock of Peter Foundation,* established by the Friars of the Atonement in connection with the *Union-That-Nothing-Be-Lost,* whereby an endowment fund of not less than one million dollars is to be accumulated to aid in the erection or maintenance of Churches and Catholic Schools in Missionary lands at home and abroad.

Gazing for a moment at the formidable document, the Holy Father shook His head as much as to say: "I have no time to examine it". But instead of rejecting the petitions altogether, he bade us place them in the hands of Cardinal Gasparri, His Secretary of State, until he should have a more convenient season and leisure in which to consider the petitions therein contained. But as far as giving the blessings we asked of him, these he freely bestowed. In fact, he blessed us two, if not three times, then giving us his hand to kiss, with a final benediction he passed his way. The experience was a brief one, but certainly for the kneeling supplicants, tense with excitement and decidedly thrilling.

17. The Passing of a Chosen Servant of God

Mother Lurana Mary Francis, S.A.

The Lamp, May, 1935

Since my last letter to you, Lurana Mary Francis, Mother General and Foundress of the Sisters of the Atonement has "entered into that rest which remaineth for the people of God" (Heb. 4:9). Predestined to bear the name and have the vocation of the Atonement she was born into the world on Tuesday in Holy Week, April 12, 1870, and she was called home on Monday in Holy Week, April 15, 1935, being aged sixty-five years and three days.

When I say that she was predestined to bear the name of the Atonement I speak advisedly. In holy baptism she was given the name of Lurana Mary; and in the commencement of her life as a religious she still bore the name as Sister Lurana Mary. But when the time came for her profession at Graymoor in 1900, she wished to receive the name of Francis because of her great devotion and love for our Seraphic Father, St. Francis of Assisi. As the future Father General of the Society of the Atonement, whose profession took place on the Mount of the Atonement on July 27th in the same year, 1900, had received from the Anglican Bishop the name of Paul James, it did not seem fitting that the Mother General should receive three names, Lurana Mary Francis. Consequently it appeared necessary that either Mary or Lurana should be dropped to make place for Francis. To discard the name of the Mother of God was unthinkable, the rejection of Lurana seemed inevitable, much as we regretted it.

The problem was happily solved by the Joint Founders of the Society of the Atonement both assuming with the permission of the Bishop the name Francis. I further said to Mother: "Lurana must have a meaning; for God never gives a name without its having some significance." I tried by my own wit and wisdom to discover what the significance was; but it was only after months of vain searching that the name came to me in a dream. Assisted by a New Testament Greek lexicon, on the feast of the Beheading of St. John Baptist, August 29, 1901, I completed the discovery; ... *Lu* the first syllable means to loose, pardon or redeem—the second *Ran* means sprinkling and is used by both St. Peter and St. Paul of the Atonement Blood. So that Lurana in New Testament Greek means "Redeemed by (the blood of) sprinkling, i.e., Atonement." After the Mother's profession had taken place on St. Francis Day, October 4th, 1900, while we were lunching together, one of the clergy present said to me: "This is Yom Kippur, the Day of Atonement." So without knowing it, the Mother Foundress was professed on the ancient day of the Atonement; and it was nearly a year later that she learned the significance of the name which she was the first to bear as a religious.

Having the name of the Atonement, she was called by God

313

to be an Atoning Victim in union with the Crucified. At the commencement of her religious life she saw herself as a slain lamb and this vision of the night was particularly fulfilled in her last long illness, extending over many months, during which time to an extraordinary and striking degree she was conformed to the image of the Lamb of God slain upon the cross. Unable to take food or drink without experiencing great nausea, she passed through a long period of fasting almost as absolute as that of Our Lord in the wilderness. She once spoke of her body as a "pain factory" and truly such it was. For a time one particular part of the body would be subjected to excruciating pain; and when it became almost unbearable, it suddenly shifted to some other portion of the body until almost every organ or member was involved in the sufferings of the Crucified. But the sufferings of Mother Lurana were not entirely physical, during the thirty-six years of her life as a Religious at Graymoor, she was called upon to pass through many periods of great mental strain, not the least acute of which served as an introduction to her last illness. Her fortitude and patience were a marvel to those of her community most intimately associated with her.

We ask the Rosarians to treasure most lovingly the memory of that valiant woman, greatly beloved of God, who was divinely chosen to be a Mother of a Religious Family, destined to grow and increase until its numbers rival the stars for multitude. Pray for the soul of Lurana Mary Francis, and may you experience the gracious power of her intercession.

All her children at Graymoor are confident that she has already attained to the Beatific Vision and knowing well her solicitude and thought for her loved ones while on the earth, we do not doubt that she will manifest the same prayerful solicitude for us in heaven.

> Rest, valiant woman, who wrought for God alone
> Thy sun of life has vanished in the west,
> Thy goal is reached, thy labors now are o'er.
> Rest, valiant woman, rest.

18. Unity with Christ

St. Anthony's Hour, April 25, 1937

I have a message for you this morning, which may sound strange and new in your ears, but which, in reality, is as old as Christianity. The message in a single word is At-one-mentism. And the Author of At-one-mentism is no less a personage than Jesus Christ, the God-Man, the Savior and Redeemer of mankind.

Satan, the usurping prince of this world, in this 20th Century has offered to the proletariat as a substitute for At-one-mentism, Communism, and he has presented it in such an attractive and fascinating way that it has captivated the mind and heart of such vast multitudes that in some nations Communist revolutionaries have seized the reins of government and established a union of Soviet republics where imperial dynasties once held sway.

Why do the common people fall for Communism? What does it offer to the proletariat? The old Red Dragon offers them the material world. He says to them: "Get done with religion! It is the dope of priests and ministers, who fatten on your sacrifices and worship of a God that does not exist. There is no life beyond the grave! It is matter alone that matters! Destroy the capitalists! Seize all land and property; divide it among yourselves; possess all wealth in common!"

It is the same old bribe that the devil offered to Christ when he took Him up to a high mountain and showed Him all the kingdoms of the earth and said to Him: "All these will I give thee, if, falling down, Thou wilt adore Me." "The Prince of this World" is just making fools of the people. The Psalmist says: "The fool hath said in his heart, 'There is no God.'" And when a man becomes an atheist he *is* a fool; and when anyone believes in the promises of fallen Lucifer he is fooling himself. Antichrist will never deliver the goods and the proletariat will never possess the earth for themselves under the standard of Antichrist!

Now what is it that Jesus Christ promises to His followers, to those who believe on Him and enroll themselves in the army of the King of kings under His standard of the cross? At-one-mentism is the answer! He promises to those that believe on Him and embrace the doctrines of His holy religion At-one-ment

315

with God. First of all, He shed His blood and laid down His life on the Cross that, rising from the dead, He might give Himself to the regenerate, for those who are baptized are born again into the Kingdom of God and become members of the Mystical Body of Christ—and He dwells in them and they in Him.

He did not promise that we would possess Him alone, but He promised also the Father and the Holy Ghost would come and take up Their abode with us and in us. His words are: "If ye love Me, keep My commandments and My Father will come and take up His abode with you together with Myself." And in the Holy Gospel for today we read His promise: "It is expedient for you that I go away, for if I go not away the Holy Ghost, the Comforter, the Paraclete, will not come to you; but if I go to the Father, I will send the Paraclete unto you." This promise was fulfilled on the day of Pentecost, that glorious Feast which we will be celebrating three weeks from today. And this is the At-One-Mentism which Jesus Christ preaches unto us—*union* or *oneness* with God!

Is not that tremendous and how joyfully ought we to accept the gifts promised by Our Divine Savior! Could any possession be greater or more precious or more to be desired than the possession of God Himself? We ought to realize that in possessing God, as the people of God, we also possess the material world as well as the eternal world beyond the grave, the New Jerusalem, also called Paradise or Heaven. Even as Our Lord said to His disciples: "In My Father's house are many mansions. I go to prepare a place for you, that where I am, there ye may be also." And He promised that he that overcame as a militant soldier of Jesus Christ in the battle with Antichrist would sit with Him on His throne, even as He overcame and is set down with His Father on His throne, the throne of unlimited power and possession for all eternity. But even the present material world belongs by Divine Decree not to the Atheists but to the At-One-Mentists, the people of God.

Jesus declared to the proletariat in His Sermon on the Mount: "Seek ye first the Kingdom of God and His Justice and all these things (food, raiment and shelter) will be given unto you." St. Paul, writing to the Corinthian Christians says: "All things are yours because you possess Christ—and Christ is God." To you, my brethren, as a part of the proletariat, I say: Enter into your God-given possession! Become in practice an At-one-

316

mentist! Do not be duped by the devil, who is a liar from the beginning. He could not tell the truth, even if he tried, because the truth is not in him. Did he not fool our Mother Eve? And when did he ever make good on his promises to any of the children of men, whom he has lured away from God and His justice by bribes and seductive prospects?—illusions all of them. My dear people, spurn with utter contempt and aversion this latest seduction of Satan—so called Communism.

19. At-one with Christ

St. Anthony's Hour, June 27, 1937

I have spoken to you several times on the subject of At-one-mentism as opposed to Communism and how we should be At-one-mentists and I have explained to you what I mean by that word or expression, how through the Incarnation and Atonement of Jesus Christ our human nature has been united with God so that it is possible for us to live a life of At-one-ment or union with God. But we Christians, as members of the Mystical Body of Christ dwelling in Him and He dwelling in us, become members one of another even as Our Lord Himself prayed after He had instituted the Sacrament of His love in the upper room on the night of His betrayal—"that they all may be one as Thou Father in Me and I in Thee, that they also may be one in Us."

It is the will of God that we should not only fulfill the first and greatest Commandment. "Thou shall love thy Lord thy God with all thy heart, mind, soul and strength." But Christ gave us a new Commandment, that we should love one another even as He has loved us.

I spoke last Sunday of how in the first days of Christianity the pagans were astonished and cried out in amazement as they beheld the loving fellowship and unity among the Christians. "Behold, how these Christians love one another." But alas, through heresy and schism division in the course of the centuries have taken place between Christians and these heresies and divisions have not only separated the Christians from each other but, often filled their hearts with vengeance and hatred so that they have persecuted and even put each other to death and given the enemies of God cause to blaspheme and to say,

"Behold how these Christians hate one another." Recognizing as we do this sad division we are all more or less fervently wishing and praying that Christians may be united again. You will recall the saying of the Good Shepherd in the Holy Gospel—"Other sheep I have which are not of this Fold, them also I must bring and they will hear My voice and there shall be one Fold and one Shepherd."

It is the particular vocation of the Society of the Atonement to reach out after the other sheep who are separated from Peter's Fold and in the name of Christ to call them back to Catholic Unity.

You have just heard read in the Gospel how our Lord made Saint Peter the foundation in union with Himself of the Catholic Church and gave into his hands the keys of the Kingdom of God, that is the Divine Society which He established among men, in a word—the Catholic Church. In giving the Keys of His Kingdom to St. Peter, Christ gave Him control of supremacy over it.

After His Resurrection, Our Lord said three times to Saint Peter, "Feed my lambs; feed my lambs; feed my sheep"; and by so doing He constituted him His Vicar, the Supreme Shepherd of the One Flock.

But Saint Peter could not live forever and so Our Lord provided successors who should receive his office and carry it on through the centuries. He led Saint Peter finally to Rome where He established the Chair of His Authority as the Universal Shepherd and Ruler over the Kingdom of Christ. And so through the centuries ever since a successor has sat from generation to generation in the Chair of Peter and that Chair constitutes the Center of Unity and it is the will of Jesus Christ that all His sheep scattered abroad over the mountains and deserts should come and enter through the gate into the One Fold of the Catholic Church. And my dear non-Catholic listeners, can you not hear the voice of Christ, the Good Shepherd, calling you to return, to cease to be one of the other sheep wandering outside but to make haste to enter through the gate into the One Fold. I can promise you that if you hearken to the voice of the Good Shepherd and enter the Catholic Church you will be very happy and will not stop thanking God through all eternity.

I received a letter since my last broadcast, written by a non-Catholic, and accusing me of having forsaken Protestant-

318

ism and entering the Catholic Church just to make money, but my friend is mistaken. I and my associates at Graymoor sought and obtained admission into the Catholic Church because we heard the voice of Christ calling us and we obeyed. We knew that we were "not of this Fold" and when we heard the Good Shepherd say: "Them also I must bring and they will hear my voice and there shall be one Fold and one Shepherd"—we most willingly harkened to the Divine Master's call and we have now been in Peter's Fold for twenty-eight years and every year we live, we thank God, increasingly for opening the door and letting us in. Our heart goes out to "the other Sheep" wishing and longing that they too for their own present and eternal happiness would hear the Good Shepherd's voice and enter the One Fold over which he appointed St. Peter and his successors, His Vicars, to feed and watch over His Sheep until the end of time. Unless all the other Sheep will do as we of Graymoor did, there is no possibility anymore of a united Christendom.

20. Thoughts on the Church

St. Anthony's Hour, November 7, 1937

During the past week. I have received a communication from some pious non-Catholic who believes that instead of being led by the light of the Holy Ghost to enter the Catholic Church that I was led by the devil to do so. Here is what he or she writes: "Dear Sir: I am enclosing a few leaflets. I wish you would study them and see how wrong you are by going over to that diabolical Roman Catholic Church with all its heresies and false doctrines. The only excuse I can think of is that you hadn't read the gospel of Christ and found Him. If you were one of His disciples and had given your heart to him you could never enter that Church with all the doctrines that are against the teachings of Christ."

I have said that the Catholic Church which has been in the world for 1900 years through the witness of her members has piled up a tremendous amount of evidence concerning the actual existence of purgatory, but like every other teaching of the Catholic Church there are texts to support the doctrine, there either in the old or New Testaments, or both. We shall not, however, take up your time this afternoon in producing the texts.

As to Purgatory being the priests' "gold mine" and the Holy Sacrifice of the Mass being offered up only for those who can afford to pay for it, let me tell you this: Protestant ministers as well as Catholic priests are supported by the offerings of the people. For the support of the Jewish priesthood God ordained the payment of tithes by the people of Israel. St. Paul says: "Know you not that they that serve the altar partake with the altar; so God ordained that they who preach the gospel should live by the gospel." No priest could ever get rich on the stipends which he receives for saying Mass. The stipend in the United States is a dollar. In some countries it is only 25 cents and as ordinarily the priest is limited to saying only one Mass a day he can only receive a dollar. I wonder how many of our layfolk would be willing to live on a dollar a day.

It is not true that the Holy Sacrifice of the Mass is refused to those who have no money to pay. The Church has been careful to provide in every Mass special prayers for the faithful dead, regardless of whether they were poor or rich, and on All Soul's Day, every priest is supposed to say three Masses for the dead and for only one is he allowed to receive a stipend.

On the past two Sundays we invited our hearers to send in their names to be remembered in the Poor Soul Masses of November, and we did not ask you to send a stipend. Whether you sent an offering or not the Masses will be said for your deceased just the same. We agree, of course, with the writer in accepting the words of Christ. We could not do otherwise. "Believe on the Lord Jesus Christ and thou shalt be saved." But there is a saving Faith as well as one that does not save. The Unitarian, for example, believes Our Lord Jesus Christ was a mere man and some people profess to believe on the Lord Jesus Christ, but they do not believe the things that He says in the Gospel.

I will give our friend an evidence of something Our Lord said that he does not believe, and to have a saving faith in Jesus he must believe that He spoke the truth and accept His teachings. It is Jesus Himself who bears witness concerning His Church in the Holy Gospel, and in the face of that witness how can my Christian friend believe that the Church which Jesus Christ founded is a diabolical institution, in spite of the promise

320

Our Lord made to guide that Church into all truth and to be with its ministers unto the end of the world.

He says: "The only excuse I can think of is that you hadn't read the Gospel of Christ." Now I have been a reader of the Gospel of Christ since my childhood. I read the Holy Bible through when I was a boy and as a minister of the gospel in the Episcopal Church I read every day of my life a chapter out of the Old Testament and one out of the New, so it was that I got saturated with the Word of God. And let me tell you, my friend, that it was this continual reading of the Gospel which made a Catholic out of me, because I could not get over the words which Our Lord said to St. Peter: "Thou art Peter and upon this Rock I will build My Church and the gates of hell shall not prevail against it." Our Lord also said: "I have prayed for thee, Peter, that thy faith fail not, and being converted, confirm thy brethren in that same Catholic Faith." And, although Peter denied Our Lord thrice, Peter's faith did not fail, for Our Lord said: "I will send the Holy Ghost and He will guide you unto all truth." And so the Catholic Church instead of teaching heresies and false doctrines teaches truth—"all truth"—and because I believe in Jesus Christ I believe His Words.

I liked the Episcopal Church and I did not care particularly about leaving her, but the words of Christ concerning His true Church in the Holy Gospel pursued me wherever I went until finally, I had to capitulate and enter the Holy Catholic Apostolic Church, which Christ founded upon Peter in union with Himself and concerning which He said the gates of hell would never prevail against it. The writer calls it "diabolical Roman Church"! If the Church which Christ founded has become diabolical then truly the gates of hell have prevailed against it and the Savior has failed to keep His word.

There is another saying of Christ as the Good Shepherd which I commend to all my non-Catholic listeners: "Other sheep I have which are not of this Fold. Them I also must bring and they shall hear my voice and there shall be One Fold and One Shepherd." I happen to have been born and brought up as one of the "Other Sheep", but I heard the voice of the Good Shepherd and He called me into the "One Fold" under the "One Shepherd".

321

21. At-one-mentism

St. Anthony's Hour, March 20, 1938

Last Sunday I spoke to you again on the subject of At-one-mentism, contrasting the At-*one*-mentist with the Communist. I said that a one-hundred-per-cent Communist had to be an atheist. One of the forerunners of Communism, at one time Premier of France, declared: "We must kill God." It is part of the Communistic program to at least destroy the faith of man in the existence of God.

At-*one*-mentists, on the contrary, instead of repudiating God, embraces God, rejoices that God became man in order that man might attain to the Heavenly Vision and enter into union with the Adorable Trinity—Father, Son and Holy Ghost —first becoming here on earth a member of the Mystical Body of Christ. And so, instead of seeking his happiness in the possession of material and perishable things, the At-*one*-mentist finds his "joy in God through Our Lord Jesus Christ by whom (he) has now received the At-*One*-Ment" or state of union with God.

Today, addressing you, my friends, as At-one-mentists, let me point out to you how God imposes on you the duty of propagating the Faith and thereby making increase of the Mystical Body of Christ. When Noah and his family came out of the ark God imposed on him and his sons the command, *"Increase and multiply and replenish the earth."* The propagation of the seed of Adam comes through sexual generation. The children of men marry, are given in marriage, and they bring forth children, sons and daughters. When Christ established His Kingdom, the society that was to be perpetuated in Heaven, He proclaimed a New Birth for every man, woman or child who should join that Society, saying to Nicodemus: "You must be born again, if you would enter into the Kingdom of Heaven." So we have the Sacrament of Regeneration, usually called holy Baptism, by which the sons and daughters of Adam are grafted into the Mystical Body of Christ, which increases and multiplies itself, and which extends into all countries and into all lands in fulfillment of the prophecy of Daniel, who saw a stone cut out of the mountain, which grew and increased until it filled the whole world.

St. Peter in his epistle, addressing the regenerate, i.e., the Children of the Atonement, reminds them that they are born again "not of corruptible seed, but incorruptible, by the Word of God, who liveth and remaineth forever." And he describes Christ as a living Stone, rejected indeed by man, but chosen and made honorable by God, and then he says: "Be you also as living Stones built up, a spiritual house, a holy priesthood, to offer up spiritual sacrifices, acceptable to God by Jesus Christ."

Our Lord gave to St. Peter, himself, the name of "the rock," saying: "Thou art Peter and upon this rock, I will build my Church," and it is interesting in the description of the new Jerusalem that it had twelve foundations, corresponding to the twelve Apostles—every one a different stone but the first stone was St. Peter—and that was jasper, and all the wells built upon that foundation were jasper, a red stone of the hue blood, symbolical of the Precious Blood of the Atonement. Now the blood is the life; so St. Peter says: "Know you that you were redeemed not with corruptible things as gold and silver, but with the Precious Blood of Christ as of a Lamb, unspotted and undefiled." And so the Mystical Body of Christ grows and expands by incorporating into its substance more and more of redeemed humanity and as the sons and daughters of our first parents, were to increase and multiply the seed of Adam by the process of carnal generation; so we At-one-mentists in the Mystical Body of Christ must increase and multiply ourselves as the sons and daughters of the Atonement.

The process, however, is not by sexual generation. It is by the propagation of the Faith, and this is done by the command of Christ through preaching. When He commanded His apostles to go into all the world and preach the Gospel to every creature, making disciples of all nations, He did not intend that command to rest upon the Apostles alone. He willed that every Child of God should become a missionary, to increase and extend the Mystical Body of Christ until as a stone hewn out of the mountain it should fill the whole world.

The children of anti-Christ, dominated by the spirit of Lucifer, are zealous propagandists. Through all kinds of weather, you will find the Communists preaching from improvised pulpits on Columbus Circle and Union Square. And you will find them preaching in halls and meeting places in season and out of season, seeking to increase and multiply the Communists until they will posses the world for the Prince of Darkness.

If we are true At-*one*-mentists the preaching should not be confined to the Priests and the Bishops. As it was in the primitive Church, so should it be now—every Catholic a missionary. If the individual Catholic cannot go as an active missionary into China, Japan, India and the islands of the sea, he should at least back up those missionaries who do go by giving of his substance, for the missionaries have to live. Moreover, to make their work effective they have to build churches, schools, and hospitals in pagan lands. Having nothing themselves, they must look back home and depend upon the faithful to support and uphold their hands by almsgiving to missions.

The Communists throughout the world are supported in the publication of their papers and the carrying on of their propaganda, it is alleged, by large supplies of cash sent from Moscow. We At-one-mentists at home should see that our missionaries receive whatever money is necessary to carry on their work of converting the heathen to Christ.

22. Be an At-one-mentist

St. Anthony's Hour, May 2, 1937

What a wonderful promise is contained in the gospel for today! Jesus saith to His disciples: "Amen, amen I say to you, if you ask the Father anything in My Name, He will give it to you." What, therefore, shall we ask? When Solomon became King over Israel and Judah in succession to his Father, David, the Lord appeared to him in a dream by night, saying: "Ask what thou wilt that I should give thee." Solomon said: "Give, therefore, to Thy servant an understanding heart, to judge Thy people and discern between good and evil." And the word was pleasing to the Lord that Solomon had asked such a thing. And the Lord said to Solomon: "Because thou hast asked this thing and hast not asked for thyself long life or riches, nor the lives of thy enemies, but hast asked for thyself wisdom to discern judgment. Behold I have done for thee according to thy words, and have given thee a wise and understanding heart, insomuch that there hath been no one like thee before thee, nor shall arise after thee."

St. Paul urges us to covet the best gift. What is the best gift that we could ask of God? Once the Lord appeared to the great Doctor of the Catholic Church, Thomas Aquinas, and said to him: "Thomas, thou hast written well concerning Me. What, therefore, shall I give thee?" And he made reply: "Nothing but Thyself, O Lord." St. Thomas coveted the best, the highest and the most supreme gift, the Gift of God, Himself. St. Paul says: "God so loved the world that He gave His only Begotten Son to the end that all that believe in Him should not perish but should have everlasting life." That is the best and the supreme gift of Divine Love, the Only-Begotten Son of God—and so we ask the Father of lights "from whom cometh down every good and perfect gift" to give us His only Son, Jesus Christ, to be our eternal possession. One night St. Francis of Assisi was invited by the righest young man in the town to be his guest overnight and his host, Bernard Quintivali, arranged that St. Francis should sleep in his room. Bernard pretended to be asleep, but his eye was on St. Francis during his night watches. No sooner did St. Francis believe that Bernard was asleep when he got up and prayed with his arms extended in the form of a cross, for a long time saying only: *Deus Meus et Omnia,* My God and my All."

St. John tells us in his Gospel: "The Word was made Flesh and dwelt among us," the Only Begotten Son of God full of grace and truth, and then he says: "He came unto His own and His own received Him not, but to as many as received Him, to them gave He the power to become the sons of God." Let us, therefore, ask of God the Father that we may possess for all eternity, Our Lord Jesus Christ, for, if we possess Christ, in Christ we possess all things. The Father hath given to the Son all power and all glory in not only this little world of ours, but the universe. The heavens and the earth—all things are Christ's.

I spoke to you last Sunday about becoming At-one-ment-ists, of entering into the possession of your inheritance in Christ Jesus by becoming partakers of the Divine Nature through Jesus Christ and possessing, not only the Second Person of the Eternal Trinity, but the Father and the Holy Ghost, and living a life of oneness or union with Them.

The greatest and most perfect At-one-mentist in the history of Christianity was St. Francis of Assisi. He was the most Christian of all Christians. He possessed Christ to such an extent

325

that in Francis and through Francis Christ lived again among men. St. Paul says of himself; "It is no longer I that live but Christ that liveth in me," and St. Francis could have said the same. When St. Francis preached to the people, young men by the thousands left the world to be his companions in the Religious houses which St. Francis established as their home, though he had abandoned all things to follow Christ and called himself, "the little poor man of Assisi." Young women also, by the thousands forsook the world and joined themselves to Lady Clare in the Convents of the Poor Clares, which sprung up all over Europe. And then the proletariat, who could not go into the Convent, asked him to give them a Rule that they also might become At-one-mentists, possessing God the Father, God the Son and God the Holy Ghost. St. Francis did give them a rule and organized them into Brothers and Sisters of Penance, until there became not only thousands of them, but tens of thousands and eventually, hundreds of thousands. And, after seven hundred years, the Tertiaries of St. Francis throughout the world, as they are called, now number 3,000,000. And that you may be true At-one-mentists I speak to you, the common people, the proletariat, and invite you to enroll yourself under the banner of the Seraphic Patriarch in his Third Order.

23. Unity in God Alone

St. Anthony's Hour, June 26, 1938

This is the Sunday within the Octave of the Feast of the Sacred Heart of Jesus and a great concourse of pilgrims are assembled here on the Mount of the Atonement. As one of the ambassadors of Christ the King I address you in His name.

A short time before the Savior of the world allowed Himself to be arrested, dragged into court, condemned, and led away to be crucified on the Mount Calvary He Himself said, "And I, if I be lifted up from the earth, will draw all men unto Me." "Greater love hath no man than this," He declared, "that he lay down His life for His friends." And Christ lifted up from the altar of the Cross as the "Lamb of God that taketh away the sins of the world" constitutes a magnet of Divine love, wooing the hearts of men.

When Jesus appeared to St. Margaret Mary, the Visitation nun, she beheld a flame of fire ascending out of His Heart as a symbol of the Divine Love that burned therein for the sons and daughters of men. It was only another way in which Jesus Christ revealed the Heart of the Divine Lover, seeking to woo the hearts of redeemed humanity to Himself, that they might be united to His own Sacred Heart in a mystical union that would persevere throughout eternity. The complaint of Christ to the Visitation nun was that the hearts of men were cold and indifferent, that they did not respond to His own burning heart, giving Him love for love.

The pathos of human life throughout the world today is the wholesale apostacy of the nations from God and the consequent misery and wretchedness that has come upon them. The world is full of wars and rumors of wars, as men, self-centered, consumed by greed and worldly ambition, slaughter each other with all kinds of instruments of destruction, and in the meantime, have forgotten God, and nations arrayed against nations, armed to the teeth, are inviting another universal war that shall transcend in its horror the World War of 1914.

A political party, international in its character, seeking to dominate the world at the present time, has actually gone so far as to profess its belief in the non-existence of God, to repudiate God altogether. As one of their French forerunners exclaimed, "We must kill God".

In the midst of this widespread apostasy in a world that was redeemed by the Blood of Christ, we cry out to our listeners to respond to the wooing of the Heavenly Bridegroom, who seeks to wed our souls to Himself and to unite our hearts to His in an indissoluble union, which will last for eternity. As the one wooed responds to the advances of the lover, and the two are joined together in holy wedlock, "two souls with but a single thought, two hearts that beat as one," so let it be with us, beholding in Our Lord Jesus Christ the Divine Lover, who took our nature into union with His Godhead, that He might incorporate us into His Majestical Body to such a degree that we actually become through communion with Him in the Blessed Sacrament bone of His Bone and Flesh of His Flesh, let us respond with alacrity to His wooing and instead of running away from Him, let us run towards Him with outstretched arms to be caught up into His Divine embrace and to give Him

327

freely and fully our poor hearts to be united with His in a union that will transcend in its intensity and fervor the burning love that sometimes coalesces the lover and the beloved in the embrace of conjugal affection.

As the ambassador of Jesus Christ I call upon you to yield yourself to the attraction of Christ Crucified, to seek to unite yourself with Him, particularly in the right reception of Holy Communion and to give Him love for love. And in counselling you to do that, I am counselling you to consult your own happiness.

We have a beautiful prayer which the Friars, Sisters and Tertiaries of the Atonement say every day. It runs as follows: "O God, Who has prepared for those who love Thee such good things as pass man's understanding, pour into our hearts such love towards Thee, that we, loving Thee in and above all things may obtain Thy promises, which exceeds all we can desire." What blindness on the part of man to reject the advances of the Divine Suitor, Our Lord Jesus Christ, asking us to enter into a union with Himself and to give Him love for love. If we decline the invitation, which He gives us to attend the marriage feast of the Lamb, which will take place throughout eternity in Heaven, we are closing the gates of paradise against ourselves and there is only alternative—hell. In heaven the divine love reigns supreme. In hell, hatred, cursing and blasphemy prevail. In the final judgment there will be a separation of the sheep from the goats. To His loved ones Christ shall say, "Come ye blessed of My Father, possess you the kingdom prepared for you from the foundation of the world." To those that have rejected Him and refused to obey the first and the Great Commandment, "Thou shalt love the Lord Thy God with all Thy Heart, mind, soul and strength," their portion will be the outer darkness, associated with the devils and the damned throughout eternity. Jesus Christ said: "I am come to kindle a fire on earth." That fire is the divine love. As Elias built an altar on Mt. Carmel and then cried to Jehovah to send the sacred fire down from Heaven to consume the sacrifice upon it, so make of your heart an altar and offer yourself as a victim of Divine love and with your arms lifted up like St. Francis of Assisi, ask God to send the fire to consume the sacrifice which you have offered on the altar of your heart to Jesus Christ, Our Savior and Redeemer.

328

24. The Union-That-Nothing-Be-Lost

Lamp, July 1912

This is the month dedicated by Holy Church to the Most Precious Blood of our Divine Redeemer. It is also, by a Providential coincidence, the birth month of the Society of the Atonement. As there can be no crown without the Cross, so there could be no Atonement without the shedding of Christ's most Precious Blood. The Precious Blood and the Atonement, therefore, are essentially and eternally related.

By the law of consequence and deduction it follows that a Society called into being to promote the mission and work of the Atonement must be, *ipso facto,* a *missionary* Society. This logical necessity is too obvious to need much exposition. St. Paul's preaching to the Athenians on Mar's Hill wished them to understand that the application of the Atonement was commensurate with the bounds of the entire human family and he said: "God (the Creator and Lord of all things) hath made of one (blood) all mankind, to dwell upon the whole face of the earth" (Acts 17:26).

In assuming flesh and blood from Mary, which was through her derived from Adam, Jesus acquired His title *Son of Man* and as He became a willing victim for the sins of the whole world the sovereign jurisdiction of the Atonement extends to every sinful child of Adam, who accepting Christ as His Savior and the Catholic Church as the City of Refuge, seeks salvation through the Precious Blood. "For the Scripture saith: whomsoever believeth in Him shall not be confounded. For there is no distinction of the Jew and the Greek: for the same is Lord over all, rich unto all that call upon Him. For whosoever shall call upon the name of the Lord, shall be saved" (Rom. 10, 11-12).

A Society therefore which is consecrated to the work of illustrating and spreading abroad the saving efficacy and the worldwide mission of Christ's Atonement, must like the great Church of which it is a very small part, be essentially a missionary organization, its members must be mission preachers and evangelists and for that end they must be trained and equipped.

How then shall they call on Him, in Whom they have not believed? Or, how shall they believe Him of Whom they have not heard? And how shall they hear without a preacher? (Rom. 10:14).

That this has been in the mind of the Friars of the Atonement from the beginning is evidenced by the following prayer of the First Congregation, which has been recited in choir every day since the Society began.

Antiphon. *Omnia pro Christo et salute ominum* (All things for Christ and the Salvation of men.)

℣. Set your affections on things above, not on things on earth.

℟. For ye are dead and your life is hid with Christ in God.

Let Us Pray

O God, Who through the preaching of Thy servants, St. John Baptist, St. Paul and St. Francis hast glorified Thy Name and saved an innumerable multitude of souls, pour out abundantly the spirit of prophecy, we pray Thee, upon the Sons of the Atonement and make them to be missionaries in all lands.

Of course it was impossible for this prayer to be answered, while the Society yet remained outside the Fold of Peter and even now years must be spent in training the religious subjects who shall join the Institute before they can become active missionaries. This autumn we hope to have our first boys come to us but it will take ten or twelve years of study before they can be ordained and commissioned to go forth into the mission field.

Meantime Divine Providence has begun to build up around our infant Institute a little army of missionary co-workers who, we confidentally believe, are destined to do much to further in every way the work of the Society. We refer to the Union-That-Nothing-Be-Lost. Not six months have passed since the rule of the U.N.B.L. was published with Episcopal sanction and already it has several hundred probationary members. The machinery of this union is so simple and its rule so practical that no long schooling is necessary before its members can become active missionaries, they have but to lift up their eyes and look about them and behold everywhere, "the field is white to harvest".

The Rule of Action:

I. To make the best use I can of every talent I possess.

II. To waste nothing—neither time, money, food, clothing nor opportunity of doing good which may be given me.

III. To spend upon myself the *minimum* rather than the *maximum* of what is at my disposal; that I may have

330

the more to give to God and to those whose need is greater than my own.

IV. To practice as strict an economy in order to lay up treasure in Heaven as the worldly-wise do in accumulating treasure on the earth.

V. To keep ever in mind the text: "That Nothing Be Lost" and for love of God and the rewards of Eternal Life, to do all the good I can, as long as life affords the privilege and opportunity of service.

And the daily prayer which the members say brings down from heaven the grace necessary to practice this rule:

O Lord Jesus Christ Who commandest Thine Apostles to gather up the fragments *that nothing be lost*, give me grace to waste nothing but to use all my time, talent, substance and opportunity to the greater Glory of God, the good of my neighbor and the salvation of souls: and all for love of Thee, O Most Sweet Lord Jesus Christ. Amen.

We promised in our last number to treat more fully in this issue of the principles embodied in our new Society, the Union-That-Nothing-Be-Lost. It is the *name* of the Society which contains its basic idea as completely as the oak tree is packed within the narrow compass of the acorn. Let us expand that idea by recalling the occasion when Jesus first issued His "no waste" orders to the Apostolic band.

It was a splendid illustration of the munificence of God when Jesus so multiplied five barley loaves and two small fishes in a desert place that after five thousand men, besides women and children, had fully satisfied their desperate hunger, there still remained quantities of broken bits of food lying all about on the ground, where the multitude had eaten. It was a no less striking illustration of the *economy* of God, Who operates a universe without the loss of an atom of its immensity, that Christ should have said to His Disciples, "Gather up the fragments lest they be lost." Thus for all time, did the Creator of heaven and earth rebuke the extravagance and reckless waste of man, and Christ imposed upon His followers the duty of using wisely and well all that we receive from the Divine bounty "that nothing be lost." Surely there never was an age or country which needed more than our own rigid observance by His followers of these words of Christ—"Gather up the fragments that remain lest they be lost."

The increasing ills of our day are mainly due to man's selfish greed, his inordinate desire to have and to hold more than his rightful share of the material wealth intended by our Father in Heaven for all His children. The spectacle over which angels weep are vast store houses erected and employed by the Shylocks of trade to corner produce of every sort, while millions of the poor are compelled to barter almost their souls to purchase at exorbitant prices the necessities of life. Along the fashionable avenues of the great city roll the equipages of the enormously rich. On either side are residences of such magnificense that kings might envy their possessors. Within these sumptuous palaces, dinners, fetes, balls, gambling bouts take place night after night, whereat the extravagant expenditure of a Cleopatra or a Caligula, is rivalled and not infrequently outdone by private individuals, who could purchase outright the Golden Palace of Nero and not miss from their exchequer the sum named in the deed of transfer.

Paralleling these avenues of wealth and stretching away into quarters of unspeakable degradation and vice are miles upon miles of huge tenement buildings in and out of which swarn, like water rats, hundreds of thousands of the poor. What indescribable wretchedness, what desperate poverty, what famine pinched faces, what rags, what disease, what corruption of soul and body, what utter misery!

The glaring extremes of unlimited wealth in the hands of the few and abject destitution the portion of tens of thousands is becoming more and more the unhappy condition of society because people professedly Christian give little or no heed to the ethical teaching of Jesus and walk not in the footsteps of His Holy, self-denying life. Jesus bade His followers do as He had done, to make themselves poor, to part with all things, to give even their lives "a ransom for many" seeking, in a word, to impoverish self in making others rich. The average Christian of our time does the exact reverse of all this, for by hook or crook, and oftentimes in flagrant violation of every law of God and man, he seeks to make others poor that he may enrich himself. David Harum's perversion of the Golden Rule, as a trader of horses, has become, among businessmen, a maxim of their daily life: "Do unto your neighbor as he would do unto you, but see you do it first."

Most of our multi-millionaires profess to be disciples of Christ, some of them are Catholic. What tongue could describe

332

the possibilities of good which lie within the grasp of these financial potentates did they waste nothing of their resources, employing the very fragments of their countless dollars for God's greater glory and the welfare of humanity, taking care not so much as a penny be lost.

We are not recommending that they go to the extremes of St. Francis of Assisi in imitating the poverty of the Son of God, stripping themselves of the very clothes on their back. Let others heed the words addressed to the rich young man in the Gospel. "If thou wilt be perfect go, sell *all* thou hast and give it to the poor." For our millionaire Christians it would mean immense treasure laid up in Heaven, if they would only "gather up the fragments that remain that nothing be lost". Let them spend on themselves, their wives and their children as much as is consistent with "living soberly, righteously and godly in this present world" and only spend the balance of their income on the poor, "that nothing be lost", and even so, who could calculate their opportunities of increasing the sum of human happiness and helping their fellow pilgrims on the road to heaven.

A few thousands a year economically administered ought to be amply sufficient to supply Dives and his family with every comfort and material need, agreeable to the profession of Christianity. What a princely revenue would remain to be expended in the furtherance of the Gospel at home and abroad, in building churches, endowing hospitals, providing better homes for the poor, clothing the naked, feeding the hungry, rescuing the perishing, visiting those in prison and setting the captive free. Then when the rich man died instead of "lifting up his eyes" in hellish torment and "seeing Lazarus afar off" what would be his happiness to hear Christ say, as He points to the multitude of the poor whom his charity had clothed and warmed and fed, "Inasmuch as you did it unto these My least brethren, you did it unto Me. Behold the friends you made by a wise use of the mammon of unrighteousness. Lazarus and his companions stand ready to receive you into everlasting habitations."

But it is not only in the banqueting halls of the rich that fragments are left after the feast. In the houses of the well-to-do, those who constitute the prosperous middle class in both England and America, there is "bread enough and to spare". Extravagance and waste are by no means confined to the very wealthy. They percolate through every strata of society and are nowhere more painfully apparent than in the wretched homes of the very poor. What so much as the bread snatched from the table of the poorest of the poor, maintains at almost every street corner the gin palace and saloon. The churches and the charities of the United States and of the United Kingdom of Great Britain could be supported ten times over by what people waste and sinfully squander. An army of a million missionaries could be maintained in the foreign field by the fragments that would be gathered together if every baptized member of His Church learned economy of Jesus Christ and took the utmost care "that nothing be lost".

The object of the Union-That-Nothing-Be-Lost is to bind together a company of Catholic men and women, drawn from every rank of society and state of life, in a united effort to make the best use they can of every talent they possess, to waste nothing, neither time, nor money, nor food, nor clothing, nor influence, nor any chance of doing good which may be given them; to spend upon self the minimum rather than the maximum, of what is at their disposal; to practice the same rigid economy in laying up treasure in heaven that the worldly wise do in accumulating treasure on the earth. To keep ever in mind the text, "That Nothing Be Lost", and for the love of God and man, and the rewards of eternal life "to do all the good they can, in all the ways they can, to whomsoever they can" till the last breath is spent and the soul is summoned before the Judgment Seat of Christ.

Selfishness starves and kills the life of Christ within us. It petrifies the heart and prepares the soul as a dead tree to be burned in hell. To deny self, to take up the cross of self-sacrifice, there is no way but this of following Jesus. Give as He gave, spend as He spent, then there will be no waste of thy substance, no loss of thy soul, and thou shalt have imperishable treasure in Heaven.